The Author

Gottfried Dietze graduated from the law school of the University of Heidelberg and received doctorates in Politics from Princeton University and in Juridical Science from the University of Virginia. He is an Associate Professor at the Johns Hopkins University, where he teaches comparative government, with a major interest in federalism and constitutional government. He has been lecturing at various European institutions. Previous publications include *Uber Formulierung der Menschenrechte* (1956), and numerous articles. A book on property rights is projected for publication in 1962.

THE FEDERALIST: A Classic on Federalism
and Free Government

The Federalist

A Classic on Federalism and Free Government

BY GOTTFRIED DIETZE

THE JOHNS HOPKINS PRESS: BALTIMORE

© 1960 by The Johns Hopkins Press, Baltimore 18, Md.

Second Printing, 1961

Distributed in Great Britain by Oxford University Press, London

Printed in the United States of America

Library of Congress Catalog Card Number 60–11204

TO WALTER JELLINEK

In Memoriam

FOREWORD

My first acquaintance with the *Federalist* dates back to my student days in Heidelberg, when I came across a copy of the essays while writing a study on the formulation of human rights. At that time, we were all very interested in problems of federalism and democracy as being relevant for a future German constitution. I found the Papers to contain a most interesting discussion of freedom in a democratic society and have ever since been fascinated by them.

After I arrived in the United States, I found literature on the *Federalist* to be scarce. This seemed amazing in view of the fact that the Papers were generally considered the American classic on government. Aware that the absence of a sizeable monograph was probably due to the difficulty of tackling the subject matter rather than to a want of interest, I decided to make an attempt to fill the gap, although I felt that the obstacles to be overcome would be considerable for any newcomer.

The present study attempts to analyze the *Federalist* as a classic on federalism and constitutional democracy. It tries to show the contribution of the work to the literature on federal government by demonstrating how the essays advance beyond the orthodox conception of the purpose of federation, by advocating federalism not only as a means for maintaining the security of the federating states from foreign powers or peace among the members, but also—and especially —as a means for securing the individual's freedom from governmental control. Federalism is thus elevated to a form of constitutionalism. It will be shown that the authors believed in the constitutional ideal of free government. This ideal implied to them a popular government which, for the sake of the rights of the individual and the minority, is restricted under law, i.e., where the democratic principle of popular participation in government, as a mere means, is subordinate to the liberal principle of the protection of the individual, as the end. The *Federalist* thus emerges as a treatise on a broadened concept of federalism, as a classic on free government in peace and security.

I should like to express my thanks to Professors Heinrich Brüning, Edward S. Corwin, William S. Carpenter, Thomas I. Cook, Hardy C. Dillard, William Y. Elliott, Carl J. Friedrich, Louis Hartz, Dean E. McHenry, Carl B. Swisher, Benjamin F. Wright and especially, Alpheus T. Mason, for advice and counsel rendered at one or another stage in the preparation of this study. I should also like to express my gratitude to the Davella Mills Foundation and the Relm Foundation for their financial support. The permission granted by the *Cornell Law Quarterly,* the *Georgetown Law Journal,* the *Jahrbuch des öffentlichen Rechts,* the *Maryland Law Review,* and the *Virginia Law Review* to reprint material that appeared in these publications is appreciated.

Charlottesville, Virginia
September 18, 1959   **GOTTFRIED DIETZE**

CONTENTS

Introduction

CHAPTER ONE

The Federalist–
A General Appreciation

I

The *Federalist* is a treatise on free government in peace and security. It is the outstanding American contribution to the literature
on constitutional democracy and federalism, a classic of Western
political thought.

Tribute has been paid to this work in the old and new worlds
alike, and its impact has been felt not only in the United States, but
also in Latin America and Europe. The American Constitution became an object of admiration for the world, as was predicted in the
Federalist.[1] Also, its famous commentary did justice to Washington's

---

[1] Hamilton expressed the idea that the adoption of the Constitution would
benefit mankind. Edward Mead Earle, ed., THE FEDERALIST (1937), No. 1 on p. 3.
(References to the text of the *Federalist* will hereinafter be cited by number and
page of this edition only, as 1, 3). Madison had a similar thought (14, 85). Hamilton also stated that the Constitution establishes "a government for posterity as
well as ourselves" (34, 208), and Madison, that it created "a system of government, meant for duration" (41, 268). Later, Gladstone referred to the Constitution as "the most wonderful work ever struck off at a given time by the hand
and purpose of man." W. E. Gladstone, "Kin Beyond the Sea," NORTH AMERICAN
REVIEW (1878), CCLXIV, 185.

prognosis that it "will merit the notice of posterity because in it are candidly discussed the principles of freedom and the topics of government which will always be interesting to mankind, so long as they shall be connected with civil society."[2]

1. Although there exists some controversy as to how far the *Federalist* played a decisive role in the ratification of the Constitution,[3] its

[2] Letter to Hamilton of Aug. 28, 1788. John C. Fitzpatrick, ed., THE WRITINGS OF GEORGE WASHINGTON (1931-44) (hereinafter WASHINGTON'S WRITINGS), XXX, 66. See also *ibid.*, XXIX, 33, 323, 407, 466.

[3] Whereas authors at the end of the nineteenth and the beginning of the twentieth centuries stressed the importance of the *Federalist* in the ratification of the Constitution, modern writers emphasized its rather small significance. Examples of the former school are John Fiske, THE CRITICAL PERIOD OF AMERICAN HISTORY (1888), 342; E. G. Bourne, ed., THE FEDERALIST (1901), ix-x. On the other hand, Charles Warren, THE MAKING OF THE CONSTITUTION (1947), 767, maintains that the Papers cannot have been very influential owing to the fact that many of the most controverted parts of the Constitution were not treated in these letters until after most of the state conventions had met. A similar view is expressed by Max Beloff, ed., THE FEDERALIST (1948), x. Frank Monaghan, JOHN JAY (1935), 291-92, states: ". . . it is easy to exaggerate the influence of the *Federalist* papers in 1787 and 1788. They were more widely read than any other tract of the controversy; those who supported the Constitution took them as their Bible; the anti-Federalist leaders felt that they were a factor to be countered. But the mere length of the *Federalist* militated against its effectiveness; its scholarly tone made little appeal to the bulk of those whom it wished to convert. A newspaper contributor, 'Countryman,' scored a point when he wrote: 'As to Mr. Publius I have read a great many of his papers, and I really cannot find out what he would be at; he seems to me as if he was going to write a history, so I have concluded to wait and buy one of his books when they come out.' " According to Douglass Adair, "The Authorship of the Disputed Federalist Papers," WILLIAM AND MARY QUARTERLY (1944), I (3rd series), 236n., *"The Federalist's* propaganda value, as first published in the newspapers, should not be overrated; the essays probably influenced few votes among the general electorate. In the Virginia and New York Conventions, however, the bound volumes were enormously valuable. The pro-Constitution party in both states was eager for a clause by clause discussion of the proposed government. Under this procedure, with Publius' systematic analysis of the document at hand, the Constitutionalist leaders were able to arrange the order of debate beforehand, to coach specific speakers to talk on the various parts of the Constitution, and generally to organize and manage its defense in a systematic way."

Here are some voices of the period under discussion. A. Stuart wrote from Richmond to Madison on Jan. 14, 1788: "Publius is in general estimation, his greatness is acknowledged universally." Gaillard Hunt, ed., THE WRITINGS OF JAMES MADISON (1900-10) (hereinafter MADISON'S WRITINGS), V, 89n. A Senator from Pennsylvania, anti-Hamiltonian in his views, wrote in his diary on June 12, 1789: *"Mem.* Get if I can the Federalist, without buying it. It is not worth it . . . (but)

quality as a political classic is hardly questioned in the United States in spite of the fact that it has been considered by many, including one of its authors, a work of advocates for a cause.[4] Jefferson called it "the best commentary on the principles of government which was ever written."[5] John Quincy Adams lauded the Papers as a "classical

It certainly was instrumental in procuring the adoption of the Constitution." William Maclay, SKETCHES OF DEBATES IN THE FIRST SENATE OF THE UNITED STATES IN 1789–90–91 (1880), 79. On Feb. 7, 1788, Washington wrote to Chevalier de la Luzerne that "a periodical Essay in the New York Gazettes, under Title of the Federalist, has advocated it with great ability." WASHINGTON'S WRITINGS, XXIX, 407. On the other hand, Maclaine wrote James Iredell of North Carolina on March 4, 1788 that Publius "is certainly a judicious and ingenious writer, though not well calculated for the common people." G. J. MacRee, ed., LIFE AND CORRESPONDENCE OF JAMES IREDELL (1857-58), II, 219. Tobias Lear wrote to Washington on June 22, 1788, that in New Hampshire "the valuable numbers of 'Publius' are not known." Quoted in Warren, *op. cit.*, 767n. Humphrey Marshall of Kentucky stated in 1788 that he had never seen a copy of "Publius" in that district. A. J. Beveridge, THE LIFE OF JOHN MARSHALL (1916-19), I, 320n.

[4] On April 17, 1824, Madison wrote to Livingston: "It cannot be denied, without forgetting what belongs to human nature, that in consulting the contemporary writings which vindicate and recommend the Constitution, it is fair to keep in mind that the authors might be sometimes influenced by the zeal of advocates." MADISON'S WRITINGS, IX, 189. William Lowndes of South Carolina said in 1818: "The FEDERALIST was the composition of three very able men who had great agency in framing the Constitution, in procuring its adoption and afterwards in administering it. It was, too, a contemporary exposition, but the exposition of jealous advocates, anxious to procure the establishment of a Government on which depended the happiness and liberty of the country. Is it to be believed that they never represented a power as less extensive, a limitation as somewhat more strict, than an impartial judge would have pronounced it? If the opinions of Patrick Henry and Mr. Monroe should be read to the Committee as evidence of the just construction of any article of the Constitution, this contemporaneous exposition would weigh but little, nor ought it to weigh. By the apprehensions of the one party, a necessary and well-guarded power was almost magnified into uncontrolled despotism; while the complacency with which the other party were disposed to view their own work, led them to believe its provisions less obnoxious to abuse than they really were. THE FEDERALIST was written by men yet warm from debates, in which all their ingenuity and talent for refinement had been employed to prove that the powers which the Constitution gave were not great enough to be dangerous. That with such powerful disturbing causes, the judgment of these distinguished men, should so often have led to the same construction of the Constitution which cool examination has since confirmed, is a rare testimony of their merit." *15th Congress, first session, March 10, 1818.*

[5] Letter to Madison of Nov. 18, 1788. Memorial ed., THE WRITINGS OF THOMAS JEFFERSON (1903) (hereinafter JEFFERSON'S WRITINGS), VII, 183. See Madison's letter to Jefferson of Feb. 8, 1825. MADISON'S WRITINGS, IX, 219.

work in the English language, and a commentary on the Constitution of the United States, of scarcely less authority than the Constitution itself."[6] Woodrow Wilson spoke of "the admirable expositions of the *Federalist*."[7]

American judges were not less complimentary. "The opinion of *The Federalist*," wrote John Marshall, "has always been considered as of great authority. It is a complete commentary on our Constitution, and is appealed to by all parties in the questions to which that instrument has given birth. Its intrinsic value entitles it to its high rank, and the part two of its authors performed in framing the Constitution put it very much in their power to explain the views with which it was framed."[8] The opinion of the great judge drew support from authors of outstanding treatises on constitutional law. Justice Story, dedicating his *Commentaries on the Constitution of the United States* to Marshall, confessed that for this work he drew largely from the *Federalist*, "an incomparable commentary of three of the greatest statesmen of their age."[9] For having done so, Story was praised by Chancellor Kent, who stated that "there is no work on the subject of the Constitution, and on republican and federal government generally, that deserves to be more thoroughly studied. . . . No constitution of government ever received a more masterly and successful vindication." "I know not, indeed," he continued, "of any work on the principles of free government that is to be compared, in instruction and intrinsic value, to this small and unpretending volume of the Federalist; not even if we resort to Aristotle, Cicero, Machiavel, Montesquieu, Milton, Locke, or Burke. It is equally admirable in the depth of its wisdom, the comprehensiveness of its views, the sagacity of its reflections, and the fearlessness, patriotism, candor, simplicity, and elegance with which its truths are uttered and recommended."[10]

Scholars were not less enthusiastic. John Fiske called the *Federalist* "perhaps the most famous of American books, and undoubtedly the most profound and suggestive treatise on government that has ever

---

[6] John Quincy Adams, AN EULOGY ON THE LIFE AND CHARACTER OF JAMES MADISON (1836), 31.

[7] Woodrow Wilson, CONSTITUTIONAL GOVERNMENT IN THE UNITED STATES (1908), 56.

[8] Cohens v. Virginia, 6 Wheaton 264, 418 (1821).

[9] Joseph Story, COMMENTARIES ON THE CONSTITUTION OF THE UNITED STATES (1833), I, v.

[10] James Kent, COMMENTARIES ON AMERICAN LAW (12th ed., 1873), 241.

been written,"[11] and Charles A. Beard thought it was "the most instructive work on political science ever written in the United States," which "ranks first in the world's literature of political science."[12] The praise of historians is matched by that of political scientists.[13]

The enthusiasm displayed by American statesmen, jurists, and scholars is vindicated by compelling facts. Decisions of the Supreme Court consistently have referred to the *Federalist* and made it the basis of judicial argument.[14] In the United States, the Papers have demonstrated a continuous validity that is matched only by the Declaration of Independence and the Constitution. The need for publication of the work has been felt in all periods of American history, from its first appearance down to our day.[15]

2.   Interest in the essays was also evident in Latin America. In 1811, the Venezuelan Manuel García de Sena is said to have published a book that contained a Spanish translation of the *Federalist,* together with translations of the Declaration of Independence, the Articles of Confederation, and the Constitution.[16] An early Latin American

---

[11] John Fiske, *op. cit.*, 341.

[12] Charles A. Beard, THE ENDURING FEDERALIST (1948), 10.

[13] For instance, George Ticknor Curtis, CONSTITUTIONAL HISTORY OF THE UNITED STATES (1896), 32, considered the *Federalist* "the most important commentary on the Constitution that was written contemporaneously with its creation and establishment." Andrew C. McLaughlin, A CONSTITUTIONAL HISTORY OF THE UNITED STATES (1936), 208-9, wrote that "the essays . . . are among the few great treatises on government ever published by political philosophers or statesmen." Carl B. Swisher, AMERICAN CONSTITUTIONAL DEVELOPMENT (1943), 41, found the Papers "the most systematic and the most celebrated defense of the Constitution," which "was and still is one of the most distinguished works in political science produced in the United States."

[14] C.W. Pierson's introduction to the 1923 reprint of H. C. Lodge's edition of the *Federalist* supplies a list of Supreme Court decisions in which the *Federalist* is quoted.

[15] Paul Leicester Ford, A LIST OF EDITIONS OF THE FEDERALIST (1886), lists twenty-three American editions, but this list is incomplete. Henry Cabot Lodge, ed., THE WORKS OF ALEXANDER HAMILTON (1904) (hereinafter HAMILTON'S WORKS), XI, xxxi-xl, gives a more detailed description of the various editions. Ever since, quite a few additional American editions of the *Federalist* have come forth, aside from works that contain excerpts from the Papers.

[16] Manuel García de Sena, LA INDEPENDENCIA DE LA COSTA FIRME JUSTIFICADA POR TOMAS PAINE TREINTA AÑOS HA: EXTRACTO DE SUS OBRAS. This information is taken from Santos Primo Amadeo, ARGENTINE CONSTITUTIONAL LAW (1943), 32n. I have been unable to take a look at García de Sena's book. However, Gustavo R. Ve-

work on federalism, published in 1826, was based mainly upon the *Federalist*.[17] A Portuguese translation was made in Rio Grande, Brazil, in 1835, followed by one published in Rio de Janeiro in 1840 and by one that appeared in 1896.[18] A few copies of the Brazilian editions are said to have found their way to Argentina.[19] In 1868 and 1887, Spanish translations were published in Buenos Aires.[20] They were followed in 1943 by one published in Mexico, which was re-edited in 1957.[21]

The *Federalist* influenced Argentine constitutional development. In the discussion over the advisability of a unitary or federal form of government, the work was appealed to as early as 1818.[22] It was known to the framers of the present Argentine constitution, which was drafted in 1853 by the Convention of Sante Fé.[23] A contemporary historian relates that during the preparatory sessions of the convention, the delegate Gutiérrez had, in the office of the secretary of the convention, looked over a copy of the *Federalist* that belonged to Rivera Indarte, but when the moment arrived to draft the constitution, the book had disappeared. The loss of such a book was considered irreparable in Santa Fé. As a substitute for the *Federalist*, the delegates turned to Alberdi's masterpiece on the organization of the Argentine Republic, and the reading of that book fixed the path

lasco, ed., EL FEDERALISTA (2nd ed., 1957), xvin., takes issue with Primo Amadeo's statement, saying that Professor Antonio Martínez Báez of the University of Mexico consulted that book at the Bancroft Library of the University of California and found that it did not include a translation of the *Federalist*, complete or partial.

[17] (No author), CARTAS DE UN AMERICANO SOBRE LAS VENTAJAS DE LOS GOBIERNOS REPUBLICANOS FEDERATIVOS (1826). This book, published in London, was an answer to the Chilean Juan Egaña's MEMORIAS POLITICAS SOBRE LAS FEDERACIONES Y LEGISLATURAS EN GENERAL Y CON RELACION A CHILE (1825).

[18] The 1835 edition by O. Pharol Paulistano is mentioned in Primo Amadeo, *op. cit.*, 33n. O FEDERALISTA (1840) appeared in Rio de Janeiro. The name of the translator or editor is not mentioned in the three-volume work. The subtitle states wrongly that Madison was a citizen of New York. The 1896 edition was published in Ouro Prêto.

[19] Zeballos, "Aproposito de las traducciones de autores americanos," LA PRENSA, Nov. 9, 1886.

[20] The translations were by J. M. Cantilo and Dr. D. Ildefonso Isla, respectively.

[21] Velasco, *op. cit.*

[22] "The writings of Franklin, *The Federalist*, and other American works are frequently quoted." H. M. Brackenridge, VOYAGE TO SOUTH AMERICA . . . IN THE YEARS 1817 AND 1818 (1820), II, 141.

[23] Amadeo, *op. cit.*, 33n.

to be followed in drafting the constitution. Alberdi was asked to draft a constitution in conformity with the principles laid down in his book, and his draft guided the committee in charge of drawing up the constitution.[24] Alberdi, in turn, was strongly influenced by American constitutionalism, and his work quotes the *Federalist*.[25] Once the Argentine constitution was adopted, the *Federalist* continued to play an influential role in the constitutional development of the country. For example, its authority has been cited in decisions of the Argentine Supreme Court.[26]

The strong federal movement in Brazil in 1840–1842 and the widespread desire to establish a federal state patterned after the United States[27] caused Brazilians to become aware of the value of the *Federalist*. It gave rise to the thought that a reading of the work and an application of its principles would lead the Brazilians to happiness.[28]

Although the Papers were probably not used as a reference in the debates of the various constitutional conventions in Mexico,[29] they occupied the interest of Mexican scholars in the nineteenth and twentieth centuries. Manuel Larrainzar claimed to have translated the *Federalist*.[30] Gamboa referred to it as a "monumental work, which can without exaggeration be called a great monument for the defense of liberty,"[31] and Rabasa called it a work of world reputation.[32] The editor of the Mexican edition maintains that as long as man does not find a form of government that is superior to constitutional government, the *Federalist* will not lose its value.[33]

---

[24] Mariano A. Pelliza, HISTORIA DE LA ORGANIZACION NACIONAL (1923), 67-68.

[25] Juan Bautista Alberdi, BASES Y PUNTOS DE PARTIDA PARA LA ORGANIZACION POLITICA DE LA REPUBLICA ARGENTINA (El Ateneo ed.), 162. In the introduction to that edition, Posada writes: "Estas Bases recuerdan por su función y hasta por su orientación, la labor maravillosa de aquel *Federalista* . . . ." *Ibid.*, lii. See also the edition by Leoncio Gianello (1957), 153-54.

[26] Amadeo, *op. cit.*, 56n, 84n.

[27] See L. de Chavagnes, "Le Brésil en 1844," REVUE DE DEUX MONDES (1844) III, 76-79.

[28] O FEDERALISTA (1840), vii.

[29] Velasco, *op. cit.*, xvii.

[30] *Ibid.*, xvin.

[31] José Maria Gamboa, LEYES CONSTITUCIONALES DE MEXICO EN EL SIGLO XIX (1901), 5.

[32] Emilio Rabasa, EL JUICIO CONSTITUCIONAL (1919), 54.

[33] Velasco, *op. cit.*, xxiv.

3. The influence of the *Federalist* was also felt in Europe. Its most immediate impact was upon France, where it became known soon after its American publication, and it was quoted on several occasions in the debates of the Constituent Assembly.[34] The second and third editions of the complete work were published in Paris in 1792. On August 26 of that year, the French assembly conferred honorary citizenship upon the main authors of the *Federalist,* Hamilton and Madison, who, together with Washington, were included in a list that started with the name of Priestley and ended with that of Schiller. The citation read as follows:

> Considering that men who, by their writing and courage, have served the cause of liberty and paved the way for the enfranchisement of man, cannot be regarded as strangers by a nation which was made free by their guiding light and courage, . . . and in view of the fact that it can be hoped that these men will one day form nothing but one single family, one single association before the law as well as before nature, we feel that the friends of liberty and universal fraternity should be as highly valued by a nation which has proclaimed its renunciation of all conquest and its desire to fraternize with all peoples.[35]

During the next year, the evaluation of the *Federalist* changed. The majority of the Convention was now haunted by the specter of a division of France, and the doctrine of federalism was looked upon with suspicion.[36] Saint-Just skeptically denied that the United States under the Constitution could possibly be one republic and considered a war among the states inevitable.[37] Michelet even reports that the condemnation of Brissot by a revolutionary tribunal was due to the latter's admiration for the *Federalist,* regretting that Brissot was judged to be an advocate for the dismemberment of France, because he had borrowed a copy of that work.[38]

[34] See Albert Esmein's preface in Gaston Jèze, ed., LE FEDERALISTE (1902), xxxiv.

[35] REIMPRESSION DE L'ANCIEN MONITEUR (1858-63), XIII, 540-41.

[36] Esmein, *loc. cit.*, xxxv. On September 25, the Convention declared the French Republic to be one and indivisible, and proposed to inflict the death penalty on those who should propose a dictatorship, a triumvirate, a tribunate or "le gouvernement fédératif." PROCES-VERBAL DE LA CONVENTION NATIONALE (no date), I, 49-50.

[37] REIMPRESSION DE L'ANCIEN MONITEUR, XVI, 396.

[38] Jules Michelet, HISTOIRE DE LA REVOLUTION FRANÇAISE (Marpon et Flammarion ed., 1879), VII, 111n. Esmein, *loc. cit.*, xxxvi, doubts Michelet's statement: "Y a-t-il là l'echo d'une tradition? Nous l'ignorons; mais nous n'avons rien trouvé de semblable ni dans le rapport de Saint-Just, du 8 juillet 1793, ni dans l'acte

But the period during which the *Federalist* had fallen into disfavor did not last long. The work was strongly recommended by Talleyrand, a man who had great respect for Hamilton.[39] The great observer of American democracy, de Tocqueville, considered the *Federalist* "an excellent book, which ought to be familiar to the statesmen of all countries."[40] He referred to it frequently in his classic work, *Democracy in America*. Guizot said that the *Federalist* was the greatest work known to him concerning the application of the elementary principles of government to practical administration.[41] Laboulaye called the *Federalist* a manual on liberty, which was so clear an exposition of the Constitution that to his day it could be ranked as one of its best commentaries.[42] By the end of the nineteenth century, a need was felt for a new edition, which appeared in 1902 under the editorship of Gaston Jèze, whose translation was far superior to those of the 1790's. The eminent jurist Esmein wrote the preface, in which he referred to the essays as "one of the best treatises of constitutional philosophy which the eighteenth century delegated to the nineteenth century."[43] In his introduction, Jèze writes that the authority of the *Federalist* was con-

---

d'accusation dressé par Amar, ni dans le concepte rendu du procès, très ample, qui publia le Moniteur. Voici simplement ce que l'on peut relever à cet égard. Le président du tribunal interrogeait Brissot au sujet de la Constitution feuillantine de Condorcet; c'est ce qu'on appelle aujourd'hui le projet de Constitution girondine: '*L'accusé Brissot*.—Cette Constitution était la plus démocratique qui ait jamais existé, et je pourrais citer celle des Etats-Unis, qui l'est bien moins qu'elle.—*Le Président*. La plus grande preuve que l'on puisse donner du projet qu'avaient les accusés de fédéraliser la République, c'est la citation que Brissot vient de faire de la Constitution des Etats-Unis, citation que les accusés faisaient sans cesse.' " See also REIMPRESSION DE L'ANCIEN MONITEUR, XVIII, 252. Trudaine de la Sablière, who was probably the translator of the French edition of the Federalist, met his death on the scaffold in 1794.

[39] John C. Hamilton, ed., THE FEDERALIST (1864), lxxxviii: "Talleyrand appreciating it, said to the Duc d'Aranda, envoy at the French Court from Spain— 'Vous avez-lu Le Fédéraliste?'—'Non,' replied d'Aranda. 'Lisez donc—lisez,' was the significant answer." Compare also Talleyrand's statement: "Je considère Napoléon, Pitt et Hamilton comme les trois plus grands hommes de notre époque, et si je devais me prononcer entre les trois, je donnerais sans hésiter la première place à Hamilton. Il avait deviné l'Europe." Le Marquis de Talleyrand-Périgord, ETUDE SUR LA REPUBLIQUE DES ETATS-UNIS D'AMERIQUE (1876), 192.

[40] Alexis de Tocqueville, DEMOCRACY IN AMERICA (4th ed., 1845), I, 119n.

[41] John C. Hamilton, *op. cit.*, lxxxviii.

[42] Edouard Laboulaye, HISTOIRE DES ETATS-UNIS (5th ed., 1870), III, 224, 227.

[43] Esmein, *loc. cit.*, vi.

siderable throughout the nineteenth century, remaining so to his day, and that an almost religious respect was attached to these essays.[44] The 1902 edition was republished in 1957 with an introduction by André Tunc.

On the other side of the Rhine, the *Federalist* found a favorable reception with a people striving for unification in freedom.[45] It became largely the basis of that country's extensive literature on federalism. We may assume that the work became known through the French translation of 1792, because in that year that edition was ranked much higher than John Adams' *Defence of the Constitutions of Government of the United States of America*.[46] Robert von Mohl, in his early work on the government of the United States, frequently drew upon the *Federalist*.[47] There is good reason to believe that the essays were admired by the members of the constitutional committee of the National Assembly in Frankfort.[48] Finally, when German unification was approaching realization, there was published in 1864, shortly before the formation of the North German League, a book on the *Federalist* that contained a partial translation of the Papers into German.[49] In the years after the National Assembly, the value of the *Federalist* as a classic on federalism had been increasingly recognized by German scholars. In his more mature treatise on

[44] Jèze, *op. cit.*, xxxix.

[45] Rotteck's statement, "Ich will lieber Freiheit ohne Einheit als Einheit ohne Freiheit," made at a meeting of liberals in Badenweiler on June 2, 1832, is characteristic of the fear of many Germans lest freedom might be the price for the unification of Germany. Quoted in Heinrich von Treitschke, DEUTSCHE GESCHICHTE IM 19. JAHRHUNDERT (1879-95), IV, 265.

[46] ALLGEMEINE LITERATUR-ZEITUNG of Dec. 27, 1792.

[47] Robert von Mohl, DAS BUNDES-STAATSRECHT DER VEREINIGTEN STAATEN VON NORD-AMERIKA (1824).

[48] The report of the *Verfassungsausschuss* of Oct. 20, 1848, mentions the work of von Mohl just referred to. After praising the United States system of federal government, the report states that no nation can take as much pride as the United States in the fact that its statesmen, equally qualified in the theory and the practice of government, have written works that comment as beautifully upon the character and details of the federal state as did such men as Hamilton, Jefferson, Story, Kent, Rawle, and Serjeant. Franz Wigard, ed., STENOGRAPHISCHER BERICHT ÜBER DIE VERHANDLUNGEN DER DEUTSCHEN KONSTITUIERENDEN NATIONALVER-SAMMLUNG ZU FRANKFURT AM MAIN (1848), IV, 2722 ff. The passage is reprinted in Ellinor von Puttkamer, FÖDERATIVE ELEMENTE IM DEUTSCHEN STAATSRECHT SEIT 1648 (1955), 106.

[49] Wilhelm von Kiesselbach, DER AMERIKANISCHE FEDERALIST—POLITISCHE STUDIEN FÜR DIE DEUTSCHE GEGENWART (1864).

American government of 1855, Robert von Mohl did not merely refer to the *Federalist,* but recognized the permanent value of that work for the science of government. Saying that the American contribution in the field of law as reflected in the works of Kent, Story, Marshall, and the authors of the *Federalist* would, in the oldest and richest literature, be among the stars of first magnitude,[50] von Mohl praised the *Federalist* for being one of the best publications in the general field of politics and public law, and one of the most famous and useful theoretical treatises on American *Staatsrecht.* "It would be difficult," he stated, "to render a more careful and more brilliant account of the principles and the essential institutions of the American Constitution, . . . and it is absolutely impossible to speak with greater clarity."[51] Two years earlier, Waitz, disappointed by the failure of the Frankfort National Assembly to unite Germany, published his classic treatise on the nature of the federal state.[52] In it, the principle of divided sovereignty, which was introduced by the *Federalist* and spread in Europe mainly by de Tocqueville,[53] found its first systematic elaboration. Waitz's—and, thereby, the *Federalist's*—concept of the federal state became generally accepted by German authors throughout the following decades. In 1865 Treitschke, who at that time still shared the theory of Waitz, admitted the original importance of the *Federalist* for the idea of the *Bundesstaat*[54] in spite of the fact that he felt that federalism in

[50] Robert von Mohl, DAS STAATSRECHT DER VEREINIGTEN STAATEN VON NORD-AMERIKA, in DIE GESCHICHTE UND LITERATUR DER STAATSWISSENSCHAFTEN (1855), 509.

[51] *Ibid.,* 548-49.

[52] Georg Waitz, "Das Wesen des Bundesstaates," ALLGEMEINE (KIELER) MONAT-SCHRIFT FÜR WISSENSCHAFT UND LITERATUR (1853), 494-530. However, only the republication of the work in GRUNDZÜGE DER POLITIK (1862), 153-218, made Waitz's treatise well known as the first systematic and scholarly discussion of divided sovereignty.

[53] On de Tocqueville's role in the spreading of the doctrine of the *Federalist* in Europe, see Siegfried Brie, DER BUNDESSTAAT (1874), 95; Heinrich von Treitschke, "Bund und Reich," PREUSSISCHE JAHRBÜCHER (1874), XXXIV, 518; Eugène Borel, ETUDE SUR LA SOUVERAINETE ET L'ETAT FEDERATIF (Dissertation, Bern, 1886), 6; Hugo Preuss, GEMEINDE, STAAT, REICH ALS GEBIETSKÖRPERSCHAFTEN (1889), 2.

[54] The term *Bundesstaat* means "federal state" (singular) and was used for a federal state in which the member states were not sovereign. A league of sovereign states is a *Staatenbund,* i.e., a "states-league." According to Godehard Josef Ebers, DIE LEHRE VOM STAATENBUNDE (1910), 99, Wheaton, ELEMENTS OF INTERNATIONAL LAW (1836), was the first author who made use of the German terminology on the other side of the Atlantic.

Germany would have to be different from that in America, due to the presence in Germany of monarchical forms of government.[55] With the replacement of the Waitzian doctrine of divided sovereignty by a younger generation of jurists through a doctrine of nationalism, the *Federalist* did by no means lose its recognition as a classic. Haenel, one of the first to take issue with the concept of divided sovereignty, and a strong adherent of a nationalistic interpretation of the imperial constitution, still credited the *Federalist* with having discovered the concept of the federal state in the first modern *Rechtsstaat*,[56] and called the work an unequalled example of juristic-political thinking.[57] A year later Treitschke, while stressing that he was no longer a follower of Waitz, still maintained that the *Federalist* had introduced the concept of the *Bundesstaat* into the science of government.[58] The *Federalist* is frequently mentioned by other German authors in that period.[59] Hugo Preuss, who became

[55] Heinrich von Treitschke, "Bundesstaat und Einheitsstaat," HISTORISCHE UND POLITISCHE AUFSÄTZE (1865), 475, 587.

[56] Stahl, who can probably be considered the originator of this specifically German concept of constitutionalism, defined *Rechtsstaat* this way: "Der Staat soll Rechtsstaat sein, das ist die Losung und ist auch in Wahrheit der Entwicklungstrieb der neueren Zeit. Er soll die Bahnen und Grenzen seiner Wirksamkeit wie die freie Sphäre seiner Bürger in der Weise des Rechts genau bestimmen und unverbrüchlich sichern und soll die sittlichen Ideen von Staatswegen, also direkt, nicht weiter verwirklichen (erzwingen), als es der Rechtssphäre angehört, d.i. nur bis zur nothwendigsten Umzäunung. Dies ist der Begriff des Rechtsstaats, nicht etwa dass der Staat bloss die Rechtsordnung handhabe ohne administrative Zwecke, oder vollends bloss die Rechte der Einzelnen schütze, er bedeutet überhaupt nicht Ziel und Inhalt des Staates, sondern nur Art und Charakter, dieselben zu verwirklichen." Friedrich Julius Stahl, DIE STAATSLEHRE UND DIE PRINZIPIEN DES STAATSRECHTS (3rd ed., 1856), 137. On the concept of *Rechtsstaat*, see also Otto Bähr, DER RECHTSSTAAT (1864); Rudolf Gneist, DER RECHTSSTAAT UND DIE VERWALTUNGSGERICHTE IN DEUTSCHLAND (1872); Walter Jellinek, VERWALTUNGSRECHT (3rd ed., 1931), paragraphs 5, 12-14.

[57] Albert Haenel, DIE VERTRAGSMÄSSIGEN ELEMENTE DER DEUTSCHEN REICHSVERFASSUNG (1873), 39.

[58] Von Treitschke, "Bund und Reich," 517.

[59] Compare Georg Jellinek, DIE LEHRE VON DEN STAATENVERBINDUNGEN (1882), 50, 178, 255, 256, 275, 283, 288, 290, 307. J. B. Westerkamp, STAATENBUND UND BUNDESSTAAT (1892), mentions the *Federalist* frequently and takes issue with its interpretation by German authors. He re-interprets the *Federalist*, which he calls a masterly interpretation and defense of the federal Constitution (468). See 69, 75, 81, 103, 139, 145, 224, 227, 231, 243, 305, 307, 316-17, 330, 372, 403, 407, 410, 411, 467-68, 474-75, 477-78, 487, 489, 491, 497-98, 500, 508. Ebers, *op. cit.*, 94-105, and Heinrich Triepel, UNITARISMUS UND FÖDERALISMUS IM DEUTSCHEN REICH (1907), 9, 82, also refer to the work.

the father of the Weimar constitution and an advocate of the division of Prussia, referred to the *Federalist* as "the canonical book of American constitutionalism."[60] A complete German edition, *Der Föderalist,* was brought out by Felix Ermacora in Vienna in 1957.

The *Federalist* also drew attention in Italy. Of course, it did not have the importance there that it had in France and Germany. This may be attributed to the fact that the Italians throughout the eighteenth and nineteenth centuries had less contact with the new world than did France, and also to the fact that the Albertian Statute had provided for a unitary form of government. Nevertheless, toward the end of the nineteenth century, the essays of Hamilton, Madison, and Jay were described as a work of great ability and the best commentary of the American Constitution so far published.[61] A decade later, the *Federalist* was acknowledged as one of the great masterpieces of American political thought.[62] In his study of the Supreme Court, Catinella often referred to the *Federalist.*[63] However, it was after World War II, when the Italians were considering decentralization, that the work achieved its greatest popularity. Aside from being mentioned frequently by modern authors, there appeared, in 1954, Aldo Garosci's study on the political thought of the authors of the *Federalist,* one of the major works written on the Papers.[64] In his preface, Garosci praised the *Federalist* as "a book of great political value," saying that few political treatises show as much natural evidence and lucidity.[65] The following year, the first Italian translation of the work was published, and Gaspare Ambrosini, a member of the Italian Constitutional Court, described the *Federalist* as "a profound and suggestive commentary on the Constitution and a great treatise of political science."[66]

This brings us to a consideration of the impression the *Federalist* made in Great Britain. An early number of the *Edinburgh Review* mentioned the *Federalist* as a "work little known in Europe, but which exhibits a profundity of research and an acuteness of understanding which would have done honour to the most illustrious

---

[60] Preuss, *op. cit.*, 18.

[61] Giacomo Grasso, LA COSTITUZIONE DEGLI STATI UNITI D'AMERICA (1894), 20-21. The work also refers to the *Federalist* on p. 102.

[62] Gennaro Mondaini, LE ORIGINI DEGLI STATI UNITI D'AMERICA (1904), 372.

[63] Salvatore Catinella, LA SUPREMA CORTE FEDERALE NEL SISTEMA COSTITUZIONALE DEGLI STATI UNITI (1934), 31 ff., 41 ff., 209 ff.

[64] Aldo Garosci, IL PENSIERO POLITICO DEGLI AUTORI DEL "FEDERALIST" (1954).

[65] *Ibid.*, ix.

[66] Gaspare Ambrosini, ed., IL FEDERALISTA (1955), xi.

statesmen of modern times."[67] In 1825, *Blackwood's Magazine* mentioned the *Federalist*, "which may be called seriously, reverently, the Bible of Republicanism. It is a work altogether, which for comprehensiveness of design, strength, clearness, and simplicity has no parallel. We do not even except or overlook those of Montesquieu and Aristotle among the writing of men."[68] John Stuart Mill called the essays "the most instructive treatise we possess on federal government,"[69] and Sir Henry Sumner Maine wrote that Chancellor Kent's praise of the work was not exaggerated.[70] A great English observer of the United States, Lord Bryce, referred to the *Federalist* as a classic commentary and defense of the Constitution[71] and often mentioned it in his classic, *The American Commonwealth*. At the beginning of this century, the first English edition of the Papers made its appearance, and the editor stated that the work "treats its subject with a philosophic breadth and general insight into political character, which have made it a political classic."[72] About half a century later, another English scholar, Max Beloff, considered the *Federalist* to be the greatest of the commentaries on the Constitution.[73]

4. While the *Federalist* has been universally recognized as being relevant for problems of constitutional government and federalism within particular nations, its importance for international federal movements has been increasingly emphasized. Shortly after World War I, it found its way into Hugan's study of international government.[74] In 1938, just before the Munich crisis, Lord Lothian stated: "The importance of the Federalist papers is that they expose, from experience and with unanswerable argument, why sovereignty is the insuperable obstacle to the organization of peace, and why the federal principle is the only way forward."[75] At the beginning

---

[67] Quoted in Henry Sumner Maine, POPULAR GOVERNMENT (1886), 203.

[68] John C. Hamilton, *op. cit.*, lxxxix. Compare also the quotation given here of the evaluation of the *Federalist* by the *Edinburgh Review*, which differs slightly from that quoted by Henry Sumner Maine.

[69] John Stuart Mill, CONSIDERATIONS ON REPRESENTATIVE GOVERNMENT (1867), 324.

[70] Henry Sumner Maine, *op. cit.*, 203-4.

[71] James B. Bryce, THE AMERICAN COMMONWEALTH (1888), I, 27.

[72] Goldwin Smith, ed., THE FEDERALIST (1901), iii. Also, Roger Foster, COMMENTARIES ON THE CONSTITUTION OF THE UNITED STATES (1896), 3, had praise for the *Federalist*.

[73] Beloff, *op. cit.*, lxvi.

[74] Jessie Wallace Hugan, A STUDY ON INTERNATIONAL GOVERNMENT (1923), 26-27.

[75] Quoted in Clarence Streit, UNION NOW (Shorter Version, 1940), 53.

of World War II, Clarence Streit started out his well-known book, *Union Now,* with a quotation from the *Federalist,* and quoted the Papers on different occasions.[76] At the end of the war, Carl van Doren pointed out that the work now "begins to be consulted for the remarkable parallel between its arguments in favor of the United States and the arguments brought forward in favor of the United Nations. We live today in an age as much concerned with the international future as the age which produced The Federalist was concerned with the national future."[77] Charles A. Beard stated three years later that the *Federalist* should be studied because federalism was a promise of a lasting world peace.[78] Garosci pointed to the importance of the work for European integration,[79] just as in the preceding decade this was done in an argument for Pan-American union.[80]

5. In the preceding pages, an attempt has been made to demonstrate the general importance of the *Federalist.* However, we should not conclude from the universal recognition of the work that its statements have met with nothing but approval. Other interpretations of the Constitution, of federalism, and of constitutional democracy have come forth, and the *Federalist* has often been under attack.[81] Nevertheless, these attacks have hardly detracted from the importance of the classic.

Moreover, the value of the work as a whole has not been affected by the relative importance that has been attributed to some of its

[76] *Ibid.,* 3, 100, 105, 147.

[77] Carl van Doren, ed., THE FEDERALIST (1945), ix-x.

[78] Beard, *op. cit.,* 1-4. Compare also Richard McKeon's remarks in Quincy Wright, ed., THE WORLD COMMUNITY (1948), 257-58. Dusan Sidjanski, DU FEDERALISME NATIONAL AU FEDERALISME INTERNATIONAL (1954), explains the ideas of the *Federalist* at great length.

[79] Garosci, *op. cit.,* ix.

[80] Ely Culbertson, TOTAL PEACE (1943), 213-14.

[81] The classic representative of the argument opposing the new Constitution is probably Richard Henry Lee, OBSERVATIONS LEADING TO A FAIR EXAMINATION OF THE SYSTEM OF GOVERNMENT, PROPOSED BY THE LATE CONVENTION; AND TO SEVERAL ESSENTIAL AND NECESSARY ALTERATIONS IN IT. IN A NUMBER OF LETTERS FROM THE FEDERAL FARMER TO THE REPUBLICAN, which appeared in various letters since October 8, 1787. Vernon Louis Parrington, MAIN CURRENTS IN AMERICAN THOUGHT (1930), I, 288, praises the calmness and fair-mindedness of Lee's LETTERS, which he contrasts with the *Federalist.* The most recent denunciation of the *Federalist* can be found in William W. Crosskey, POLITICS AND THE CONSTITUTION (1953), I, 3-14. The classic argument against the Constitution's interpretation in the *Federalist* was probably made by John C. Calhoun.

parts in various places at various times. For instance, in the United States prior to the Civil War the most prominent essays were the ones dealing with the federal structure of the nation, whereas in later years those concerned with the separation of powers gained greater prominence. Likewise, to give only two examples of the different appreciation of the Papers in different nations, the importance of the work has been seen, in unitary France, primarily in its statements concerning popular government, and, in federal Germany, in its comments on sovereignty. International federalists, on the other hand, have stressed the classic's ideas on federalism as a means for the preservation of peace among the federating nations and for their security from foreign aggression. Thus different writers saw the value of the work in different things, depending upon the environment they lived in and upon their political leanings. On the whole, however, it can be said that in the literature of the various countries the Papers appear to be mainly concerned with the protection of the individual from the government, with peace among the members of the federal state, and with security from foreign powers. Even though all these aspects of the work may not always have been stressed, its value as an outstanding American treatise for free government in peace and security has not been denied.

II

1. In view of the general appreciation of the *Federalist,* it is not surprising that the work has occupied the interest of scholars. Valuable contributions have been made on various aspects of the Papers, such as the disputed authorship, the "split personality" of the *Federalist,* its opinion on the nature of man, essay ten, and the authors' new evaluation of natural law.

The discussion of the disputed authorship of some of the essays seems to have come to a conclusion through the research of Douglass Adair.[82] Whereas Jay's contribution has been firmly established,

---

[82] Douglass Adair, "The Authorship of the Disputed Federalist Papers," WILLIAM AND MARY QUARTERLY (1944), I (3rd series), 97-122; 235-264. Adair's findings are accepted by Beard, *op. cit.,* vii; Alpheus T. Mason, "The Federalist—A Split Personality," AMERICAN HISTORICAL REVIEW (1951-52), LVII, 625-43, on p. 631. This author is also inclined to accept Adair's findings.

this could not, for a long time, be said about the writings of the main authors. Probably for political reasons, neither Hamilton nor Madison were inclined to identify the particular numbers they wrote, under the pseudonym of Publius, for some years after publication.[83] Only two days before his fatal duel with Burr, Hamilton concealed in his lawyer's bookcase a paper identifying the authors of the various numbers, claiming to have written sixty-three essays himself.[84] However, in 1818 Jacob Gideon published a corrected list, claiming twenty-nine essays for Madison instead of the fourteen conceded to him by Hamilton. Since the Gideon edition was checked and approved by Madison himself, editors of later editions were accustomed to attribute the disputed numbers to Hamilton or Madison. Taking issue with the work done by Henry Cabot Lodge[85] and building upon the research of E. G. Bourne,[86] Adair makes it reasonably clear that aside from the five essays written by Jay, Madison wrote twenty-six essays, as compared with Hamilton's fifty-one. Three essays appear to have been the result of the joint effort of Madison and Hamilton.[87]

In his work on the disputed authorship, Adair speaks of the "split personality" of the *Federalist*.[88] This is actually an old idea, and Adair considers it a by-product of his research on the disputed authorship. Written in haste, which prevented the authors from consulting each other as to what each was going to write,[89] the *Federalist*

[83] Alpheus T. Mason, FREE GOVERNMENT IN THE MAKING (1949), 267.

[84] The list reads as follows: "Nos. 2, 3, 4, 5, 54 by J. Nos. 10, 14, 37, to 48 inclusive, M. Nos. 18, 19, 20, M. &. H. jointly. All the others by H." For an account on the hiding and the discovery of the list, see John C. Hamilton, *op. cit.*, xcvi.

[85] See Lodge's introduction to the *Federalist* in HAMILTON'S WORKS, XI, XV-XXXI.

[86] E. G. Bourne, "The Authorship of *The Federalist*," ESSAYS IN HISTORICAL CRITICISM (1901), 113-56.

[87] According to Adair, *op. cit.*, Jay wrote five essays (2-5 and 64); Hamilton did numbers 1, 6-9, 11-13, 15-17, 21-36, 59-61 and 65-85, inclusively. Essays 18, 19, and 20 appear to have been the result of Hamilton's and Madison's joint effort. In spite of Adair's findings, the fact remains that Hamilton's quantitative contribution to the *Federalist* is considerably greater than Madison's. In the Earle edition, the former's contribution would amount to about 342 pages, as compared with about 176 pages of Madison's writing. Jay's contribution covers about 25 pages.

[88] Adair, *op. cit.*, 242.

[89] On Aug. 10, 1788, Madison wrote Jefferson: "Though carried on in concert, the writers are not mutually answerable for all the ideas of the other, there

was not likely to be characterized by uniformity. Madison himself was aware of this as early as 1787, when he wrote John Randolph: "The enclosed paper contains two numbers of the Federalist. . . . You will probably discover marks of different pens."[90] Jefferson noticed the split personality a year later, writing: "I read it with care, pleasure, and improvement, and was satisfied that there was nothing in it by one of those hands, and not a great deal by a second. It does the highest honor to the third."[91] In 1830, John Mercer, viewing the *Federalist,* insisted that

> he who studies it with attention, will perceive that it is not only argumentative, but that it addresses different arguments to different classes of the American public, in the spirit of an able and skilful disputant before a mixed assembly. Thus from different numbers of this work, and sometimes from the same numbers, may be derived authorities for opposite principles and opinions. For example, nothing is easier to demonstrate by the numbers of Publius than that the government . . . is, or is not a National Government; that the State Legislatures may arraign at their respective bars, the conduct of the Federal Government or that no state has any such power.[92]

Six years later, John Quincy Adams remarked that "written in separate numbers, and in unequal proportions, it has not indeed that entire unity of design, or execution which might have been expected had it been the production of a single mind."[93]

The essays of Jay on the one hand and of Hamilton and Madison on the other hand are distinguished from each other in the fact that the former deal mainly with the international advantages the adoption of the Constitution would offer, whereas the latter are mainly

being seldom time for even a perusal of the pieces by any but the writer before they were wanted at the press, and sometimes hardly by the writer himself." MADISON'S WRITINGS, V, 246. "It frequently happened," Madison recalled later, "that, whilst the printer was putting into type parts of the number, the following parts were under the pen and to be furnished in time for the press." (From an unpublished memorandum entitled "TF," drawn up by Madison after he retired from the presidency. Quoted in John C. Hamilton, ed., *op. cit.,* lxxxvin.) For a good account on the haste in which the Papers were written, see Adair, *op. cit.,* 239-40.

[90] Letter of Dec. 2, 1787. MADISON'S WRITINGS, VII, 183.

[91] To Madison on Nov. 18, 1788. JEFFERSON'S WRITINGS, VII, 183.

[92] PROCEEDINGS AND DEBATES OF THE VIRGINIA STATE CONVENTION OF 1829-30 (1830), 187.

[93] John Quincy Adams, *op. cit.,* 31.

concerned with the domestic improvement. This can be accounted for by the fact that Jay had been closely involved in the diplomacy of the Confederation, for which he had acted as ambassador to Spain and as Secretary for Foreign Affairs, and thus knew all the disadvantages to which the Confederation was exposed in foreign relations. Hamilton and Madison confined their essays mainly to internal problems, which, in the preceding years, they had most directly and keenly experienced, while, on the other hand, not absolutely ignoring the international situation of the United States. However, the division between Jay's essays and those of Hamilton and Madison is not what is understood by the term "split personality." Rather, that split personality reveals itself in a difference of opinion between Hamilton and Madison. Such a difference was already evident before and during the Philadelphia Convention. In the *Federalist,* it comes to light even more conspicuously, as was observed by John Quincy Adams: "In examining closely the points selected by these two great co-operators to a common cause and their course of argument for its support, it is not difficult to perceive that diversity of genius and character which afterwards separated them so widely from each other on questions of political interest, affecting the construction of the Constitution which they so ably defended, and so strenuously urged their countrymen to adopt."[94]

It is the merit of Alpheus T. Mason to have first elaborated the idea of the split personality.[95] Showing Hamilton's and Madison's attitudes toward various subjects relevant to free government, Mason points out fundamental agreements, for instance, on the nature of man and the inequality of property, and distinguishes them from such points of disagreement as the value of power, political pluralism, the deficiencies of the Articles of Confederation, and the change brought about by the Constitution. Mason's contribution is most helpful for a true understanding of the *Federalist* as a treatise on constitutional government. It is indispensable for an analysis of the *Federalist.*

Benjamin F. Wright deals with the nature of political man as viewed in the *Federalist.*[96] Through an analysis of the Papers, he arrives at the conclusion that the authors view man through the eyes

[94] *Ibid.,* 31-32. See also MADISON'S WRITINGS, v, 55.

[95] Alpheus T. Mason, "The Federalist—A Split Personality."

[96] Benjamin F. Wright, *"The Federalist* on the Nature of Political Man," ETHICS (1948-49), LIX, No. 2, Part II, 1-31.

of statesmen, and not philosophers, depicting him as he is, not as he should be. Man is defective, and his shortcomings are a constant. According to Wright, the more perfect Union and the separation of legislative, executive, and judicial powers under the Constitution were for the authors nothing but means for securing a certain degree of individual happiness in spite of man's own shortcomings. By no means does the Constitution attempt to improve human nature. Rather, by taking that nature into account, it establishes a government which is likely to work satisfactorily for man's own good. Self-government, of course, presupposes certain good qualities in man, the existence of which is admitted in the *Federalist.* No doubt Wright illuminates a very essential aspect of the Papers. However, it appears doubtful whether he is right when he maintains that "the aspect of *The Federalist* which is of universal applicability is not its discussion of the separation of powers, or constitutionalism, or judicial review, or the representative principle, or even federalism, although there is much of importance in it on all these subjects, and on some of them its theory has been influential far beyond the limits of this country. The universal element is its recognition of the importance of human nature in politics, together with its remarkably penetrating analysis of the motives and the behavior of men in a free society."[97]

Wright's thesis is based largely upon what came to be one of the most famous numbers of the *Federalist,* essay ten.[98] According to him, that essay contains passages that are the most searching in all American political analysis.[99] In discussing that number, Wright also takes issue with Charles A. Beard, who used the tenth essay as proof for his economic interpretation of the Constitution. That interpretation is attacked at greater length by Adair.[100] By describing the intellectual climate in which Beard wrote, Adair shows why that historian was only slightly concerned with Madison's theory as theory, but found in essay ten the doctrine of class struggle that,

[97] *Ibid.,* 31. Wright's article was complemented by James P. Scanlan, "The Federalist and Human Nature," REVIEW OF POLITICS (1959), XXI, 657. Scanlan stresses the importance of human motives.

[98] *Ibid.,* 17-26. For the increase of popularity of essay 10, see Douglass Adair, "The Tenth Federalist Revisited," WILLIAM AND MARY QUARTERLY (1951), VIII (3rd series), 48-67.

[99] Wright, *op. cit.,* 20.

[100] Adair, "The Tenth Federalist Revisited."

taken out of context, served the political causes of 1913 dear to Beard's heart. Adair takes issue with the argument that the tenth *Federalist* proves that theories are unimportant in politics. Rightly, he refutes the economic interpretation of the essay, an interpretation that in the 1920's and 1930's came to be accepted by historians as the master theory of the whole Constitution, and that over-emphasized the importance of this particular essay. Thus Adair substantiates the doubt of modern authors that the tenth *Federalist,* or, for that matter, the whole *Federalist,* demonstrates an economic determinism of the Founding Fathers. While Adair seems to be astonished by Beard's elevation of the tenth essay to the position of the most important one of the Papers, he writes, on the other hand, that that essay can be considered "the final flowering" of Madison's political theory prior to the writing of the *Federalist.*[101] He thus seems to indicate that the tenth number is the outstanding Madisonian contribution to the *Federalist,* if not the most important essay of the whole work. Such emphasis on the importance of a single essay is a risky undertaking, especially when that essay is being dealt with in isolation.

Mario d'Addio's contribution on the *Federalist* and the defeat of the natural rights school is again concerned with the whole *Federalist.*[102] The article is in many respects similar to that written by Wright. D'Addio deals largely with the nature of political man. He juxtaposes the *Federalist's* "concrete," historical, and positive concept of man in society with the allegedly "panjuristic" and "passionless" conception of human nature of the natural rights philosophy. According to d'Addio, there is no room in the *Federalist* for natural law, but only for positive law. In opposition to the representatives of the natural law school, the authors of the *Federalist* are said to stress the value of positive governmental power. Government is no longer a mere instrument of coercion from which the individual can claim his unalienable rights. Rather, it appears as the basis of all state organization, of stability and security, the guardian not so much of individual rights, but of individual interests. Human rights are not something in the heavens, but are created by the people themselves. The written preamble of the Constitution is their best recognition. *Jusnaturalista* is superseded by a new vision of politics,

[101] *Ibid.,* 67.

[102] Mario d'Addio, "Il Federalista e il superamento del giusnaturalismo politici," in Ambrosini, *op. cit.,* 625-47.

based upon the reality of history and on social factors. Untenable as
d'Addio's thesis is, it is an interesting *geistesgeschichtlicher* attempt,
although as narrow in its approach as was Beard's in 1913.

Martin Diamond deals with the attitude of the *Federalist* toward
democracy. Being of the opinion that the *Federalist* is demonstrative
of the political ideas of the Founding Fathers, Diamond takes issue
with the thesis that the Constitution embodied a reaction against
the democratic principles espoused in the Declaration of Independence. He maintains that the Founders and the *Federalist* accepted
popular government as the very premise for their discussions and
plans and that their concepts of democratic and republican government are nothing but variations of popular government. The so-
called undemocratic features of the Constitution, Diamond says, are
mere means to secure a good popular government, which is not
necessarily the most democratic popular government.[103]

2.   In addition to essays dealing with specific aspects of the Papers,
there have appeared various treatises on the *Federalist* as a whole.
Their great majority are introductions to editions of the work.
Although most of them deal mainly with the problem of the disputed authorship, there are some that are concerned with the essence
of the work.[104]

In his introduction to the English edition of 1901, Goldwin Smith
emphasizes the influence of the British constitution upon the American Constitution and its defenders in the *Federalist*. The new American form of government, as interpreted in its classic commentary, is
for Smith, as far as the main features of the national government are

---

[103] Martin Diamond, "Democracy and *The Federalist:* A Reconsideration of the
Framers' Intent," AMERICAN POLITICAL SCIENCE REVIEW (1959), LIII, 52. Diamond
thus follows the opinion in Gottfried Dietze, "Hamilton's Federalist—Treatise for
Free Government," CORNELL LAW QUARTERLY (1957), XLII, 516-17. Compare in this
connection Maynard Smith, "The Principles of Republican Government in *The
Federalist*" (Dissertation, 1951, The New School), and Irvin Weaver, "The Social
Philosophy of *The Federalist*" (Dissertation, 1953, Boston University).

[104] Longer introductions to the *Federalist*, consisting largely of discussions of
the disputed authorship, can be found in Henry B. Dawson, ed., THE FEDERALIST
(1863), lx-lxxxix (discussion of the authorship, xxv-lv); John C. Hamilton, ed.,
op. cit., ix-cxxxviii (discussion of the authorship, xc-cxxxviii); Henry Cabot
Lodge, ed., THE FEDERALIST (1888), xxiii-xlv (discussion of the authorship, xxiii-
xxxv), and in the subsequent editions by these three authors. Also, in Paul
Leicester Ford, ed., THE FEDERALIST (1898), vii-xli (discussion of the authorship,
xxix-xxxix).

concerned, largely an imitation of its English counterpart. Quite naturally Montesquieu, the great observer of English institutions, is considered to be the outstanding philosopher who influenced American constitutionalism. However, Smith credits the authors of the *Federalist* for not having adopted the extreme version of Montesquieu's concept of the separation of powers, by upholding the executive's veto on legislation and the participation of the Senate in the treaty-making process. Aside from its merit of being a treatise on the institutional separation of powers, Smith feels that the exposition of federalism is perhaps the best part of the essays. Besides, he praises the authors' vindication of the Supreme Court as the bulwark of a limited constitution against legislative encroachments.[105]

The evaluation of the Papers by the French jurist Esmein is quite similar. In his preface for the edition of 1902, Esmein looks for a genesis of the Constitution, as viewed in the *Federalist*. The great innovations brought about by the fundamental law are for him, first, the federal state; second, the presidential system; and third, the organization of the judiciary and judicial review. Esmein traces the origins of these institutions and evaluates them in the light of the writings of political philosophers. He rightly stresses that the *Federalist* is a work on the theory, and not merely the practice, of federalism. However, he fails to clarify his own opinion on the Papers, except for statements on what he considers to be the main points of the work.[106]

In his introduction to the edition of 1937, Edward M. Earle points to what he feels are, according to the *Federalist*, the main features of the Constitution. For Earle, federalism and the concept of divided sovereignty seem to rank before other factors of importance, such as the protection of property, political liberties, representative government, and judicial review.[107]

Gustavo R. Velasco, the editor of the Mexican edition, sees in the Papers primarily a defense of limited government, or a government of law, or constitutionalism. In the second place, he feels the authors stressed the merits of republican representative government, which according to Velasco is the only form of government under which "objective law" is being observed and the protection of individual rights secured. Other features of the new system that merited the

[105] Goldwin Smith, ed., *op. cit.*, iii-ix.
[106] Esmein, *loc. cit.*
[107] Earle, *op. cit.*, v-xxv.

main attention of the authors of the *Federalist* were listed by Velasco in the following order: the federal state; the division of powers with its corollary, the presidential system; the announcement in the fundamental law of the essential individual rights; the creation of an independent judiciary.[108]

The most comprehensive introduction to the essays is that by Max Beloff. After examining the circumstances surrounding the composition of the Papers and furnishing a guide to the text in which he comments, one by one, upon the various numbers, Beloff attempts to formulate the structure of general political ideas underlying the work and gives some indication of its place in the history of political theory. Beloff, who feels that "the *Federalist* was written for a practical purpose and to be read by practical men,"[109] sets forth a historicist interpretation of the work. According to him, the authors were acutely conscious that to them and their contemporaries had been given the chance of constructing a new political society, of proving by experiment what had been hitherto only food for abstract speculation; that the social contract was no mere anthropological figment or a logical abstraction, but the actual basis of the American union. Beloff regrets that "this sense of novelty, this rejection of the ties of tradition and history, is paralleled by an unawareness of history as a continuing process and by a rejection of any notion that this process affects political ideas."[110] He blames the authors of the *Federalist* for thinking in absolute terms; for declaring that political science, like other sciences, has developed since ancient times, while not bringing forth a parallel idea of the development of society; for not conceiving of the possibility that society may further develop and that this may call for a further revision of political ideas. "The rigidity of the *Federalist* in this respect," he maintains, "has been perhaps as potent as the more-often discussed rigidity of the Constitution, in giving to American political and social thought its peculiarly absolutist quality."[111] As to the essence of the political thinking of the authors of the *Federalist*, Beloff points to the fact of its essential duality.

There is, on the one hand, an analytical study of society and social

[108] Velasco, *op. cit.*, vii-xxiv.
[109] Beloff, *op. cit.*, xxviii.
[110] *Ibid.*, xlvii.
[111] *Ibid.*, xlvii.

psychology—on the whole empirical, cautious, realistic. On the other hand, there is a profound and unquestioned belief in a system of natural rights whose preservation is the object of government, and the true function of law. The business of political science is to use the data of social psychology to construct institutions which shall maintain these rights unimpaired. Thus, political science is a function of human reason; the right kind of government can be worked out from a knowledge of its objective and of the means to hand. And the authors of the Federalist neither admitted their commitments to republicanism nor took the step of submitting their own political prescriptions to the same kind of psychological analysis as they applied to men at large. Action is conditioned; thought is free. It was the paradox which later generations were to find so irritating, and so difficult to get around without self-stultification.[112]

From among the values that are defended in the *Federalist,* Beloff feels that justice occupies a central position. A guarantee of the fruits of inequality, it ranks above political liberty. Rejecting absolute majority rule as a rule by the poor that is productive of equality and its resultant injustice, the authors are said to be advocates of a limited government characterized by an institutional separation of powers and federalism. The theory of federalism as expounded in the Papers is considered "an inseparable commentary upon the federal constitution itself which is the core of the work."[113] According to Beloff, the authors conceive of federalism as having three objectives. First, federalism provides a counterpoise for dangerous movements that might gain control in a smaller and more homogeneous unit. "As a corollary of this defensive function," Beloff remarks, "federations must clearly have a general measure of agreement as to the nature and purposes of the society so organized—or, if one prefers it, as to the definition of natural rights they are prepared to accept."[114] Second, federalism is a means for the defense of the member states against foreign nations. As a consequence, the federal government must control the important aspects relevant to defense and foreign relations. Third, federalism maintains the union of the component parts. To fulfill that function, the federal government must exercise jurisdiction over all matters that may lead to internecine disputes. Beloff concludes his introduction with a discussion of the

[112] *Ibid.,* xlviii.
[113] *Ibid.,* liv.
[114] *Ibid.,* lv.

place of the essays in the history of political philosophy, and stresses
that "because of the practical context of the *Federalist* it is not surprising that it is history rather than philosophy which is the authors'
favorite court of appeal. It is for the factual material contained in
their works that such European thinkers as Montesquieu, Delolme
and Mably are called upon. The text indicates a solid groundwork
of historical knowledge in spite of the essentially unhistorical nature
of its theoretical foundations."[115]

Beloff's historicist interpretation came under attack in a country
where, strangely enough, the historicist tradition is probably stronger
than anywhere else. Garosci's study on the political thought of the
authors of the *Federalist,* a more comprehensive study in book
form on the work as a whole,[116] not only refutes Beard's economic
interpretation with arguments that are similar to those used by Benjamin F. Wright and Douglass Adair, it also takes issue with Beloff's
criticism that the authors of the *Federalist* did not take into consideration the impact of the historical process upon political ideas
and that they thought in "absolute terms." Garosci points out that
any writer who is concerned with political philosophy rather than
history is likely to take the approach the authors took, just as any
historicist who poses theoretical problems must give an answer that
is formulated in general terms and is valid for any period. "Political
theory cannot have the flexibility of history," he adds, "for if it is
an instrument for measuring it cannot be at the same time deformed
by the objects that it measures, since in such a case it would no
longer measure anything."[117] Garosci is probably the first writer on
the Papers to give full credit to Jay's contribution. From among
the main authors of the work, Hamilton, who is said to have reserved for himself the discussion of the general political theory of
the federal state, is considered the more important one. He is given
credit for dealing with the basic concepts of a federal republic, i.e.,
a body politic in which individual citizens and states enjoy freedom.
The comments upon the executive and judicial branches of government, upon the position of the federal state in international affairs,
and upon the essence of liberty and the separation of powers are
regarded as the major contribution of that author, who is described
as a man with a profoundly political and, on the whole, Machiavel-

[115] *Ibid.,* lviii.
[116] Garosci, *op. cit.*
[117] *Ibid.,* 320-21.

lian turn of mind.[118] Madison's writing in the *Federalist* appears to be of less significance, though by no means unimportant. In Garosci's opinion, it contains the argument that a republic extending over a large area is conducive to freedom. Great significance is attributed to essay ten, while number fourteen, "the other essay on general politics," is considered to be of less importance.[119] However, the Virginian's major effort is seen in his analysis of the federal compromise and the federal structure of the new system, as it comes to light in his discussion of the "federal" and "national" features of the Constitution and in his comments upon the powers of the national government. Also, Madison's remarks on the separation of powers are evaluated highly in view of the central position that institution occupies in the realm of constitutional law. On the whole, it can also be said that Madison appears as an opponent of majoritarianism and an advocate of political compromise.[120]

In contrast to his compatriot, Ambrosini does not distinguish between the political ideas of the authors. To him, the *Federalist* constitutes one organic whole, and the reproach of its split personality is ill-founded. The writings of Publius represent the expression of one will because the authors were devoted to one common cause. Consequently, Ambrosini analyzes the essays irrespective of their authorship. For him, the outstanding features of the work are its pessimism and realism, its discussion of democracy and conservatism, the advantages of the Union, the federal system, representative government and direct democracy, the necessity of efficient government, the separation of powers, and—last, but not least—the Supreme Court as the guardian of the Constitution.[121]

3.   An examination of the literature on the *Federalist* reveals a diversity of approaches to the work. A variety of attempts to tackle specific aspects of the Papers is matched by many different evaluations of the classic as a whole. While the discussion of concrete subjects does not usually fail to include the general content of the essays, more comprehensive treatises on Publius' complete commentary often result in emphasis upon specific aspects of the work. The two approaches thus do not differ too much. It seems as if the more gen-

[118] *Ibid.*, 267-96.
[119] *Ibid.*, 296-305.
[120] *Ibid.*, 306-16.
[121] Ambrosini, *op. cit.*, lxxxiii-cxix.

eral approach, which has been undertaken especially since the beginning of this century,[122] preceded the more specific one and that, due to the various studies that have come forth in the past decades on more or less limited subjects, the standards of more comprehensive treatises on the *Federalist* improved.[123] On the whole, it can be said that the Papers have increasingly attracted the interest of scholars. Thus the importance attributed to them by the whole world has been matched more and more by a continually improved elucidation of the work of Publius by members of the academic profession in the various nations.

In spite of the great variety of approaches to the *Federalist,* certain definite evaluations of that work have crystallized over the years. They fall into a number of groups, depending upon their respective orientations. Thus some authors have maintained that the Papers deal with the practice of government, whereas others have felt that theory had a definite place in them. Writers who emphasized the split personality were opposed by those who felt that the work of Publius constituted one organic whole. Aside from these distinctions, others of a less technical character have been made. The influence of the historical process upon the authors has been evaluated differently. The *Federalist* has been described as a work in which there was no room for natural law, a thesis that challenged the opinion of other scholars. An economic interpretation of the essays has been countered by those who felt that such an interpretation was one-sided and not corresponding to the actual content of the Papers. The nature of political man has been seen in a different light, with some writers displaying a greater degree of pessimism than others. As to the purpose and the essence of the work, it has been stressed, on the one hand, that the essays were written for the sake of union, whereas, on the other hand, union has been considered to be nothing but a means for the achievement of certain further ends. These ends have been conceived largely to be such things as security from foreign attack, good relations among the members of the federal state, and the protection of individual rights from governmental encroachment. Different writers have stressed the various aspects in different ways, just as their particular leanings might induce them to. The *Federal-*

[122] Nineteenth-century literature on the *Federalist* was largely concerned with a discussion of the disputed authorship. See *supra.,* note 104.

[123] The works of Beloff and Garosci are demonstrations of such an improvement. On the other hand, Esmein's study is also one of high caliber.

ist's concept of constitutionalism has by no means been beyond the realm of interpretation, and neither has its doctrine of federalism, which some students have considered in a more nationalistic vein than others.

The literature on the *Federalist* thus unfolds a wide panorama not only of approaches, but also of evaluations. The diversity of the attitudes of scholars that have made the Papers the subject of their research may well be said to match that of those statesmen, jurists, historians, and political scientists who have merely commented upon the work.[124] This must raise the question as to what is the proper approach in order to obtain a comprehension of the *Federalist,* to which we now turn.

III

1.   A comprehension of the *Federalist* presupposes a comprehensive study of the work. Useful as treatises on specific subjects may have proven, they run the risk of providing for only a part of the story, of losing sight of the whole, and, consequently, of giving a more or less one-sided picture. They are as risky an undertaking as partial editions of the *Federalist,* which were published every so often, although Chancellor Kent had admitted that his own attempt to abridge the Papers was fruitless.[125]

As to the technique of a general approach, there appear to be, first of all, no alternatives to an analytical approach. The *Federalist* is primarily a commentary on a constitution. As such, it exists in black on white, having an intrinsic value of its own and being as independent as the law it defends. The fact that it was the work of advocates for a cause[126] does not detract from its quality. All laws are, since they set up norms, advocating definite ends, and no one would think of denying their validity on that account. It was the exposition of the *Federalist,* its words and sentences as they appeared in print, that became the classic interpretation of the Constitution. Whenever the *Federalist* served as a guide for the interpretation of the Constitution, as happened quite frequently,[127] it was the phrasing

---

[124] See *supra,* pp. 3 ff.
[125] Kent, *op. cit.,* I, 256.
[126] See *supra,* p. 5.
[127] See *supra,* pp. 6-7.

of the work that was taken into consideration rather than what was possibly in the back of the authors' minds when they put their ideas on paper. Once these ideas had flown from their originators' pens, they became independent statements that were merely interdependent upon other parts of the commentary, and upon nothing else. With its promulgation, a subjective expression became an objective truth that can be considered wiser than its creators.[128]

Analysis means thorough analysis. While studies on the *Federalist* have largely taken the analytical approach and do thus confirm our thesis of the necessity of such an approach, their analytical efforts are far from painstaking. Words and sentences are quoted, but often in a careless manner. Proof is hardly furnished that they were compared with and weighed against other statements of the work. It appears as if in many cases the writer simply chose certain passages that were useful for the support of his argument, irrespective of the context in which they were actually used in the *Federalist* and without being too much concerned about their real validity. Such a procedure can easily lead to misunderstandings. To be protected against them, it is necessary to apply a method that carefully evaluates the various statements of the work, be they words or sentences, in their relation to each other and with respect to their meaning. This may require an occupation with semantics[129] and result in a rather legal-formalistic discussion.[130] However, since it is, after all, a commentary on a constitution that is being analyzed, such an analytical method can hardly be out of place if it serves to find the truth.

A thorough analysis implies a systematic analysis. Hastily written,[131] the essays are (the literary style is here of no concern)[132] not too systematically arranged.[133] Beard is right when he comments

---

[128] Compare Gustav Radbruch, RECHTSPHILOSOPHIE (4th ed., 1950), 211.

[129] See, for instance, *infra,* p. 125, n. 85.

[130] See, for instance, *infra,* pp. 146 ff.

[131] See *supra,* note 89.

[132] Comp. Mabel G. Benson, SOME RHETORICAL CHARACTERISTICS OF THE FEDERALIST (Dissertation, Chicago, 1948).

[133] The "systematic" arrangement of the *Federalist* consists merely in a subject-by-subject discussion. A general introduction is followed by a discussion of the following subjects: Dangers from foreign force and influence; dangers from dissensions between the states; the consequences of hostilities between the states; the Union as a safeguard against domestic faction and insurrection; the utility of the Union in respect to commercial relations and to a navy, to revenue, to economy in government; objections to the proposed Constitution from extent of

that the *Federalist* "lacks in many places the finish" the authors "could have given it, had they commanded greater leisure. It is more than occasionally repetitious and defective in logical structure. . . . The most profound and instructive of the observations contained in its pages are frequently buried in passages respecting practices no longer observed."[134] The diversity of authorship did not contribute to a systematic work.[135] Writers dealing with the *Federalist,* just as they have not been too thorough in their analytical efforts, have also not been too systematic in their approach. The organization of their studies often appears to be arbitrary, and one has the feeling that they felt not quite sure on where to start and where to end, because they did not recognize what was the central idea of the commentary.[136] In view of the want of system in the Papers, it thus seems to

territory; the insufficiency of the present confederation to preserve the Union; other defects of the present confederation; the necessity of a government as energetic as the one proposed to the preservation of the Union; the powers necessary for the common defense; the militia; taxation; the difficulties of the Convention in devising a proper form of government; the conformity of the new Constitution to republican principles; the powers and actions of the Federal Convention; the powers of the new government; restrictions on the authority of the several states; the alleged danger from the powers of the Union to the state governments; the influence of the state and federal government; the separation of powers; the House of Representatives; the Senate; the executive; the judiciary; miscellaneous objections to the Constitution; and a concluding remark.

[134] Beard, *op. cit.,* 10. When in March, 1788, Hamilton wrote the preface for the first volume of the first edition of the *Federalist* in book form, he apologized: "The particular circumstances under which these papers have been written, have rendered it impracticable to avoid violations of method and repetitions of ideas which cannot but displease a critical reader. The latter defect has even been intentionally indulged, in order the better to impress particular arguments which were most material to the general scope of reasoning. Respect for public opinion, not anxiety for the literary character of the performance, dictates this remark." (iii-iv.)

[135] See *supra,* pp. 18-21.

[136] Thus Goldwin Smith, *op. cit.,* centers his discussion around the authors' concept of the separation of powers and thereby stresses the institutional division of power out of proportion to its actual importance in the Papers. On the other hand, after having dealt with the separation of powers at greater length, he mentions that the exposition of federalism is perhaps the best part of the essays. However, he does not dwell on the subject of federalism and fails to point out its relevance for the separation of powers. Later on, he mentions judicial review as a bulwark of a limited Constitution and a means to check legislative encroachments, a subject that belongs to the discussion of the separation of powers. Similarly Esmein, *op. cit.,* while assigning the first place to federalism, does not

be necessary for a writer who plans to make a comprehensive study of the *Federalist* to create such a system. This, in turn, presupposes a knowledge of the core of the work.

2. The *Federalist* was written in order to secure the ratification of a constitution providing for a more perfect Union. Throughout the

show its implications on what he considers the other important features of the Constitution, namely, the presidential system and the organization of the judiciary. Likewise, a central focus is missing in the study of Earle, *op. cit.*, who stresses, side by side, such aspects as federalism and divided sovereignty, the protection of property, political liberties, representative government, and judicial review. Velasco, *op. cit.*, offers a more defensible system. Considering the *Federalist* primarily a treatise on constitutional government, he maintains that, in the second place, it is a defense of republican representative government, which is most conducive to the protection of individual rights. From here he proceeds to enumerate various means by which constitutionalism may be achieved, namely: federalism; the separation of powers with its corollary, the presidential system; the affirmation of essential individual rights; and the independent judiciary. This order is acceptable: The constitutional representative republic appears as the government ideally suited for individual protection under law, and the end of government—individual protection—is centered between the primary means to achieve such protection—federalism and the separation of powers—and the guarantee for a constitutional working of these means, an independent judiciary with the power of judicial review. However sound Velasco's approach may be, it does not seem to give due credit to the *Federalist's* character as a classic on federalism. Max Beloff, *op. cit.*, on the other hand, seems to assign a central position to the authors' discussion of federalism (liv). He also points out the function of federalism to insure individual freedom, peace among the member states, and security from foreign nations. However, he refrains from putting federalism in the center of his discussion. As a matter of fact, it appears as if he regards other concepts, such as justice and constitutional government, to be central to the argument of the *Federalist*. Possibly, Beloff was not too much concerned with giving a systematic picture of the work. One part of his introduction consists in a number-by-number discussion of the essays, a procedure which indicates that the author was inclined to accept the "system" provided by the *Federalist* itself. Garosci, *op. cit.*, fails to give a systematic analysis largely due to his author-by-author discussion of the work, which prevents an evaluation of the *Federalist* as a whole. The study of his compatriot, Ambrosini, *op. cit.*, in which the split personality of the *Federalist* is denied, suffers from a rather arbitrary selection of topics and their unsystematic and partly repetitious arrangement. Of course, a systematic treatise on the *Federalist* is not possible in studies on specific aspects of the Papers. On reading these studies, however, one often feels that their authors do not have a clear concept of the *Federalist* either. Compare, for instance, the rather strange arrangement of the essential features of the essays in Wright, *op. cit.*, *supra*, p. 22, which appears to be very arbitrary indeed.

Papers, the idea of the more perfect Union occupies a front stage. This has led some students to believe that the idea of union is the core of the *Federalist*. However, this is true only in a qualified sense. It is possibly Hamilton himself who laid the groundwork for this misconception. He starts the first essay saying that the deliberation on the Constitution is a subject that "speaks its own importance; comprehending in its consequences nothing less than the existence of the UNION, the safety and welfare of the parts of which it is composed," and ends the same essay saying, "I propose . . . to discuss the following . . . particulars:—*The utility of the UNION to your political prosperity—The insufficiency of the present Confederation to preserve that Union—The necessity of a government at least equally energetic with the one proposed, to the attainment of this object—The conformity of the proposed Constitution to the true principles of republican government—Its analogy to your own State constitution* and lastly, *The additional security which its adoption will afford to the preservation of that species of government, to liberty, and to property.*"[137] The purpose of the *Federalist* seems to be the idea of union, which is the only word that is, in the introductory essay, spelt in capital letters. A closer scrutiny, however, reveals that advocacy of the Union is the purpose of the *Federalist* only in a relative sense. "Union" and the "safety and welfare of the parts of which it is composed" are depicted as inseparable, and the Union appears as a means to achieve the safety and welfare of its parts. Toward the end of the essay, Hamilton again stresses the *utility* of the Union to political prosperity and the security of liberty and property. Union being a means to an end rather than an end in itself, the idea of union, important as it may be in the *Federalist*, can hardly be the core of that work, at least not in an absolute sense. It would be more correct to say that, like the idea of union itself, the *Federalist* turns around the objects which the more perfect Union is supposed to achieve, and that these objects rather constitute the core of the Papers. This does in no way decrease the importance of the Union which, as the means, remains inseparably connected with its ends and thus close to the core of the *Federalist*. It would be folly indeed to deny the relevance in the essays of the more perfect Union, the federal state that was advocated by men who called themselves federalists and who felt that for a defense of that state there was no better title than *The Federalist*.

[137] 1, 3; 1, 6.

It should not be forgotten that the essays were written for a constitution providing for a federal government.

If we now ask for the ends that the more perfect Union is to
achieve, according to the *Federalist,* we receive a direct answer
from the authors themselves. Aside from Hamilton's statements in
the first essay, there are others in later numbers. In the sixth essay,
Hamilton points out the necessity of the Union for security "from
the arms and arts of foreign nations," for the prevention of "dissensions between the States themselves," and for the protection
"from domestic factions and convulsions."[138] Madison gives a similar
enumeration in essay forty-one,[139] and in number forty-five he states
that the Union is "essential to the security of the people of America
against foreign danger; . . . to their security against contentions and
wars among the different States; . . . to guard them against those
violent and oppressive factions which embitter the blessings of
liberty, and against those military establishments which must gradually poison its very fountain; . . . in a word, . . . essential to the
happiness of the people of America."[140] These statements agree that
the ends of the Union are mainly three: first, freedom of individual
rights; second, peace within the federation; and third, security from
foreign nations. The more perfect Union is advocated in order to
achieve free government in peace and security. Studies on the *Federalist* have, on the whole, failed to elevate the concept of "free
government in peace and security through Union" to the central
position where, according to the authors of the *Federalist,* it belongs.[141] As a result, certain aspects of the work received an attention
that was out of proportion to their actual importance, whereas
others were slighted.[142] This distorted the picture of the whole work
and prevented the systematic approach that is essential to a comprehensive analysis of the Papers. It is therefore proposed to analyze
the *Federalist* as a treatise for a federal government that provides
for free government in peace and security.

The *Federalist* is not only the classic exposition of a specific federal state. It is also a classic on federalism in general. In a word, it
is a work on the practice and theory of federalism. The tendency

[138] 6, 27.
[139] 41, 261.
[140] 45, 298.
[141] See *supra,* pp. 18 ff.
[142] See *supra,* p. 31.

among writers to deny the existence of theory in the *Federalist* was a misconception that rendered a systematic analysis impossible.[143] Jefferson can possibly be regarded the originator of the belief that the commentary was dealing with the practice of government only. In a letter to his nephew Thomas Mann Randolph he distinguishes the *Federalist* from the theoretical writings of Locke when he writes, after discussing Locke's philosophy: "Descending from theory to practice, there can be no better book than the Federalist."[144] However, the authors by no means considered their work a mere treatise on governmental practice. In their essays, a distinction between theory and practice is often drawn. "Theoretical reasoning . . . must be qualified by the lessons of practice," Madison writes,[145] and he also states that the Philadelphia Convention "must have been compelled to sacrifice theoretical propriety to the force of extraneous considerations."[146] In a similar vein, Hamilton distinguishes between "theory and practice"[147] and puts "theory against fact and reality,"[148] saying also that "to give a minority a negative upon the majority . . . is one of those refinements which, in practice, has an effect the reverse of what is expected from it in theory."[149] A study on the *Federalist* can thus be divided into a theoretical and a practical part, the former dealing with federalism as a means to achieve free government in peace and security, the latter with the nonexistence of that form of government under the Articles of Confederation and its achievement under the Constitution.

3.   A conclusion has now been reached on how to undertake an analysis of the *Federalist*. Federalism will be examined as a means for establishing free government, as a means for securing peace within the federal state, and as a means for maintaining security

---

[143] The importance of the *Federalist* for political theory was generally recognized by continental authors in the nineteenth century. American writers have stressed that the Papers comment on the practice of government. This different evaluation is probably a reflection of different approaches to political problems and constitutional law, with American authors preferring a rather pragmatic approach, in contrast to their continental colleagues.

[144] Letter of May 30, 1790. JEFFERSON'S WRITINGS, VIII, 31.

[145] 43, 284.

[146] 37, 231.

[147] 31, 190.

[148] 34, 203.

[149] 22, 135.

from the threats of foreign powers. Wherever it appears to be necessary and advisable, the split personality of the Papers will be taken into account. Always, however, a distinction will be drawn between the authors' opinion on the theory of federalism, which includes their comments on historical experiences, and their opinion on federal practice, as existing in America. We are aware that such an approach is likely to result in repetitions. Federalism as a means to achieve free government will in many instances also appear as a means to achieve peace and security, which is not surprising in view of the fact that, after all, it is supposed to achieve all these ends, and not just one of them. Therefore, arguments used in one connection might turn up in another. The same applies to our discussion of the theory and practice of federalism. Very often, the distinction between the two is not clearly drawn by the authors, which is, again, only natural in view of the fact that their suggestions for the practice of federal government were largely influenced by their knowledge of theory and historical experience. Still, it is felt that occasional repetitions are a price that ought to be paid for the sake of clarity, which can be attained only through systematic analysis.

The analytical approach does by no means imply a rejection of history as a factor relevant to an understanding of the Papers. The *Federalist* was definitely the product of its time, and its authors were influenced by the thinking and the events of their age. Consequently, a historical part will precede the analytical one, showing the general atmosphere of the years prior to the writing of the essays and the degree to which the authors were under the spell of that atmosphere.

Also, the analytical approach does not mean that the present study will not take into consideration the writings of political philosophers other than the authors. The influence of these thinkers on Hamilton, Jay, and Madison can be seen in the pages of their work. The *Federalist,* in turn, left its mark upon the literature of subsequent generations not only of the United States, but also of other parts of the world. Therefore, this analysis of the Papers shall be followed by a theoretical evaluation of the commentary.

A systematic analysis of the Papers, set against a historical background and accompanied by a discussion of the work's place in political theory, will, it is hoped, contribute to an appreciation of the *Federalist* as a classic on federalism.

BOOK ONE

Historical Setting

CHAPTER TWO

The American Revolution
and Union

The period of the American Revolution was characterized by a
quest for security from foreign nations, for peace among the American states, and for individual freedom.

Although there existed many currents and cross-currents in the
political, social, and economic life during the eventful years from
the colonists' struggle with England to the adoption of the Constitution, they were, on the whole, connected with security, peace, and
freedom. Depending upon the relative threats to these values, the
intensity of the desire for any one of them would vary from time to
time and from section to section. Often the striving for one would be
closely connected with the quest for another, and it would be difficult to keep them apart. Still, no matter how much the distinction
was blurred, the various desires would never completely lose their
identity and would sooner or later emerge from temporary decline.
It was, above all, the desire for security, peace, and freedom that led
to the more perfect Union under the Constitution.

I

1. The hope to enjoy security through union was already evident in the colonial period. Fear of attacks from the Dutch, the French, and the Indians led to the formation of the New England Confederacy in 1643.[1] William Penn's proposal of 1698, for the establishment of an American federation, was motivated by the dangers arising from the presence of the French in Canada and the West.[2] It was defended by Charles Davenant, an Englishman, who also recognized the value of union for security.[3] In 1701, a Virginian published in London *An Essay upon the Government of the English Plantations on the Continent of America*. While this book criticized the plans of Penn and Davenant, it agreed with their urging union as a means for security.[4] In the same year, Robert Livingston of New York recommended union to the Lords of Trade, mainly for defense purposes.[5] The proposal by the Earl of Stair of 1721 was motivated

[1] The first two paragraphs of the Articles of Confederation read: ". . . whereas we live encompassed with people of several nations and strange languages which hereafter may prove injurious to us or our posterity. And foreasmuch as the natives have formerly committed sundry insolence and outrages upon several Plantations of the English and have of late combined themselves against us: and seeing by reason of those sad distractions in England which they have heard of, and by which they know we are hindered from that humble way of seeking advice, or reaping those comfortable fruits of protection, which at other times we might well expect. We therefore do conceive it our bounden duty, without delay to enter into a present Consociation amongst ourselves, for mutual help and strength in all our future concernments. . . . The said United Colonies for themselves and their posterities do jointly and severally hereby enter into a firm and perpetual league of friendship and amity, for offence and defence, mutual advice and succor. . . ." Francis N. Thorpe, ed., THE FEDERAL AND STATE CONSTITUTIONS, COLONIAL CHARTERS, AND OTHER ORGANIC LAWS (1909), I, 77. Also, the following paragraphs show that these Articles were concerned primarily with security.

[2] According to Paragraph 6 of the plan, the colonial congress was "to consider the ways and means to support the union and safety of these provinces against the public enemies," and to "better adjust and balance their affairs in all respects for their common safety." Henry Steele Commager, ed., DOCUMENTS OF AMERICAN HISTORY (5th ed., 1949), 39-40.

[3] Charles Davenant, "Discourse on the Plantation Trade," in Sir Charles Whitworth, ed., THE POLITICAL AND COMMERCIAL WORKS OF THAT CELEBRATED WRITER CHARLES D'AVENANT, etc. (1771), II, 1-76.

[4] Louis B. Wright, ed., AN ESSAY UPON THE GOVERNMENT OF THE ENGLISH PLANTATIONS ON THE CONTINENT OF AMERICA (1945), 51.

[5] Letter of May 13, 1701. Richard Frothingham, THE RISE OF THE REPUBLIC OF

by similar considerations.[6] Two decades later, Daniel Coxe, who held several high posts in New Jersey, drew public attention to the designs of France. For the protection of the English colonies, he urged union "for their mutual defence and safety."[7] In 1752, Archibald Kennedy, the receiver-general of New York, recommended union in order to secure the general defense,[8] and Governor Dinwiddie of Virginia recommended the formation of a Northern and a Southern confederacy together with a scheme of alliance between the Indians and all the British Indians in America, obviously having the security of the colonies in mind.[9] Last but not least, the Albany Congress met to encounter threats from the French and the Indians.[10] Four years later, Dr. Samuel Johnson, president of King's College, proposed union for the common defense.[11]

With the collapse of French power in North America the spirit of co-operation would probably have waned had it not been for the colonial policy of the British government, of which parliamentary taxation of the colonies became an outstanding feature. This again prompted the colonies to unite. Whereas Great Britain had desired

THE UNITED STATES (1872), 116. See also Hampton L. Carson, ed., HISTORY OF THE CELEBRATION OF THE ONE HUNDREDTH ANNIVERSARY OF THE PROMULGATION OF THE CONSTITUTION OF THE UNITED STATES (1889), II, 459-60.

[6] Carson, *op. cit.*, II, 460-62.

[7] "A Description of the English Province of Carolina," Carson, *op. cit.*, 465-66. Attributing the fall of the ancient Britons and of Rome to disunity, Coxe adds: "If the English colonies in America were consolidated as one body, and joyn'd in one common interest, as they are under one gracious sovereign, and with united forces were ready and willing to act in concert, and assist each other, they would be better enabled to provide for and defend themselves, against any troublesome ambitious neighbor or bold invader. For union and concord increase and establish strength and power, whilst division and discord have the contrary effects." *Ibid.*, 466-67.

[8] Archibald Kennedy, IMPORTANCE OF GAINING AND PRESERVING THE FRIENDSHIP OF THE INDIANS (1752).

[9] Frothingham, *op. cit.*, 116-17.

[10] Compare the provisions of the Albany Plan concerning the power to raise troops, build forts, and equip vessels for defense purposes. Thorpe, *op. cit.*, I, 85.

[11] In 1760, Dr. Samuel Johnson, president of King's College, sent suggestions concerning the union of the colonies to the Archbishop of Canterbury, in which he stated: "As the disunited state of our Colonies was found attended with many disadvantages at the beginning of the War, and was one great occasion of our ill success at first, and would at any time and on any occasion be attended with many fatal effects; Qu: Whether some scheme could not be pitched upon that for the future, might be a principle of Union?" Carson, *op. cit.*, 484.

the colonies to speak collectively to the French, they now spoke collectively to her, in the Stamp Act Congress of 1765 and the First Continental Congress of 1774. The Second Continental Congress got beyond speech and brought forth the Declaration of Independence. Security was now being sought from the mother country. Congress assumed the powers necessary for the direction of the policy of the United States as a whole and supervised the conduct of the war. Desirous of basing the union of the states upon a legal foundation and a written constitution, Richard Henry Lee moved as early as June 7, 1776 that Congress prepare a plan of confederation. Shortly after independence had been declared, a committee consisting of one member from each state reported the first draft of the Articles of Confederation. After various amendments, Congress agreed to the instrument proposed in November, 1777 and submitted it to the states for ratification. By 1781, the Articles had been ratified by all the states.

2.   The security motive is evident in the text of the Articles. Articles one and two, giving the name of the Confederacy and asserting the principle of state sovereignty, are followed by a statement on the first purpose of the confederation: "The said states hereby enter into a firm league of friendship with each other for their common defence, the security of their liberties and their mutual and general welfare; binding themselves to assist each other against all force offered to, or attacks made upon them, or any of them, on account of religion, sovereignty, trade, or any other pretence whatever."[12]

Once the war against England was won, security from foreign nations was still precarious. It appears doubtful whether the ally in the struggle for independence, France, did not now constitute a threat to America.[13] She had entered the alliance primarily to further her own ends and had, from the beginning, misgivings about American greatness. As early as 1778 Vergennes had written to Montmorin in Spain: "We do not desire by a great deal that the rising new republic remain exclusively mistress of this whole immense continent. Self-sufficient before long for her own needs, the other nations would be likely to reckon with her, because she, able to do without

[12] Art. 3.
[13] See, on the whole, Arthur B. Darling, OUR RISING EMPIRE 1763-1803 (1940), esp. 115-22.

everything, would very certainly make a very hard law for them."[14]
France's effort to deny American claims to the Mississippi Valley
were stopped temporarily by the provisional treaty of 1782, which
transferred British title there to the United States. But hopes remained alive with the French population of Quebec, Illinois, and
Louisiana that France would return. Likewise, the French in the
mother country kept an interest in that area, as was borne out by
later events.[15]

Spanish interests constituted an even greater threat to American
security. From the beginning, Spain had been less enthusiastic about
the Americans' fight for independence than France. American republican principles were considered a menace to the Spanish empire,
and the talk of American diplomats that their country had a natural
right to the outlets through Spanish territory was resented. As the
war progressed, American troops were coming closer to Spanish possessions, and Spanish suspicions grew.[16] After the Peace of Paris,
Spain saw in the feebleness of the American confederation an opportunity for her own intentions east of the Mississippi. She took
under her protection Indian tribes that were natural enemies of the
advancing American pioneers, and used them for the defense of
Louisiana, Florida, and Mexico. Like England in the Northwest,
Spain was laboring on the American Southwestern border to divert
the allegiance of settlers west of the Alleghanies, who strongly opposed a project pending before Congress to barter American rights
in the Mississippi for certain commercial privileges mainly of advantage to the North. She made attempts to foster a Spanish party
in Kentucky, and perhaps in the settlements on the Cumberland and
the Tennessee southward, to rebel against Congress.[17]

However, the most serious threat to American security came from
England. After the treaty of peace, relations with the mother country
remained strained.[18] Both nations were now competitors in the field
of commerce. John Adams, ambassador to the Court of St. James,
was snubbed by the King. His attempts to settle the problems con-

[14] Letter of Oct. 30, 1778. Henry Doniol, HISTOIRE DE LA PARTICIPATION DE LA
FRANCE A L'ETABLISSEMENT DES ETATS-UNIS D'AMERIQUE (1886-99), III, 561-62.

[15] Compare Francis P. Renaut, LA QUESTION DE LA LOUISIANE, 1796-1806 (1918).

[16] See, on the whole, Darling, *op. cit.*, esp. 27-44.

[17] *Ibid.*, 100-10. Compare also Arthur P. Whitaker, THE SPANISH-AMERICAN
FRONTIER: 1783-95 (1927).

[18] See, on the whole, Darling, *op. cit.*, esp. 110-15.

cerning the Northwestern ports, the compensation for the slaves that had been taken away by the British, the reciprocal agreements on shipping and goods, and the fisheries were encountered by stubborn questions about the compensation of the loyalists and old American debts to British merchants. Not only were relations between the two countries strained in the field of diplomacy, but also an imminent military threat from the British continued to exist. Pitt was thinking of a British future in the Mississippi Valley, from the Great Lakes to the Gulf. Consequently, the British tried to prevent American expansion to the West. In defiance of the Treaty of Paris, British troops remained in the Northwest Territory, alleging infractions of the treaty by the Americans. The English entertained hopes that the pioneers in western Pennsylvania, Kentucky, and the Northwest would tend toward England rather than the United States. They continued to incite the Indians against the Americans. Although Lord Sidney felt that "to afford the Indians active assistance would at the present moment be a measure extremely imprudent," he stressed that "at the same time it would not become us to refuse them such supplies of ammunition as might enable them to defend themselves." He observed that the Indians were in great want of ammunition and that, "circumstanced as they now are, there cannot be any objection to . . . furnishing them with a supply, causing it to be done in a way the least likely to alarm the Americans, or to induce the Indians to think that there is a disposition on our part to incite them to any hostile proceedings."[19] George Washington had quite a different opinion as to the British "reluctance" to induce the Indians to acts of hostility against the Americans. In a letter to Lafayette, he complained about the British occupation of the Western ports and said, concerning British activities, that he had "not the smallest doubt, but that every secret engine is continually at work to inflame the Indian mind, with a view to keep it at variance with these States."[20]

3.   The threat to American security from foreign nations was one of the reasons for the desire for a more perfect Union. Although the

[19] Letter to Lord Dorchester of April 5, 1787. George Bancroft, HISTORY OF THE FORMATION OF THE CONSTITUTION OF THE UNITED STATES OF AMERICA (1882), II, 416.
[20] Letter of May 10, 1786. WASHINGTON'S WRITINGS, XXVIII, 423. For a general discussion of the position of the new nation vis-à-vis foreign powers, see Merrill Jensen, THE NEW NATION (1950), 154-78.

security motive was, in the months preceding the Philadelphia Convention, probably not as strong as was the desire for peace among the American states and for the freedom of the individual, its relevance for the revision of the Articles of Confederation can hardly be denied.[21] The credentials of the delegates to the Federal Convention speak of the necessity of rendering the Articles adequate to the exigencies of the Union, and the idea of defense from foreign powers was obviously too much considered part of these exigencies to be mentioned in so many words. Only New Hampshire deemed it necessary to state expressly that the delegates were "enabled to avert the dangers which threaten our existence as a free and independent People."[22]

In the Convention, the fear of foreign intrusion and war could be noticed. Colonel Mason opposed a three-year citizenship as a sufficient qualification for members to the House of Representatives, fearing that "it might . . . happen that a rich foreign Nation, for example Great Britain, might send over her tools who might bribe their way into the Legislature for insidious purposes."[23] Governor Morris mentioned the possibility of a war with Spain for the Mississippi,[24] and he referred to the fisheries and the Mississippi as "the two great objects of the Union."[25] These problems could be solved only through concessions by foreign nations.

Defense against foreign powers was an important consideration in the framing of the new charter. In his speech opening the main business of the Convention, Randolph mentioned first that the new government was to achieve security against foreign invasion, and elaborated the respective shortcomings of the Articles of Confederation.[26] The idea of common defense was in the foreground during the next day of the debates.[27] The Pinckney Plan started out by saying that the states established a confederacy "under one general superintending Government for their common Benefit and for their Defense and Security against all Designs and Leagues that may be injurious to their Interests and against all Force (or Foes) and At-

---

[21] This is rarely debated by historians.
[22] Max Farrand, ed., THE RECORDS OF THE FEDERAL CONVENTION (1911), III, 573.
[23] *Ibid.*, II, 216, 271.
[24] *Ibid.*, I, 604.
[25] *Ibid.*, II, 548.
[26] *Ibid.*, I, 18-20.
[27] *Ibid.*, I, 30, 33, 38-41.

tacks offered to or made upon them or any of them."[28] The importance of the security motive is, finally, evident in the Convention's product, where the preamble states that the Constitution is ordained and established in order to provide for the common defense.

II

1. Like the desire for security from non-American powers, the quest for peace among the English colonies was connected with the idea of union at an early stage. The New England Confederacy was conceived to be "a firm and perpetual league of friendship and amity," and the Commissioners for that confederation were authorized to "endeavor to frame and establish agreements . . . for preserving of peace among themselves, for preventing as much as may be all occasion of war or differences with others."[29] William Penn planned to establish an intercolonial assembly, which was to promote harmony between the colonies, safeguard commerce, and take measures for the general tranquility.[30] Charles Davenant and the Virginian author of the essay on the government of the English plantations agreed with Penn as to the usefulness of a union for better relations among the colonies.[31] The peace motive can be recognized in the plans for union offered by Robert Livingston and the Earl of Stair.[32] Coxe's design shows a desire for peace when it says that the proposed union will "lay a sure and lasting foundation of dominion, strength and trade sufficient . . . to secure and promote the prosperity of the plantations."[33] Dr. Samuel Johnson desired union partly in order to "preserve as far as possible a spirit of

---

[28] *Ibid.,* II, 134.

[29] Paragraph 8. Thorpe, *op. cit.,* I, 80.

[30] Compare Paragraph 6 of Penn's plan: "That their business shall be to hear and adjust all matters of complaint or difference between province and province. As, 1st, where persons quit their own province and go to another, that they may avoid their just debts, though they be able to pay them; 2d, where offenders fly justice, or justice cannot be had upon such offenders in the provinces that entertain them; 3rd, to prevent or cure injuries in point of commerce; . . ." Commager, *op. cit.,* 39-40.

[31] Carson, *op. cit.,* II, 455; Louis B. Wright, *op. cit.,* 31, 47-48.

[32] The plan of union, submitted by the Lords of Trade to the King on Sept. 8, 1721, also says that through union the colonies would be rendered "mutually subservient to each other's support." Carson, *op. cit.,* II, 464.

[33] *Ibid.,* II, 466.

harmony, mutual indulgence and forbearance, with regard to each other, avoiding everything unkind and invidious."[34]

Although the need for union as a means for the preservation of peace among the colonies had been recognized throughout the colonial period, a union hardly existed during that time. Plans for unification were either short-lived or not realized at all. European travelers were struck by this disjunction. Kalm, the Swede, noted in 1749-1750 that frequently, "while some Provinces have been suffering from their enemies, the neighboring ones were quiet and inactive, and as if it did not in the least concern them." There were "provinces who were not only neuter in these circumstances, but who even carried on a great trade with the Power which at that very time was attacking and laying waste some other Provinces."[35] A decade later, Burnaby felt that fire and water were not more antagonistic than some of the colonies: "Such is the difference of character, of manners, of religion, of interest in the various colonies, that I think, if I am not wholly ignorant of the human mind, were they left to themselves, there would soon be civil war from one end of the continent to the other."[36] Americans were, on the whole, not more optimistic. James Otis was afraid in 1765 that the colonies' separation from England would usher in "a terrible scene. Were these Colonies left to themselves to-morrow, America would be a mere shambles of blood and confusion before little petty States could be settled."[37] The fear of civil war was one of the favorite arguments of the Tories against separation from England.[38]

[34] *Ibid.*, II, 485.

[35] Allan Nevins, THE AMERICAN STATES DURING AND AFTER THE REVOLUTION (1924), 545.

[36] *Ibid.*, 545.

[37] James Otis, BRIEF REMARKS ON THE DEFENCE OF THE HALIFAX LIBEL, ON THE BRITISH-AMERICAN COLONIES (1765), 16.

[38] In the First Continental Congress, Galloway expressed fears of open hostilities among the colonies: "They are at this moment only suppressed by the authority of the parent state; and should that authority be weakened or annulled, many subjects of unsettled disputes, and which in that case can only be settled by an appeal to the sword, must involve us in all the horrors of civil war." JOURNALS OF THE CONTINENTAL CONGRESS, Sept. 28, 1774. Tories in Maryland declared that "Our independency may produce endless wars among ourselves, and with them, a certain loss of liberty is to be sustained from our foreign foes." MARYLAND JOURNAL, July 22, 1777. In Virginia, they stated that the destruction of "the finest constitution in the world" would bring about "a dreadful train of domestic convulsions in each republic; of jealousies, dissensions, wars, and all their

The dispute with the mother country united the colonies by necessity rather than inclination.[39] During the War of Independence, the states fought side by side without any notable disharmony. Under the Articles of Confederation, they were united in a "firm league of friendship." Also, these Articles provided for means "to secure and perpetuate mutual friendship and intercourse among the people of the different States in this Union."[40]

2. In spite of these provisions, tensions among the states continued.[41] Even during the war, Congress complained that the drafting of the Articles of Confederation was "attended by uncommon embarrassments and delay," and that "to form a permanent union, accommodated to the opinions and wishes of so many States, differing in habits, produce, commerce, and internal police, was found to be a task which nothing but time and reflection, conspiring with a disposition to conciliate, could mature and produce."[42] Once the war was over, the states increasingly exhibited much petty jealousy and even quarrelsomeness. The reasons were manifold. Jefferson stated that "broils among the States may happen in the following ways: First, a State may be embroiled with the other twelve by not complying with the lawful requisitions of Congress. Second, two States may differ about their boundaries. . . . Third, other contestations may arise between two States, such as pecuniary demands, affrays between their citizens, and whatever else may arrive between two nations."[43] He could have added quarrels over trade, commerce and finance, war burdens, and the Western lands.

Disputes over trade probably were the most constant. They account for the effort to bring about a comprehensive congressional regulation of trade, led by Massachusetts in 1783. Tariffs became responsible for an increasing deterioration of the relations between

attendant miseries, in the neighboring republics; in which forms of government they seem to imagine that Nature breeds: All monstrous, all prodigious things . . . /Gorgons, and hydras, and chimeras dire." VIRGINIA GAZETTE, April 12, 1776.

[39] The Stamp Act Congress of 1765 and the Continental Congress of 1774 were both demonstrations of American unity.

[40] Articles 3 and 4.

[41] See Nevins, *op. cit.*, 544-605.

[42] *Ibid.*, 544.

[43] "Answers to Questions Propounded by Monsieur de Meusnier, Jan. 24, 1786," JEFFERSON'S WRITINGS, XVII, 120-21.

the states. During the war, Virginia alone had levied duties on a broader scale, and at the end of the struggle Patrick Henry had expressed hope that commerce between the states would not be fettered at all through taxation.[44] On the whole, it can be said that up to 1785 the states imposed duties on imports only to lighten taxes. However, once home industries had developed in New England and the Middle states, the states of these areas sought to protect their goods from foreign imports by raising tariffs. On the other hand, the Southern states, not having built up industries, depended largely upon imported manufactured goods. With the exception of Virginia, they refrained from making their tariffs protective. Due to different tariff policies, the feeling between some of the states became bitter, even hostile. It became more and more evident that some of them did not mind injuring their neighbors as long as they could profit from it. By 1786, the prediction of the Pennsylvania legislature, made in 1783, that "the local exercise within the States of the powers of regulating and controlling trade can result only in discontent systems productive of internal jealousies and competitions, and illy calculated to oppose or counteract foreign measures, which are the effect of a unity of council,"[45] was borne out in all parts of the United States.

The problem of navigation on the Mississippi proved to be another source of tension. Jay's proposal to surrender navigation for almost thirty years to Spain in return for that country's opening her ports to American goods was received with enthusiasm by the Northern merchants, shippers, and farmers. In the South and Southwest, the plan was considered a demonstration of sectional selfishness. When Congress, by a majority of seven Northern against five Southern states, virtually authorized Jay to negotiate the proposed treaty, intense anger was manifested in Virginia, the Ohio Valley, and western Pennsylvania. The nation was split apart over that issue.

Different currencies created commercial and financial difficulties that resulted in ill-feeling among the citizens of the various states. This feeling was enhanced by the unreliability of paper currencies, the value of which depreciated with every new legislative session.

---

[44] "Why, why should we fetter commerce? Fetter not commerce, Sir; let her be as free as the air—she will range the whole creation, and return on the wings of the four winds of heaven to bless the land with plenty," Patrick Henry is said to have remarked. Nevins, *op. cit.*, 557-58.

[45] Bancroft, *op. cit.*, I, 335.

Other disputes arose from the enactment of laws infringing upon the obligation of contracts.[46] Stay laws, under which debtors were allowed extensions of time to meet their obligations, amounting to virtual moratoriums, were another source of interstate tensions.[47]

The states' different disposition toward requisitions by Congress also contributed to frictions. Already during the war it had become evident that some of the states shirked from their obligations to the national cause, and this remained so in the years after the war. In 1785, Gerry blamed unfair taxation for the low value of Massachusetts lands.[48] In New York, ill-feeling existed toward New Hampshire for not having paid a cent into the national treasury since the peace, in spite of the fact that she had not suffered from invasions during the war. North Carolina was accused of having been equally delinquent.[49] On the other hand, a North Carolinian in 1784 opposed the cession of land to the nation on the grounds that his home state had not been given financial credit for her military assistance to Virginia and South Carolina and to the Indian wars, while other states had been rewarded for similar efforts.[50]

Territorial disputes were another case in point. They caused spectacular quarrels between the states, and the two major ones actually involved bloodshed. These were the dispute among New York, New Hampshire, and Massachusetts over Vermont, and the dispute between citizens of Pennsylvania and Connecticut over the Wyoming Valley. Both controversies did not really jeopardize the sovereignty of the states concerned, but, since they raised questions over the actual ownership of land, they provoked bad feeling among the rival states. Territorial disputes of less significance occurred over boundaries between Georgia and South Carolina, North Carolina and Virginia, Virginia and Maryland, New York and Massachusetts, and Pennsylvania and New York. The Western lands issue was

[46] For instance, stay laws passed in Rhode Island resulted in strong retaliatory measures against the citizens of that state by Massachusetts and Connecticut.

[47] These laws took their most reprehensible form in Virginia and South Carolina.

[48] Letter to Rufus King of April 23, 1785. C. R. King, ed., THE LIFE AND CORRESPONDENCE OF RUFUS KING (1894-1900), I, 89-90. Later, Rufus King reproached other states for not doing their share in the support of the Union. Jonathan Elliot, ed., THE DEBATES IN THE SEVERAL STATE CONVENTIONS ON THE ADOPTION OF THE FEDERAL CONSTITUTION (1876), II, 56.

[49] Elliot, op. cit., II, 232.

[50] Nevins, op. cit., 577-78.

another source of friction. New York, Connecticut, and Massachusetts as well as Virginia asserted title to some of the lands northwest of the Ohio River, Georgia and South Carolina to parts of the southwestern territory. More threatening than these claims were the irritations of those states that had no rights to the Western land at all, but were apprehensive as to the future power and growth of the other states.

These examples show that after the war, peace among the states did hardly exist. Richard Henry Lee's pessimism, expressed in 1777, concerning the precarious situation of interstate relations, remained justified in later years.[51] In 1785, Knox wrote Washington that "the different States have not only different views of the same subject, but some of them have views that sooner or later must involve the country in all the horrors of civil war."[52] Before the meeting of the Philadelphia Convention, the Connecticut *Courant* said that in case of a dissolution of the Union

> it is by no means an improbable supposition that real and imaginary injuries would occasion mutual complaints and accusations among the States; that they would become more and more unfriendly; that animosities would begin, and rise higher and higher; that fresh provocations would embitter the minds of the people in one State against those in another; that . . . they would have recourse to arms; that the war becoming more fierce, one side, in danger of being conquered, would call a foreign nation to its aid; that the foreigners would be victorious, subdue those States which were hostile to them, and oppress those whom they came to assist.[53]

The year before, Washington had written to Governor Harrison

[51] In a letter to Patrick Henry of May 26, 1777, Lee stated: ". . . Our enemies, & our friends too know that America can only be conquered by disunion—The former, with unremitting art had endeavored to fix immovable Discord between the Southern & Eastern Colonies, and in truth Sir they had so far prevailed, that it required constant attention and a firmness not to be shaken, to prevent the malicious art of our enemies from succeeding—I am persuaded as I am of my existence, that had it not been for Virginia and New Jersey, with Georgia sometimes, that our Union would . . . now have been, by this means, broken like a Potters Vessel dashed against a Rock—And I heartily wish that this greatest of all evils may not yet take place before a safe and honorable peace is established. . . ." James Curtis Ballagh, ed., THE LETTERS OF RICHARD HENRY LEE (1911), I, 301.

[52] Letter of Jan. 31, 1785. Francis S. Drake, LIFE AND CORRESPONDENCE OF HENRY KNOX (1873), 145.

[53] (New York) JOURNAL, March 29, 1787.

of Virginia that the "unreasonable jealousy" the states showed of each other was threatening "our downfall as a nation."[54]

Tensions among the states were matched by those among the various sections of the country. In 1784, Richard D. Spaight informed Governor Martin of North Carolina that the New England states, by trying to increase their own importance, were pressing so hard upon the national framework that "I imagine it will break before they are well aware of it."[55] A year later, Rufus King expressed fears lest the eight Northern states might quarrel with the five Southern states over the regulation of trade by Congress, feeling that they could form, and "in the event must form, a sub-confederation remedied of all their present embarrassment."[56] General Lincoln felt that a division between North and South was inevitable.[57] A few weeks before the meeting of the Federal Convention, more and more proposals for a division of the Union into sectional confederacies came to the fore. Bingham of Pennsylvania suggested that the country be divided into "several distinct federacies—its great extent and various interests being incompatible with a single government."[58] A Boston newspaper advocated an independent confederation of the five New England states in order that Massachusetts might be bound no longer to the wretched measures of Congress and be a prey to the jealousy of Pennsylvania and New York.[59]

3. By 1787, the threat to peace from state and regional jealousies had become an even stronger motive for the creation of the more perfect Union than the fear of foreign nations. It was from a commercial dispute between Maryland and Virginia that the desire for the Annapolis Convention arose. That convention, in turn, proposed the Federal Convention.[60] The recommendation of Annapolis spoke of the necessity "to render the constitution of the Federal Government adequate to the exigencies of the Union," and this purpose is

[54] Nevins, *op. cit.*, 555.

[55] NORTH CAROLINA STATE RECORDS, XVII, 172-75. In the opinion of Spaight, the Wyoming and Vermont disputes had "sown the seeds of dissension which I think will not end without a civil war."

[56] Letter to John Adams of Nov. 2, 1785. King, *op. cit.*, I, 13.

[57] Compare Lincoln's letter to Rufus King of Feb. 11, 1786. *Ibid.*, I, 156-60.

[58] William C. Rives, HISTORY OF THE LIFE AND TIMES OF JAMES MADISON (1859-68), II, 187.

[59] Nevins, *op. cit.*, 603-4.

[60] Nevins considers this a "symbolic fact." *Ibid.*, 572.

evident in the credentials of the delegates to the Philadelphia meeting. It can hardly be disputed that the adequacy of the Constitution to the exigencies of the Union was largely connected with the preservation of the Union, i.e., with the preservation of peace among its parts.

In the Convention, the fear of division cast its shadow over the proceedings. The discussions were dealing with problems that caused tensions between the states and the regions, such as the regulation of commerce and trade, finance, territorial claims, etc. In his opening speech, Randolph stressed that one of the main tasks ahead was the establishment of a government that could prevent "dissentions between members of the Union."[61] In tune with this suggestion, which was expressive of a general feeling, the discussions were largely concerned with matters relevant to the preservation of good relations among the members of the United States. The Constitution paid due tribute to the idea of internal peace. It was framed "in order to . . . insure domestic tranquility."

III

1. Unlike the security and peace motives, the desire for the freedom of the individual from governmental oppression is hardly evident in plans for union brought forth during the colonial era. Individual liberty was protected under the charters of the various colonies and was not considered to be one of the purposes of union. As a matter of fact, the creation of the important New England Confederacy indicates that individual rights were not conceived to be of concern to the government of the confederacy. Rhode Island was excluded from the union because of her different concepts of freedom. The members of that confederation strongly desired union in order to enjoy security and peace. However, they preferred to be isolated from the religious and political radicals of Rhode Island rather than to attempt, through union, to bring them into line with their own way of life. One was careful to stress that the regulation of individual freedom was left to the jurisdiction of the members of the New England Confederacy.[62] Similarly, Coxe's plan of union, while stressing the security and peace motives, made it clear that the union was not

[61] Farrand, *op. cit.*, I, 18.
[62] Art. 3 of the New England Articles of Confederation.

thought to guarantee the individual's freedom from his respective colonial government. "Powers and authorities, respecting the honour of His Majesty, the interest of the plantations, and the liberty and property of the proprietors, traders, planters and inhabitants . . . are not thought fit to be touch'd on or inserted" in his plan of union, but are left to the regulation of the colonial governments, although it was not denied that they could conceivably be regulated by the government of the union "according to the laws of England."[63] The omission, even rejection, of the idea of individual freedom in colonial plans for union is probably due to the fact that the inhabitants of the various colonies were, on the whole, able to enjoy the rights of Englishmen. If the governments of particular colonies occasionally infringed upon the rights of their citizens, this would, in all likelihood, not happen in the other colonies at the same time. Where there is no common danger, there is no common cause. Consequently, the need for common action would hardly be felt, and union was not likely to be considered a means for the individual's emancipation.

The need for common action for the sake of individual rights was recognized only when those rights were endangered not just in one colony, but in all the colonies, i.e., when acts of Parliament were felt to be oppressive of the colonists' cherished rights of Englishmen, their lives, liberty, and property. Now a common fear created a common cause and led to common action through union, which was now conceived to be as conducive to individual freedom as it was to peace and security.[64]

In the first great demonstration of an American will, the First Continental Congress, the desire for liberty was obvious. According to their credentials, the delegates of New Hampshire were sent "to secure . . . [the colonies'] rights, liberties and privileges"; those of Massachusetts, "for the recovery and establishment of their just rights and liberties, civil and religious"; those of Pennsylvania, for "ascertaining American rights."[65] During the proceedings, it was resolved "that a Committee be appointed to State the rights of the Colonies in general."[66] The delegates read an address by the people

[63] Carson, *op. cit.*, 466.

[64] Compare *infra.*, pp. 62 ff.

[65] Worthington Chauncey Ford, ed., JOURNALS OF THE CONTINENTAL CONGRESS (1904-37), I, 15, 16, 20.

[66] *Ibid.*, I, 26.

of Massachusetts to General Gage, in which an act of Parliament is declared "dangerous in an extreme degree . . . to the civil rights and liberties of America."[67] Congress requested merchants in the colonies not to send any order for goods to Great Britain, "until the sense of the Congress, on the means to be taken for the preservation of the liberties of America, is made public."[68] A plan was proposed to the King under which "the Rights and Liberties of America" would be secured.[69] The delegates spoke of a "despotism, which is preparing to destroy those rights, which God, Nature, and compact, have given to America." Considering themselves the "guardians [of the Bostonians'] rights and liberties," the delegates called certain statutes "destructive of American rights."[70] In an address to the people of Quebec, they considered "the violation of your rights . . . as a violation of our own."[71]

Similarly, the delegates asserted that "Congress are deliberating on the most peaceable means for restoring American liberty" and requested the agents of Congress "to call in the aid of such Noblemen and Gentlemen as are esteemed firm friends to American liberty."[72] John Adams wrote to his wife that the people of Massachusetts were "universally acknowledged, the saviours and defenders of American liberty."[73] Richard Henry Lee expressed hope that the vigor of the proceedings "will prove the ruin of our Ministerial Enemies and the salvation of American Liberty."[74]

What are these liberties, or their sum total, American liberty? There is no clear-cut definition. However, aside from the fact that the delegates abhorred despotic, arbitrary government, they indicated the main components of freedom. "The first grand right is that of the people having a share in their own government by their representatives chosen by themselves, and, in consequence, of being ruled by laws, which they themselves approve, not by edicts of men over whom they have no control."[75] "The foundation of English liberty,

[67] *Ibid.*, I, 35.
[68] *Ibid.*, I, 41.
[69] *Ibid.*, I, 49.
[70] *Ibid.*, I, 60, 61, 66.
[71] *Ibid.*, I, 113.
[72] *Ibid.*, I, 57, 104.
[73] Edmund C. Burnett, ed., LETTERS OF THE MEMBERS OF THE CONTINENTAL CONGRESS (1921-36), I, 31.
[74] *Ibid.*, I, 37.
[75] Worthington C. Ford, *op. cit.*, I, 107.

and of all free government, is the right of the people to participate
in their legislative council." [76] We may thus say that popular participation in government is one component of American liberty.

Its second component is the individual's protection from the government. Delaware regretted the "new-modelling the government of
Massachusetts-Bay, and the operation of the same on the property,
liberty and lives of the Colonists."[77] Congress resolved that the inhabitants of the colonies are "entitled to life, liberty, and property."[78] They wanted redress for the grievances "which threaten
destruction to the lives, liberty and property of his majesty's subjects."[79] Asserting the rights of trial by jury, the delegates said that
"this provides, that neither life, liberty nor property can be taken
from the possessor."[80] Samuel Adams, speaking of the act for regulating the government of Massachusetts and of the act for the more
impartial administration of that province, wrote that "both or
either of them if put into execution will shake the Foundations of
that free and happy Constitution which is the Birthright of English
subjects, and totally destroy the inestimable Blessing of Security in
Life, Liberty and Property."[81] James Duane rejected certain statutes
because they "would effectually destroy all Security of the Lives,
Liberties and Properties of the Colonists."[82] The meaning of the
rights of life, liberty, and property is partly described in detail.[83]
There is no evidence that the members of the First Continental
Congress attributed a different value to any one of those particular
rights. All three are usually mentioned in one breath, and the pre-
sumption of their being considered equal is borne out upon closer
inspection.[84]

[76] *Ibid.*, I, 68.
[77] *Ibid.*, I, 22.
[78] *Ibid.*, I, 67.
[79] *Ibid.*, I, 107.
[80] *Ibid.*, I, 107.
[81] Burnett, *op. cit.*, I, 68.
[82] *Ibid.*, I, 43.
[83] The rights of life are dealt with by the delegates in a rather general way
only in connection with property, trial by jury, and liberty. (Worthington C.
Ford, *op. cit.*, I, 85, 82, 107; Burnett, *op. cit.*, I, 21.) Liberty includes liberty of
the person, i.e., freedom from seizure and imprisonment, as well as freedom of
the press and religion. (Worthington C. Ford, op. cit., I, 107, 108, 33, 100.) As to
property, the delegates felt it should be free from seizure and taxation. (*Ibid.*,
I, 56, 58, 111.)
[84] There is no evidence that the rights of life were considered more important
than those of liberty. As to the relative importance of liberty and property, the

Also, there is no evidence that either one of the two main components of American freedom would have ranked higher than the other. The right to participate in government, one may argue, seems to possess primacy before the protection of life, liberty, and property in view of the fact that it was referred to as the *first* grand right. But this apparent preference can probably be explained in the light of the then prevalent belief that participation in government was the best guarantee to secure life, liberty, and property. It does not conceal the fact that popular government was, after all, nothing but a means for individual protection. As such, it could hardly be superior to its end.

The meaning attributed to the general concept of freedom in the decade before the First Continental Congress is the same. Here also we find a quest for participation in government connected with the desire for the protection of the individual and the rights of the minority.[85] The same applies to the Second Continental Congress.[86] The document that declared independence, again, had no different concept of freedom. As Jefferson wrote Richard Henry Lee many years later, the Declaration of Independence was "an expression of the American mind," fusing "the harmonizing sentiments of the day, whether expressed in conversation, in letters, printed essays, or in elementary books of public right, as Aristotle, Cicero, Locke, Sidney, etc." Not intending "to find out new principles, or new arguments, never before thought of," Jefferson sought, as he put it, only "to place before mankind the common sense of the subject," and to do so "in terms so plain and firm as to command their assent, and justify ourselves in the independent stand we (were) impelled to take."[87] Quite naturally, the Declaration speaks of the inalienable rights of

latter is mentioned on the same level as other rights, such as religious freedom and life. (*Ibid.*, I, 82, 83, 86.) In an address to the inhabitants of Quebec, no distinction between the value of life, liberty, and property is made. The same applies to the delegates' petition to the King. (*Ibid.*, I, 105-13, 115-21.) The equality of property with the other rights is also confirmed by a proposed letter of Samuel Adams to General Gage. (Burnett, *op. cit.*, I, 68.)

[85] The slogan, "no taxation without representation" is probably the outstanding demonstration of the close connection between popular participation in government and the individual's protection. For the relation of that ideal to the rights of Englishmen, compare Charles H. McIlwain, THE AMERICAN REVOLUTION, A CONSTITUTIONAL INTERPRETATION (1923).

[86] An examination of the journals of that Congress does not indicate a different evaluation of values from that existing in the First Continental Congress. Consult Worthington C. Ford, *op. cit.*, and Burnett, *op. cit.*

[87] Letter of May 8, 1825. JEFFERSON'S WRITINGS, XVI, 118.

man, that among these are life, liberty and the pursuit of happiness. And, at the same time, it advocates a government that is based upon the consent of the governed. Which one of the two main components of freedom is superior, the Declaration does not state. But, again, it is obvious that the protection of the individual is the end, and his participation just a means to achieve that end.

We may conclude: In the revolutionary struggle up to the Declaration of Independence freedom was considered to consist of two main components, namely, the right of the individual to participate in and to be protected from the government. No primacy of the participation principle over the protection principle was recognized. On the contrary, it can admit of no doubt that popular participation, being considered a remedy against the infringements upon the individual's life, liberty, and property by Parliament and the Crown, was nothing but a means for the protection of the individual.

2. The situation changed after 1776. It is true that in the Articles of Confederation the desire for liberty is still evident. While being based upon the principle of popular government, these Articles proclaim that the states "enter into a firm league of friendship with each other, for . . . the security of their liberties, and their mutual and general welfare."[88] However, in spite of this fundamental recognition of the fact that the protection of the individual's life, liberty, and property was at least as important as popular participation in government, the relation between the two principles changed while the Articles were in operation. Individual freedom became more and more jeopardized under the new democratic governments in the states, where the will of the sheer majority soon reigned supreme, often without giving due consideration to the rights of the minority.

Individual rights were increasingly being drowned in the legislative vortices of the states, where the majority held full sway. As early as 1777 one Benjamin Hichborn delivered a speech in Boston in which he defined "civil liberty" to be not "a government of laws, made agreeable to charters, bills of rights or compacts, but a power existing in the people at large, at any time, for any cause, or for no cause, but their own sovereign pleasure, to alter or annihilate both the mode and essence of any former government, and to adopt a new

---

[88] Art. 3. The Articles of Confederation thus reflect the political credo of the new state constitutions.

one in its stead."[89] Within most of the states, a struggle arose in the
following years between a paper-money faction composed of small
farmers, debtors, and artisans, and a hard-money faction composed
of creditors, merchants, and large planters. In seven states the "rag
money" party triumphed outright and the legislatures passed acts
fixing prices in paper and making it a misdemeanor to refuse paper
currency at its face value. These conditions had aroused severe
criticism from the beginning. Jefferson, in his *Notes on Virginia*,
bitterly assailed that state's constitution because of its concentration
of power in the assembly, which was to him "precisely the definition
of despotic government." It made no difference that such powers
were vested in a numerous body "chosen by ourselves," since "one
hundred and seventy-three despots" were "as oppressive as one," and
since "an elective despotism was not the government we fought for."[90]
Benjamin Rush expressed similar thoughts with respect to the constitution of Pennsylvania. "By the Constitution of Pennsylvania," he
complained, "the whole of our liberty and property . . . may be taken
from us, by the hasty and passionate decision of a single assembly.
. . . The liberty, the property and life of every individual in the State
are laid prostrate . . . at the feet of the Assembly. This combination
of powers in one body has at all ages been pronounced a tyranny. To
live by one man's will became the cause of all men's misery; but
better, far better, would it be to live by the will of one man, than to
live, or rather die, by the will of a body of men."[91] The report of the
Pennsylvania Council of Censors of 1784 revealed the same point of
view.[92] John Adams' *Defence of the Constitutions of Government of*

[89] Hezekiah Niles, ed., PRINCIPLES AND ACTS OF THE REVOLUTION (1822), 27, 30.

[90] JEFFERSON'S WRITINGS, II, 162-63.

[91] "Observations on the Government of Pennsylvania" (1777), in Dagobert D.
Runes, ed., THE SELECTED WRITINGS OF BENJAMIN RUSH (1947), 68, 70. Compare also
57: "I shall now . . . say a few words upon particular parts of the Constitution.
In the second section, 'the supreme legislature is vested in a "single" House. . . .'
By this section we find, that the supreme, absolute, and uncontrolled power of
the State is . . . in the hands of *one body* of men. Had it been lodged in the
hands of one man, it would have been less dangerous to the safety and liberties
of the community. Absolute power should never be trusted to man. . . . I should
be afraid to commit my property, liberty and life to a body of angels for a
whole year. . . ." To Wayne, Rush wrote on May 9, 1777: "A single legislature is
big with tyranny. I had rather live under the government of one man than of
72." Lyman H. Butterfield, ed., LETTERS OF BENJAMIN RUSH (1951), 148.

[92] PROCEEDINGS RELATIVE TO THE CALLING OF THE CONVENTIONS OF 1776 AND 1790
(1825), 83 ff.

the United States of America was less an answer to Turgot's criticism that the American constitutions represented an unreasonable imitation of the usages of England than an exhortation to constitutional reform in other states along the lines that Massachusetts had already taken under Adams' own guidance, i.e., toward a restriction of majority rule.[93] Though these voices were receiving no slight attention, Shays's Rebellion sounded alarm throughout the country. The insurgents' creed was, wrote Henry Knox, then Secretary of War, to Washington,

> that the property of the United States has been protected from the confiscations of Britain by the joint exertions of all, and therefore ought to be common property of all; and he that attempts opposition to this creed is an enemy to equality and justice, and ought to be swept from the face of the earth. . . . In a word, they are determined to annihilate all debts public and private, and have agrarian laws, which are easily effected by the means of unfunded paper money, which shall be a tender in all cases whatsoever. . . . This dreadful situation . . . has alarmed every man of principle and property in New England. . . . What is to give us security against the violence of lawless men? Our governments must be braced, changed or altered to secure our lives and property. . . . The men of property and . . . station and principle . . . are determined to endeavor to establish (a government which shall have power to) protect them in their lawful pursuits; and, what will be efficient in all cases of internal commotions or foreign invasions, they mean that liberty shall form the basis,— liberty resulting from an equal and firm administration of law. They wish for a general government of unity, as they see the local legislatures must necessarily tend to retard the general government. We have arrived at the point of time in which we are forced to see our own humiliation, as a nation, and thus a progression in this line cannot be productive of happiness, private or public.[94]

3.   By 1787, the men who advocated independence in order to secure the colonists' rights to life, liberty, and property had found out that these rights were, under the new popular governments, far from safe, since they were increasingly infringed upon by the ruling majority. Benjamin Rush's address to the American people, made in January,

---

[93] Charles Francis Adams, ed., THE WORKS OF JOHN ADAMS (1850-56) (hereinafter JOHN ADAMS' WORKS), IV, 273 ff. (John Adams' "Defence, etc." was written in January, 1787.)

[94] Letter of Oct. 23, 1786. F. S. Drake, LIFE AND CORRESPONDENCE OF HENRY KNOX (1873), 91-93.

1787, is an example of the misgivings of those who felt that through a democratic majoritarianism the fruits of the Revolution might be lost. In that speech, the father of American medicine stated: "There is nothing more common than to confound the terms of the American Revolution with those of the late American War. The American War is over: but this is far from being the case with the American Revolution. On the contrary, nothing but the first act of the great drama is closed. It remains yet to establish and perfect our new forms of government; and to prepare the principles, morals, and manners of our citizens, for these forms of government, after they are established and brought to perfection . . . THE REVOLUTION IS NOT OVER."[95] Frightened, like many of his compatriots in this critical period of American history, by the alarming events occurring in various states, Rush warned that "in our opposition to monarchy, we forgot that the temple of tyranny has two doors. We bolted one of them by proper restraints; but we left the other open, by neglecting to guard against our own ignorance and licentiousness."[96] He felt that just as the Americans could revolt against monarchical tyranny eleven years earlier, they could and should proceed now to take steps against the new democratic despotism. Rush urged this in as much as "the Confederation, together with most of our state constitutions, were formed under very unfavorable circumstances."[97] If changes of the state constitutions were not feasible, the Articles of Confederation could be revised so as to create a stronger national government that would be in a position to prevent a despotic majoritarianism in the states.[98] This would not amount to a new revo-

[95] Niles, *op. cit.*, 402. The speech was made in January, 1787, and its ideas were already expressed by Rush a year earlier in a letter of May 25, 1786, to Richard Price. Butterfield, *op. cit.*, 388. Later, on July 4, 1787, the same position was taken by Joel Barlow in an oration at Hartford, Conn. Niles, *op. cit.*, 386.

[96] Niles, *op. cit.*, 402.

[97] *Ibid.*, 402.

[98] Rush expressed strong sentiments for Union as early as 1776, when he stated on the floor of the Continental Congress: "We are now a new nation. Our trade, language, customs, manners don't differ more than they do in Great Britain. The more a man aims at serving America, the more he serves his colony. . . . We have been too free with the word independence; we are dependent on each other, not totally independent States. . . . I would not have it understood that I am pleading the cause of Pennsylvania; when I entered that door, I considered myself a citizen of America." Burnett, *op. cit.*, VI, 1081. In his address to the American people in 1787, he maintained that the states under the Articles of Confederation are by no means sovereign and independent, claiming that any state was inde-

lution. It would be nothing but another act of the American Revolution, aiming to preserve the ideals of that revolution, which
conceived of popular government as a mere means for the protection
of the individual's freedom.

The friends of freedom were probably not too unhappy that the
Annapolis Convention was not too much of a success.[99] Its failure
paved the way for the meeting at Philadelphia, of which considerably more could be expected. Under Rush's theory of the unfinished
revolution, the delegates could now overthrow the Articles of Confederation and, by creating a more perfect Union, crack down on
what had been called "the devil's own government"—absolute democracy.[100]

According to the resolutions of Annapolis, it was the task of the
Federal Convention "to take into consideration the situation of the
United States, to devise such further provisions as shall appear to
them necessary to render the constitution of the federal government
adequate to the exigencies of the Union."[101] This clearly states cause
and effect. Union would result from an existing situation, a means
to improve that situation. Union could thus only in a relative sense
be the end of the Federal Convention. As some form of government,
it was there to achieve further ends, including the freedom of the
individual. Cause for the Convention was "the situation of the

pendent only with her sister states in Congress. Niles, *op. cit.,* 403. When the
Constitution was before the ratifying conventions, Rush pointed out the necessity
for a more perfect Union as a remedy against democratic despotism. See *infra,*
note 100.

[99] See the letter of the French chargé d'affaires Otto to Count Vergennes of
Oct. 10, 1786. Quoted in Alpheus T. Mason, FREE GOVERNMENT IN THE MAKING,
190.

[100] In March or April, 1788, Benjamin Rush wrote Ramsay: "Is not history as
full of the vices of the people, as it is of the crimes of kings? What is the present
moral character of the citizens of the United States? I need not describe it. It
proves too plainly that the people are as much disposed to vice as their rulers;
and that nothing but a vigorous and efficient government can prevent their degen-
erating into savages, or devouring each other like beasts of prey. A simple
democracy has been aptly compared . . . to a volcano that contained within its
bowels the fiery materials of its own destruction. A citizen . . . of Switzerland . . .
refused in my presence to drink 'the commonwealth of America' as a toast, and
gave as a reason for it, 'that a simple democracy was the devil's own government.' The experience of the American states, under the present Confederation,
has, in many instances, justified these two accounts of a simple popular government." Butterfield, *op. cit.,* 454.

[101] Elliot, *op. cit.,* I, 118.

United States" and the disadvantages ensuing from it. That situation was defective in a different way. And whereas the Annapolis resolutions enumerate specific defects of the Articles, they do not specify "other" shortcomings. However, it is beyond doubt that the existence of too much democracy in the states was one of those defects. There is no reason to believe that the task before the Philadelphia Convention arose primarily from the inadequacies of the Articles of Confederation with respect to such things as security from foreign nations and peace among the states. For instance, if a regulation of commerce—a means for better relations among the states—had been that urgent, there is no evident reason why the Annapolis Convention did not improve commerce among the states represented at that convention. A uniform regulation for four states would probably have been better than no regulation at all and would have precluded neither other states from joining, nor the meeting of a general convention. Furthermore, an improvement of the Articles toward a more perfect Union—with respect to commerce a mere technical task—could have been achieved at Philadelphia in accordance with the authorizations of the states. To do just this, there was no need for the delegates to meet in secret for fear the people might, as Patrick Henry put it, smell a rat. The task of the Convention was more deeply rooted. Having its cause largely in the threat to individual rights, the Convention wanted the Union mainly for the preservation of free government from democratic despotism.

While the adherents of absolute democracy conceived of freedom in the sense of Hichborn,[102] the Founding Fathers, constituting a countermovement against democratic excesses, understood it in the sense of Rush. To the former, it meant freedom of the majority to infringe upon minority rights; to the latter, freedom from absolute democracy for the protection of those rights, among which the right of property played a prominent role.[103] Every antagonism of the

---

[102] See *supra*, pp. 60-61.

[103] Charles A. Beard, AN ECONOMIC INTERPRETATION OF THE CONSTITUTION (1913), brought forth the thesis that the Founding Fathers, when framing and ratifying the new Constitution, were largely prompted by a materialistic self-interest. Beard's thesis, which was a product of the progressive climate of the time when it was pronounced (Compare Adair, "The Tenth Federalist Revisited"), is one-sided and does not do justice to the actual motives of the Founders. For them, the protection of private property was not merely desirable from a materialistic and an egoistic point of view, but also from an idealistic and altruistic one. The protection of private property meant to them a basic guarantee of individual

delegates against democracy is therefore a protagonism for individual rights, especially those of private property. And a strong antagonism against democracy was there indeed.

The Fathers' fear of democracy was based on recent experience with the aggressive farmers and the lower strata of society in the cities, and on their study of history and politics.[104] Still under the influence of Shays's Rebellion, Theodore Sedgwick wrote to Rufus King: "Every man of observation is convinced that the end of government, security, cannot be attained by the exercise of principles founded on democratic equality. A war is now actually levied on the virtue, property, and distinctions in the community, and however there may be an appearance of a temporary cessation, yet the flame will again and again break out."[105] Through their studies of history, leading members of the Convention had reached the conclusion that government by the common people led to tumults, attacks on persons and property, and finally to despotism. The belief was that democracy could only be a transitory stage of government, and would evolve into a tyranny of the rich demagogue who patronized the common people.[106] During the discussions on the superiority of the national over the state governments and the election of the legislature, the fear of democracy was most obvious. Edmund Randolph,

liberty and of an orderly society, and was thus a prerequisite for what Jefferson in the Declaration of Independence referred to as "the pursuit of happiness." John Adams expressed that sentiment when, in his "Defence of the Constitutions of Government," he wrote: "Property is surely a right of mankind as really as liberty. . . . The moment the idea is admitted into society that property is not as sacred as the laws of God, and that there is not a force of law and public justice to protect it, anarchy and tyranny commence." JOHN ADAMS' WORKS, VI, 8-9. For a good recent refutation of Beard, see Robert E. Brown, CHARLES BEARD AND THE CONSTITUTION (1956); Forrest McDonald, WE, THE PEOPLE (1958).

[104] For a survey of the delegates, see Warren, *op. cit.*, 55 ff.

[105] *Ibid.*, 231. See also NEW YORK INDEPENDENT JOURNAL, June 2, 1787; MASSACHUSETTS CENTINEL, June 9, 1787; NEW HAMPSHIRE SPY, June 9, 12, 1787; CONNECTICUT COURANT, June 11, 1787; SALEM MERCURY, June 12, 1787; VIRGINIA INDEPENDENT CHRONICLE, June 13, 1787; INDEPENDENT CHRONICLE (Boston), June 14, 1787; AMERICAN MUSEUM, June, 1787, I. The GAZETTEER, the GAZETTE and the JOURNAL printed an article that read: "A foederal Shays may be more successful than the Shays of Massachusetts Bay. . . . This view of our situation is indeed truly alarming. We are upon the brink of a precipice." Quoted in Warren, *op. cit.*, 152.

[106] Compare the statement of Governor Morris: "Give the votes to the people who have no property, and they will sell them to the rich who will be able to buy them." Quoted in Charles A. Beard, PUBLIC POLICY AND THE GENERAL WELFARE (1941), 58.

regretting that the existing federal government was not superior to the state constitutions, complained: "Our chief danger arises from the democratic parts of our constitutions. . . . None of the constitutions have provided sufficient checks against democracy."[107] In the debate on the election of the second branch of the national legislature, Sherman opposed election by the people, who should have as little as possible to do about the government.[108] Elbridge Gerry left no doubt that "the evils we experience flow from the excess of democracy," adding that in Massachusetts it had been fully confirmed by experience that the people are daily misled into the most baneful measures and opinions by the false reports that were circulated by designing men. Mentioning that it was a maxim of democracy to starve the public servants, Gerry added that experience had shown that the state legislatures drawn immediately from the people did not always possess their confidence.[109] Pinckney moved "that the first branch of the National Legislative be elected by the State Legislatures, and not by the people," contending that the people were less fit judges.[110]

In view of this antagonism to democracy, some authors stressed that there was another side to the picture, since some delegates also expressed their belief in popular government in so many words. Of course, George Mason said that "notwithstanding the oppression and injustice experienced . . . from democracy, the genius of the people is in favor of it, and the genius of the people must be consulted." Although Mason admitted that people had been too democratic, he feared that "we should incautiously run into the opposite extreme."[111] James Wilson expressed similar views, saying that the ultimate power of the government must of necessity reside in the people.[112] Elbridge Gerry was as principled against monarchy and aristocracy as he was against democracy.[113] However, it is misleading to speak, in view of these statements, of another side to the picture. The issue confronting the Convention was not the re-institution of some form of monarchic or aristocratic government as an antidote against democracy. Although such tendencies may have existed, they

[107] Farrand, *op. cit.*, I, 26.
[108] *Ibid.*, I, 48.
[109] *Ibid.*, I, 48-50.
[110] *Ibid.*, I, 132.
[111] *Ibid.*, I, 49.
[112] *Ibid.*, I, 49, 132, 151, 361.
[113] *Ibid.*, I, 132.

were exceptional.[114] The Fathers accepted popular government as the very premise for their deliberations. Their problem was how to prevent too much democracy. It was a democratic absolutism that was feared, and of absolute democracy a man like Mason, who complained of "the oppression and injustice experienced from democracy," was as afraid as were men like Gerry and Randolph, just as the latter no more wanted an abolition of popular government than did Mason. Gerry complained about the excess of democracy only, and Randolph wished for checks upon, and by no means the abolition of, democracy. For the protection of the individual's rights the colonies had thrown off the tyranny of the British. It was now up to the Federal Convention—to paraphrase Rush—to bolt the other door to the temple of tyranny and to secure those rights from a despotism of a democratic kind. Under the theory of the unfinished revolution,[115] the delegates could venture into some revolutionary action. Although they were authorized only to reform the Articles, they virtually overthrew the existing system. Their work set up the new federal state. Being ordained and established by the people of the United States, "in order to . . . establish justice, . . . and secure the blessings of liberty,"[116] the Constitution bears the mark of the freedom motive.[117]

IV

In the preceding pages, an attempt has been made to demonstrate how the revolutionary era was characterized by a quest for security from foreign nations, for peace in America, and for individual freedom. These values, it was hoped, could be achieved by united action. And whereas earlier plans of union were largely motivated by a desire for security and peace, those of the period under consideration saw the appearance of the freedom motive. That motive came to the

[114] See Alpheus T. Mason, FREE GOVERNMENT IN THE MAKING, 188 ff.; Warren, *op. cit.,* 17-19, 43-45, 58, 378-79, 436-44, 771.

[115] See *supra,* pp. 62-63.

[116] For the relation of justice to liberty, see *infra,* pp. 116 f., 146 ff.

[117] Freedom means here, of course, the protection of the individual from the government rather than his right to participate in government, since such participation had been taken for granted ever since 1776, and since individual freedom was threatened through excessive participation rather than by a lack of participation.

fore during the colonists' struggle with England and was recognized by the Articles of Confederation. In the arguments leading to the calling of the Federal Convention, as well as in the debates at Philadelphia, the freedom motive probably occupied first rank, with the peace motive running second and the security motive, third. Symbolically, this sequence found expression in the Constitution. After mentioning the formation of the more perfect Union, the preamble states that the Constitution is ordained, first, in order to establish justice; second, to insure domestic tranquility; third, to provide for the common defense. So as if to elaborate and to emphasize again the first point, the preamble concludes by stating that the Constitution establishing the more perfect Union was formed in order to secure the blessings of liberty to Americans and their posterity. Justice and liberty, two values complementary to each other and expressive of individual freedom, are mentioned, respectively, in the beginning and the end of the preamble and thus provide the framework for the other motives that contributed to the creation of the more perfect Union. The arrival of the freedom motive marks an innovation in American plans for union or federalism. Resulting from a desire to secure individual liberty from monarchical as well as democratic oppression, it can indeed be considered a progress of constitutionalism that was born in a Revolution that was characterized by the desire for free government[118] in peace and security.

[118] Free government could thus be defined as a popular government where the majority is, for the sake of individual and minority rights, bound by a constitution and where popular participation in government, while generally accepted, is only a means for the protection of the individual's life, liberty, and property, i.e., where, in order to prevent sheer majority rule or democratic despotism, the democratic participation principle, while accepted, is inferior to the liberal protection principle.

CHAPTER THREE

The Federalist–An Outgrowth
of the American Revolution

The political thinking of the authors of the *Federalist* was formed
during the American Revolution, a period distinguished by the
quest for individual freedom, for peace among the states, and for
security from foreign nations.

Whereas Jay, serving at intervals as a delegate to the Continental
Congress of 1774 and to the Congress that declared independence,
took an active part in giving a start to the Revolution and played a
more passive role in the postwar period, the reverse is the case with
his younger collaborators.[1] Although Madison and Hamilton were
by no means inactive before and after the war, "they were of a succeeding generation, men formed in and by the revolution itself."[2]
Their influence on the political scene could be felt especially during
the latter years of the war and thereafter. As believers in the freedom
of the individual, the three authors would be adherents of a popular
government under which minority rights were protected from the

[1] Jay was born in 1745; Madison, in 1751; Hamilton, in 1757 or 1755.
[2] John Quincy Adams, *op. cit.*, 16.

majority. As American patriots, they would be interested in good relations among the states and in the safety of the American people from foreign powers. The desire for a free government in peace and security is evident in the authors' speeches and writings prior to the publication of the *Federalist*. It was, above all, this desire that prompted Jay, Madison, and Hamilton to criticize the Articles of Confederation for their failure to provide for a government that corresponded to the authors' ideal. Likewise, their advocacy of a more perfect Union can be largely explained as a result of their desire for free government in peace and security.

I

1. John Jay was a staunch defender of liberty.[3] One of the signers of the letter to the Committee of Correspondence at Boston, he expressed himself "for the security of our common rights" as early as 1774.[4] An address to the people of Great Britain, drafted by him in the same year, speaks of the sacrosanctity of private rights,[5] as does his draft of an address of the New York Convention to the people of New York.[6] In a charge to the grand jury of Ulster county, Jay spoke of the protection of lives, liberties, and property.[7] In 1780, he praised the state constitutions for guaranteeing security to civil and religious liberty and for making "effective provision for the rights of justice and the due exercise of the necessary powers of government."[8] Having experienced the ascendency of sheer majority rule in the following years, he became less confident with respect to the state governments, but continued to be a stout advocate of vested rights. To Washington, he wrote in 1786:

> Our affairs seem to lead to some crisis. . . . I am uneasy and apprehensive, more so than during the war. . . . New governments have not the aid of habit and hereditary respects, and being generally the result of preceding tumult and confusion, do not im-

[3] Characteristically, Frank Monaghan, *op. cit.*, gave his biography of Jay the subtitle, "Defender of Liberty."

[4] Henry P. Johnston, ed., THE CORRESPONDENCE AND PUBLIC PAPERS OF JOHN JAY (1890-93) (hereinafter JAY'S CORRESPONDENCE), I, 13 ff.

[5] *Ibid.*, I, 17 ff.

[6] *Ibid.*, I, 102 ff.

[7] *Ibid.*, I, 158 ff.

[8] Letter to Florida Blanca of April 25, 1780. *Ibid.*, I, 284.

mediately acquire stability or strength. . . . What I most fear is, that the better kind of people, by which I mean the people who are orderly and industrious, . . . will be led by the insecurity of property, the loss of confidence in their rulers, and the want of public faith and rectitude, to consider the charms of liberty as imaginary and delusive. A state of fluctuation and uncertainty must disgust and alarm such men, and prepare their minds for almost any change that may promise them quiet and security.[9]

Aware of the democratic vogue in the states, which made government ineffective,[10] Jay, in view of Rhode Island laws embracing "the doctrine of the political transsubstantiation of paper into gold and silver,"[11] and afraid that "similar symptoms will . . . soon mark a like disease in several other States,"[12] blamed the Articles of Confederation for admitting too much democracy. "Experience has pointed out errors in our national government which call for correction, and which threaten to blast the fruit we expected from our tree of liberty," he wrote to Washington.[13] Later, he expressed his distrust of the legislative body: "Large assemblies often misunderstand or neglect the obligations of character, honour, and dignity, and will collectively do or omit things which individual gentlemen in private capacities would not approve. . . . Our government should in some degree be suited to our manners and circumstances, and they, you know, are not strictly democratical."[14]

Not *strictly* democratical, Jay said: While observing with concern the ascendancy of the democratic element, he wanted democracy limited only to the degree that the individual's protection required.

[9] Letter of June 27, 1786. *Ibid.*, III, 204-5. Shocked by Shays's Rebellion, Jay wrote Jefferson on Oct. 27, 1786: "A spirit of licentiousness has infected Massachusetts, which appears more formidable than some at first apprehended. . . . A reluctance to taxes, an impatience of government, a rage for property and little regard to the means of acquiring it, together with a desire of equality in all things, seem to actuate the mass of those who are uneasy in their circumstances." *Ibid.*, III, 212.

[10] See the letters to Jefferson of Aug. 18, 1786 and Feb. 9, 1787. *Ibid.*, III, 211, 232; to Gouverneur Morris of Sept. 24, 1783. *Ibid.*, III, 85.

[11] Letter to John Adams of Nov. 1, 1786. *Ibid.*, III, 214.

[12] Letter to Jefferson of Oct. 27, 1786. *Ibid.*, III, 212. See also his letters to John Adams of Feb. 21, 1787 and to Jefferson of April 24, 1787. *Ibid.*, III, 234, 244.

[13] Letter of March 16, 1786. *Ibid.*, III, 186.

[14] Letter to Washington of Jan. 7, 1787. *Ibid.*, III, 226. See also his letter to Jefferson of Aug. 18, 1786. *Ibid.*, III, 210.

Although he expressed the thought that if democracy were not soon restricted it might be expedient to replace it with some other form of government,[15] Jay hesitated in going to the other extreme. "Shall we have a king?" he wrote Washington in 1787, continuing, "not in my opinion while other experiments remain untried . . . no alterations in the government should . . . be made, nor if attempted will easily take place, unless deducible from the only source of just authority—the People."[16]

2. Aside from being a believer in free government, Jay was a promoter of peace within the United States. In 1779, he regretted that Congress, being instituted mainly for the purpose of opposing the tyranny of Britain and for establishing independence, had no authority to interfere in the particular quarrels of the states, feeling that this prevented Congress from settling disputes among the states. Consequently, he was happy when Congress recommended that Massachusetts, New Hampshire, and New York pass laws expressly authorizing the government of the Confederation to hear and settle all boundary differences among the states, hoping that such an action would facilitate the settlement of the Vermont dispute.[17] He pleaded with his friends in New York to settle state boundary questions quickly and amicably, in order that all causes of dissension between the states might be removed.[18] Two years later, he criticized the constitution of Massachusetts for describing that state "as being in New England, as well as in America," and wrote that "perhaps it would be better if these distinctions were permitted to die away,"[19] as tending to perpetuate undesirable sectional differences.[20] His biographer relates that Jay even rejoiced that various families were intermarrying with those of other states, because this was conducive

[15] See the letters to Washington of June 27, 1786; to Jefferson of Oct. 27, 1786; to John Adams of Nov. 1, 1786. *Ibid.*, III, 205, 213, 214.

[16] Letter of Jan. 7, 1787. *Ibid.*, III, 226.

[17] Letter to Governor Clinton of Sept. 25, 1779. *Ibid.*, I, 237.

[18] On Dec. 14, 1782, Jay wrote to Robert R. Livingston: "The boundaries between the States should be immediately settled, and all causes of discord between them removed." On Sept. 24, 1783, he advised Gouverneur Morris: "Settle your boundaries without delay. It is better that some improper limits should be fixed, than any left in dispute." *Ibid.*, III, 7, 85.

[19] Letter to Elbridge Gerry of Jan. 9, 1781. *Ibid.*, I, 458.

[20] Monaghan, *op. cit.*, 280.

to friendship among the states.[21] Prior to the meeting of the Philadelphia Convention, Jay clipped from the *Daily Advertiser* a few verses from the "Anarchiad":[22]

> Shall lordly Hudson part contending powers,
> And broad Potomac lave two hostile shores?
> Must Alleghany's sacred summits bear
> The impious bulwarks of perpetual war?
>
> Ere death invades, and night's deep curtain falls,
> Through ruined realms the voice of Union calls . . .

and he underscored the two concluding lines:

> On you she calls! attend the warning cry:
> "Ye Live United, or Divided Die!"

3.   As Jay recognized the necessity for peace within the United States, he was very much concerned about his country's security from foreign nations. That concern already had found expression in a letter to the Committee of Correspondence of Boston, drafted two years before the colonies declared their independence from the mother country.[23] The idea of defense stands in the foreground in Jay's appeal to the people of New York of December, 1776.[24] It is evident in Jay's activities during the first years of the war.[25] In 1779, Jay was sent to the Spanish Court as an ambassador. After serving in that post for more than two years, he participated in the peace negotiations in Paris. During his stay abroad, he became aware of the position of the United States in international relations and again recognized the necessity for his country's security from foreign powers. In letters to his friends in America, such as William and Robert Livingston, Robert and Gouverneur Morris, Philip Schuyler, Egbert Benson, and Hamilton, Jay's suspicions of the designs of European nations against the United States are obvious. "I have no

[21] When Rufus King married a daughter of the Alsop family in New York in 1786, Jay remarked: "I am pleased with these intermarriages; they tend to assimilate the States, and to promote one of the first wishes of my heart, viz., to see the people of America become one nation in every respect." Nevins, *op. cit.,* 605.

[22] Monaghan, *op. cit.,* 281-82.

[23] JAY'S CORRESPONDENCE, I, 13-15.

[24] *Ibid.,* I, 102 ff.

[25] Monaghan, *op. cit.,* 51 ff.

faith in any Court in Europe," he wrote Secretary Livingston. "There are circumstances which induce me to believe that Spain is turning her eyes to England for a more intimate connection. They are the only two European powers which have continental posses- sions on our side of the water, and Spain I think wishes for a league between them for mutual security against us."[26] "Jealousy and suspi- cion never sleep in governments of a certain denomination," he wrote a few months later, probably expressing his distrust of France and Spain,[27] and in the fall of 1783 he warned Gouverneur Morris that "America is beheld with jealousy, and jealousy is seldom idle."[28] As Secretary for Foreign Affairs, Jay continued to voice his concern for American security.[29]

4. In Jay's opinion, free government in peace and security could best be achieved through union. No matter whether he argues for the freedom of the individual, for peace among the states, or for se- curity from foreign nations, the necessity of union is always stressed. This is obvious in his statements concerning security. He advocated union for the fight against England during the first years of the war.[30] While in Europe, he viewed with concern the reluctance with which the American states payed the necessary taxes, writing to Governor Livingston that

> it injures both their reputation and interest abroad, as well as at home, and tends to cherish the hopes and speculations of those who wish we may become and remain an unimportant, divided people. The rising power of America is a serious object of appre- hension to more than one nation, and every event that may retard it will be agreeable to them. A continental, national spirit should therefore pervade our country, and Congress should be enabled, by a grant of the necessary powers, to regulate the commerce and general concerns of the confederacy; and we should remember that to be constantly prepared for war is the only way to have peace.[31]

He warned Benson that "many foreign nations would rejoice to see us split to pieces, because we should then cease to be formidable,

---

[26] Letter of April 22, 1783. JAY'S CORRESPONDENCE, III, 42-43.
[27] Letter to Egbert Benson of July 10, 1783. *Ibid.*, III, 51.
[28] Letter of Sept. 24, 1783. *Ibid.*, III, 85.
[29] Monaghan, *op. cit.*, 244 ff.
[30] *Ibid.*, 51 ff.
[31] Letter of July 19, 1783. JAY'S CORRESPONDENCE, III, 55.

and such an event would afford a fine field for their intrigues."[32] To Gouverneur Morris, Jay pointed out that for the sake of security "no time is to be lost in raising and maintaining a national spirit in America. *Power to govern the confederacy, as to all general purposes, should be granted and exercized.* . . . In a word, every thing conducive to union and constitutional energy of government should be cultivated, cherished, and protected."[33] When he was Secretary for Foreign Affairs, Jay was no less unequivocal in his advocacy of a more perfect Union. He resented the restraints on trade that existed under the Articles of Confederation, hoping, on the other hand, that something positive might result from them, namely, a feeling of American solidarity. "Good will come out of evil," he wrote, continuing, "these discontents nourish federal ideas." Foreign restrictions and exclusions, bad as they were, "will tend to press us together, and strengthen our bands of union," Jay felt,[34] and thus be productive of a greater security of the United States from foreign danger. His position enabled Jay to see, with distressing clarity, how much the weak Confederation was exposed on the international scene. Desirous of the United States taking her place among the nations, he knew that this was impossible without a fundamental change of the Articles of Confederation. "To be respectable abroad, it is necessary to be so at home; and that will not be the case until our public faith acquires more confidence, and our government more strength."[35]

Similarly, Jay considered union a prerequisite for peace within America. The thirteen states were confederated not only for the purpose of conducting the Revolutionary War, but also for the promotion of good relations among the states. In 1779, Jay stated that the enemies of the United States "are mistaken when they suppose us kept together only by a sense of present danger," and that the Union is not to end with the war. He was happy to note that "the people of these States were never so cordially united as at this day," and continued: "By having been obliged to mix with each other, former prejudices have worn off, and their several manners become blended. A sense of common permanent interest, mutual affection (having been brethren in affliction), the ties of consanguinity daily extend-

---

[32] Monaghan, *op. cit.*, 221.

[33] Letter of Sept. 24, 1783. JAY'S CORRESPONDENCE, III, 85.

[34] Letter to Lafayette of July 15, 1785. *Ibid.*, III, 160.

[35] Monaghan, *op. cit.*, 269.

ing, constant reciprocity of good offices, similarity in language, in governments, and therefore in manners, the importance, weight, and splendour of the Union,—all conspire in forming a strong chain of connection, which must for ever bind us together."[36] He was in favor of a stronger national government that would be in a position to settle disputes between the various states.[37] While in France, Jay expressed his feeling that union and energy in the national government would be conducive to peace among the American states.[38] He confirmed this sentiment shortly before the Federal Convention met at Philadelphia.[39]

Last, but not least, Jay considered the Union as a means for the protection of individual liberty. This was obvious as early as 1774, when, in view of the oppressive acts of the English Parliament, he stated that "from a virtuous and spirited union much may be expected, while the feeble efforts of a few will only be attended with mischief and disappointment to themselves and triumph to the adversaries of liberty."[40] His appreciation of the Union did not change during the war, no matter whether he was in the United States or abroad.[41] After his return to America, Jay continued to be a staunch advocate of a strong national government as a means for the protection of the individual's life, liberty, and property. In a letter to Washington, written in 1786 and obviously influenced by the democratic vogue in the states, he voiced concern lest the American people "are wofully and, in many instances, wickedly misled." After denouncing the present democratic rage with its threat to private

[36] Circular Letter from Congress to their Constituents. JAY'S CORRESPONDENCE, I, 230-31.

[37] Letter to Governor Clinton of Sept. 25, 1779. *Ibid.,* I, 237 ff. On pp. 240-41, Jay claims the invalidity of "the doctrine that the Union (independent of the articles of confederation) had no other object than security against foreign invasions."

[38] Letter to John Jay of Sept. 24, 1783. *Ibid.,* III, 85.

[39] *Supra.,* p. 74.

[40] Letter to the Committee of Correspondence, Boston, of May 23, 1774. JAY'S CORRESPONDENCE, I, 14.

[41] Monaghan, *op. cit.,* 51 ff., 86 ff., 107 ff., 125 ff., 142 ff. To Egbert Benson, Jay wrote on Sept. 12, 1783: "The people of America must either govern themselves according to their respective constitutions and the confederation, or relinquish all pretensions to the respect of other nations. The newspapers in Europe are filled with exaggerated accounts of the want of moderation, union, order, and government which they say prevails in our country." JAY'S CORRESPONDENCE, III, 75.

property, Jay, referring to the state legislatures, stated that "representative bodies will ever be faithful copies of their originals, and generally exhibit a chequered assemblage of virtue and vice, of abilities and weakness. The mass of men are neither wise nor good, and the virtue like the other resources of a country, can only be drawn to a point and exerted by strong circumstances as ably managed, or a strong government ably administered." Here is a clear expression of Jay's skepticism toward the behavior of the state legislatures and their threats to the rights of the minority, and of his hope that a stronger national government might, for the sake of the individual's freedom, alter the situation. A similar sentiment prevails throughout the letter, in which it is also stated that the variety of circumstances that brought about the Confederation "would not, almost miraculously, have combined to liberate and make us a nation for transient and unimportant purposes."[42] For Jay, the purpose of the Union was not merely to have security from foreign powers and peace within the United States, but also to secure the freedom of the individual from governmental oppression.[43]

II

1. James Madison was as staunch a defender of individual rights as Jay. In favor of "defending liberty and property" against the English in 1774,[44] and active in the Virginia Assembly that framed the constitution of 1776, Madison expressed himself for the protection of the individual's rights at the very beginning of his public career.[45] Later, on the floor of Congress in 1783, he advocated "complete justice to the public creditors,"[46] and drafted his famous Address to the States.[47] Seeing government instituted for the protection of individual rights, Madison denounced legislative evils in the states: "As far as laws are necessary to mark with precision the duties of those who are to obey them, and to take from those who are to administer them a discretion which might be abused, their

---

[42] Letter of June 27, 1786. *Ibid.*, III, 203-5.
[43] Compare his letter to Jefferson of Oct. 27, 1786. *Ibid.*, III, 212-13.
[44] Letter to W. Bradford of Jan. 24, 1774. MADISON'S WRITINGS, I, 18.
[45] See the "Journal of the Virginia Convention in 1776." *Ibid.*, I, 34.
[46] Debates in Congress on Jan. 28, 1783. *Ibid.*, I, 336.
[47] *Ibid.*, I, 454 ff., esp. 459.

number is the price of liberty. As far as laws exceed this limit, they are a nuisance; a nuisance of the most pestilent kind. . . . Try the Codes of the several States by this test, and what a luxuriancy of legislation do they present."[48] The multiplicity of laws was an evil; their mutability was worse. Madison complained of "vicious legislation" that brought "into question the fundamental principle of republican government, that the majority who rule . . . are the safest Guardians both of public Good and private rights."[49] Legislative behavior was not all he disliked. He observed with concern that "the late turbulent scenes in Massachusetts and infamous one in Rhode Island have done inexpressible injury to the republican character in that part of the U. States"[50] and accused the insurgents of having "an abolition of debts . . . and a new division of property . . . in contemplation."[51]

However, Madison was interested in a restriction of democracy only to the degree to which the protection of the individual required it. "It seems indispensable that the mass of citizens should not be without a voice in making the laws which they are to obey, and in choosing the magistrates who are to administer them," he said in the Federal Convention,[52] adding that it was "politic as well as just that the interests and rights of every class should be duly represented

[48] "Vices of the Political System of the United States," April 1787. *Ibid.*, II, 365.

[49] *Ibid.*, II, 366. Similar views were expressed in a letter to Jefferson of Oct. 24, 1787. *Ibid.*, V, 27-29. On October 5, 1786, Madison wrote to Monroe: "There is no maxim in my opinion which is more liable to be misapplied, and which therefore more needs elucidation than the current one that the interest of the majority is the political standard of right and wrong. Taking the word 'interest' as synonymous with 'ultimate happiness,' in which sense it is qualified with every necessary moral ingredient, the proposition is no doubt true. But taking it in the popular sense, as referring to immediate augmentation of property and wealth nothing can be more false. In the latter sense it would be the interest of the majority in every community to despoil & enslave the minority of individuals; and in a federal community to make a similar sacrifice of the minority of the component States. In fact it is only re-establishing under another name and a more specious form, force as the measure of right. . . ." *Ibid.*, II, 273.

[50] Letter to Edmund Pendleton of Feb. 24, 1787. *Ibid.*, II, 319.

[51] Letter to James Madison of Nov. 1, 1786. *Ibid.*, 278. See, in this connection, Madison's essay on property in the NATIONAL GAZETTE of March 29, 1792, in which he distinguished, as did Locke, property in a broader and narrower sense, the former comprising the total of vested rights. *Ibid.*, VI, 102-3.

[52] Richard Hofstadter, THE AMERICAN POLITICAL TRADITION AND THE MEN WHO MADE IT (1948), 6.

and understood in the public councils."[53] He favored popular election of congressmen,[54] popular ratification of the Constitution,[55] and popular election of the executive.[56]

On the other hand, Madison left no doubt about his antipathy to monarchy when he, the advocate of a more perfect Union, referred to a partition of the Union into several confederacies as "the lesser evil," if compared with monarchy.[57] To Washington he wrote that those who "lean towards a Monarchical Government . . . are swayed by very indigested ideas" and "will of course abandon an unattainable object whenever a prospect opens of rendering the Republican form competent to its purposes."[58] Madison was opposed to monarchy out of principle, probably more so than his two collaborators in the *Federalist*.[59]

2.   Madison was not only a believer in free government. He was also an advocate of peace within the United States. In 1780, he complained about the selfishness of Connecticut with respect to its territorial claims, fearing that it might be productive of tensions.[60] A month later, he reproached Maryland for her jealousy on the same grounds.[61] In the fall of the following year, Madison expressed concern lest Congress might take action invading the Western interests of his home state.[62] His letters to Jefferson in the following months reveal a similar feeling.[63] To Randolph, he complained of the obstinacy of Maryland and about reciprocal state jealousies.[64] Madison's desire to secure peace within America was also evident in his role in Congress. On April 9, 1783, he warned Congress not to excite in the states irritations and jealousies on the issue of the Western

[53] *Ibid.*, 14.
[54] Farrand, *op. cit.*, I, 49.
[55] *Ibid.*, I, 122.
[56] *Ibid.*, II, 56.
[57] Letter to Edmund Pendleton of Feb. 24, 1787. MADISON'S WRITINGS, II, 319.
[58] Letter to Washington of Feb. 21, 1787. *Ibid.*, II, 315. See also his letters to Jefferson of March 19, 1787 and to James Madison of April 1, 1787. *Ibid.*, II, 326, 335.
[59] See *supra*, pp. 70-71.
[60] Letter to Joseph Jones of Nov. 28, 1780. MADISON'S WRITINGS, I, 107.
[61] Letter to Joseph Jones of Dec. 12, 1780. *Ibid.*, I, 115.
[62] Letters to Edmund Pendleton of Oct. 30 and Nov. 13, 1781. *Ibid.*, I, 160-61.
[63] Letters to Jefferson of Nov. 18, 1781, Jan. 15 and April 16, 1782. *Ibid.*, I, 62, 170, 186. See also his letter to Edmund Randolph of May 1782. *Ibid.*, I, 190.
[64] Letters of Aug. 13 and 27, 1782. *Ibid.*, I, 225, 228.

territory.[65] A few days earlier, he disapproved of conventions in which only the states of a particular section of the United States participated, "not as absolute violations of the Confederacy, but as ultimately leading to them and in the meantime exciting pernicious jealousies."[66] His notes for a speech in the Virginia House of Delegates in November, 1785, reveal a fear of war between the states,[67] and in the spring of the following year "the present anarchy of our commerces" is denounced as being responsible for tensions in America.[68] Madison's "Vices of the Political System of the United States," written shortly before the meeting of the Philadelphia Convention, enumerates various kinds of trespasses of the states on the rights of each other, such as laws of Virginia restricting foreign vessels to certain ports and laws of Maryland in favor of vessels belonging to her own citizens.

> Paper money, instalments of debts, occlusion of Courts, making property a legal tender, may likewise be deemed aggressions on the rights of other States. As the Citizens of every State aggregately taken stand more or less in the relation of Creditors or debtors, to the Citizens of every other State, Acts of the debtor State in favor of debtors, affect the Creditor State, in the same manner as they do its own citizens who are relatively creditors towards other citizens. . . . The practice of many States in restricting the commercial intercourse with other States, and putting their productions and manufactures on the same footing with those of foreign nations, though not contrary to the federal articles, is certainly adverse to the spirit of the Union, and tends to beget retaliating regulations, not less expensive and vexatious in themselves than they are destructive of the general harmony.[69]

Aside from trespassing on the rights of other states, the states also encroach on the federal authority and thus further endanger peace within the United States.[70]

3. Just as he desired peace within America, Madison wanted the United States to be safe from foreign nations. Upon his return to his home state in 1774, the youthful Madison was appalled by Indian

[65] *Ibid.*, I, 444. For the whole problem of the Western territory, see Gaillard Hunt, THE LIFE OF JAMES MADISON (1902), 44 ff.

[66] MADISON'S WRITINGS, I, 438-39.

[67] *Ibid.*, II, 196.

[68] Letter to Jefferson of March 18, 1786. *Ibid.*, II, 228.

[69] *Ibid.*, II, 362-63.

[70] *Ibid.*, II, 361-62.

atrocities on the frontier.[71] This feeling did not change in the following years.[72] As to the English, Madison expressed himself in favor of defending the colonists' liberty and property as early as 1774,[73] and his attitude remained the same throughout the War of Independence.[74] Even when peace was about to come, Madison was still skeptical and voiced his apprehensions lest "some tricks would be tried by the British Court notwithstanding their exterior fairness of late."[75] In a similar manner, the Virginian recognized the possibility of threats from Spain, as is evident in the instructions of the Continental Congress to John Jay in 1780, concerning the boundaries and free navigation of the Mississippi, which were drafted by him.[76] After the peace treaty, he continued to be concerned about the security of his country. In the spring of 1787, he summed up his experience of the preceding years. "From the number of Legislatures, the sphere of life from which most of their members are taken, and the circumstances under which their legislative business is carried on," he stated, violations of the law of nations and of treaties

> must frequently happen. Accordingly not a year has passed without instances of them in some one or other of the States. The Treaty of Peace—the treaty with France—the treaty with Holland have each been violated. . . . The causes of these irregularities must necessarily produce frequent violations of the law of nations in other respects. As yet foreign powers have not been rigorous in animadverting on us. This moderation, however cannot be mistaken for a permanent partiality to our faults, or a permanent security against those disputes with other nations, which being among the greatest of public calamities, it ought to be least in the power of any part of the community to bring on the whole.[77]

4. Like Jay, Madison believed that free government in peace and security could be best achieved through union. The necessity of union is evident in his statements concerning the security of America. Recognizing the threats to the colonists' liberty from the mother country, Madison expressed his confidence in the Union as early as 1775. "When I consider the united virtue of that illustri-

---

[71] Letter to William Bradford of July 1, 1774. *Ibid.*, I, 25.

[72] Letter to Jefferson of June 2, 1780. *Ibid.*, I, 64.

[73] Letter to William Bradford of Jan. 24, 1774. *Ibid.*, I, 18-19.

[74] This is evident in his writings during that period. *Ibid.*, I.

[75] Letter to Jefferson of Feb. 18, 1783. *Ibid.*, I, 372n.

[76] *Ibid.*, I, 82 ff.

[77] "Vices of the Political system of the U. States," *ibid.*, II, 362.

ous body [Congress]," he wrote to Bradford, "every apprehension of danger vanishes. The signal proofs they have given of their integrity and attachment to liberty, both in their private and Confederate capacities, must triumph over jealousy itself. However, should it come to the worst I am persuaded that the union, virtue and love of liberty at present prevailing throughout the Colonies is such that it would be as little in the power of our treacherous friends as of our avowed enemies, to put the yoke upon us."[78] In the middle of the War of Independence, Madison, prompted by the precarious military situation, wrote to his father that "no exertions . . . ought to be omitted to testify our Zeal to support Congress in the prosecution of the War."[79] In the spring of 1780, he complained to Jefferson about the weak position of Congress vis-à-vis the states,[80] and six months later he noted with satisfaction that Congress entered on a plan for finally ratifying the Confederation, hoping that this would help the American war effort.[81] The instructions of Congress to Jay, written by Madison, voice concern lest disunity between Congress and the states "might greatly embarrass the public councils of the United States and give advantage to the common enemy."[82] After Yorktown, when the British had laid down their arms, Madison wrote to Edmund Pendleton that "it would be particularly unhappy, if any symptoms of disunion among ourselves should blast the golden prospects which the events of the campaign have opened to us."[83] Once the war was over, the Virginian continued to advocate the Union for the sake of security. Commenting upon the situation on the Mississippi, he stated that Spain's *"permanent security seems to lie in the complexity of our federal government and the diversity of interests among the members of it which render offensive measures improbable in council and difficult in execution. If such be the case when thirteen States compose the system ought she not to wish to see the number enlarged to three and twenty?"*[84] Before the meeting of the Philadelphia Convention, Madison blamed "the number and independent authority of the States" for the evils experienced both during the war and since the establishment of peace with respect

[78] Irving Brant, JAMES MADISON (1941-   ), I, 170. See also 172-74.
[79] Letter to James Madison of Dec. 8, 1779. MADISON'S WRITINGS, I, 56.
[80] Letters to Jefferson of March 20 and May 6, 1780. *Ibid.,* I, 59 and 61.
[81] Letter to Edmund Pendleton of Sept. 12, 1780. *Ibid.,* I, 67.
[82] *Ibid.,* I, 85-86.
[83] Letter of Oct. 30, 1781. *Ibid.,* I, 161.
[84] Letter to Jefferson of Aug. 20, 1784. *Ibid.,* II, 70 (italics for ciphers).

to the security of the United States.[85] His opinion did not change
throughout the proceedings of the Federal Convention.[86]

Madison also advocated union for the sake of peace within the
United States. Commenting upon the Vermont question, he felt that
the government of the Union should bring about a settlement of the
problem, "and in a style marking a due firmness and decision in
Congress."[87] As to the Mississippi Valley, Madison was against Congress' relinquishing territory that was within the charter limits of
particular states, fearing that such a cession would excite discussion
between Congress and the states concerned and jeopardize American harmony.[88] In 1781, he complained that Delaware did not
merely refrain from contributing its share to the national treasury,
but enriched herself at the expense of those states that fulfilled their
duty. As a remedy, he suggested that Congress be armed with
coercive powers to prevent "the shameless deficiency of some of the
States,"[89] which was detrimental to the good relations among the
component parts of the Union. The role of Congress to prevent a
revival of the controversy between Connecticut and Pennsylvania
was pointed out by him,[90] as was its function to bring about a
friendly compromise between the United States and its members concerning the Western territory.[91] In 1785, Madison advocated the

[85] "Vices of the Political system of the U. States," *ibid.*, II, 361-62. Two
years earlier, in a letter to James Monroe of Aug. 7, 1785, Madison pointed out
the necessity of a regulation of trade by Congress as a defense measure against
the commercial policy of Great Britain. "Viewing in the abstract the question
whether the power of regulating trade . . . ought to be vested in Congress, it
appears to me not to admit of a doubt, but that it should be decided in the
affirmative. If it be necessary to regulate trade at all, it surely is necessary to
lodge the power where trade can be regulated with effect; and experience has
confirmed what reason foresaw, that it can never be so regulated by the States
acting in their separate capacities. They can no more exercise this power separately than they could separately carry on war, or separately form treaties of
alliance or commerce." *Ibid.*, II, 156. On p. 157, Madison shows why a regulation
of trade by the government of the Union is necessary for the sake of security
from Great Britain.

[86] Hunt, *op. cit.*, 116 ff., 127 ff.

[87] Letter to Joseph Jones of Sept. 19, 1780. MADISON'S WRITINGS, I, 70.

[88] "Instructions to John Jay" of Oct. 17, 1780. *Ibid.*, I, 85-86.

[89] Letter to Jefferson of April 16, 1781. *Ibid.*, I, 130. See also his letter to
Pendleton of Jan. 22, 1782. *Ibid.*, I, 174-75.

[90] Letter to Edmund Randolph of July 2, 1782. *Ibid.*, I, 213.

[91] Letter to Edmund Randolph of Sept. 10, 1782. *Ibid.*, I, 233.

regulation of trade by Congress as being conducive to friendship among the states. "Commercial interests of the States . . . meet in more points than they differ," he stated. Consequently, he was in favor of "submitting the commercial interest of each State to the direction and care of the Majority" in Congress.[92] In a letter to Jefferson, written in the same year, Madison's advocacy of union for the sake of peace within the United States is again evident. "I find with much regret," he wrote, that the affairs of the confederacy "are as yet little redeemed from the confusion which has so long mortified the friends to our national honor and prosperity. Congress has kept the Vessel from sinking, but it has been by standing constantly at the pump, not by stopping the leaks which have endangered her. All their efforts for the latter purpose have been frustrated by the selfishness or perverseness of some part or other of their constituents." Madison then enumerates "the desiderata most strongly urged by our past experience & our present situation," all of which are conducive to internal peace.[93] Half a year later, congressional regulation of trade is advocated in order to end the "commercial warfare among the States."[94] When, shortly before the Federal Convention, Madison outlined the shortcomings of the political system of the United States, he complained of the want of harmony within the country. Again, the remedy he suggested was union.[95]

Aside from considerations of security and peace,[96] Madison wanted the Union in order to secure the freedom of the individual. This desire was evident in his attitude throughout the War of Independence. In the postwar period, he increasingly conceived of a stronger national government as a means for curbing democratic excesses in

[92] Letter to James Monroe of Aug. 7, 1785. *Ibid.*, II, 159.

[93] Letter of Oct. 3, 1785. *Ibid.*, II, 178-79. The desiderata were, "1. a final discrimination between such of the unauthorized expences of the States as ought to be added to the common debt, and such as ought not. 2. a constitutional apportionment of the common debt, either by a valuation of the land, or a change of the article which requires it. 3. a recognition by the States of the authority of Congress to enforce payment of their respective quotas. 4. a grant to Congress of an adequate power over trade."

[94] Letter to James Monroe of April 9, 1786. *Ibid.*, II, 235.

[95] "Vices of the Political system of the U. States." *Ibid.*, II, 361 ff.

[96] In his letter to Richard Henry Lee of Dec. 25, 1784, Madison stated: "In general I hold it for a maxim that the Union of the States is essential to their safety against foreign danger, & internal contention; and that the perpetuity and efficacy of the present system cannot be confided in." *Ibid.*, II, 99-100.

the states. In November, 1786, when he noted with concern Shays's Rebellion,[97] Madison made a speech in the Virginia House of Delegates in defense of private property, in which he stated not only that paper money would be unjust, pernicious, and incompatible with the constitution of his home state, but also that it would be "antifederal," i.e., in conflict with the Articles of Confederation.[98] Early in the following year, he wrote Edmund Pendleton that he hoped the danger of a partition of the Union into smaller confederacies, considered by many as a remedy against democratic excesses in the states, "will rouse all the real friends of the Revolution to exert themselves in favor of such an organization of the confederacy as will perpetuate the Union, and redeem the honor of the Republican name."[99] He was in favor of equipping the national government with "a negative *in all cases whatsoever* on the legislative acts of the States," feeling that a "happy effect of this prerogative would be its control on the internal vicissitudes of State policy, and the aggressions of interested majorities on the rights of minorities and of individuals."[100] Again, his paper on the vices of the political system of the United States shows that a strengthening of the national government was considered by Madison to be conducive to free government. The very title of the essay sets out the problem of reform in its totality. Since "the political system of the United States" was *one*,

[97] Letter to James Monroe of Nov. 1, 1786. *Ibid.*, II, 277-78.

[98] *Ibid.*, II, 279-81. Madison's notes read: "Antifederal. Right of regulating coin given to Congress for two reasons. 1. for sake of uniformity. 2. to prevent fraud in States towards each other or foreigners. Both these reasons hold equally as to paper money."

[99] Letter of Feb. 24, 1787. *Ibid.*, II, 319-20. Madison's use of the term "real friends of the Revolution" is significant. These friends are, of course, those people who believe in the protection of life, liberty, and property. By contrast, the "false" friends of the Revolution would be those who believe, like Hichborn (*supra*, p. 60) in equality and the sheer will of the majority.

[100] Letter to Washington of April 16, 1787. *Ibid.*, II, 346. The letter continues: "The great desideratum which has not yet been found for Republican Governments seems to be some disinterested & dispassionate umpire in disputes between different passions & interests in the State. The majority who alone have the right of decision, have frequently an interest, real or supposed in abusing it. . . . Might not the national prerogative here suggested be found sufficiently disinterested for the decision of local questions of policy, whilst it would itself be sufficiently restrained from the pursuit of interests adverse to those of the whole Society. There has not been any moment since the peace at which the representatives of the Union would have given an assent to paper money or any other measure of a kindred nature."

the problem was not only one of reforming organizational defects of the federal government, but also one of improving the conditions within the states. Such an improvement would not only be beneficial for security from foreign nations and peace in America, but also for the safety of the individual's life, liberty, and property from the onslaught of an equalitarian majoritarianism. One of the great short-comings of the Articles of Confederation was, Madison felt, the "want of a guarantee to the States of their constitutions and laws against internal violence," a clear recognition by the Virginian of the necessity of the more perfect Union for the protection of individual rights in a popular government.[101]

III

1. Like his two collaborators, Hamilton defended the freedom of the individual from the very beginning of his career. In his first pamphlet, *A Full Vindication,* written in 1774, the student at King's College took issue with Samuel Seabury's *Letters of a Westchester Farmer* and made a strong confession to the colonists' natural rights, maintaining that their lives and properties are protected by the law of nature, the genius of the British constitution, and the colonial charters.[102] Admonishing his countrymen to die rather than to submit to an infringement upon their property, Hamilton warned that not only property was endangered, but also their lives and religious

[101] *Ibid.,* II, 361 ff. The quotation is on p. 363. The view here expressed is that of Edward S. Corwin, "The Progress of Constitutional Theory between the Declaration of Independence and the Meeting of the Philadelphia Convention," AMERICAN HISTORICAL REVIEW (1924-25) XXX, 534 ff. Madison expressed his point even more clearly five months later in a letter to Jefferson of Oct. 24, 1787: "A constitutional negative on the laws of the State seems . . . necessary to secure individuals against encroachments on their rights. The mutability of the laws of the State is found to be a serious evil. The injustice of them has been so frequent and flagrant as to alarm the most steadfast friends of Republicanism. I am persuaded I do not err in saying that the evils issuing from these sources contributed more to that uneasiness which produced the Convention, and prepared the Public mind for a general reform, than those which accrued to our national character and interest from the inadequacy of the Confederation to its immediate objects. A reform therefore which does not make provision for private rights, must be materially defective." MADISON'S WRITINGS, V, 27. Compare also Randolph's speech opening the Federal Convention. Farrand, *op. cit.* I, 18 ff.

[102] HAMILTON'S WORKS, I, 7.

freedom.[103] A few months later, Hamilton answered a reply from the *Westchester Farmer* in *The Farmer Refuted*. Here again, he came forth with a full-scale enunciation of the natural rights philosophy: "THE SACRED RIGHTS OF MANKIND . . . ARE WRITTEN, AS WITH A SUNBEAM, IN THE WHOLE VOLUME OF HUMAN NATURE, BY THE HAND OF THE DIVINITY ITSELF, AND CAN NEVER BE ERASED OR OBSCURED BY MORTAL POWER."[104]

Hamilton remained a staunch advocate of the protection of the individual's life, liberty, and property during and after the war. When, in 1782, a proposal was before Washington to execute a captured officer of Cornwallis' army by way of retaliation for the murder of the patriot Captain Huddy, Hamilton wrote General Knox that "a sacrifice of this sort is entirely repugnant to the genius of the age we live in, and is without example in modern history."[105] He asked the general to prevent the execution, which was never authorized by Washington. As a defender of liberty, Hamilton came forth in favor of the freedom of the press. When, on the eve of the revolution, Connecticut minutemen, led by Isaac Sears, raided the shop of James Rivington, a royalist printer, Hamilton protested strongly.[106] Private property was considered by Hamilton "the great and fundamental distinction in society."[107] In the later years of the war, Hamilton proved his belief in the sacrosanctity of property by taking the side of the public creditors[108] and the army.[109] He even wanted the rights of the Tories under the Treaty of Paris to be protected, maintaining that there was "no option, on the part of the particular states, as to further confiscations, prosecutions, or injuries of any kind, to person, liberty, or property, on account of anything done in the war," and observing "with great regret, the intemperate proceedings among

[103] *Ibid.* I, 35-37.

[104] *Ibid.*, I, 113.

[105] Letter of June 7, 1782. *Ibid.*, IX, 256.

[106] See his letter to John Jay of Nov. 26, 1775 (Hamilton manuscripts, New York Public Library), and his letters to Robert R. Livingston of March 18 and 22, 1789 (Robert R. Livingston Collection, New York Historical Society).

[107] HAMILTON'S WORKS, I, 410. According to Madison's Papers, Hamilton said that "it was certainly true, that nothing like an equality of property existed; that an inequality would exist as long as liberty existed, and that it would unavoidably result from that very liberty itself. This inequality of property constituted the great and fundamental distinction in society."

[108] See his letters to Robert Morris of Sept. 28, 1782 and to Washington of Feb. 7 and March 17, 1783. *Ibid.*, IX, 292, 310, 323.

[109] See his letters to Washington of Feb. 7 and March 25, 1783. *Ibid.*, IX, 310, 330.

the people in different parts of the State" of New York.[110] Also, irrespective of political consequences, he defended property of the Tories against an act of the New York legislature.[111]

In view of his belief in individual rights, it can hardly be surprising that Hamilton should come forth at a time when, under the Confederation, these rights were increasingly infringed upon by majorities who controlled some of the state legislatures, with statements against such sheer majority rule or, as it was then called, democracy. Gouverneur Morris stated that Hamilton "detested" democracy, "because he believed it must end in despotism, and, be in the same time, destructive of public morality."[112] "Individuals have been already too long sacrificed to public convenience," wrote Hamilton to Governor Clinton in 1783, when the debtor element was ascendant, and "it will be shocking, and indeed an eternal reproach to this country, if we begin the peacable enjoyment of our independence by a violation of all the principles of honesty and true policy."[113] To Washington, Hamilton spoke of the democratic vogue as "the present epidemic frenzy" which he hoped would subside.[114] He wanted government to "check the impudence of democracy," charging that "the turbulent and changing" mass of the people "seldom judge or determine right."[115]

From these polemics against democracy we should not, however, conclude that Hamilton was in favor of an exclusion of the people in government. As early as 1774, he expressed the necessity of popular participation in the legislative process as a means for securing the protection of the colonists' rights.[116] Later, when the popular govern-

[110] Letter to Governor Clinton of June 1, 1783. *Ibid.*, IX, 343.

[111] In Rutgers v. Waddington (1784). See his two "Phocion Letters," *ibid.*, IV, 230 ff.

[112] A. C. Morris, ed., DIARY AND LETTERS OF GOUVERNEUR MORRIS (1889), II, 523.

[113] Letter of May 14, 1783. HAMILTON'S WORKS, IX, 342. Compare also his resolutions for a general convention of June 30, 1783. *Ibid.*, I, 305 ff.

[114] Letter of Sept. 30, 1783. *Ibid.*, IX, 386.

[115] Speech in the Federal Convention on June 18, 1787. *Ibid.*, I, 401.

[116] "The only distinction between freedom and slavery," he wrote in *A Full Vindication,* "consists in this: In the former state a man is governed by the laws to which he has given his consent, either in person or by his representative; in the latter, he is governed by the will of another. In the one case, his life and property are his own; in the other, they depend upon the pleasure of his master. It is easy to discern which of these two states is preferable. No man in his senses can hesitate in choosing to be free, rather than a slave. That Americans are entitled to freedom is incontestable on every rational principle. All men have one

ments under the Articles of Confederation infringed upon individual
rights, Hamilton became more skeptical. Nevertheless, in principle
he remained an adherent of popular government. Although he stated
in the Federal Convention that he despaired that a republican form
of government could remove the difficulties existing under the present system, he hastened to add: "Whatever may be my opinion, I
would hold it, however, unwise to change that form of government."
His remarks on the merits of the British government were merely a
praise of a limited monarchy in which the will of the people was
checked for the sake of "public strength and individual security,"
but by no means ignored.[117] As a matter of fact, Hamilton expressed
concern about monarchical tendencies only a few weeks later.[118] He
was no doubt in favor of a political equilibrium with power poised
in one center, favoring a strong executive and a senate, elected for
life, as against the popular branch of the legislature. Although
Hamilton denounced the excess of democracy, he wanted Congress,
a fundamentally democratic representation, to continue.[119] He complained that the Articles' main defect was want of power in Congress[120] and thus implied that a remedy against the centrifugal forces
had to be based on the principle of popular government. His propositions for a constitution of government, introduced on the floor of
the Federal Convention, restricted the power of the popular branch
of the national legislature, it is true. Nevertheless, they recognized
popular government. The assembly was to be elected by the people
directly, both senate and executive indirectly.[121] Hamilton was opposed to democracy only to the degree it threatened individual
rights. In principle, he accepted popular government.

2. Hamilton, the advocate of free government, was also a believer
in peace within the United States. During the war, he feared dis-

common original: they participate in one common nature, and consequently have
one common right. No reason can be assigned why one man should exercise any
power or preeminence over his fellow creatures more than another, unless they
have voluntarily vested him with it. Since, then, Americans have not, by any act
of theirs, empowered the British Parliament to make laws for them, it follows
they can have no just authority to do it." *Ibid.*, I, 5-6. See also his "The Farmer
Refuted," *ibid.*, I, 64, 113.

[117] Compare his letter to Col. Wadsworth of Aug. 20, 1787. *Ibid.*, IX, 422.

[118] Letter to James Duane of Sept. 3, 1780. *Ibid.*, I, 213.

[119] Letter to James Duane of Sept. 3, 1780. *Ibid.*, I, 213.

[120] In the Federal Convention on June 18, 1787. *Ibid.*, I, 391.

[121] *Ibid.*, I, 381 ff.

sensions among the members of the Confederation. Stating that the republics of the Greek leagues as well as the Swiss cantons were continually at war with each other in spite of the vicinity of foreign powers, Hamilton warned that the danger of interstate tensions was considerably greater in America, due to the absence of strong neighbors.[122] He was concerned about disputes over state boundaries, and regretted that the prospects of future tranquility were not flattering.[123] In *The Continentalist,* published in 1782, Hamilton again reproached the states for their mutual jealousy.[124] When he congratulated Washington on the occasion of the conclusion of the preliminaries of peace, he added a note of caution, saying that "the centrifugal is much stronger than the centripetal force in these States—the seeds of disunion much more numerous than those of union."[125] He remained concerned about the harmony among the states in the following years.[126]

Like Madison, Hamilton was afraid that combinations of states might also endanger peace. In *The Continentalist,* he voiced fears of a contest of arms between distinct combinations of members of the Union against each other.[127] Later, he joined Madison on the floor of Congress in disapproving conventions of a restricted number of states, feeling that such partial meetings would excite pernicious jealousies and be detrimental to the Confederacy.[128]

Hamilton's skepticism concerning harmony among the states was matched by a fear of tensions between the Union and its component

[122] "A little time hence some of the States will be powerful empires; and we are so remote from other nations, that we shall have all the leisure and opportunity we can wish to cut each other's throats." Letter to James Duane of Sept. 3, 1780. *Ibid.,* I, 217.

[123] *Ibid.,* I, 218. For Hamilton's role in the settlement of boundary disputes, see Broadus Mitchell, ALEXANDER HAMILTON—YOUTH TO MATURITY 1755-88 (1957), 373 ff.

[124] HAMILTON'S WORKS, I, 287.

[125] Letter of March 24, 1783. *Ibid.,* IX, 327.

[126] In 1787, he stated before the New York legislature: "If these States are not united under a Federal Government they will infallibly have wars with each other." *Ibid.,* II, 222-23. He continued: "The human passion will never want objects of hostility. The Western territory is an obvious and fruitful source of contest. Let us also cast our eye upon the map of this State, intersected from one extremity to the other by a large navigable river. In the event of a rupture with them, what is to hinder our metropolis from becoming a prey to our neighbors? Is it even supposable that they would suffer it to remain the nursery of wealth to a distinct community?"

[127] *Ibid.* I, 286.

[128] On April 1, 1783. MADISON'S WRITINGS, I, 438-39.

parts. His letter to James Duane, written in 1780, shows grave concern about that problem.[129] Two years later, Hamilton, aware of the egoism of the states, felt that "a mere regard to the interests of the Confederacy will never be a principle sufficiently active to crush the ambition and intrigues of different members." While he thought that the use of force against the states could hardly secure a better support of the federal government, he suggested that conditions could be improved "by interesting such a number of individuals in each state in support of the Federal Government as will be counterpoised to the ambition of others, and will make it difficult for them to unite the people in opposition to the first and necessary measures of the Union."[130] In his "Resolutions for a General Convention," prepared in 1783, Hamilton complained that the Articles of Confederation withheld from the federal government "that efficacious authority and influence . . . which are indispensable to the harmony and welfare of the whole," and that the phrasing of the Articles tended "to create jealousies and disputes respecting the proper bounds of the authority of the United States, and of that of the particular States, and a mutual interference of the one with the other."[131]

3.   Closely connected with Hamilton's advocacy of peace within the United States was his concern for his country's security from foreign nations. Often, he mentioned the necessity for peace and security in one breath. "There is something noble and magnificent in the perspective of a great Federal Republic, closely linked in the pursuit of a common interest, tranquil and prosperous at home, respectable abroad," he wrote in the sixth number of *The Continentalist,* continuing, "but there is something proportionably diminutive and contemptible in the prospect of a number of petty States, with the appearance only of union, jarring, jealous, and perverse, without any determined direction, fluctuating and unhappy at home, weak and insignificant by their dissensions in the eyes of other nations."[132] Hamilton's concern for security is the keynote of his first major works, *A Full Vindication* and *The Farmer Refuted,* written when he was still under twenty years of age. It is evident in his discourse

---

[129] Letter of Sept. 3, 1780. HAMILTON'S WORKS, I, 213 ff.
[130] "The Continentalist," *ibid.,* I, 286.
[131] *Ibid.,* I, 305.
[132] *Ibid.,* I, 286-87.

on the government set up under the Articles of Confederation, sent to James Duane in the fall of 1780.[133] A year later, the New Yorker noted that British troops were making an alarming progress in the Southern states, warning his countrymen to be on their guard.[134] In 1783, he complained that "the powers reserved to the Union in the Confederation are unequal to the purpose of effectually drawing forth the resources of the respective members, for the common welfare and defence: whereby the United States have . . . been exposed to the most critical and alarming situations; have wanted an army adequate to their defence . . . ; have, on account of that deficiency, seen essential posts reduced, others eminently endangered, whole States, and large parts of others overrun and ravaged by small bodies of the enemy's forces. . . ."[135] Hamilton's concern for security did not abate in the following years. When in the spring of 1787 he made a speech on acceding to the independence of Vermont, he stated that he was "solicitous to guard against danger from abroad."[136] He voiced similar sentiments in the Federal Convention.[137]

4.   For the sake of security from foreign nations, Hamilton wanted a union of the American states. The idea of union stands in the foreground in his arguments against Samuel Seabury prior to the Declaration of Independence, in which he attacked the designs of the British.[138] In the first years of the war, Hamilton stressed the importance of preserving a national character, feeling that the states' violations of faith would have an ill effect upon foreign negotiations.[139] Two years later, he wrote James Duane: "The Confederation . . . is defective, and requires to be altered. It is neither fit for war nor peace. . . . The entire formation and disposal of our military forces ought to belong to Congress. It is an essential cement of the union; and it ought to be the policy of Congress to destroy all ideas of State attachments in the army, and make it look up wholly to them. It may be apprehended that this may be dangerous to liberty. But nothing appears more evident to me than that we run much

---

[133] *Ibid.,* I, 213 ff.

[134] "The Continentalist," *ibid.,* I, 255.

[135] "Resolutions for a General Convention." *Ibid.,* I, 311-12.

[136] Richard B. Morris, ed., ALEXANDER HAMILTON AND THE FOUNDING OF THE NATION (1957), 97.

[137] HAMILTON'S WORKS, I, 381 ff.

[138] "A Full Vindication" and "The Farmer Refuted." *Ibid.,* I, 3 ff., 55 ff.

[139] Letter to George Clinton of March 12, 1778. *Ibid.,* IX, 129-30.

greater risk of having a weak and disunited federal government, than one which will be able to usurp upon the rights of the people."[140] He continued with a warning that the Greek republics, loosely federated, for want of union fell prey to their neighbors. Likewise the Swiss cantons were spared the same fate only because the powers in their neighborhood were too jealous of one another.[141] In another passage, Hamilton, after having urged a convention of the states for the establishment of a stronger national government, wrote: "A Convention may agree upon a Confederation; the States individually hardly ever will. We must have one at all events, and a vigorous one, if we mean to succeed in the contest [against England]."[142] Toward the end of his discourse on the Articles of Confederation, he stated that a solid confederation, a permanent army, and a reasonable prospect of subsisting it, would give the United States treble consideration in Europe, and produce peace before the winter was over.[143] His *Continentalist,* written in the following years, also depicts the Union as a prerequisite for American security.[144] The Address of the Annapolis Convention saw in a more perfect Union a means for improving the prestige of the United States in international relations.[145] Shortly before the Federal Convention, he told the legislature of New York that if the states were not united, their divisions would subject them to all the mischiefs of foreign influence and intrigue.[146]

Similarly, Hamilton felt that the Union was necessary for the preservation of peace within the United States. His letter to James Duane shows his great concern about the states' jealousy of power, which "has led them to exercise a right of judging in the last resort of the measures recommended by Congress, and of acting according to their own opinions of their propriety, or necessity." Likewise, he blamed Congress' diffidence of their own powers, "by which they have been timid and indecisive in their resolutions, constantly making concessions to the States, till they have scarcely left themselves

[140] Letter to James Duane of Sept. 3, 1780. *Ibid.,* I, 215-16.
[141] *Ibid.,* I, 217.
[142] *Ibid.,* I, 223-24.
[143] *Ibid.,* I, 237.
[144] *Ibid.,* I, 243 ff.
[145] *Ibid.,* I, 335 ff.
[146] *Ibid.,* II, 222. Also, in April, 1787, he said before the legislature of New York, in his speech on acceding to the independence of Vermont, that a more perfect Union was necessary as a defense against the British in Canada. *Ibid.,* VIII, 57-58.

the shadow of power" to be responsible for facilitating state ambitions that are not conducive to peace within the confederation. The Articles established a government that was not fit for peace, to say nothing about its ability to conduct war: "The idea of an uncontrollable sovereignty in each State over its internal police will defeat the other powers given to Congress, and make our union feeble and precarious. There are instances without number where acts, necessary for the general good, and which rise out of the powers given to Congress, must interfere with the internal police of the States; and there are as many instances in which the particular States, by arrangements of internal police, can effectually, though indirectly, counteract the arrangements of Congress." Under the existing system, there was a strong competition for power between the national and state governments. For Hamilton, there was but one remedy, namely, a stronger national government in a more perfect Union.[147] In *The Continentalist,* Hamilton expressed similar thoughts.[148] The year after, he wrote that the restricted powers of the national government were detrimental to the harmony of the whole. Again, he suggested a more perfect Union.[149] A stronger national government would not only decrease tensions between nation and states, it would also help to eliminate dissensions among the states themselves. Hamilton favored "a confederacy capable of deciding the differences and compelling the obedience of the respective members."[150] His attitude toward union as a means for the preservation of peace did not change in the years after the war. His letters, written in the year before the Federal Convention, the Address of the Annapolis Convention, and the New Yorker's speeches in Philadelphia are ample proof of this.

Last, but not least, Hamilton wanted the Union for the sake of individual freedom. Already his *A Full Vindication* had concluded with an exhortation that the Americans unite for the defense of their rights. "If you join with the rest of America in the same common measure," he wrote when the colonists' freedom was threatened by the English, "you will be sure to preserve your liberties inviolate, but if you separate from them, and seek redress alone, and unseconded, you will certainly fall a prey to your enemies, and repent

---

[147] Letter of Sept. 3, 1780. *Ibid.,* I, 213-15.
[148] *Ibid.,* I, 286-87.
[149] *Ibid.,* I, 305.
[150] Letter to James Duane of Sept. 3, 1780. *Ibid.,* I, 213.

your folly as long as you live."[151] In *The Farmer Refuted,* he spoke
in defense of the rights of Americans, irrespective of the particular
colonies they lived in. Once these rights had become safe from the
British, the specter of their suppression by majoritarianism arose.
Now Hamilton, true to his principles, advocated a more perfect
Union in order to meet the democratic challenge in the states. For
the protection of the individuals' rights, among which those of private property played an important role at that time, the New Yorker
urged an alteration of the Articles, the insufficiency of which[152] made
it only "palpable, that the people have lost all confidence in our
public councils."[153] Although Hamilton stressed the organizational
defects of the Confederation, especially the disadvantages of an
imperium in imperio ensuing from a want of power in Congress,[154]
he wanted a more effective national government not only for the
security from foreign nations and peace within the United States, but
also for the protection of the individual's rights from governmental
encroachment. The re-establishment of national credit,[155] through a
funding of the national debt[156] and the creation of a national taxing
power[157] did deal a heavy blow to state pretensions. In the long run,
it created a basis for giving the individuals what was theirs: *E Pluri-*
bus Unum not only for the sake of union as a means to security and
peace, but also for the maintenance of the principle *pacta sunt*
servanda, which secures the protection of individual rights.[158] To-

[151] *Ibid.,* I, 52.

[152] See his letters to James Duane of Oct. 18, 1780, to Governor Clinton of July
27, 1783, to Washington of Sept. 30, 1783. *Ibid.,* IX, 225, 382, 386.

[153] Letter to Robert Morris of April 30, 1781. John C. Hamilton, ed., THE WORKS
OF ALEXANDER HAMILTON (1850-51), I, 223. See also the Annapolis Resolutions, HAM-
ILTON'S WORKS, I, 335 ff., and the beginning of Hamilton's speech in the Federal
Convention on June 18, 1787. *Ibid.,* I, 381.

[154] See Hamilton's letter to Robert Morris of April 30, 1781. John C. Hamilton,
ed., THE WORKS OF ALEXANDER HAMILTON, I, 223. Compare also Hamilton's speech
of June 18, 1787. HAMILTON'S WORKS, I, 381 ff.

[155] See the letters to Robert Morris of April 30, 1781, John C. Hamilton, ed.,
THE WORKS OF ALEXANDER HAMILTON, I, 224; to Washington of March 17 and April
11, 1783. *Ibid.,* I, 347, 356.

[156] See the letters to Washington of March 17, 1783, and to Governor Clinton of
May 14, 1783. *Ibid.,* I, 347, 366.

[157] See the letters to Washington of April 11, 1783, and to Governor Clinton of
Feb. 24 and May 14, 1783. *Ibid.,* I, 356, 333, 366-67. Also, for the bad state of finances
and currency, the letters to Robert Morris of about 1781 and 1782, and the letter
to Washington of Feb. 7, 1783. *Ibid.,* I, 116 ff., 286, 327.

[158] To Governor Clinton, Hamilton wrote on May 14, 1783: "I hope our State

ward the end of the war, Hamilton wrote to Washington: "There are good intentions in the majority of Congress, but there is not sufficient wisdom or decision. There are dangerous prejudices in the particular States opposed to those measures which alone can give stability and prosperity to the Union. There is a fatal opposition to Continental views. Necessity alone can work reform. But how produce that necessity, how apply it, and how keep it within salutary bounds? I fear we have been contending for a shadow." Denouncing the "internal weaknesses, disorders, follies, and prejudices" that make America stand on precarious ground, Hamilton spoke out against a democratic despotism that was made possible through the shortcomings of the Articles of Confederation.[159] The more the democratic vogue increased, the greater his concern over the protection of individual rights and the greater his emphasis on the necessity of a more perfect union. The Address of the Annapolis Convention largely advocated a general convention in order to bring about a stronger national government for the sake of the individual's protection. Similarly, Hamilton's activities in Philadelphia were often prompted by his deep concern lest private rights might be lost in the legislative vortices of the states.

IV

1. Jay's, Madison's, and Hamilton's advocacy of the Union as a means to secure free government in peace and security in the years preceding the publication of the *Federalist* raises the question as to what appeared to them the most important value to be secured through union. Was it security from foreign nations, or peace within the United States, or the freedom of the individual from governmental control? While, as the preceding pages have demonstrated, the authors were keenly interested in the realization of all three values, emphasis seems to have shifted over the years toward a concern for free government. For instance, Jay, although noticing the

will consent to the plan proposed, because it is her interest . . . to promote the payment of the public debts on continental funds (independent of the general considerations of union and propriety)." *Ibid.*, I, 367. As to Hamilton's advocacy of Union, see his letters to Washington of March 17 and 24, and April 11, 1783. *Ibid.*, I, 346, 348, 357.

[159] Letter of March 17, 1783. HAMILTON'S WORKS, IX, 324-25. See also his letter to Washington of March 24, 1783. *Ibid.*, IX, 327.

disadvantages of a feeble Union with respect to peace and security throughout the war, was not too emphatic in urging a reform of the Articles up to the end of the war, hoping that "time and experience will . . . eventually remedy" the imperfections of the existing governments.[160] However, after he had become conscious of the increasing infringement upon individual rights by the states in the years following peace, he became more ardent and definite in his advocacy of a change toward a more perfect Union. On July 4, 1787, he wrote John Adams with respect to the Philadelphia Convention that "it is much to be wished that the result of their deliberations may place the United States in a better situation, for if their measures should either be inadequate or rejected, the duration of the Union will become problematical." He wanted "a national government, as strong as may be compatible with liberty."[161] In the case of Madison, a similar shift in emphasis can be noted. Whereas in earlier years the Virginian showed about an equal concern over security, peace, and liberty, this changed with the increasing infringement of minority rights in some of the states. His "Vices of the Political System of the United States," written in April, 1787, is indicative of the greater importance he now attributed to the freedom of the individual from the ruling majority. While that treatise stresses the value of a more perfect Union for peace and security, it deals at considerably greater length with the function a stronger national government could fulfill in the liberation of the individual from democratic despotism, describing the latter in detail. With Hamilton, the situation was not much different. Naturally, Washington's *aide-de-camp* would see the value of the Union primarily in a harmony within the United States that was conducive to a successful warfare against the English. However, once the struggle had been brought to a successful conclusion, his concern over security and peace took second rank behind his desire to see the individual free in an increasingly oppressive society and to see his vested rights protected. In 1783, when Hamilton congratulated Washington on the happy conclusion of the general's labors, he had written him: "It now only remains to make solid establishments within, to perpetuate our Union, to prevent our being a ball in the hands of European powers, bandied against each other at their pleasure; in fine to make our

[160] Quoted in Max Farrand, THE FRAMING OF THE CONSTITUTION (1913), 43.
[161] JAY'S CORRESPONDENCE, III, 248.

independence truly a blessing."[162] By the time of the Philadelphia Convention, Hamilton's quest for solid establishments that would not be endangered by the mutable policy of changing popular majorities had, due to the conditions in the states, more and more come to the fore.

2.   The authors of the *Federalist,* then, considered the Union as a means for the establishment of a free government in peace and security. No matter how different their careers may have been up to the eventful year in which the Philadelphia Convention drafted the Constitution, the fight for the ratification of the Constitution saw the three side by side.

Although it was, when the Federal Convention adjourned, everybody's guess how the new government would be received by the people,[163] the first public reaction showed an approval of the Con-

[162] Letter of March 24, 1783. HAMILTON'S WORKS, IX, 327.

[163] A month before publication of the first number of the *Federalist,* Hamilton made a coolly detached forecast of the alignment of forces, pro and con, and of the Constitution's probable reception in the states: "The new Constitution has in favor of its success these circumstances: A very great weight of influence of the persons who framed it, particularly in the universal popularity of General Washington. The good will of the commercial interests throughout the States, which will give all its efforts to the establishment of a government capable of regulating, protecting, and extending the commerce of the Union. The good will of most men of property in the several States, who wish a government of the Union able to protect them against domestic violence, and the depredations which the democratic spirit is apt to make on property, and who are besides anxious for the respectability of the nation. The hopes of the creditors of the United States, that a general government possessing the means of doing it, will pay the debts of the Union. A strong belief in the people at large of the insufficiency of the present Confederation to preserve the existence of the Union, and of the necessity of the Union to their safety and prosperity; of course, a strong desire of a change, and a predisposition to receive well the propositions of the convention.

Against its success is to be put the dissent of two or three important men in the convention, who will think their characters pledged to defeat the plan; the influence of many *inconsiderable* men in possession of considerable offices under the state governments, who will fear a diminution of their consequence, power, and emolument, by the establishment of the general government, and who can hope for nothing there; the influence of some *considerable* men in the office, possessed of talents and popularity, who, partly from the same motives, and partly from a desire of *playing a part* in a convulsion for their own aggrandizement, will oppose the quiet adoption of the new government (some considerable men out of office, from motives of ambition, may be disposed to act the same part). Add to these causes the disinclination of the people to taxes, and of course to a

vention's work in most states, including New York. As late as the middle of October Hamilton could inform Washington that "the new Constitution is as popular in this city as it is possible for anything to be, and the prospect thus far is favorable to it throughout the state." However, he saw even then the opposition that was forming, and added, "but there is no saying what turn things may take when the full flood of official influence is let loose against it."[164] This cautious remark was only too justified. Aside from the opposition of such critics as Elbridge Gerry in Massachusetts, Luther Martin in Maryland, George Mason and Richard Henry Lee in Virginia, and Robert Yates and John Lansing in New York,[165] there was a growing opposition to ratification in New York, where by the end of October Governor Clinton was openly opposing the new government. Hamilton's letter to Washington of October 30 sounds, with regard to the chances of ratification, doubtful, if not pessimistic: "The constitution proposed has in this state warm friends and enemies, the first impressions everywhere are in its favor, but the artillery of its opponents makes some impression. The event cannot yet be foreseen."[166]

The ratification of the Constitution in New York was vital for the success of the Convention's plan. The Empire State could, through

strong government; the opposition of all men in debt, who will not wish to see a government established, one object of which is to restrain the means of cheating creditors; the democratical jealousy of the people, which may be alarmed at the appearance of institutions that may seem calculated to place the power of the community in few hands, and to raise a few individuals to stations of great pre-eminence; and the influence of some foreign powers, who, from different motives, will not wish to see an energetic government established throughout the States.

In this view of the subject it is difficult to form any judgment whether the plan will be adopted or rejected. It must be essentially a matter of conjecture. The present appearances and all other circumstances considered, the probability seems to be on the side of its adoption." *Ibid.*, I, 420-22.

[164] Letter of October, 1787. *Ibid.*, IX, 425. This letter is undated, but it was written before Oct. 15.

[165] See, for example, Luther Martin, "The Genuine Information," in Farrand, RECORDS, III, 172 ff.; Elbridge Gerry, "Observations on the New Constitution and on the Federal and State Conventions," in Paul Leicester Ford, ed., PAMPHLETS ON THE CONSTITUTION OF THE UNITED STATES (1888), 8-14; Richard Henry Lee, "Letters from the Federal Farmer to a Republican," *ibid.*, 282; Robert Yates and John Lansing, "To the Governor of New York Containing their Reasons for not Subscribing to the Federal Constitution," SENATE DOCUMENTS, 60th Congress, second session, Dec. 7, 1908–March 4, 1909, 191.

[166] HAMILTON'S WORKS, IX, 425.

its geographical position, easily split the new Union in twain. It was recognized by all that any system omitting New York would be destructive of the framers' work. In this crucial situation Hamilton became convinced of the need to encounter the arguments of the adversaries of the Constitution. Pressed for time, he joined with him John Jay to undertake the task of vindicating the Constitution to the New York electorate. In his letter of October 30 to Washington he was already able to enclose an essay that he described as "the first number of a series of papers to be written in its [the Constitution's] defense."[167] This paper had appeared in the *Independent Journal* three days earlier. It was the first essay of the *Federalist*. During the time the first numbers of the *Federalist*, written by Hamilton and Jay, appeared, Hamilton was looking for other collaborators. Gouverneur Morris, although he was "warmly pressed by Hamilton to assist in writing *The Federalist*,"[168] refused to do so. William Duer wrote several papers, but they were too poor to use. Therefore, sometime toward the middle of November, Hamilton turned to Madison, and the Virginian agreed to participate.[169]

Prevented by sickness, Jay wrote only a few essays, leaving the main work to Hamilton and Madison. Nevertheless, his contribution is by no means unimportant. Jay's prestige was greater in 1787 than

---

[167] *Ibid.*, IX, 425.

[168] Letter of Gouverneur Morris to W. H. Wells of Feb. 24, 1815. Jared Sparks, ed., THE LIFE OF GOUVERNEUR MORRIS (1832), III, 339.

[169] "The undertaking was proposed by Alexander Hamilton to James Madison with a request to join him and Mr. Jay in carrying it into effect. William Duer was also included in the original plan; and wrote two more papers, which though intelligent and sprightly, were not continued, nor did they make a part of the printed collection." (From Madison's memorandum entitled "The Federalist," quoted in J. C. Hamilton, ed., THE FEDERALIST (1866), lxxxvii). In spite of Madison's praise, Duer's essays are undistinguished in style and thought. Madison was not taken into the Federalist partnership until after the middle of the month, for during the week of November 12 he traveled to Philadelphia and considered going on from there to Virginia. (Letter to Randolph of Nov., 1887, MADISON'S WRITINGS, V, 56.) "The fact that Hamilton did not ask Madison to take part in the enterprise earlier throws an interesting light on the relationship of the two men. Their personal tastes, amusements, habits of life, and political ideas were poles apart; at no period except while *The Federalist* was being written, were they intimate. It was natural when *The Federalist* was first projected, for Hamilton to call on Jay, Morris and Duer, who were close friends and political allies, for their aid. He seems to have approached Madison only as a last resort when the others failed him." (Douglass Adair, "The Authorship of the Disputed Federalist Papers," *loc. cit.*, 247.)

either Hamilton's or Madison's. Furthermore, since it was sickness only that prevented him from taking a more active part in the writing of the *Federalist*[170] and not disagreement with the purpose and content of the work, he remained associated with the enterprise to the end, which was of real significance for the effect of the *Federalist* on the people. As a third collaborator, Hamilton could hardly have found a better man than Madison, Father of the Constitution. And whereas Jay was a key participant because of his extensive knowledge and experience in international affairs, Madison, who had gained unrivaled command of the proceedings of the Philadelphia Convention through his note-taking, was indispensable because he was "the best informed Man of any point in debate."[171]

The three authors had conscientiously lived through the American Revolution with its quest for security, peace, and freedom. By 1787, the order of these values, with respect to their relative importance, had become reversed. Consequently, the *Federalist* advocates the more perfect Union primarily for the sake of securing individual rights in a free government; second, as a means for preserving peace among the members of the Union; and third, as a device for maintaining the security of the United States from foreign nations.

[170] Jay was desperately sick before the end of November; and as late as the following February the excruciating pains he suffered prevented any continuous writing. (Monaghan, *op. cit.*, 290.) Compare also Madison's letter to Jefferson of Aug. 10, 1788: "*It* [the *Federalist*] *was undertaken last fall by Jay, Hamilton, and myself. The proposal came from the two former. The execution was thrown, by the sickness of Jay, mostly on the two others*." MADISON'S WRITINGS, v, 246. (Italics for cipher.)

[171] "Notes of Major William Pierce on the Federal Convention of 1787," AMERICAN HISTORICAL REVIEW (1897-98), III, 331.

BOOK TWO

Analysis

CHAPTER FOUR

Jay on Free Government

I

Jay's contribution to the *Federalist* on the subject of free government is rather slim. The five essays from his pen are mainly concerned with the value of the more perfect Union for security from
foreign nations and can thus receive full credit only in a later chapter.[1] Still, Jay leaves no doubt that the Union has a further end to
achieve, namely, the people's "safety and happiness."[2] The Federal
Convention was convened because the people wanted their threatened liberty protected,[3] and the men at Philadelphia "joined with
the people in thinking that the prosperity of America depended on
its Union."[4] Jay urges the ratification of the Constitution because
"an entire and perfect union will be the solid foundation of lasting
peace: It will secure . . . religion, liberty, and property, . . . our

[1] See *infra*, pp. 219 ff.   [2] 2, 8.

[3] The quality of the Union as a means for the protection of liberty is indicated
at 2, 10: "This intelligent people perceived these defects [of the Articles]. Still
continuing no less attached to union than enamored to liberty, they observed the
danger which immediately threatened the former and more remotely the latter;
and being persuaded that . . . security for both could only be found in a national
government more wisely framed, they, as with one voice, convened the late convention at Philadelphia, to take that important subject under consideration."

[4] 2, 12.

present and future happiness."[5] At first sight, it may appear as if
Jay's mentioning such ends of the Union as the people's safety and
happiness, their life, liberty, and property, means only that these
rights will be guaranteed from foreign attacks. However, if we consider the polemics of the time in which the challenge of individual
rights had its origin mainly in the oppressive majority rule which
existed in some of the states, and Jay's acute awareness of that situation, we seem to be justified in thinking that Jay, when pleading for
the prosperity of America and the rights of her citizens, recognized
the danger arising from the then existing democratic despotism and
wanted the individual protected from that quarter as much as from
the dangers threatening from foreign nations. This is confirmed by
him in so many words when he states that the Union, as established
under the Constitution, is securing "the preservation of peace and
tranquility" not only "against dangers from foreign arms and influence," but also "from dangers of the like kind arising from domestic
causes,"[6] that is, from those factions that were threatening individual
rights in the states. There is no reason to believe that Jay conceives
of faction in a different way than his co-authors,[7] when, obviously
having in mind the infringements upon minority rights under the
Articles of Confederation, he complains that "the prospect of present loss or advantage may often tempt the governing party in one
or two states to swerve from good faith and justice" and is glad that
"those temptations, not reaching the other States, and consequently
having little or no influence on the national government, the tempta-
tion will be fruitless, and good faith and justice be preserved."[8] Jay
continues: "Even if the governing party in a State should be disposed to resist such temptations, yet, as such temptations may, and
commonly do, result from circumstances peculiar to the State, and
may affect a great number of the inhabitants, the governing party
may not always be able, if willing, to prevent the injustice meditated,
or to punish the aggressors. But the national government, not being
affected by those local circumstances, will neither be induced to
commit the wrong themselves, nor want power or inclination to
prevent or punish its commission by others."[9] Thus Jay's opinion

---

[5] 5, 22-23   [6] 3, 13.

[7] Madison gives an exposition of factions in essay 10. Although Hamilton in the
Federalist nowhere defines faction, there can, from the context in which he uses
the term, be no doubt that it has for him the same meaning as for Madison.
Compare 9, 47; 26, 163; 65, 424; 70, 454; 78, 508-9; 27, 167; 65, 428; 15, 92; 85, 568.

[8] 3, 15.   [9] 3, 15-16.

on the dangers arising from local factions and the remedy against them has great resemblance to statements made by Hamilton and Madison in their famous essays nine and ten. That similarity appears especially interesting in view of the fact that Jay, when writing the remarks just quoted, was obviously mainly concerned with the infringements upon the property of the minority as they occurred at that time.[10] The same apprehension can be noticed in Madison's and Hamilton's essays. Therefore, it can hardly admit of any doubt that Jay, in the *Federalist,* is as fearful of majoritarianism as are his co-authors.

II

This fear is based on Jay's opinion of man, which is by no means an entirely favorable one. He bitterly complains about man's egoism,[11] depicts man as jealous,[12] and says that human beings, motivated by the "dictates of personal interest,"[13] will "swerve from good faith and justice."[14] There will often be "little room for . . . calm and mature inquiries and reflections,"[15] and people are likely to be deceived and deluded.[16] On the other hand, Jay admits that there are positive qualities in man. He is glad to note that the majority of the American people, when accepting certain recommendations of Congress in 1774, "reasoned and decided judiciously,"[17] and that "this intelligent people perceived and regretted" the defects of the Articles of Confederation.[18] The Federal Convention, he feels, was composed of men many of whom "had become highly distinguished by their patriotism, virtue, and wisdom," who were not

[10] Compare his letters to John Adams of Nov. 1, 1786 and Feb. 21, 1787; to Jefferson of Aug. 18 and Oct. 27, 1786, April 24, 1787; to Washington of Jan. 7, 1787. JAY'S CORRESPONDENCE, III, 214, 234, 210, 212, 244, 226. In the *Federalist,* Jay says that "the case of the treaty with Britain adds great weight" to this reasoning (3, 15), probably having in mind the infringement of the rights of Englishmen and former loyalists.

[11] Compare 4, 18: "It is too true, however disgraceful it may be to human nature, that nations in general will make war whenever they have a prospect of getting any thing by it, nay, absolute monarchs will often make war when their nations are to get nothing by it but for purposes and objects merely personal, such as a thirst for military glory, revenge for personal affronts, ambition, or private compacts to aggrandize or support their particular families or partisans."

[12] 5, 23-25.   [15] 2, 10.   [18] 2, 10.
[13] 2, 11.   [16] 2, 11.
[14] 3, 15.   [17] 2, 11.

"awed by power, or influenced by any passions except love for their country."[19] Also, Jay expresses his confidence in the new national government, trusting that, since it will be composed of the "best men in the country,"[20] its administration, political counsels, and judicial decisions will be "more wise, systematical, and judicious than those of the individual States,"[21] and wisdom and prudence will govern its decisions.[22]

By not committing himself completely on the nature of man, Jay puts himself in a position that is advantageous for an adherent of free government. By depicting man as bad and passionate, he can denounce the system under the Articles of Confederation for being too democratic and thus oppressive of minority rights. On the other hand, by describing man as good and reasonable enough to be trusted with self-government, he can come forward with his advocacy of the new government.

III

1. The new system is to be recommended because it diminishes, while remaining a popular government, the chances of faction and democratic despotism. This is due to a selective process by which the national government will become a refined body. While "town or country, or other contracted influence, may place men in State assemblies, or senates, or courts of justice, or executive departments, yet more general and extensive reputation for talents and other qualifications will be necessary to recommend men to offices under the national government—especially as it will have the widest field of choice, and never experience that want of proper persons which is not uncommon in some of the States."[23] Owing to its superior composition, the national government is unlikely to be swayed by passions that result in violence.[24] Rather, its proceedings will be characterized by "moderation and candor."[25] Being "more temperate and cool" in their deliberations,[26] the national government will be relatively free from those local factions that result in grave injustice toward minorities in the states.[27]

[19] 2, 10. See also 3, 13; 3, 15.   [24] 3, 16.
[20] 3, 14.   [25] 3, 17.
[21] 3, 15.   [26] 3, 16.
[22] 3, 16.   [27] 3, 15.
[23] 3, 14-15. A similar statement is made at 4, 20.

Seeing the danger to the protection of individual rights arise mainly from the legislative body, Jay is careful to point out the refined character of that branch of the national government in essay sixty-four, where he comments on the treaty-making power. It is in this essay that Jay's distrust of democracy seems to be most evident. On the whole, it may be said that his skepticism toward popular government increases with the immediacy of that government. Jay is happy to note that the power to approve treaties is not vested under the Constitution in the popular assembly, which is elected directly by the people. Rather, it is vested in the Senate, the members of which are appointed by the state legislatures,[28] which "will in general be composed of the most enlightened and respectable citizens," whose votes "will be directed to those men only who have become the most distinguished by their abilities and virtue, and in whom the people perceive just grounds for confidence."[29] Since the Constitution excludes men under thirty from the office of senator, "it confines the electors to men of whom the people have had time to form a judgment, and with respect to whom they will not be liable to be deceived by those brilliant appearances of genius and patriotism, which, like transient meteors, sometimes mislead as well as dazzle."[30] Treaties and laws will thus bear the mark of human wisdom rather than passion, because they are cautiously formed.[31]

2. In a polemic against majority despotism, both Madison and Hamilton denounce, in the *Federalist*, the mutability of the laws. In a like manner Jay considers the instability of treaties destructive of public morale. He lauds the new system for matching a wise mode of election by good provisions pertaining to the tenure of senators, which will contribute to a steady policy. "A popular assembly, composed of members constantly coming and going in quick succession, . . . must necessarily be inadequate to the attainment of those great objects, which require to be steadily contemplated in all their relations and circumstances, and which can only be approached and achieved by measures which not only talents, but also exact information, and often much time, are necessary to concert and execute,"[32] Jay writes, and he is glad that the Convention was so wise as to provide "not only that the power of making treaties should be committed to able and honest men, but also that they should continue in place a sufficient time to become perfectly acquainted with our

[28] 64, 417-18.　　　[30] 64, 417.　　　[32] 64, 418.
[29] 64, 417.　　　[31] 64, 419.

national concerns, and to form and introduce a system for the management of them."[33] Finally, Jay praises the Convention for providing for a partial renewal of the Senate only, "for by leaving a considerable residue of the old ones in place, uniformity and order, as well as a constant succession of official information, will be preserved."[34]

Although Jay likes the idea of vesting the treaty-making power in a high-caliber legislative chamber like the Senate, he opposes those who argue that this power should reside exclusively in that body, since treaties have the force of law. In this connection, he comes forth with a strict denial of legislative supremacy. Reminding the inhabitants of New York that the judgments of the courts, and the commissions constitutionally given by the governor, are as valid and as binding on all persons whom they concern as the laws passed by the legislature, Jay states that

> all constitutional acts of power, whether in the executive or in the judicial department, have as much legal validity and obligation as if they proceeded from the legislature; and therefore, whatever name be given to the power of making treaties, or however obligatory they may be when made, certain it is, that the people may, with much propriety, commit the power to a distinct body from the legislature, the executive, or the judicial. It surely does not follow that because they have given the power of making laws to the legislature, that therefore they should likewise give them power to do every other act of sovereignty by which the citizens are to be bound and affected.[35]

Therefore, the Constitution is praised for giving the president a substantial share in the conclusion of treaties. Since the chief executive is elected by a process that is even more selective than the one used for the election of senators,[36] he is likely to be a man of great integrity who in many cases will be able to assume the leadership of the Senate. Jay, being afraid that the size of the Senate might prevent an effective foreign policy under circumstances that make an immediate action imperative, is glad to note that "those matters which in negotiations require the most secrecy and the most despatch," can be dealt with by the president directly, and that, on the other hand, should any circumstances occur that require the advice and consent of the Senate, that body could easily be convened by the president.[37] The Constitution thus provides for the compatibility of

[33] 64, 418.   [35] 64, 420-21.   [37] 64, 420.
[34] 64, 419.   [36] 64, 417-18.

an effective foreign policy with the democratic process, while, at the same time, making sure that even the more conservative chamber of the most democratic branch of government will be checked in the exercise of its treaty-making power. Once treaties are approved and ratified against the will of the sheer majority, Jay comments in a concluding remark, "they are just as binding, and just as far beyond the lawful reach of the legislative acts now, as they will be at any future period."[38]

IV

The preceding pages have demonstrated that Jay's *Federalist*, although it is mainly concerned with aspects of international relations, also recognizes the threat to individual freedom in society. There can be noticed a distrust of sheer majority rule and democratic despotism stemming from an apprehension lest the individual's life, liberty, and property might be oppressed. The more perfect Union, while increasing the prestige of the nation abroad, also has the function of securing freedom at home. Thus Jay's contribution to the *Federalist* is a defense of free government, as are the essays of Madison and Hamilton, which will now be considered.

[38] 64, 421.

CHAPTER FIVE

Madison on Free Government

I

1.   The orgins of free government go back, for Madison, to the very foundation of civil society. Man, living in the anarchic state of nature in which "the weaker individual is not secured against the violence of the stronger,"[1] reflects on human nature and man's greed and selfishness and becomes convinced of the necessity of a government[2] that can control individual passions.[3] The desire to end the *bellum omnium contra omnes* does not come from the weak only, since "even the stronger individuals are prompted, by the uncertainty of their condition, to submit to a government which may protect the weak as well as themselves."[4]

Madison does not state in the *Federalist* how the state of nature is left and government created. We may assume, however, that his opinion does not differ here from what has been called the core of his philosophy,[5] namely, the compact theory of the foundation of the state. This theory was generally accepted at the time the essays were written, whereas the organic theory was hardly known. Madison adhered to it even when it was being abandoned by most

[1] 51, 340.   [3] 49, 331.
[2] 51, 337.   [4] 51, 340.
[5] E. M. Burns, JAMES MADISON, PHILOSOPHER OF THE CONSTITUTION (1938), 29.

112

European theorists, and called it "a fundamental principle of free government."[6] Furthermore, the acceptance of the compact theory in the *Federalist* can be concluded from the fact that Madison, who recognizes a parallel between the formation of the state by individuals and the formation of a confederacy by states,[7] calls the Confederation "a compact among the States."[8] Madison's distinction between a compact by which society is formed and one by which society establishes a government is of no concern here.[9] However, he says that the compact is a voluntary one, since the weak, having naturally the greater interest to be protected, are in no position to force the strong to conclude the compact, and the strong want a government in order that the rule of force might be replaced by a rule of justice, which is "the end of government . . . [and] of civil society."[10]

As the protection element may be seen in the establishment of government, so the principle of popular participation in government may also be recognized. The people's activity does not end with the social compact. Being "the only legitimate fountain of power,"[11] "the fountain of authority,"[12] the people are not only government-creating, but also government-sustaining by constantly nourishing government through their participation. Both the protection and the participation principles retain their validity once society and government are established. From the former as the motive for the foundation of government follows the conception of government as a means to an end. From the latter follows the right of the individuals to participate in government. Before we turn to an explanation of both

[6] Letter to N. P. Trist of Feb. 15, 1830. MADISON'S WRITINGS, IX, 335n. For a discussion of the philosophy of the social contract at that time, see William S. Carpenter, THE DEVELOPMENT OF AMERICAN POLITICAL THOUGHT (1930), 1 ff.

[7] "As the weakness and wants of man naturally lead to an association of individuals under a Common Authority, whereby each may have protection . . . and enjoy . . . the advantages of social intercourse . . . ; in like manner feeble communities, independent of each other have resorted to a Union . . . with common Councils." "Origin of the Constitutional Convention," MADISON'S WRITINGS, II, 391. In the *Federalist*, Madison says that "one nation is to another what one individual is to another." (62, 405.)

[8] 43, 287.

[9] "The original compact is the one implied or presumed, but nowhere reduced to writing, by which the people agree to form one society. The next is a compact, here for the first time reduced to writing, by which the people in their social state agree to a Govt. over them." Letter to Trist of Feb. 15, 1830. MADISON'S WRITINGS, IX, 355n.

[10] 51, 340.   [11] 49, 327.   [12] 51, 336.

principles, we shall consider their implementation in the relation between people and government. That relation is seen by Madison under a teleological, a static-factual, and a dynamic-legal aspect.

2. The relation between people and government from the teleo- logical point of view follows from the fact that the object of govern- ment is the happiness of the people.[13] Madison maintains that "the safety and happiness of society are the objects at which all political institutions aim, and to which all such institutions must be sacri- ficed,"[14] and he denounces "the impious doctrine in the Old World that the people were made for kings, not kings for the people."[15]

The static-factual relation results from the establishment of gov- ernment *ipso facto*. The people, when leaving the state of nature, become civil society[16] under a government.[17] Justice being the end of government and civil society,[18] government and society, serving an identical purpose and established for identical reasons, must be concomitant. This means an inseparable connection of one society with one government, and *argumentum e contrario* the impossibility of one society having several governments. This amounts to a con- ception of society as pertaining to a particular state or the denial that several states may have one society. In a word, society is an intrastate phenomenon.

We shall now, dealing with Madison's view on the dynamic-legal aspect of the relation between society and government, inquire into the nature of the co-existence of society and government and con- sider the implementation of the protection and participation prin- ciples. Madison presents three possibilities: Absolute dependence of the government on society; absolute independence of the govern- ment from society; and a compromise between the two.

---

[13] 62, 404.

[14] 43, 287. Also, Madison refers to "the objects of government" etc. (63, 408). The idea that governments are nothing but means to further the interests of the indi- vidual is évident throughout his essays.

[15] 45, 299.

[16] Madison often uses for this term such terms as "the public," "society."

[17] The subtlety of Madison's distinction between a compact establishing civil society and a compact by which civil society establishes a government is evident in the *Federalist*. When he says that "justice is the end of government, . . . of civil society" (51, 340), he does not only eliminate the distinction by identifying the end of government and civil society, but it even appears as if government is founded before civil society.

[18] 51, 340.

An absolute dependence of the government on society must be rejected. Since people established government to control their passions,[19] a government absolutely dependent on society would be in no position to achieve this end for want of that stability which is "essential . . . to that repose and confidence in the minds of the people, which are among the chief blessings of civil society."[20] Such a government would neither be a power nor an authority,[21] and would be incompatible with the protection principle. An absolute independence of the government from the people is not feasible either. Although it would constitute an authority to protect the individual, it would be incompatible with the participation principle. Rejecting extremes, Madison favors a government consistent with the individual's protection as well as popular participation in government. In this compromise he ascribes primacy to the protection principle, owing to its quality as the end of government. Government must be sufficiently independent from society to be able to protect the individual. To the degree in which that protection is not endangered, there must exist a dependence upon the people, as reflected in their participation in government: "You must first enable the government to control the governed, and in the next place oblige it to control itself. A dependence on the people is, no doubt, the primary control on the government."[22] Madison wants that dependence according to a constitution.[23]

Madison's view on the relation between people and government has important consequences. From his conception of government as a means follows not only the primacy of the individual's protection before popular participation in government, but also that his *Federalist,* advocating the Union, can be a treatise on the Union only in a relative sense and must, in an absolute sense, be a treatise for the individual's rights. His conception of society as an intrastate

[19] 49, 331.   [20] 37, 227.

[21] 49, 327; 51, 336. Compare also: "Frequent appeals [to the people] would, in a great measure, deprive the government of that veneration which time bestows on every thing, and without which perhaps the wisest and freest governments would not possess the requisite stability" (49, 328). "The internal effects of a mutable policy . . . are . . . calamitous. It poisons the blessings of liberty itself. . . . No government . . . will long be respected without being truly respectable; nor be truly respectable, without possessing . . . order and stability" (62, 406).

[22] 51, 337.

[23] See essay 49, esp. p. 348: ". . . a constitutional road to the decision of the people ought to be marked out and kept open, for certain great and extraordinary occasions. . . ."

phenomenon must influence his view on the nature of confederations and the Union. Finally, from the necessity of the independence of the government from the people follows the possibility that government abuses its power. In that case the people, possessing "the transcendent and precious right . . . to 'abolish or alter their governments as to them shall most likely to effect their safety and happiness',"[24] may resort to revolution. Furthermore, from the subjection of government under a constitution follows the existence of two sorts of man-made law; that by which the government is bound (society-made, fundamental, constitutional law), and that by which the government binds the people (government-made, ordinary, statute law). All man-made law is—and this follows from Madison's admission of a right of revolution—subservient to the "transcendent law of nature and of nature's God, which declares that the safety and happiness of society are the objects to which all political institutions aim, and to which all such institutions must be sacrificed."[25]

3. We shall now proceed to Madison's explanation of the protection and participation principles and their concomitance in the state. Owing to its quality as the end of government, the protection principle can be explained through an inquiry into what Madison considers the end of government to be. What he calls "justice" in essay fifty-one is referred to also as "the happiness of the people,"[26] "the common good of society,"[27] "the public good,"[28] "the safety and happiness of society."[29] More concretely, the people's good, safety, or happiness mean the protection of their "liberties," their "private rights," their "sacred rights."[30] That these liberties or rights are largely vested rights follows from essay ten, in which Madison sees them endangered by government. Complaining that the public good and the rights of other citizens may be sacrificed by the passions of the ruling faction, he adds that it is "the great desideratum . . . to secure the public good and private rights . . . and at the same time to preserve . . . popular government."[31]

[24] 40, 257.   [26] 62, 404.   [28] 37, 225.
[25] 43, 287.   [27] 57, 370.
[29] 43, 287. For the identity of "people," "society," "the public," see *supra.*, page 114, note 16. The identity of "happiness" and "good" follows from their being mentioned in the same connection in 41, 260, as does the identity of "safety" and "happiness" in 43, 287. Madison speaks of "justice and the general good" (51, 341) and of "justice and the public good" (10, 57).
[30] 14, 84-85.   [31] 10, 57.

Madison docs not clearly define vested rights.[32] However, since he distinguishes life from liberty[33] and property from liberty,[34] we may conclude that vested rights are the individual's rights of life, liberty, and property. As to the importance of "personal rights" (life and liberty) and the "rights of property,"[35] Madison does not only emphasize that "government is instituted no less for the protection of the property, than of the persons of individuals,"[36] he also leaves no doubt that property rights are especially important, saying that the protection of the faculties from which the rights of property originate is the first object of government.[37] The pre-eminence of property rights can also be concluded from other parts of essay ten.[38]

The participation principle, in practice, amounts to popular government. Aside from attributing such factors as propensity to faction, instability, injustice, confusion,[39] and an "insecurity of rights"[40] to it, Madison defines popular government as a majority government, which follows from his considering a minority rule as incompatible with popular government.[41] It may be the rule of an "interested and overbearing majority."[42]

4.   It remains to show Madison's explanation of the co-existence of these two principles. A protection particularly directed to property rights by an interested and overbearing majority will amount to a

[32] Madison uses the words "liberties," "liberty," "rights," for the total of vested rights without stating what specifically these terms comprise. For instance, he speaks of governments "which have crushed the liberties of . . . mankind" (14, 85) and of members of the legislature as "guardians of the rights and liberties of the people" (49, 330); he denies that biennial elections would be "dangerous to the public liberties" (52, 345); he says that "there can be no liberty where the legislative and executive power arc united" (47, 314). See also 10, 53; 10, 55; 14, 84; 14, 85; 47, 315; 48, 322; 50, 335; 51, 340; 52, 344; 52, 346; 53, 347; 53, 348.

[33] 47, 315.

[34] 10, 55; 10, 56; 10, 57. "Liberty" is here used in a narrow sense and does not mean the total of vested rights. (Compare 47, 315.)

[35] 54, 357.   [36] 54, 357.   [37] 10, 55.

[38] Since "liberty is to faction what air is to fire," it would be "folly to abolish liberty, which is essential to political life." Therefore, if the "causes of faction cannot be removed," factions have to be taken as granted within society. Now, "the most common and durable source of factions has been the various and unequal distribution of property." Consequently, since liberty is the source of faction, the most important part of the individual's liberty must be those rights under which such various and unequal distribution of property may be achieved, namely, the rights to acquire and make free use of property.

[39] 10, 53.   [41] 58, 383.

[40] 51, 340.   [42] 10, 54.

rule of the many poor over the few rich and thus seems more than
questionable. The same applies to other rights. This problem is seen
by Madison, who considers it a great desideratum, "to secure the
public good and private rights . . . and at the same time to preserve
the spirit and the form of popular government."[43] In accordance with
his decision for the primacy of the individual's protection over popular participation in government Madison solves the problem by
restricting popular government to the degree required for the
protection of life, liberty, and property.[44] That form of government
is "free government."[45] It is Madison's ideal of government.[46]

[43] 10, 57.

[44] "Popular government" without any restriction is to Madison a government
under which an infringement on vested rights is not only possible, but probable.
This is expressed by him when he speaks of the "insecurity of rights under the
popular form of government" (51, 340) and complains about the existence of
"instability, injustice, and confusion" (10, 53) under it. Popular government is
not a government to which the protection of vested rights is intrinsic. This follows from essay 10. Whereas in the beginning Madison speaks of "popular government," he continues that "the protection of these faculties [to acquire prop-
erty] is the first object of government": "Popular government" is not necessarily
a government protecting the individual's rights, as otherwise Madison would
have used the word "popular" in the second sentence too. A few pages later,
Madison expresses this idea more directly: "When a majority is included in a
faction, the form of popular government . . . enables it to sacrifice to its ruling
passion or interest both the public good and the rights of other citizens." (10, 57.)

[45] To Madison, free government is a government in which the people participate. He expresses this idea when he speaks of "free government, of which fre-
quency of elections is the cornerstone" (54, 348), or asserts that in case the majority
would not rule, "the fundamental principle of free government would be reversed" (58, 382). On the other hand, in a free government vested rights are protected: "In a free government the security for civil rights must be the same as
for religious rights." (51, 339.) On Oct. 24, 1787, Madison wrote to Jefferson: "A
distinction of property results from that very protection which a free Government
gives to unequal faculties of acquiring it." MADISON'S WRITINGS, v, 29. Compare also
Madison's remarks in the Virginia Convention on June 7, 1788. Ibid., v, 144-45.

[46] The quality of free government as an ideal, approached to a greater or
smaller degree by existing governments, is evident when he speaks of "free" and
"freest" governments (49, 328), and of "free governments" (plural), 43, 285; 49, 328;
63, 409. See also his Fifth Annual Message of Dec. 7, 1813, where he speaks of
"our free Government, like other free governments." MADISON'S WRITINGS, VIII, 274.
As an ideal, free government was and is possible in all times: in Rome (63, 415),
in the future (43, 285); it is possible in a large as well as in a small, in a unitary
as well as in a federal state: in Rome (63, 415), New Hampshire (47, 316), the
United States (43, 285).

The distinction for Madison between "free" and "good" government (I was
unable to find a definition by him of these terms in his speeches and writings)

It is necessary to consider the factors by which vested rights, popular government, and free government are threatened. There is one main enemy, faction, i.e., "a number of citizens, whether amounting to a majority or minority of the whole, who are united and actuated by some common impulse of passion, or of interest, adverse to the rights of other citizens, or to the permanent and aggregate interest of the community."[47] Faction is free government's Frankenstein's monster. Resulting from vested rights[48] and popular government,[49] factions are "the natural offspring of free government."[50] They are a threat to free government.[51]

From this concept of faction two rules emerge. First, from the fact

seems to be that "good government," while being—to a greater or smaller degree —a free government, is a real, existing government with *power*, as seems to follow from these passages: "A good government implies two things: first, fidelity to the object of government, which is the happiness of the people; secondly, a knowledge of the means, by which that object can be best attained" (62, 404); "energy in government is essential to that security against external and internal danger, and to that prompt and salutary execution of the laws which enter into the very definition of good government" (37, 227). See also his essay on the Government of the United States of 1792 in which he calls the separation of powers "a first principle of free government." MADISON'S WRITINGS, VI, 91. In the *Federalist*, Madison refers to the separation of powers as a "sacred maxim of free government" (47, 320). According to these last quotations, Madison attributes power to a free government too, and not only to a "good" government. His distinction between "free" and "good" government is thus not quite clear.

[47] 10, 54. "Faction" is for Madison identical to "party." This can be concluded from his using both words in the same sense in essays 10 and 50. "Liberty is to faction what air is to fire, an aliment without which it instantly expires" (10, 55), and "an extinction of parties necessarily implies either a universal alarm for the public safety, or an absolute extinction of liberty" (50, 335); "The regulation of . . . various . . . interests forms the principal task of . . . legislation, and involves the spirit of party and faction in the necessary and ordinary operations of the government" (10, 56). Compare also his essay on Parties of Jan. 23, 1792. MADISON'S WRITINGS, VI, 86.

[48] "Liberty is to faction what air is to fire, an aliment without which it instantly expires" (10, 55); "the most common and durable source of factions has been the various and unequal distribution of property" (10, 56).

[49] Popular governments have a "propensity to this dangerous vice," factions (10, 53).

[50] 43, 280.

[51] Madison complains that owing to factions, "instability, injustice and confusion . . . have . . . been the mortal diseases under which popular governments have everywhere perished" (10, 53-54). Factions also threaten vested, especially property rights: "To secure . . . private rights against . . . faction . . . is the great desideratum" (10, 57); "the most common and durable source of factions has been the various and unequal distribution of property" (10, 56).

that free government creates factions, it follows that factions grow in proportion to the freedom of that government. The more a concrete government realizes the ideal of free government, the more factions it will spawn. Second, the exposure of free government to factions makes protection of government from factions imperative. Of the "two methods curing the mischiefs of faction: the one, by removing its causes; the other, by controlling its effects,"[52] the former is not feasible, since it would mean the abolition of free government itself.[53] "The *causes* of faction cannot be removed, and . . . relief is only to be sought in the means of controlling its *effects*."[54] We may conclude that free government is secure to the degree that it controls factions.

Summarizing Madison's opinions on the nature of free government as expressed in the *Federalist,* we may say that the individuals, motivated by self-interest, leave the state of nature in order to live under justice in a free government that, primarily, protects their lives, liberty, and property and—to the degree compatible with the security of those rights—permits people to participate in government under a constitution. The main threat to free government arises from its own creation, factions, the control of which is of vital importance. The latter observation has important implications for Madison's inquiry into the compatibility of concrete governments with the ideal free government. In his search for the government that is most likely to realize that ideal, he need only look for a government under which factions are controlled.

II

1. The type of government most likely to realize free government is one in which power is opposed to power. Power-balance implies the existence of power and its division. Madison understood that the existence of power measures the government's effectiveness, while division of power is manifested in a system of territorial and institutional balances.

Governmental effectiveness is an antidote for faction.[55] This is

---

[52] 10, 54.   [53] See essay 10.   [54] 10, 57.

[55] After stressing the necessity for power in the governments of the Achaean league and the Lycian confederacy, Madison continues: "We know that the ruin of one of them proceeded from the incapacity of the federal authority to prevent the dissensions [factions] . . . of the subordinate authorities" (45, 300).

closely connected with the government's stability and energy, which are requisites for government,[56] and are, besides, antidotes against faction in their own right: "Energy in government is essential to that security against external and internal danger [i.e., factions] and to that prompt and salutary execution of the laws which enter into the very definition of good government. Stability in government is essential to national character and to the advantages annexed to it, as well as to that repose and confidence in the minds of the people [with respect to the protection of their life, liberty and property!] which are among the chief blessings of civil society."[57] It remains to show the utility of the territorial and institutional divisions of power, the former resulting in a federal state, the latter in that "sacred maxim of free government," the separation of powers.[58]

2.   Madison's theory that territorial division of power is conducive to free government is based on an inquiry into the probable ability of different governments to control factions. Considering, under that point of view, a democracy, a republic, a large unitary and a federal republic, he arrives at the conclusion that the chances for free government grow with the degree of a territorial power-balance, which in turn increases with the degree of compound government.

A pure democracy,[59] which is "a society consisting of a small num-

[56] 37, 227.

[57] 37, 227. The necessity of stability in government for the protection of life, liberty, and property is evident in 62, 406-7: "The internal effects of a mutable policy are . . . calamitous. It poisons the blessings of liberty itself. . . . Great injury results from an unstable government. The want of confidence in the public councils damps every useful undertaking, the success and profit of which may depend on a continuance of existing arrangements. What prudent merchant will hazard his fortunes in any new branch of commerce when he knows not but that his plans may be rendered unlawful before they can be executed? What farmer or manufacturer will lay himself out for encouragement given to any particular cultivation or establishment, when he can have no assurance that his preparatory labors and advances will not render him a victim to an inconstant government? . . . No government . . . will long be respected without possessing a certain portion of order and stability." As to energy, Madison, in a later essay on the Spirit of Governments, maintains not only that a government possesses energy by reason of military establishments, but also that it can derive its energy from the will of society. For such a government, "philosophy has been searching, and humanity been fighting, from the most remote ages." MADISON'S WRITINGS, VI, 94.

[58] 47, 320.

[59] The identity of "pure democracy" and "democracy" follows from the use of both terms in essay 10. Speaking of a republic, Madison says: "Let us examine

ber of citizens, who assemble and administer the government in person,"[60] is not conducive to free government, since it is "incompatible with personal security or the rights of property."[61] Democracy tends to be the rule of an "interested and overbearing majority,"[62] which does not consider the rights of the minority[63] and is incompatible with the protection principle. It also is incompatible with the principle of popular participation in government, since it has a tendency to degenerate into tyranny.[64] Besides, it can admit of no cure for the mischiefs of faction.[65]

A republic, which is distinguished from a democracy[66] by its extension over a greater number of citizens and over a greater sphere of country,[67] as well as by representative government,[68] the latter being a consequence of the former,[69] "opens a different prospect, and promises the cure" against faction.[70] While a republic is a popular government,[71] it is compatible with the individual's protection, since there is, in spite of majority rule,[72] much less of a possibility of

the points in which it varies from pure democracy." In the next sentence, he continues: "The two great points of difference between a democracy and a republic are: . . ." (10, 59.)

[60] 10, 58. "The natural limit of a democracy is that distance from the central point which will just permit the most remote citizens to assemble as often as their public functions demand, and will include no greater number than can join in those functions" (14, 81). Although democracy seems to be a nonrepresentative government (48, 322), Madison feels that in a democracy, the executive can be the representative of the people (63, 412).

[61] 10, 58.   [63] 10, 58.   [65] 10, 58.

[62] 10, 54.   [64] 48, 322.

[66] In a letter to Jefferson of Oct. 24, 1787, Madison identifies a "simple democracy" with a "pure republic." MADISON'S WRITINGS, v, 28. See also his speech in the Virginia Convention on June 5, 1788. *Ibid.*, v, 126.

[67] 10, 59. See 14, 80.   [68] See 10, 59; 14, 80.

[69] "As the natural limit of a democracy is that distance from the central point which will just permit the most remote citizens to assemble . . . , so the natural limit of a republic is that distance from the centre which will barely allow the representatives to meet" (14, 81). In reversed logic: "In a democracy, the people meet and exercise the government in person; in a republic, they assemble and administer it by their representatives and agents. A democracy, consequently, will be confined to a small spot. A republic may be extended over a large region" (14, 80).

[70] 10, 59.

[71] "We may define a republic to be . . . a government which derives all . . . powers directly or indirectly from the great body of the people. . . . It is essential . . . that it be derived from the great body of the society, not from an inconsiderable proportion . . . of it" (39, 243). See also 37, 227; 48, 322; 57, 371.

[72] 10, 60.

majoritarian oppression than in a democracy. Representative government refines and enlarges the public views "by passing them through
the medium of a chosen body of citizens, whose wisdom may best
discern the true interest of their country, and whose patriotism and
love of justice will be least likely to sacrifice it to temporary or partial considerations."[73] Furthermore, a greater number of citizens and
extent of territory may be brought within the compass of republican
than of democratic government, and it is this circumstance, principally, that renders factious combinations less to be dreaded in the
former than in the latter.

> The smaller the society, the fewer probably will be the distinct
> parties and interests composing it; the fewer the distinct parties
> and interests, the more frequently will a majority be found of the
> same party; and the smaller the number of individuals composing
> a majority, and the smaller the compass within which they are
> placed, the more easily will they concert and execute their plans
> of oppression. Extend the sphere, and you will take in a greater
> variety of parties and interests; you make it less probable that a
> majority of the whole will have a common motive to invade the
> rights of other citizens; or if such a common motive exists, it will
> be more difficult for all who feel it to discover their own strength,
> and to act in unison with each other.[74]

Madison goes on to show that free government is most likely to
be realized in a large unitary republic and, even more so, in a federal republic. In an ordinary representative body "men of factious
tempers, of local prejudice, or of sinister designs may . . . betray the
interests of the people."[75] Just as a representative body is a refinement of society and a remedy against factions, a refinement of that
representative body must be a further step toward free government.
Additional refinement can be achieved in an extensive republic,
which is "more favorable to the election of proper guardians of the
public weal"[76] than a small republic.[77]

[73] 10, 59.

[74] 10, 60. For Madison's opinion on a republic, see also his essay "Charters" of
1792, and his essay "Who are the best keepers of the people's liberties?" of the
same year. MADISON'S WRITINGS, VI, 85, 120.

[75] 10, 59.

[76] 10, 59.

[77] "However small a republic may be, the representatives must be raised to a
certain number, in order to guard against the cabals of the few; and . . . however large it may be, it must be limited to a certain number, in order to guard
against the confusion of a multitude. Hence, the number of representatives in
the two cases not being in proportion to that of the two constituents, and being

If a large republic is more conducive to free government than a small one because the individual's rights are more likely to be protected, the degree and quality of popular participation in government are not similarly increased. Madison regrets that "by enlarging too much the number of electors, you render the representative too little acquainted with all their local circumstances and lesser interests, as by reducing it too much, you render him unduly attached to these."[78] Therefore, Madison wants a large republic in which there are representations of both local and collective interests, where the power surrendered by the people is divided between two different governments.[79] He wants "a compound republic, partaking both of the national and federal character,"[80] a "confederated republic."[81] This type of government forms a happy combination; the great and aggregate interests being referred to the national, the local, and particular to the state representations.[82] Madison emphasizes the protection of life, liberty, and property in a federal republic:

> Whilst all authority in it will be derived from and dependent on society, the society itself will be broken into so many parts, interests and classes of citizens that the rights of individuals, or of the minority, will be in little danger from interested combinations of the majority. In a free government the security for civil rights must be the same as that for religious rights. It consists in the one case in the multiplicity of interests, and in the other in the multiplicity of sects; and this may be presumed to depend on the extent of the country and number of people comprehended under the same government. This view of the subject must particularly recommend a proper federal system to all sincere and considerate friends of republican government.[83]

Further, factious insurrections happening in one part are more likely to be quelled in a federal state than in a large republic, since here the particular states, i.e., organized political units and not only some

proportionally greater in the small republic, it follows that, if the proportion of fit characters be not less in the large than in the small republic, the former will present a greater option, and consequently a greater possibility of a fit choice. In the next place, as each representative will be chosen by a greater number of citizens in the large than in a small republic, it will be more difficult for unworthy candidates to practice with success the vicious arts by which elections are too often carried; and the suffrages of the people being more free, will be more likely to center in men who possess the most attractive merit and the most diffusive and established characters" (10, 59-60). See also 10, 61.

78 10, 60.   80 62, 401.   82 10, 60.

79 51, 338-39.   81 63, 410.   83 51, 339.

other vague power, act as a counterpoise.[84] The federal state[85] comes into existence through a compact between the individual states.[86]

[84] 43, 285. See also 63, 410.

[85] Or "confederate." Madison makes no clear distinction between such terms as "federal" on the one hand and "confederate," "confederation," and "confederacy" on the other hand.

To Madison in the *Federalist,* the United States under the Articles of Confederation is a "Confederation," a "federal pact" (43, 287-88), in which there exists a "federal council" (46, 306).

Likewise, the United States under the Constitution is called a "Confederacy" under a "federal Constitution" (54, 357), a "confederate republic" (43, 285), a "confederacy," which is a "federal coalition" (43, 282).

The equal meaning of these different terms can also be seen in 39, 245, where they are distinguished from "national."

Although Madison does not distinguish a league of states under national law from one under international law by terminology, there can be no doubt that he was aware of the difference. The distinction does not lie in the fact that a league under international law is a *league,* and one under national law not, or vice versa, since both organizations may be leagues: The United States under the Articles of Confederation is a league (43, 288), as is the Achaean league, although here "the federal head had a degree and species of power which gave it a considerable likeness to the government" set up under the Constitution (45, 300). Nor does the distinction lie in the exclusive quality of a league under national law and one under international law as a *union,* for the United States is a union under the Articles (14, 83; 14, 84; 14, 85; 40, 252; 41, 269; 44, 289; 44, 297) as well as under the Constitution (44, 297; 45, 298; 45, 299; 14, 83; 40, 251).

The distinction lies in the *intimacy* of the union. (Compare 43, 282.) Although both a confederation under international law and one under national law come into existence through a compact between the states (the United States under the Articles as well as under the Constitution came into being by compact, 43, 287-88; 39, 249), it is important for Madison that the compact forming a league under national law comes into being by an act of the different societies, i.e., by *the people within the states,* whereas a league under international law is created by a compact between (branches of) the governments of the states. The United States under the Articles is for him "a compact between independent sovereigns, founded on ordinary legislative authority" (43, 288), whereas the United States under the Constitution will be a compact "by the people, not as individuals composing one entire nation, but as composing the distinct and independent States to which they respectively belong" (39, 246).

This greater intimacy of a union under national law has as a consequence a greater power of the federal government. That government can now act directly upon the individuals in the states and not only upon the states as political entities. Madison is glad that the powers of the federal government to act immediately upon individuals are extended under the Constitution (40, 254).

A government coming into existence through a compact not only of the governments, but of the people of the states has, furthermore, greater power against the member states. Complaining that ancient confederacies were probably ruined be-

3.   A system of territorial balances does not suffice, however, for a realization of free government. Believing that "ambition must be made to counteract ambition,"[87] Madison wants also a separation of powers, that "sacred maxim of free government."[88] Calling the accumulation of legislative, executive, and judicial power in the same hands, whether of one, a few, or many and whether hereditary, self-appointed, or elective, the very definition of tyranny,[89] Madison considers their separation essential to the preservation of liberty.[90] Quoting Montesquieu, he points out that when the legislative and executive powers are united there can be no liberty, because apprehensions may arise lest the same monarch or senate should enact tyrannical

cause of "the incapacity of the federal authority to prevent the dissensions, and finally the disunion, of the subordinate authorities" (45, 300), and that the Amphictyonic league, the Germanic, Swiss, and Dutch confederate governments as well as the New England Confederacy had no energy, and remarking that governments destitute of energy will ever produce anarchy, Madison sees in the greater energy and power of the federal government vis-à-vis the states another characteristic of the federal state under national law. That state is an "improvement" (14, 85) over a league under international law, because an "invigoration" of the powers of the federal government has taken place (45, 303).

With the greater intimacy of the union and the greater power of the federal government over individuals as well as states Madison connects the concept of the "nation" and thus makes it clear that the federal state is *one* state composed of several states. It partakes "both of the national and federal character" (62, 401).

The federal state as it was established by the Constitution is referred to as "an extended republic" (14, 85), "the republic" (43, 285) (note that Madison always uses the singular!). It is a political *novum*, an "experiment made for the 'glory of America,'" one of the "numerous innovations displayed on the American theatre . . . in favor of private rights and public happiness" (14, 85).

(When, in the following pages, we speak of a "federal state," we shall understand under that term, unless stated differently, a federation under national law.)

[86] For the parallel between the formation of the state by individuals leaving the state of nature and the formation of a federal state by different states, see *supra.*, p. 113. For the distinction between a compact concluded by the people of the states or the governments of the states, see the preceding note. Logically, that distinction seems hardly tenable, since a representation of the people is, in the last analysis, the people. It seems as if the distinction was made by Madison for political reasons as a polemic against the too democratic legislatures in the states. However, here he is caught in another logical trap, because he practically admits that pure democracy is preferable to a republic, i.e., to representative government, which is contrary to his theory of government. It is remarkable, however, that despite his fear of too much democracy Madison steadfastly adheres to the principle of popular government when he wants the federal compact to be made by the people.

[87] 51, 337.   [88] 47, 320.   [89] 47, 313.

[90] 51, 335. See also 47, 313; 47, 315.

laws to execute them in a tyrannical manner.[91] Furthermore, "were the power of judging joined with the legislative, the life and liberty of the subjects would be exposed to arbitrary control, for *the judge would then be the legislator.* Were it joined to the executive power, the judge might behave with all the violence of an oppressor."[92]

While adhering to popular government, Madison leaves no doubt that the separation of powers is a device primarily for the protection of the individual's life, liberty, and property. For this protection he wants a division of the legislature, i.e., an emasculation of that branch of government that embodies popular government to the highest degree. "The tendency of republican governments is to an aggrandizement of the legislative at the expense of the other departments,"[93] for "in republican government, the legislative authority necessarily predominates."[94] Therefore, one should divide the legislature into different branches, and render these, by different modes of election and different principles of action, as little connected with each other as the nature of their common functions and their common dependence on the society will admit.[95] The upper chamber should then be "an anchor against popular fluctuations," and "a defence to the people against their own temporary errors and delusions."[96]

The separation of powers must not be absolute. After showing in essay forty-seven that Montesquieu did not advocate a complete separation, Madison says that only a "degree of separation" is "essential to a free government."[97] However, a blending is wanted to prevent an entire consolidation of power in one department.[98]

Madison believes that "a mere demarcation on parchment of the constitutional limits of the federal departments is not a sufficient guard against those encroachments which lead to a tyrannical concentration of all powers of government in the same hands"[99] and that occasional or periodical appeals to the people would be unworkable.[100] He proposes, therefore, to secure an effective separation of powers by so contriving the interior structure of the government

[91] 47, 315. [94] 51, 338. [96] 63, 411; 63, 409.
[92] 47, 315. [95] 51, 338. [97] 48, 312.
[93] 49, 330.

[98] Before the first Congress, Madison said on June 17, 1789 that the principle of the separation of powers "is to be found in the political writings of the most celebrated civilians and is everywhere held as essential to the preservation of liberty . . . ; and if in any case they are blended, it is in order to admit a partial qualification, in order more effectually to guard against an entire consolidation." MADISON'S WRITINGS, v, 398. See Burns, *op. cit.*, 128.

[99] 48, 326.   [100] Essays 49 and 50.

that its several constituent parts may, by their mutual relations, be the means of keeping each other in their proper places.[101] He rejects appointments of the executive, legislative, and judiciary by the people "through channels having no communications whatever with one another,"[102] for practical reasons. Believing that the main threat of a usurpation of power arises in the legislative, he does not suggest an absolute veto-power of the (weaker) executive. However, he favors "some qualified connection between this weaker department and the weaker branch of the stronger department by which the latter may be led to support the constitutional rights of the former, without being too much detached from the rights of its own department."[103] Madison does not want an institutional balance by isolating the different powers, but by intertwining them. The departments are not balanced and regulated through mere "parchment" or referenda, but actually check each other. They derive their power from the people.[104]

4. We may say, then, that the protection of the individual's life, liberty, and property through a popular government requires the existence of governmental power coupled with territorial and institutional division of that power. This has important consequences. Since internal division of power will result in an impairment of the government's external quality as a power, a system of power-balances can, if a state of anarchy is to be prevented, only be admitted to a degree that does not impair the government's quality as a power.

For the system of territorial balances this qualification means that the federal state must have authority to prevent anarchy. In a republic, this amounts to the superiority of the national over the state legislature and to a recognition of the principle that federal law supersedes state law. This implies also the necessity of some federal authority that can render a final verdict on problems of federalism. For the system of institutional balances, the qualification means that there must be some authority that can decide upon the competency of the different departments. We have here a recognition by Madison to that linchpin of federalism, found in most federal constitutions, the supremacy clause, as well as an appreciation of judicial review.

In the *Federalist,* Madison mentions only the supremacy provision when he attributes the ruin of an ancient confederacy to the want

---

[101] 51, 336.   [102] 51, 336.   [103] 51, 338.
[104] See 49, 327; 49, 328; 51, 336; 51, 337.

of power in the federal government[105] and says that without a supremacy provision the world would have seen "a system of government founded on an inversion of the fundamental principles of all government; it would have seen the authority of the whole society everywhere subordinate to the authority of the parts; it would have seen a monster, in which the head was under the direction of the members."[106] Madison does not specifically mention judicial review. But could a specific remark be expected in view of the fact that all the essays dealing with the judiciary are written by Hamilton? Madison, like most of the Founding Fathers, accepted judicial review.[107] Its recognition in the *Federalist* follows logically from the concomitance of the existence and division of power. It is hinted at in the distinction between the superior constitutional and the inferior statute law and in Madison's distrust of the legislature as a proper guardian for vested rights.[108]

Having brought to a conclusion the theoretical part of Madison's *Federalist*, we shall now turn to the practical side of his essays and deal with the negation of free government under the Articles of Confederation and its achievement under the Constitution. Here, Madison's view on the theoretical realization of free government has important implications. If free government can be realized in a

---

[105] 45, 300.   [106] 44, 296.

[107] In the Federal Convention, Madison said on July 23 that "a law violating a treaty ratified by pre-existing law, might be respected by the judges as a law, though an unwise or perfidious one. A law violating a constitution established by the people themselves, would be considered by the judges as null and void." Farrand, RECORDS, II, 93. For the attitude of the Founding Fathers toward judicial review, see Charles A. Beard, THE SUPREME COURT AND THE CONSTITUTION (1912), 17 ff., and Edward S. Corwin, THE DOCTRINE OF JUDICIAL REVIEW (1914), 17.

[108] In the first Congress, after having introduced amendments to constitute a bill of rights, Madison declared that the courts would "consider themselves in a peculiar manner the guardians of those rights; they would be an impenetrable bulwark against every assumption of power in the Legislative or Executive; they will be naturally led to resist every encroachment upon rights stipulated for in the Constitution by the declaration of rights." ANNALS OF CONGRESS, I, 43(. On April 1, 1833, Madison wrote to J. C. Cabell: "The federal judiciary is the only defensive armour of the Federal government, or, rather for the Constitution and laws of the United States. Strip it of that armour, and the door is wide open for nullification, anarchy, and convulsion." LETTERS AND OTHER WRITINGS OF JAMES MADISON (Congressional ed., 1884), IV, 296-97. Although admitting judicial review in principle, Madison's acceptance of that institution was a qualified one. See his remarks on Jefferson's Draught of a Constitution for Virginia. MADISON'S WRITINGS, IX, 284-94; his report on the Virginia Resolutions, *ibid.*, VI, 349; Farrand, RECORDS, II, 430.

government that constitutes a power and in which power is counter-poised by power, in which "ambition [is] made to counteract ambition"[109] in both territorial and institutional respects, a negation of free government must be due mainly to the absence of a federal state and the separation of powers. Likewise, free government must be achieved if a constitution provides for a federal state and the separation of powers.

III

1.   The situation of the United States under the Confederation is regarded by Madison as peculiarly critical.[110] He complains about the "opprobrium" under which the government "has so long labored,"[111] and decries the existence of a system founded on fallacious principles.[112] The crisis existed mainly because the Articles did not provide for a government that, according to Madison's theory, was most likely to realize free government. In the Confederation, a failure to separate powers resulted in the instability and mutability of the government and in a threat to the rights of the individual.[113] Neither was there a federal government that could prevent the state governments from encroaching upon these rights.

2.   After the Revolution had brought about the collapse of the royal judicial system and the decline of executive power, the legislature had, under the new state constitutions, become the most powerful branch of the government. Having taken over most of the judicial functions,[114] the legislature, more and more influenced by the debtor element, started to interfere with the processes of the courts, suspended judicial actions, modified or annulled judgments, and determined the merits of disputes. It is against this situation that Madison speaks out, when he complains that in the states "the legislative department is everywhere extending the sphere of its activity, and drawing all power into its impetuous vortex."[115] One is reminded of Benjamin Rush's address to the people of the United States when

[109] 51, 337.   [111] 10, 58.
[110] 37, 225.   [112] 37, 226.
[113] Madison mainly considers the absence of a separation of powers in the states, not in the Union. This is natural in view of the fact that he did not consider the United States under the Articles as *one* state.
[114] See Corwin, "The Progress of Constitutional Theory etc.," *loc. cit.,* 515.
[115] 48, 322.

Madison points out that although the draftsmen of the state constitutions have never turned their eyes from the danger to liberty from the overgrown and all-grasping prerogative of an hereditary magistrate, at the same time they have failed to appreciate the danger from legislative usurpations, which must lead to the same tyranny.[116] He warns that in a representative republic the "people ought to indulge all their jealousy and exhaust all their precautions" against the enterprising ambition of the legislature.[117]

Pretending that he might collect vouchers in abundance from the records and archives of every state in the Union to prove the existence of legislative usurpations,[118] Madison complains about the mutability in the public councils, the internal effects of which he describes as calamitous. It poisons the blessings of liberty, hampers individual enterprise, disregards the principle *pacta sunt servanda,* and leaves property insecure.[119] In the Confederation, Madison sees the public good disregarded in the conflict of rival parties and measures decided not according to the rules of justice and the rights of the minor party, but according to the superior forces of an interested and overbearing majority.[120] The "prevailing and increasing distrust of public engagements, and alarm for private rights, which are echoed from one end of the continent to the other," are "chiefly, if not wholly, effects of the unsteadiness and injustice with which a factious spirit has tainted our public administrations."[121] There exists in the Confederation, owing to an absence of the separation of powers in the states, a democratic despotism that encroaches upon all vested rights, especially those of property. Popular participation in government is increased to such an extent as to be incompatible with free government.

3.   This negation of free government could not be stopped by a government of the Union as set up under the Articles, since the Union, having come into existence through "a compact between independent sovereigns, founded on ordinary acts of legislative authority, can pretend to no higher validity than a league or treaty between the parties."[122] The government of the Union has, aside from its defects in organizational matters,[123] no means to prevent a

[116] 48, 322.   [119] 62, 406.   [121] 10, 54.
[117] 48, 323.   [120] 10, 54.   [122] 43, 288.
[118] 48, 323.

[123] That topic will be dealt with more extensively in the following part on the achievement of free government. It is necessary to say here only that Madison saw

majoritarian tyranny in the states. Madison hopes to achieve this through a national veto power over state laws, to be vested either in the president or in Congress, by which the states would be prevented from oppressing the weaker party within their respective jurisdictions,[124] and through a guarantee by the federal government to the states against internal violence to their constitutions and laws.[125]

4. For the protection of the individual's rights Madison wants a more perfect Union.[126] In order that this Union might be achieved, he does not only concede to the delegates of the Federal Convention a right of revolution, but even admits their duty to revolt for "the happiness of the people of America."[127] Just how far the Articles were "revised"[128] and their tendency to a negation of free government "reduced" by decreasing their centrifugal content,[129] or, what amounts to the same thing, how far the Articles were "invigorated" in their affirmation of free government and in their national or centripetal content,[130] shall now be examined.

IV

1. The invigoration of the Articles toward a greater realization of free government does not reach perfection in the Constitution. In accordance with his conception of free government as an ideal, Madison admits, though praising the Founders for having surmounted many difficulties,[131] that "a faultless plan was not to be expected."[132] The Convention was "compelled to sacrifice theoretical propriety to the force of extraneous considerations, [and] forced into some devia-

the organizational defects of the Confederation mainly in the restrictions upon the federal government to act directly upon the individuals (see 40, 254, also Elliot, *op. cit.*, II, 200), and effectually against the states (see 38, 241; 54, 358; 44, 296 [supremacy provision]; 42, 274 [commerce]; Elliot, *op. cit.*, II, 199).

[124] Farrand, RECORDS, I, 164-65. See the letters to Jefferson of March 19 and Oct. 24, 1787. MADISON'S WRITINGS, II, 326-27; V, 27.

[125] "Vices of the Political System of the U. States," *ibid.*, II, 365 ff.

[126] For Madison's conception of the Union as a means to an end, see 45, 299: "Were the Union . . . inconsistent with the public happiness . . . [my voice] would be, Abolish the Union."

[127] Essay 40.

[128] 40, 251. See also his letter to Noah Webster of Oct. 12, 1804. MADISON'S WRITINGS, VIII, 163, 166.

[129] 40, 253.   [131] 37, 231.

[130] 40, 255; 45, 303.   [132] 37, 226.

tions from that artificial structure and regular symmetry which an abstract view. . . . might lead an ingenious theorist to bestow on a Constitution, planned in his closet or his imagination."[133] The Constitution, blending inconveniences with political advantages[134] and at points being faulty,[135] provides, as compared with the Articles, only for "the GREATER, not the PERFECT, good."[136] The improvement lies in the fact that the Constitution comes closer to that form of government that theoretically is more conducive to a realization of free government than do the Articles, because it provides for an effective government as well as for territorial and institutional balances.[137] Madison praises the members of the Federal Convention for having made corrections in the "structure of the Union"[138] by creating a more effective federal government. Although he assures his readers that the great principles of the Constitution may be considered less as absolutely new than as an expansion of the principles that are found in the Articles of Confederation, Madison admits that under the Constitution there is so great an enlargement of federal power as to give "to the new system the aspects of an entire transformation of the old."[139]

The Constitution gave the United States a new aspect indeed. An "experiment" made for the "glory of America," one of "the numerous innovations displayed on the American theatre, in favor of private rights and public happiness,"[140] it transformed what had been a compact between independent sovereigns, a mere league or treaty between the states,[141] into one republic,[142] "partaking both of the national and federal character."[143] It created a nation resting "on the assent and ratification of the people of America, . . . as composing the distinct and independent States to which they respectively belong."[144]

2. The change was effected by the grant to the national government of powers that were required by the exigencies of a closer Union. Madison mentions the powers necessary for security from foreign nations and for peace within the United States, making it clear that

[133] 37, 231.   [136] 41, 260. See also 37, 228-29.
[134] 41, 260.   [137] See 14, 85; 38, 236; 42, 271; 44, 290.
[135] 43, 286.   [138] 14, 85.
[139] 40, 255. See 37, 224-25; 40, 253; 54, 358.
[140] 14, 85.   [142] 14, 82.
[141] 43, 288.   [143] 62, 401.
[144] 39, 246. For the Union under the Constitution, Madison also uses the terms "extended republic" (14, 85), "confederate republic" (43, 285).

any grant of power to the federal government is also given for the achievement of free government. In Philadelphia "it was of most importance to the happiness of the people of America, that the articles of Confederation would be disregarded, and an adequate government be provided, and the Union preserved."[145] The Union is created not for its own sake, but for the happiness of the people.[146] The Constitution gives to the federal government the power to advance the public happiness and creates an effective government for the "public good."[147] It is thus not surprising to find Madison devoting relatively little space to federal powers that are organizationally necessary for the Union, and dwelling longer on those powers that are more directly concerned with the protection of the individual, no matter whether they are granted to the federal government or denied to the states.

Scolding the paper-money factions that had come to power in several states, Madison says that the Constitution's prohibiting the states from emitting bills of credit "must give pleasure to every citizen, in proportion to his love of justice and his knowledge of the true springs of public prosperity." "The loss which America has sustained since the peace," he continues, "from the pestilent effects of paper money on the necessary confidence between man and man, on the necessary confidence in the public councils, on the industry and morals of the people, and on the character of republican government, constitutes an enormous debt against the States chargeable with this unadvised measure, which must long remain unsatisfied; or rather an accumulation of guilt, which can be expatiated not otherwise than by a voluntary sacrifice on the altar of justice, of the power which has been the instrument of it."[148] Bills of attainder, ex-post-facto laws, and laws impairing the obligation of contracts are considered contrary to the first principles of the social compact and to every principle of sound legislation.[149] In an argument against infringements upon vested rights by the state legislatures, Madison says concerning Article 1, Section 10, clause 1: "Our own experience has taught us . . . that . . . fences against these dangers ought not to be omitted. Very properly, therefore, have the convention added this

[145] 40, 252.

[146] See 37, 232 and essay 40. For the fact that the Union is considered a mere means, see 37, 225; 40, 252; 45, 298-99.

[147] 41, 260. The "public good," which was the motive for the framing of the Constitution, amounts to a protection of the individual's vested rights.

[148] 44, 290.   [149] 44, 291.

constitutional bulwark in favor of personal security and private rights. . . . The sober people of America are weary of the fluctuating policy which has directed the public councils. They have seen with regret and indignation that sudden changes and legislative interferences, in cases affecting personal rights, become jobs in the hands of enterprising and influential speculators, and snares to the more-industrious and less-informed part of the community."[150] Finally, reminding his countrymen that a recent and well-known event has warned them to be prepared for emergencies,[151] a reference to Shays's Rebellion, Madison says that to the powers granted to the federal government the power to insure the states' "protection against domestic violence is added with great propriety."[152]

Efficacy is given to the specific grants of power by two, more general, provisions, the "necessary and proper" and the "supremacy" clauses. As to the former, Madison, being of the opinion that "without the *substance* of this power, the whole Constitution would be a dead letter,"[153] deals only with the question whether the clause is in proper form. He rejects the use of the word "expressly" in the second of the Articles of Confederation. He also opposes a positive enumeration of the powers comprehended under the general term "necessary and proper" as well as a negative enumeration, by specifying the powers excepted from it.[154] He goes so far as to say that even if the clause had been omitted, the power it grants would be in the federal government by unavoidable implication because "no axiom is more clearly established in law, or in reason, than that wherever the end is required, the means are authorized; wherever a general power to do a thing is given, every particular power necessary for doing it is included."[155] Without the supremacy clause the Con-

---

[150] 44, 291.   [151] 43, 286.

[152] 43, 283. Again Madison's fear of democratic excesses in the states can be noted when he continues: "At first view, it might seem not to square with the republican theory, to suppose, either that a majority have not the right, or that a minority will have the force, to subvert a government; and consequently that the federal interposition can never be required, but when it would be improper. But theoretic . . . reasoning must be qualified by the lessons of practice. Why may not illicit combinations, for purposes of violence, be formed as well by a majority of a State . . . as by the majority of a country; . . . and if the authority of the State ought, in the latter case, to protect the local magistracy, ought not the federal authority, in the former, to support the State authority?" (43, 283-84.)

[153] 44, 292.   [154] 44, 293 ff.

[155] 44, 294. Marshall's words in McCulloch v. Maryland were: "Let the end be legitimate, let it be within the scope of the Constitution, and all means which are

stitution would have been radically defective, since the new Congress would have been reduced to the same impotent condition as its predecessors.[156] Madison thus considers the clause not only necessary for the unity of law with respect to national statutes and treaties,[157] but also as a grant of power, enabling the national government to check state legislation.

Although Madison considers a strong federal government as a remedy for democratic despotism, he accepts popular government as long as it is compatible with free government. Expressing himself against "aristocratic or monarchical innovations," he praises the Constitution for granting to the national government the power to guarantee to every state a republican form of government[158] to which the elective mode of obtaining rulers is characteristic.[159] This form of government "derives all its powers directly or indirectly from the great body of the people, and is administered by persons holding their offices during pleasure, for a limited period, or during good behavior. It is *essential* to such a government that it be derived from

appropriate, which are plainly adapted to that end, which are not prohibited, but consist with the letter and spirit of the Constitution, are constitutional." 4 Wheaton 159, 206 (1819). In spite of the similarity of his language and comments on the necessary and proper clause in the *Federalist,* Madison attacked Marshall's decision, saying that "it was anticipated . . . by few if any of the friends of the Constitution, that a rule of construction would be introduced as broad and pliant as what has occurred. And those who recollect, and still more those who shared in what passed in the State Conventions, thro' which the people ratified the Constitution, with respect to the extent of powers vested in Congress, cannot easily be persuaded that the avowal of such a rule would not have prevented its ratification." Letter to Spencer Roane of Sept. 2, 1819. MADISON'S WRITINGS, VIII, 450-51. Burns, *op. cit.,* 110, saying that "this was undoubtedly true," does not take into account Madison's comments in the *Federalist,* and thus creates the impression that Madison always interpreted the clause as he did in 1819.

[156] 44, 296. It is interesting to note that Madison proves the necessity of a supremacy clause on the hypothetical supposition that "the supremacy of the State constitutions had been left complete by a saving clause in their favor" (44, 295-96). In a word, he identifies the nonexistence of state supremacy with the existence of national supremacy, or vice versa. Supremacy is either here or there, it cannot be in both the state and federal governments. This amounts to a recognition of the indivisibility of sovereignty. It may thus not be correct to call Madison a believer in divided sovereignty. Sovereignty can be divided only to the degree as the sovereign permitted it, which means, however, that sovereignty was actually not divided. Since under the Constitution sovereignty resides in the national government owing to the supremacy clause, the states were sovereign only to the degree the Constitution permitted it. In this qualified sense only do they have part of the sovereignty, is sovereignty "divided." See also 45, 299.

[157] 44, 296.   [158] 43, 282.   [159] 57, 370.

the great body of the society, not from an inconsiderable proportion, or a favored class of it."[160] Madison lauds the Constitution for creating a government in which the House of Representatives is elected immediately by the people, the Senate derives its appointment indirectly from the people, the president is indirectly chosen by the people, and the judges with all other officers of the Union are also the choice of the people.[161] Only popular government can be reconciled with the genius of the people of America and with the fundamental principles of the Revolution.[162]

The Union is an extended federal republic. Madison does not only believe that, due to the Union's extent, there will be a refined national legislature;[163] also, he sees in the Union the conservator of peace among Americans,[164] because there exist many powers, which by counterpoising each other maintain political equilibrium: "In the extent and proper structure of the Union, . . . we behold a republican remedy for the diseases most incident to republican government"[165]—factions, the violance of which the Union "breaks and controls."[166] Greater security will be afforded by a greater variety of parties, against the event of any one party being able to outnumber and oppress the rest, and greater obstacles will be opposed to the concert and accomplishment of the secret wishes of an unjust and interested majority.[167] "A religious sect may degenerate into a political faction in a part of the Confederacy; but the variety of sects dispersed over the entire face of it must secure the national councils against any danger from that source."[168] Through these power-balances, Madison sees one part of the society guarded against the injustices of the other part.[169]

[160] 39, 243-44.

[161] 39, 244-45. In essay 46, Madison says that both federal and state governments must be considered "as substantially dependent on the great body of the citizens of the United States, . . . [being] but different agents and trustees of the people." (46, 304-5.) Under the Constitution, all authority in the United States "will be derived from and dependent on . . . society" (51, 339). See also 57, 371-73 for the democratic character of the House of Representatives, 63, 416 with reference to the Senate.

[162] 39, 243.   [165] 10, 62.   [167] 10, 61.
[163] 10, 61.   [166] 10, 53.   [168] 10, 61-62.
[164] 14, 79.

[169] 51, 339. "The society . . . will be broken into so many parts, interests and classes of citizens, that the rights of individuals, or of the minority, will be in little danger from interested combinations of the majority. In a free government the security for civil rights must be the same as that for religious rights. It consists in the one case in the multiplicity of interests, and in the other in the multi-

Also, the states counterbalance the national government as well as each other. Since, in view of the states' role in the election of the president, the Senate, and the House,[170] each of the principal branches of the federal government will owe its existence to the favor of the state governments, there will be no consolidated government, but one in which the states will retain a very extensive portion of active sovereignty.[171] The powers of the federal government being "few and defined," and those of the states "numerous and indefinite,"[172] ambitious encroachments of the federal government on the authority of the state governments would not excite the opposition of a single state, or of a few states only. They would be signals for general alarm. Every state would espouse the common cause. Plans of resistance would be concerted. One spirit would animate and conduct the whole.[173]

In view of the powers of the federal government, we may thus say that both the federal and state governments possess the "faculty . . . to resist and frustrate the measures of each other."[174] The states also balance each other. "The influence of factious leaders may kindle a flame within their particular states, but will be unable to spread a general conflagration through the other states,"[175] the latter performing a shock-absorbing function. Fearing democratic excesses in the states, Madison is happy that under the Constitution "a rage for paper-money, for an abolition of debts, for an equal distribution of property, or for any other improper or wicked project, will be less apt to pervade the whole body of the Union than a particular member of it."[176]

3. In addition to territorial balances, there are institutional balances. Ascribing the crisis under the Confederation mainly to the omnipotence of the legislatures, Madison lauds the Constitution for realizing that "sacred maxim of free government,"[177] the separation of powers. Although its establishment under the Constitution does not correspond perfectly to that outlined in his theory,[178] it does so

plicity of sects. The degree of security in both cases will depend on the number of interests and sects; and this may be presumed to depend on the extent of country and number of people comprehended under the same government." 51, 339-40.

[170] 44, 297.   [173] 46, 309.   [176] 10, 62. See also 54, 358-59.
[171] 45, 300-1.   [174] 46, 306.   [177] 47, 320.
[172] 45, 303.   [175] 10, 61.

[178] For instance, under the Constitution there is no veto power of the President *and* the Senate against the House, as proposed by Madison theoretically (51, 338).

in general. Executive, legislative, and judiciary are separated, but not absolutely so, and ambition is made to counteract ambition.[179] Separation is "essential to the preservation of liberty,"[180] and Madison sees it mainly as a device to check democratic tyranny. He rejects the idea that the people themselves should be the judge over breaches of the Constitution by one of the three departments, because they are strongly influenced by the members of the legislature and, therefore, the "constitutional equilibrium" would be destroyed and "the *passions, . . .* not the *reason,* of the public would sit in judgment."[181] He wants the legislature, which in republican government necessarily predominates,[182] divided into a Senate and a House, the former being a salutary check on the latter, which, like all numerous assemblies, has a propensity to yield to the impulse of sudden and violent passions, and to be seduced by factious leaders into intemperate and pernicious resolutions.[183] The dissimilarity of the two legislative bodies renders "sinister combinations" improbable.

4.   The territorial and institutional balances do not work totally independently of each other, but are so integrated as to render the system of checks and balances more complete in order to make the "constitutional equilibrium"[184] a perfect one.[185] To the balances created by federalism and the separation of powers is thus added a balance *among* territorial and institutional balance factors.

The discrepancy arising from the concomitance of the government's constituting a power and the division of that power is only partly corrected in the language of the Constitution, as in the case of federalism. The supremacy clause secures the superiority of national legislation and thus makes certain that the territorial power division does not impair the quality of the national government as a power. This is noted by Madison with satisfaction.[186] Another provision that he considers necessary, namely, that in controversies relating to the boundary between state and national jurisdictions the tribunal that is ultimately to decide is to be established under the general government,[187] amounts to a similar guarantee of national power. However, the Constitution is silent in the case of the institu-

---

[179] 51, 335.   [181] 49, 330-31.   [183] 62, 403.
[180] 51, 335.   [182] 51, 338.   [184] 49, 330.
[185] This integration is evident in essay 51 where Madison deals with the advantage of power-balances in both territorial and institutional respects, connecting both. See Beard, THE ENDURING FEDERALIST, 8, 23.
[186] 44, 295-96.   [187] 39, 249.

tional separation of powers. It does not mention judicial review. Also
Madison refrains from connecting that institution with the Constitution. It can be assumed, however, that he considered judicial review existent under the new law.[188]

Concluding our inquiry into how, according to Madison's *Federalist,* free government is achieved under the Philadelphia document,
we may say that through the establishment of an effective national
government there is created a remedy for the crisis arising from a
majoritarian tyranny in the states. By providing for federalism and
the separation of powers, the Constitution creates a system of checks
and balances through which the effects of factions are controlled. In
spite of these measures against democratic excesses, provision is
made for popular government. Democracy, while being fundamentally recognized, is restricted for the sake of the individual's rights.

[188] When Madison writes: "What is to restrain the House . . . from making legal
discriminations in favor of themselves . . . ? I answer: the genius of the whole
system; the nature of just and constitutional laws" (57, 373), he admits that the
House can pass unconstitutional laws. The restraint on the passage of such laws
must therefore come from some power outside the House. Such restraint may
exist in two forms. Either some nonlegislative power prevents the unconstitutional
law from taking effect, or the House, aware of that possibility, restrains itself
and does not pass unconstitutional laws. In both cases, the power to declare a law
unconstitutional exists *outside* of the legislature. Madison, saying that "the success of the usurpation [by the legislature] will depend on the executive and judicial departments, which are to expound and give effect to the legislative acts"
(44, 295), strongly hints at judicial review, because the interpretation of the laws
precedes their taking effect through an act of the executive. When he further speaks
of "the . . . distinction . . . between a Constitution established by the people and
unalterable by the government," continuing, "where no Constitution, paramount
to the government, either existed or could be obtained, no constitutional security
similar to that established in the United States, was to be attempted" (53, 348-49),
he says that there exists security when the legislature is bound by a constitution.
It is but a step further to recognize a review of legislative acts by some authority
outside the legislature, in all probability the judiciary.

CHAPTER SIX

Hamilton on Free Government

I

1. Since in the state of nature[1] man's actions do "not conform to the dictates of reason and justice," individuals become induced "to the establishment of civil power"[2] and "enter into a state of society" the laws of which become "the supreme regulator of their conduct."[3] Security for individual rights and privileges is attainable in civil society, but not in the state of nature.[4] Hamilton nowhere specifies in

---

[1] That term is mentioned in "The Farmer Refuted," written in 1775. Hamilton says here that the colonists, when going to the new world, "looked upon themselves as having reverted to the state of nature." HAMILTON'S WORKS, I, 102. See also *ibid.*, III, 291.

[2] 15, 92. [3] 33, 201.

[4] 28, 173. Since "the laws of . . . society" are "the supreme regulator" of the individual's conduct (33, 201), and since there are no such laws in the state of nature, the state of nature must be a state of anarchy. It is interesting to note in that connection Hamilton's discussion of Hobbes in "The Farmer Refuted." Hobbes held, Hamilton writes, that man in the state of nature was "perfectly free from all restraint of *law* and *government*. Moral obligation, according to him, is derived from the introduction of civil society; and there is no virtue but what is purely artificial, the mere contrivance of politicians for the maintenance of social intercourse. But the reason he ran into this absurd and impious doctrine was that he disbelieved in the existence of an intelligent, superintending prin-

141

the *Federalist* how the state of nature is left behind. However, we may assume that he was an adherent of the social contract theory. This follows from his recognition of a parallel between the formation of a state by individuals and of a confederacy by states,[5] the latter coming into existence by compact.[6] The compact by which the people subject themselves to a "civil power"[7] (Hamilton's distinction between a social compact proper and a compact between society and government is of no major relevance here[8]) is a voluntary pact concluded by weak and strong individuals alike.[9] It can thus be said that the individuals subject themselves to the "constraint" of a government[10] in order to have the rule of force replaced by the rule of "the laws of . . . society"[11] under which they will "conform to the dictates of reason and justice."[12] Like Madison, Hamilton sees the protection principle at the very founding of society.

ciple, who is the governor, and will be the final judge, of the universe. . . . To grant that there is a Supreme Intelligence who ruled the world and has established laws to regulate the actions of his creatures, and still to assert that man, in a state of nature, may be considered as perfectly free from all restraints of *law* and *government*, appears, to a common understanding, altogether irreconcilable." HAMILTON'S WORKS, I, 61-62. The word "law" is here used in the sense of natural law. More frequently, law is for Hamilton "a rule which those to whom it is prescribed are bound to observe" (33, 201), i.e., something that has a sanction. Since such positive law does obviously not exist, in Hamilton's opinion, in the state of nature, the state of nature must be a state of anarchy. R. C. Mulford, THE POLITICAL THEORIES OF ALEXANDER HAMILTON (1903), 20, does not recognize this distinction between natural and positive law and thus arrives at the conclusion that to Hamilton the state of nature was not anarchic.

[5] "If individuals enter into a state of society, the laws of that society must be the supreme regulator of their conduct. If a number of political societies enter into a larger political society, the laws which the latter may enact . . . must necessarily be supreme over those societies" (33, 201).

[6] For the fact that the Confederation came into existence by compact, see 21, 125; 22, 140-41; 24, 149; 30, 183. For the fact that the United States under the Constitution will come into being by a compact, see 85, 571.

[7] 15, 92.

[8] When Hamilton speaks of "a voluntary compact between the rulers and the ruled" ("The Farmer Refuted," HAMILTON'S WORKS, I, 63), he must presuppose a compact by which the ruled, able to conclude a compact with the rulers, come into existence as a party to that compact.

[9] "The origins of all civil government . . . must be a voluntary compact between the rulers and the ruled. . . . What original title can any man, or set of men, have to govern others, except their own consent?" "The Farmer Refuted," *loc. cit.*, I, 63. From this can be concluded that for Hamilton, also, the social contract is a voluntary one.

[10] 15, 92.   [11] 33, 201.   [12] 15, 92.

The same applies to the participation principle. After establishing civil society, the people as the "pure, original fountain of all legitimate authority"[13] do not become politically passive. Rather, they constantly nourish government through participation.

The concomitance of the protection and participation principles at the beginning of civil society is for Hamilton as natural a coincidence as it is for Madison. The individuals, leaving the state of nature in order to be protected, do not want to replace the *bellum omnium contra omnes* by a *bellum regis contra subiectos*. Consequently, they choose a government that is most likely to protect their rights, i.e., one in which they participate.

If we consider the relation of the two principles under the criterion of cause and effect, their co-existence at the beginning of civil society has important implications with regard to their concomitance within society. Government is nothing but a means for the individual's protection. Popular participation in government can thus be justified only in so far as the rights of the individual are not endangered. This amounts to a primacy of the people's protection before their participation in government. Before we explain the protection and participation principles, we shall consider how they are implemented in the relation between people and government. Like Madison, Hamilton considers that relation from a teleological, a static-factual, and a dynamic-legal point of view.

2.   As to the first point of view, government was instituted for the public happiness,[14] a means to an end: "A government ought to contain . . . every power requisite to the . . . accomplishment of the objects committed to its care, and to the complete execution of the trusts for which it is responsible, free from every other control but regard to the public good and to the sense of the people."[15]

The static-factual relation follows from the fact that the people, when leaving the state of nature, become society[16] under a government. Hamilton's words, "if individuals enter into a state of society, the laws of that society must be the supreme regulator of their conduct,"[17] have important consequences. If individuals enter into a state of society, they become the objects upon which those laws operate, the subjects of the state they brought into being. They are under the civil power of that particular state only. In agreement

---

[13] 22, 141.   [14] 71, 464.   [15] 31, 190.

[16] Or "civil society" (28, 172-73), or "the public" (83, 544).

[17] 33, 201.

with Madison, Hamilton considers society as confined within the bounds of one body politic.[18]

This brings us to the relation between society and government from a dynamic-legal point of view and the implementation of the protection and participation principles. Like Madison, Hamilton rejects the government's absolute dependence upon as well as its absolute independence from society and expresses himself in favor of a compromise theory. Government, being instituted "because the passions of men will not conform to the dictates of reason and justice, without constraint,"[19] must possess, in order that "the laws of . . . society" may be the "supreme regulator,"[20] the power to enforce those laws. A government absolutely dependent on society would not constitute a power that could constrain the people. It could not provide that "security for the rights and privileges of the people, which is attainable in civil society."[21] It would be inconsistent with the protection principle. On the other hand, a government absolutely independent of society is not acceptable either, since it is incompatible with the principle of popular participation in government.

Hamilton favors a government that is compatible with both the protection and participation principles, the latter, as a means, being secondary to the former, as the end. A dependence of the government upon the people can be suffered only in so far as the protection of the individual is not hazarded. Although "the deliberate sense of the community should govern the conduct of those to whom they intrust the management of their affairs," Hamilton expresses himself against the government's "unqualified complaisance to every sudden breeze of passion, or to every transient impulse which the people may receive from the arts of men, who flatter their prejudices and betray their interests."[22] While fundamentally accepting a de-

---

[18] The quality of society as an intrastate phenomenon follows from such passages as: "If a number of political societies enter into a larger political society" (33, 201); "a confederate republic . . . is a kind of assemblage of societies that constitute a new one" (9, 50-51); "a federal government, which is a composition of societies" (83, 545); "a large state or society" (85, 574). Further, Hamilton speaks of "the society" of a particular state (12, 75; 17, 103; 35, 215; 36, 217; 36, 222; 60, 391; 65, 424; 66, 435; 68, 443; 71, 464; 74, 483; 75, 488; 78, 504; 78, 509; 78, 510), of "society" as existent in one particular state (16, 100; 21, 127; 24, 150; 25, 158; 34, 206; 35, 214; 60, 390; 79, 513; 83, 554; 85, 569; 13, 77; 6, 271; 6, 33; 9, 48), and of "societies" of different states (1, 3; 27, 167; 28, 170). He calls the Union a "civil society upon an enlarged scale" (28, 172).

[19] 15, 92.   [20] 33, 201.   [21] 28, 173.

[22] 71, 464. "The people commonly *intend* the PUBLIC GOOD," Hamilton con-

pendence of the government on the people, Hamilton wants the government sufficiently independent to fulfill its purpose, namely, the protection of the individual's rights. Popular participation in government is restricted by a constitution.[23]

When Hamilton shows government as a means to an end, this does not merely mean that popular participation in government must be secondary to the individual's protection. It also means that his *Federalist,* written for the adoption of a system of government, must largely be a treatise for the end this government has to fulfill, namely, the protection of the individual. The quality of society as an intrastate phenomenon must have a bearing upon Hamilton's theory on the nature of confederacies. Furthermore, the relative independence of government from the people opens on to the perspective of a government that abuses its power. Against such a government Hamilton, although aware of the dangers of popular uprisings,[24] admits a right of revolution: "If the representatives of the people betray their constituents, there is then no resource left but in the exertion of that original right of self-defence which is paramount to all positive forms of government."[25] Finally, the sub-

tinues, but they do not always *"reason right* about the *means* of promoting it," because they are "beset . . . by the wiles of parasites and sycophants, by the snares of the ambitious, the avaricious, the desperate, by the artifices of men who possess their confidence more than they deserve it" (71, 464-65).

[23] Although this is nowhere expressly stated in the *Federalist,* it follows from Hamilton's rejection of the government's absolute dependence upon and its absolute independence from society: If the people, as represented in the government, were at liberty to decide the degree of their participation in government (for instance, by ordinary laws), the government would be absolutely dependent upon the people. On the other hand, had the government an absolute power to regulate (and forbid) the people's participation, it would be absolutely independent of society, like a dictatorship. The restriction of participation under a constitution can further be concluded from the fact that in essay 78 Hamilton accepts judicial review, which means that the branch of government in which popular participation is most reflected, is bound by a constitution: "The Constitution ought to be the standard of construction for the laws, and . . . wherever there is an evident opposition, the laws ought to give place to the Constitution" (81, 524).

[24] 26, 159.

[25] 28, 173. See also 33, 200: "If the federal government should overpass the just bounds of its authority and make tyrannical use of its powers, the people, whose creature it is, must appeal to the standard they have formed, and take such measures to redress the injury done to the Constitution as the exigency may suggest and prudence justify." If unjust election laws were passed, "citizens, . . . conscious of their rights, would . . . overthrow their tyrants, and . . . substitute

ordination of government under a constitution shows the existence of two sorts of man-made law,[26] namely, "the Constitution and the laws."[27] The former is made by society and is fundamental; the latter, made by the government, is ordinary. All positive law is under natural law.[28]

3.   It remains to explain the protection and participation principles and their relation to each other in the state. Since Hamilton considers the individual's protection the end of government, an explanation of the protection principle can be derived from his specification of that end. Government being instituted for the distribution of justice,[29] Hamilton explains the end of government more concretely as "the public happiness,"[30] the "public good."[31] He connects the existence of justice with the well-being of the people, majority and minority alike.[32] More specifically, the people's happiness means the protection of their "general liberty," their "rights," their "private rights."[33] From his distinction between liberty and prop-

men who would be disposed to avenge the violated majesty of the people" (60, 395).

[26] The term "positive" law is used at 28, 173; 78, 507.

[27] 78, 510.

[28] This follows from Hamilton's admission of a right of revolution. For Hamilton's conception of positive law, see 33, 201: "A LAW, by the very meaning of the term, includes supremacy. It is a rule which those to whom it is prescribed are bound to observe"; also 15, 91: "It is essential to the idea of a law, that it be attended with a sanction; or, in other words, a penalty or punishment for disobedience." In "The Farmer Refuted," *loc. cit.*, I, 63, Hamilton quotes Blackstone in his definition of natural law, "which, being coeval with mankind, and dictated by God himself, is . . . superior in obligations to any other. It is binding over all the globe, in all countries, at all times. No human laws are of any validity, if contrary to this; and such of them as are valid, derive their authority . . . from this original."

[29] 15, 92.   [30] 71, 464.   [31] 31, 190.

[32] Hamilton considers the permanency of the judicial office as "the citadel of the public justice and the public security" (78, 505). He speaks of "justice or the public good" (79, 514), of "the ends of public justice and security" (81, 533).

[33] 78, 504; 78, 508-9. Hamilton often uses the terms "liberties," "rights," and "liberty" (when he speaks of the total of vested right) without specifically stating the meaning of those terms, as, for instance, when he speaks of the "liberties of the great community" (26, 164), of "our liberties" (26, 165), of "rights" (26, 159; 28, 173; 28, 174), of the "liberty of the States . . . against domestic faction and insurrection" (9, 47), of the "vigor of government" which "is essential to the security of liberty." Compare also, for "liberty," 9, 48; 70, 462; 71, 467; 78, 504; for "general liberty," 84, 563; 85, 573.

erty[34] and life and property[35] follows Hamilton's classification of those rights into the categories commonly used in his time, namely, the rights of life, liberty, and property.

Of these rights, those of property are most important. Their greater weight, as compared with the rights of liberty,[36] follows from Hamilton's enumeration, in order of importance, of the advantages of an energetic executive. He mentions, first, the protection of the community against foreign attacks; second, the steady administration of the laws; third, the protection of property against irregular and high-handed combinations that sometimes interrupt the ordinary courts of justice; and fourth, the security of liberty.[37] Hamilton thus puts the protection of property before the security of liberty and connects it more closely with that all-embracing end of government, justice. The prevalence of property before liberty is confirmed when Hamilton states that among vested rights, those concerning life and property are most important.[38] When, finally, he refers hardly ever to the right of life and very often to that of property, the conclusion can be drawn that he attributes a greater weight to the latter, which he once referred to as "the great and fundamental distinction of society."[39]

Although "an actual representation of all classes of the people, by persons of each class, is altogether visionary,"[40] the government should be in the hands of the representatives of the people. Hamilton feels that this is the essential and only efficacious security for the rights and privileges of the people that is attainable in civil society.[41] "Popular government"[42] is a majority government.[43] In its "ex-

---

[34] 1, 6; 25, 156; 70, 454; 83, 545; 85, 567-68.

[35] 8, 24; 17, 103.

[36] "Liberty" is here used in a narrow sense, exclusive of the rights of life and property. It comprises such rights as the freedom of the press (84, 560; 85, 567), trial by jury (83, 543).

[37] 70, 454.   [40] 35, 213.

[38] 17, 103.   [41] 28, 173.

[39] HAMILTON'S WORKS, I, 410.

[42] For the use of that term, see 12, 72; 18, 110; 83, 543.

[43] Hamilton speaks of "the fundamental maxim of republican government, which requires that the sense of the majority should prevail" (22, 134). Since "republican government" is a popular government, popular government must be majority government too. Compare also 22, 135: "To give a minority a negative upon the majority (which always is the case where more than a majority is requisite to a decision) is . . . to subject the sense of the greater number to that of the lesser," a "poison."

cesses"[44] it may be a tyranny of the popular magistrates,[45] the rule of an "overbearing majority."[46] Susceptible to "every sudden breeze of passion,"[47] it may proceed to "oppressions of the minor party."[48]

4.   While fundamentally accepting it, Hamilton wants popular government restricted under a constitution so as to secure the protection of the individual's rights from the majority. This ideal[49] form of government he calls "free government."[50]

[44] 70, 458.   [46] 60, 390.   [48] 78, 508.
[45] 83, 543.   [47] 71, 464.

[49] Hamilton's opinion of free government as an ideal can be concluded from the fact that the only criteria of free government are for him its constituting elements, namely, the individual's protection and popular participation in government, i.e., elements which may exist in different forms of existing governments. He speaks of "a" free government (70, 458; 70, 461; 71, 468; 73, 478; 78, 510), or just of "free government" (83, 543), but never of *one* concrete free government. Free government may exist at all times; it was possible in ancient Greece and Italy (9, 47-48), as it is possible in Hamilton's time under the new Constitution (70, 458; 70, 461). It is not bound to a particular form of a state, but possible in the "petty republics of Greece and Italy" (9, 47-48), in England (71, 468), in the United States (70, 458; 70, 461).

[50] The conformity of free government to the participation principle is expressed when Hamilton speaks of "the superior weight and influence of the legislative body in a free government" (73, 478) and when he says that "upon the principles of a free government" there must exist a numerous legislature (70, 458) and that "a voluminous code of laws [made by that branch of government which mainly reflects popular government] is one of the inconveniences necessarily connected with the advantages of a free government" (78, 510). On the other hand, free government is consistent with the protection principle when Hamilton says that the trial by jury is represented "as the very palladium of free government" (83, 543) or that in a free government there must be liberty of the press (84, 560). In some passages Hamilton even mentions both the protection and participation principles in connection with free government. For instance, he says that "from the disorders . . . [in ancient] republics the advocates of despotism have drawn arguments, not only against the forms of republican [i.e., popular] government, but against the very principles of civil liberty. They have decried all free government as inconsistent with the order of society" (9, 48). See also 70, 461; 71, 467.

"Good government," while being a free government ("It is one thing to be subordinate to the laws, and another to be dependent on the legislative body. The first comports with, the last violates, the fundamental principles of good government" [71, 465-66]), seems for Hamilton to be a concrete government with power when he says that "the true test of a good government is its aptitude and tendency to produce a good administration" (68, 444) and that "energy in the executive is a leading character in the definition of good government" (70, 454), and, further, when he considers the independence of the judges as characteristic of a good government (78, 511; 79, 512). See also, for the use of the term "good government," 1, 3; 22, 140.

Free government is mainly threatened by factions. Although Hamilton nowhere defines that term, there can be no doubt, from the context in which he uses it, that it has for him the same meaning as for Madison.[51] Hamilton does not demonstrate the origin of faction as elaborately as Madison. When, however, he says that seditions and insurrections are maladies as inseparable from the body politic, i.e., from any form of government, as tumors and eruptions from the natural body,[52] we may conclude that even more so must factions have their roots in a free government. Protecting the individual's rights, this form of government enables people to make full use of those rights, and to become Protestant, Catholic, debtor, and creditor factions, to name only a few. Furthermore, free government in principle accepts the rule of the majority faction over the minority faction.

As maladies of free government, factions are not an essential part, but only a consequence of that form of government. Being its "tumors and eruptions," they constitute a threat both to individual rights and to popular government.[53] Consequently, free government can be secured only by controlling the effects of factions. This means that free government exists to the degree that it checks factions. Factions—and here Hamilton goes further than Madison—are in their

[51] "Faction" is for Hamilton identical to "party." He speaks of the "tempestuous waves of sedition and party rage" (9, 47) and says that "the spirit of party, in different degrees, must be expected to infect all political bodies" (26, 163). With respect to political offenses, he says that "the prosecution of them . . . will . . . agitate the passions of the . . . community and . . . divide it into parties . . . [and] in many cases will connect itself with the pre-existing factions" (65, 424).

[52] 28, 170-71.

[53] The threat of factions to individual rights is expressed when Hamilton thinks an energetic executive necessary "to the protection of property against those irregular and high-handed combinations [factions] which sometimes interrupt the ordinary course of justice; to the security of liberty against the enterprises and assaults of ambition, of faction, and of anarchy" (70, 454). In 78, 508, Hamilton says that "the independence of the judges is . . . requisite to guard . . . the rights of individuals from the effects of those ill humors, which the arts of designing men, or the influence of particular conjectures, sometimes disseminate among the people . . . and which . . . have a tendency . . . to occasion . . . serious oppressions of the minor party," continuing that "occasional ill humors, or contemporary prejudices and propensities . . . frequently contaminate the public councils" (27, 167). "It ought not to be forgotten that the demon of faction will, at certain seasons, extend his sceptre over all numerous bodies of men" (65, 428). "A spirit of faction . . . is apt to mingle its poison in the deliberations of all bodies of men" (15, 92). An ambitious individual, by controlling a strong faction, may become a despot of the people (85, 568).

consequences not confined within the bounds of one body politic, but may affect other states and may lead to war.[54]

Concluding, we may say that Hamilton's view on the nature of free government is very similar to that of Madison. The individuals leave the anarchic state of nature out of self-interest in order to live under a free government that, while being a popular government, restricts democracy under a constitution for the protection of the individual's life, liberty, and property. Threatened mainly by its own creature, faction, free government exists to the degree that it controls its effects. There is, however, one dissimilarity to be noted. For Hamilton, the effects of faction are not only felt within one particular body politic, but may also lead to war with other states.

From the fact that free government exists to the degree that it controls factions it follows that free government can best be realized under a concrete government that is likely to control factions. Furthermore Hamilton, by pointing out that factions may lead to war, admits that factions in one state may not be peacefully absorbed by other states and thus prevents himself from pronouncing a system of territorial balances as a remedy for factions, a scheme that Madison thinks so efficient. What concrete form of government Hamilton considers to be most conducive to free government shall now be examined.

II

1. Hamilton regards a government in which power is conspicuous and poised in one center as most conducive to free government. Since a concentration of power presupposes power factors that can be concentrated, the question is to what degree a concentration should exist. Although Hamilton concedes a division of power in both territorial and institutional respects, he permits this division only in so far as the quality of the government as a power is not jeopardized.

---

[54] Among the causes of hostility among nations are those "which take their origin entirely in private passions; in the attachments . . . , interests . . . of leading individuals in the communities of which they are members" (6, 28), i.e., in factions. The connection of interior factions with war is demonstrated in essay 6. Also, in an argument against the too democratic legislation in the states, Hamilton says in 7, 40 that "laws in violation of private contracts, as they amount to aggressions on the rights of those States whose citizens are injured by them, may be considered as another probable source of hostility" between states.

He emphasizes—to a much greater extent than Madison—the necessity of a concentration of power.

"The vigor of government" is "essential to the security of liberty."[55] In order that this vigor, or power, may exist, there must be, since "every government ought to contain in itself the means of its own preservation," governmental stability. Also, to be effective, the government must possess energy.[56] Both qualities are conducive to free government. According to Hamilton, only a strong government can possess energy and stability and fulfill the purposes of its institution. Only a strong government can possess confidence at home and undertake or execute liberal or enlarged plans for the public good.[57]

In view of Hamilton's emphasis on governmental power it is not surprising that he considers territorial and institutional power-division as of minor importance for a realization of free government. Therefore, when an inquiry is now made into the tendency of concrete governments to promote free government, the leitmotiv of power-concentration will be encountered as often as was the leitmotiv of power-balance in Madison's *Federalist*.

2.   The popular government (other governments such as monarchy or aristocracy are *a priori* excluded because of their inconsistency with the participation principle) most conducive to free government

---

[55] 1, 5.

[56] For proof that energy is necessary for a government, see 13, 77: "When the dimensions of a State attain to a certain magnitude, it requires the same energy of government . . . which [is] requisite in one of much greater extent." "The citizens of America have too much discernment to be argued into anarchy. And . . . experience has . . . wrought a deep . . . conviction . . . that greater energy of government is essential to the welfare . . . of the community" (26, 160): A government without energy is an anarchy, no government at all. See also 77, 502: "The executive department . . . combines . . . all the requisites to energy."

[57] 30, 186. The conduciveness of stability to free government is evident when Hamilton identifies stability with the "peace of society" (21, 127) and the "peace of the community" (72, 471), which, if not identical to, is at least very closely connected with "the public good or happiness." At 70, 454, Hamilton says: "Energy in the executive is a leading character in the definition of good government. It is essential . . . to the steady administration of the laws; to the protection of property against . . . irregular and high-handed combinations, . . . to the security of liberty against the enterprises . . . of faction." He recommends unity in the executive, because if the executive consisted of a plurality of persons, "they might split the community into the most violent and irreconcilable factions" (70, 457).

is a republic.[58] Believing that the possibility to realize free government grows with the extent of the republic, Hamilton considers pure democracy in a "petty" republic[59] and representative democracy in a republic, a large unitary republic and a federal republic.

A pure democracy[60] as it existed in the "petty republics of Greece

[58] Hamilton does not make a clear-cut statement as to the relation between democratic (popular) and republican government. There can be no doubt, however, that to him republican government *is* a popular (democratic) government. Speaking of the prohibition of titles of nobility, he says that "this may truly be denominated the corner-stone of republican government; for so long as they are excluded there can never be serious danger that the government will be any other than that of the people" (84, 557). To Hamilton, who speaks of "the fundamental maxim of republican government which requires that the sense of the majority should prevail" (22, 134), "the republican principle demands that the deliberate sense of the community should govern the conduct of those to whom they intrust the management of their affairs" (71, 464). The fact that republican government is to him popular government is further evident when he says that in "every government, partaking of the republican genius," the most popular branch will be a full match for every other member of the government (66, 431), that "in a republic . . . every magistrate ought to be personally responsible for his behavior in office" (70, 461), and calls the executive's "dependence on the people" a "safety in the republican sense" (70, 455). There are even strong hints in Hamilton's *Federalist* that republican government is identical with popular government to such a degree as to correspond only to the participation principle, i.e., possibly endangering vested rights, when in 9, 48 "the forms of republican government" are distinguished from the "principles of civil liberty," or in 84, 557, "liberty" from "republicanism." In a republic, there may be either direct or indirect democratic government, or pure representative democracy: When in essay 9 Hamilton distinguishes a republican government in which the people are represented in a legislature, from the "petty republics of Greece and Italy," it follows that in the latter there was no representation. (Compare also his "Brief of Argument on the Constitution of the United States" of 1788, where he says: "Democracy in my sense, where the whole power of the government is in the people. 1. Whether exercised by themselves, or 2. By their representatives. . . ." He calls the government under the Constitution a "representative democracy," whereas in other places he calls the United States a republic. HAMILTON'S WORKS, II, 92-93).

[59] 9, 47.

[60] Speaking about pure democracy (a term he does not use in the *Federalist*), Hamilton said on the floor of the New York convention on June 21, 1788: "It has been observed that a pure democracy, if it were practicable, would be the most perfect government. Experience has proved, that no position in politics is more false than this. The ancient democracies [which Hamilton calls the "petty republics of Greece and Italy" in the *Federalist*], in which the people themselves deliberated, never possessed one feature of good government. Their very character was tyranny; their figure deformity. When they assembled, the field of debate presented an ungovernable mob, not only incapable of delibera-

and Italy" is plagued by "tempestuous waves of seditions and party rage, [by] domestic faction and insurrection," and is "in a state of perpetual vibration between the extremes of tyranny and anarchy."[61] It is inconsistent with both the protection and the participation principles, and Hamilton concedes even to his opponents that the unfavorable portraits they have sketched of republican government are just copies of the original from which they were taken.[62]

A representative democracy offers a brighter picture. In it, the excellences of republican government may be retained and the requirement of the participation principle be met. Besides, the imperfections inherent in popular government, for instance, the rule of an overbearing and selfish majority, or infringements upon vested rights by a powerful faction, may be lessened or avoided.[63] Thus protection exists to a higher degree than under the pure democracy of a small republic. However, even here an unjust infringement upon the individual's rights is possible because "the representatives of the people, in a popular assembly, seem sometimes to betray strong symptoms of impatience and disgust at the least sign of opposition."[64] Therefore, to the factors that "tend to the amelioration of popular systems of civil government" in favor of a greater protection of the individual, Hamilton adds another one, namely, "the ENLARGEMENT of the ORBIT within which such systems are to revolve, either in respect to the dimensions of a single State, or to the consolidation of several smaller States into one great Confederacy."[65]

In a large republic the probability of an encroachment on the rights of the minority by the passionate legislative majority is reduced, since the representative body will be refined. Candidates, in order to get elected, will have to possess qualifications enabling them to extend their influence beyond the narrow circles of personal intrigue.[66] Being persons of good reputation—preferably proprietors of land, merchants, and members of the learned professions[67]—the

tion, but prepared for every enormity. In these assemblies the enemies of the people brought forward their plans of ambition systematically. They were opposed by their enemies of another party; and . . . the people subjected themselves to be led blindly by one tyrant or by another." HAMILTON'S WORKS, II, 22. The similarity of that passage with the beginning of essay 9 of the *Federalist* is striking and justifies my speaking of the "pure democracy" in the "petty republics of Greece and Italy."

[61] 9, 47.   [64] 71, 466.   [66] 9, 50.
[62] 9, 48.   [65] 9, 49.   [67] 36, 216.
[63] 9, 49.

representatives in a large republic will be guided in their decisions
by reason rather than passion. Should it happen that they betray
their constituents, the people have a good chance to resist success-
fully. Since "the obstacles to usurpation and the facilities of resistance increase with the increased extent of the state, provided the
citizens understand their rights and are disposed to defend them,
the natural strength of the people in a large community, in proportion to the artificial strength of the government, is greater than in a
small, and of course more competent to a struggle with the attempts
of the government to establish a tyranny."[68]

It is, however, a special form of a large republic that appears to
be most conducive to free government, namely, "the consolidation
of several smaller States into one great Confederacy."[69] Complain-

[68] 28, 173-74.

[69] 9, 49. When Hamilton speaks of a *consolidation* of states into a *confederacy*,
he shows that the distinction between a federation under national and one
under international law is not known to him by terminology. Consequently,
there is no clear distinction in his writings between such terms as "federal" on
the one hand and "confederate" on the other hand.

To Hamilton in the *Federalist*, the United States under the Articles is a "confederation" (15, 89; 15, 94; 18, 106; 21, 125; 21, 127; 22, 134; 22, 139; 23, 143; 25, 154;
30, 183; 75, 490; 78, 502; 80, 519; 84, 564) or a "confederacy" (6, 32; 7, 35; 7, 36;
8, 41; 8, 43; 11, 66; 15, 93; 16, 97; 21, 126; 22, 132; 27, 168; 27, 169; 29, 175; 69, 451),
which has a "federal" government (15, 87; 25, 155; 83, 548; 84, 564), a "federal"
authority (15, 89; 15, 92). He calls the confederacy a "federal plan" (21, 126), the
"existing federal system" (22, 131; 22, 140).

Similarly the United States under the Constitution is a "confederacy" (9, 52;
27, 168; 27, 169; 29, 175; 69, 448) with a "federal" government (9, 52; 16, 98;
23, 141; 23, 142; 23, 145; 24, 147; 26, 163; 29, 176, 29, 177; 29, 178; 29, 180; 30, 182;
31, 191; 32, 194; 33, 202; 36, 222; 26, 223; 59, 384; 76, 493), under a "federal" authority (27, 166), a "federal" power (35, 210; 61, 397).

If Hamilton does not distinguish between a federation under national and
one under international law by terminology, that distinction does not lie in the
fact that the former is a league and the latter not. To Hamilton, both may be
leagues. The United States under the Articles is a league (15, 91; 15, 96), as are
the Lycian and Achaean leagues (16, 95). Nor does the distinction lie in the
quality of union, since the United States is for Hamilton a union under the
Articles (1, 6; 8, 46; 11, 64; 15, 86; 22, 134; 23, 143; 23, 146; 25, 154; 30, 183; 30, 185;
85, 568), just as it is a union under the Constitution (1, 3; 13, 78; 17, 101; 17, 103;
23, 141; 23, 144; 25, 154; 33, 203; 36, 220; 59, 385; 85, 574).

In spite of these similarities, Hamilton saw the difference between a federation
under national law and one under international law. Although both types of
federation come into being by compact (like the United States under the Articles,
21, 125; 22, 141; 24, 149; 30, 183; or the United States under the Constitution,
85, 571), he emphasizes that the United States under the Constitution would
come into existence through the "ratification by the PEOPLE" (22, 140), and

ing of "the spirit of faction and . . . those occasional ill-humors, or temporary prejudices . . . which, in smaller societies, frequently contaminate the public councils, beget injustice and oppression of a part of the community, and engender schemes which, though they gratify a momentary inclination or desire, terminate in general dis-

would "rest on the solid basis of THE CONSENT OF THE PEOPLE" because "the streams of national power ought to flow immediately from that pure, original fountain of all legitimate authority" (22, 141). "Immediately," he says, meaning that the assent was to be given by the *American* people, irrespective of state boundaries. On the other hand, the United States under the Articles came into being by a compact between "the several legislatures" (22, 141) and was based on a "compact between the States." (21, 125.)

Resting on the more solid foundation of the assent of the people, the power of the government of a federation under national law is, as compared with that under international law, increased, since the government can act directly upon individuals. Complaining that "the great and radical vice in the construction of the existing Confederation is the principle of LEGISLATION for STATES or GOVERNMENTS, in their CORPORATE or COLLECTIVE CAPACITIES, and as contradistinguished from the INDIVIDUALS of which they consist" (15, 89), Hamilton is glad that the Constitution deviates from that principle which "is in itself evidently incompatible with the idea of GOVERNMENT" (15, 90).

Parallel to the greater power toward individual citizens, of the government of the federation under national law, there exists a greater power toward the member states, since resistance to the laws of the federal government by the commonwealths can be remedied by the national government's acting directly on the citizens. Being independent of the assistance of the states, the federal government is "empowered to employ the arm of the ordinary magistrate to execute its own resolutions" (16, 95). Through its greater power, the federal government prevents the states from falling into a state of anarchy and civil war (16, 95) and thus the confederacy from dissolution. A strong federal government is more likely to slay "the political monster of imperium in imperio" (15, 89); see also essays 16 and 22.

Due to its greater intimacy and power in the national government, the federation under national law is, in contradistinction to one under international law, a nation, i.e., one state with one government. Although Hamilton concedes that the United States under the Articles has a national government, he leaves no doubt that this government exists only in form, not in fact. Of the opinion that legislation for states is "incompatible with the idea of GOVERNMENT" (15, 90), Hamilton says that "all the wheels of the national government" are "arrested" (15, 95), and denies the existence of a national government under the Articles altogether (15, 87; 85, 574), which means that he denies the existence of a *nation*. On the other hand, Hamilton makes it clear that under the Constitution there will be one national government and thus one nation, a "majesty of . . . national authority" (16, 98; see also 85, 574), one "American republic" (70, 461), one federal state.

When in the following we speak of a "federal state," we shall understand under that term—unless stated differently—a federation under national law, "an association of two or more states into one state" (singular!) (9, 52).

tress, dissatisfaction and disgust,"[70] Hamilton praises the "utility of a Confederacy . . . to suppress faction and to guard the internal tranquility of the States."[71] Aside from having a popular government, a federal republic affords an increased protection of the individual. Since "the extension of the spheres of election will present a greater option, or latitude of choice, to the people" for the election of representatives for the lower house, and since the representatives in the upper house will be elected by the state legislatures, which "are elect bodies of men,"[72] the probability of a refined representation is greater even than in a large republic. So is the chance of the people to resist usurpation: "In a single state, if the persons intrusted with supreme power become usurpers, the different parcels, subdivisions, or districts of which it consists, having no distinct government in each, can take no regular measures for defence."[73] "But in a confederacy the people, without exaggeration, may be said to be entirely the masters of their own fate. Power being almost always the rival of power, the general government will at all times stand ready to check the usurpations of the state governments, and these will have the same disposition towards the general government. The people, by throwing themselves into either scale, will infallibly make it preponderate. If their rights are invaded by either, they can make use of the other as the instruments of redress."[74]

While Madison considers a federal state as conducive to free government mainly because it creates power-balances, Hamilton does so mainly for another reason. While admitting the advantages of an internal power-division in the words of Montesquieu,[75] he is reluctant to stress the blessings of a power-balance and rather emphasizes those of power-concentration. There is in his *Federalist* no concert of powers that is so distinct a feature of Madison's. Not praising the tendency of different parts, interests, and classes of citizens as well as sects to balance each other, as Madison had done,[76] Hamilton emphasizes mainly one power rivalry, namely, that between the states and the federal government. His statement, "power being almost always the rival of power, the general government will at all times stand ready to check the usurpations of the state governments, and these will have the same disposition towards the general government,"[77] means, applied to the polemics of the time, simply this: Democracy being excessive in the states, the general government will

[70] 27, 167.   [73] 28, 173.   [76] 51, 339.
[71] 9, 49.   [74] 28, 174.   [77] 28, 174.
[72] 27, 167.   [75] 9, 51.

and must stand ready to check the too democratic state governments. It will have the *power* to do so. In a word, there will be enough power concentrated in it to enable it, for the sake of the individual, to deal the death blow to that "political monster," *imperium in imperio.*[78]

3. Though the people's representation is refined in a federal state, Hamilton wants, as a further check upon the legislature, an institutional division of power. "It is a fundamental maxim of free government, that the three great departments of power, *legislative, executive,* and *judiciary,* shall be essentially distinct and independent, the one of the other," he wrote in 1801.[79] In a similar vein, in the *Federalist* he calls for the regular distribution of power into distinct departments and the introduction of legislative balances and checks, great improvements in the science of politics,[80] seeing in the separation of powers mainly a device for checking the department most susceptible to democratic excesses, i.e., the legislature. Since there is a "superior weight and influence of the legislative body in a free government,"[81] the legislature, "the favorite of the people,"[82]

[78] 15, 89. This interpretation of the passage in essay 28 is not only compatible with, but even follows from, Hamilton's constantly emphasizing the relative badness of representative government in smaller societies, as was just shown. Further, his desire for a concentration of power in the federal government is reflected in his regretting the want of power in the general government under the Articles (15, 94; 15, 87; 85, 574).

[79] "Examination of Jefferson's Message to Congress of Dec. 7, 1801," HAMILTON'S WORKS, VIII, 333. In essay 66 of the *Federalist,* Hamilton uses a similar language, when he speaks of "that important and well-established maxim which requires a separation between the different departments of power." (66, 429.)

[80] 9, 48.   [81] 73, 478.

[82] 66, 432. Similar 71, 466: "The tendency of the legislative authority to absorb every other, has been fully displayed. . . . In governments purely republican, this tendency is almost irresistible." Hamilton's distrust of the legislature is evident when he continues that "the representatives . . . in a popular assembly, seem sometimes to fancy that they are the people themselves, and betray strong symptoms of impatience and disgust at the least sign of opposition from any other quarter; as if the exercise of rights, by either the executive or judiciary, were a breach of their privilege and an outrage to their dignity. They often appear disposed to exert an imperious control over the other departments; and as they commonly have the people on their side, they always act with such momentum as to make it very difficult for the other members of the government to maintain the balance of the Constitution" (71, 465-66). See also 66, 431-32. To Hamilton, all three departments derive their power from that "fountain of all legitimate authority" (22, 141), the people. Compare, with respect to the executive, 70, 455; 70, 461; the judiciary, essay 78.

the "AARON'S ROD most likely to swallow up" the other departments,[83] has to be checked for the protection of the individual. This
is possible if the partition of powers is so contrived as to render one
power independent of the other.[84] "To what purpose separate the
executive or the judiciary from the legislative, if both the executive
and the judiciary are so constituted as to be at the absolute devotion
of the legislative?" Hamilton asks, feeling that such a separation
must be merely nominal and incapable of producing the ends for
which it was established, i.e., to check a majoritarian despotism for
the sake of the individual. "It is one thing to be subordinate to the
laws, and another to be dependent on the legislative body. The first
comports with, the last violates, the fundamental principles of good
government; and, whatever may be the forms of the Constitution,
unites all power in the same hands."[85]

A further security against democratic excesses is seen in a division
of the legislature. "In the legislature, promptitude of decision is
oftener an evil than a benefit. The differences of opinion, and the
jarrings of the parties in that department . . . , though they may
sometimes obstruct plans, . . . often promote deliberation and circumspection, and serve to check excesses in the majority."[86] Hamilton sees in the division of the legislative branch a device for a more
mature legislation. The upper chamber serves as a check on the
lower, although "the most *popular* branch" will remain "a full
match, if not an overmatch, for every other member of the Government."[87]

The separation of powers need not be absolute. There may exist
"a partial intermixture" of the departments "for special purposes,"
which is, "in some cases, not only proper but necessary to the mutual

[83] "Examination of Jefferson's Message," HAMILTON'S WORKS, VIII, 290.

[84] 71, 465.

[85] 71, 465-66. In his "Examination of Jefferson's Message," Hamilton says that
the "CONCENTRATION of the powers of the different departments in the
LEGISLATIVE BODY . . . is precisely the DEFINITION OF DESPOTISM."
HAMILTON'S WORKS, VIII, 348-49.

[86] 70, 458.

[87] 66, 431-32. The necessity for Hamilton of a division of the legislature can be
concluded from 66, 431-32. When A. J. Mulford, *op. cit.*, 44-45, says that "a
single assembly . . . would be inconsistent with all the principles of good government," he overlooks the fact that Hamilton did not have in mind here the
disadvantages of a unicameral against a bicameral legislature, but the disadvantages arising from a concentration of *all* power in one assembly, as was the
case under the Articles, where Congress had legislative, executive, and judicial
functions.

defence of the several members of the government against each other."[88] Thus Hamilton considers an absolute or qualified negative in the executive upon the acts of the legislative body as indispensable[89] for the defense of the executive against the depredations of the legislature by which he might gradually be stripped of his authorities by successive revolutions or annihilated by a single vote.[90] Besides, an executive veto is "a salutary check upon the legislative body, calculated to guard the community against the effects of faction, precipitancy, or of any impulse unfriendly to the public good, which may happen to influence a majority of that body."[91] Hamilton concedes to the legislature the power of impeachment as an essential check upon the encroachments of the executive.[92]

No doubt Hamilton considers institutional power-balances as conducive to free government. In later years he extensively quoted Madison's essay fifty-one with its conspicuous emphasis on institutional power-balances.[93] Nevertheless, on reading the *Federalist,* one feels that Hamilton considers the separation of powers not so much as a device for the sake of power-balance *per se,* but rather as a means for deconcentrating power from the legislature. While advocating possibilities for a decrease of legislative power, he demonstrates the necessity of power-concentration in the executive. And whereas he thought that in the legislature, promptitude of decision is oftener an evil than a benefit,[94] he considers energy in the executive to be a leading character in the definition of good government, quite essential to the steady administration of the laws, to the protection of property, and to the security of liberty against faction.[95] In order to have an energetic or powerful executive, Hamilton wants unity,[96] duration,[97] and an adequate provision for its support.[98] Madison considered the accumulation of all powers, legislative, executive, and judicial, in the same hands to be tyranny.[99] Hamilton, on the other hand, concentrates his attack on an all-powerful legislature. For him, a concentration of power in the legislature is despotism.[100] While Madison is against a concentration of power in any department and thus opens the way for his system of power-balances, Hamilton is primarily opposed to a concentration of power

[88] 66, 429. [90] 73, 476. [92] 66, 430.
[89] 66, 429-30. [91] 73, 477.
[93] "Examination of Jefferson's Message, etc."
[94] 70, 458. [96] Essay 70. [98] Essay 73.
[95] 70, 454. [97] Essays 71 and 72. [99] 47, 313.
[100] See *supra.,* p. 158, note 85.

in the legislative body. To him, power-concentration in the executive need not result in tyranny.

4. Thus Hamilton, while recognizing the advantages of both territorial and institutional power-divisions, leaves no doubt that a concentration rather than a division of power is conducive to free government. This attitude becomes even more evident when he considers the implications of the concomitance of the internal division and the external existence of power in the state. In a federal state, this concomitance means that the government, in order to constitute a power, must possess the authority to "break the fatal charm" of "the political monster of *imperium in imperio*."[101] This amounts to the superiority of federal over state legislation and the possibility of the execution of federal law within the states. The superiority of federal law in turn implies the existence of some federal authority that can decide matters arising from the complex of federalism. Hamilton here recognizes the supremacy provision. In a state where the separation of powers is carried out, the concomitance of internal power-division and external power-existence requires the recognition of an authority that can decide upon the scope of the powers in the different departments. This authority is the judiciary with the power of judicial review.

The supremacy provision "only declares a truth, which flows immediately and necessarily from the institution of a federal government."[102] "If a number of political societies enter into a larger political society, the laws which the latter may enact, pursuant to the powers intrusted to it by its constitution, must necessarily be supreme over those societies, and the individuals of whom they are composed. It would otherwise be a mere treaty, dependent on the good faith of the parties, and not a government, which is only another word for POLITICAL POWER AND SUPREMACY."[103] Therefore, state officials have to observe federal law.[104] Since "laws are a dead letter without courts to expound and define their true meaning and operation," Hamilton, in order to prevent the states from jeopardizing the power of the federal government, wants, for the interpretation of federal law, a supreme tribunal that is instituted under the very authority which makes that law.[105] It is a *federal* supreme court that has to decide on matters arising out of

[101] 15, 89.   [103] 33, 201.   [105] 22, 138.
[102] 33, 202.   [104] 27, 169.

the federal structure of the nation,[106] and the danger of a diminution of federal power is thus reduced to a minimum.

As the supremacy provision secures power-concentration in the
federal government, judicial review secures the power of the constitution. Hamilton emphasizes that *de iure* judicial review does not
amount to a superiority of the judicial to the legislative power.[107]
Still, saying that "the interpretation of the laws is the proper and
peculiar province of the courts,"[108] and giving the courts the right to
declare legislative acts void, he *de facto* enthrones the judiciary over
the legislature. Considering the judiciary as "the citadel of the public justice and the public security,"[109] he feels that judicial independence is "an excellent barrier to the encroachments and oppressions of the representative body."[110] For the protection of the
individual, Hamilton wants the power-concentration in the legislature replaced by a power-concentration in the judiciary. The judiciary is a bulwark for the protection from "legislative encroachments" on a "limited Constitution,"[111] a constitution "which
contains certain specific exceptions to the legislative authority; such,
for instance, as that it shall pass no bills of attainder, no *ex-post-facto*
laws, and the like."[112] Judicial review thus becomes the guarantor of
free government against democratic excesses, against mobocracy.[113]
Not the voice of the people, as reflected in the legislature, is the
voice of God,[114] but that of the judges in whom the requisite knowledge is combined with the requisite integrity[115] and who, when invalidating an act of the legislature, "do their duty as faithful
guardians of the Constitution, where legislative invasions of it had
been instituted by the major voice of the community."[116]

Hamilton's opinion on the theoretical realization of free government has important implications. If free government can best be
realized in a state that, while federal, has power concentrated in the
national government, and that, while adhering to the principle of
the separation of powers, has power concentrated in the nonlegislative departments, the negation of free government in a concrete state

---

[106] Essays 22 and 80.   [109] 78, 505.   [111] 78, 508.
[107] 78, 506.   [110] 78, 503.   [112] 78, 505.
[108] 78, 506.

[113] Essay 78 is as much a treatise for the protection of the individual's rights
from democratic excesses as it is an advocacy of judicial review, a symbol of
the close relation between the two.

[114] Hamilton in the Federal Convention on June 18. HAMILTON'S WORKS, I, 401.
[115] 78, 511.   [116] 78, 509.

must mean the existence of an omnipotent legislature and the absence of a strong federal government. Conversely, the achievement of free government must mean the absence of power-concentration in the legislature and a concentration of power in the federal government. How free government is seen in Hamilton's *Federalist* as negated under the Articles and achieved under the Constitution shall now be examined.

III

1.   The situation under the Articles is depicted by Hamilton as "precarious."[117] The people of the United States have been conducted to the very brink of a precipice and are about to plunge into the abyss.[118] The country has "reached almost the last stage of national humiliation."[119] This crisis Hamilton attributes to "material imperfections in our national system" and warns that "something is necessary to be done to rescue us from impending anarchy."[120] "Let the point of extreme depression to which our national dignity and credit have sunk, let the inconveniences felt everywhere from a lax and ill administration of government, let the revolt of a part of . . . North Carolina, the late menacing disturbances in Pennsylvania, and the actual insurrections and rebellions in Massachusetts, declare—!" Hamilton complains about the existing plight.[121] Due to democratic excesses in the states, minority rights are disregarded by the majority and anarchy is impending. Owing to the shortcomings of the existing national system, the federal government, unable through its lack of power to provide for more than "a lax and ill administration," is in no position to check "domestic faction and insurrection."[122] It is unable to halt democratic insurrections occurring in the states and to prevent the tyrannic acts of the legislatures.[123]

[117] 85, 570.   [119] 15, 87.   [121] 6, 33.
[118] 15, 88.   [120] 15, 87.   [122] 9, 47.

[123] Like Madison, Hamilton considers the disadvantages of the absence of a separation of powers mainly as they exist in the states, which is not surprising in view of the fact that in a strict sense he denies the United States under the Articles the quality of a federal state with one government (15, 87), and thus precludes a separation of powers in that (nonexistent) government. There can be no doubt, however, that the problem of the states, too much democracy, is for Hamilton identical to that of the United States. The decline of "national dignity" is a consequence of "the revolt of . . . North Carolina, the insurrections . . . in Massachusetts" (6, 33). Likewise, as we shall see, the remedy for too much democracy in the states is a strong national government. When Hamil-

2. The rule of these legislatures is viewed by Hamilton with concern. Seeing them "tainted with the spirit of faction" and contaminated with "those occasional ill-humors, or temporary prejudices and propensities, which . . . beget injustice and oppressions of a part of the community,"[124] Hamilton complains of "those practices . . . of the State governments which have undermined the foundations of property and credit, have planted mutual distrust in the breasts of all classes of citizens, and have occasioned an almost universal prostration of morals."[125] Under the Articles, there exists in the states an oppressive rule of the debtors. Motivated by "momentary inclination or desire"[126] rather than by considerations of justice, they encroach upon the rights of the minority. Free government is negated because the existence of too much democracy, in which the pestilent breath of the powerful debtors' faction poisons the fountains of justice,[127] amounts to a primacy of the participation before the protection principle.

3. For lack of power, the federal government is in no position to meet this situation with effective countermeasures. Having come into existence not through "a ratification by the PEOPLE" and "having no better foundation than the consent of the several legislatures, it has been exposed to frequent and intrinsic questions concerning the validity of its powers."[128] While the ghost of an *imperium in imperio*[129] hovered over the ratification of the Articles, it became a sad reality through the Articles' "radical vice, . . . the principle of LEGISLATION for STATES or GOVERNMENTS, in their CORPORATE or COLLECTIVE CAPACITIES, and contradistinguished from the INDIVIDUALS of which they consist."[130] With the states being sovereign, national disorder, poverty, and insignificance were as natural as the reduction of the federal government to imbecility and a mimic sovereignty.[131] To Hamilton, the Confederation offered the "awful spectacle" of "a nation, without a national government."[132]

ton speaks of the "material imperfections of our national system" (singular!) (15, 87), he has the same outlook on the problem of reform as does Madison in his "Vices of the Political System of the United States."

[124] 27, 167. [126] 27, 167. [128] 22, 140-41. [130] 15, 89.
[125] 85, 568. [127] 81, 525. [129] 15, 89. [131] 15, 88.

[132] 85, 574. "We have neither troops, nor treasury, nor government" says Hamilton in 15, 87, continuing that the principle of legislation for states is "evidently incompatible with the idea of GOVERNMENT" (15, 90). Hamilton denies further that under the Articles there is a federal government, because the laws enacted by Congress have no sanction (15, 92; 21, 125-26).

For the debtors in the states, the weakness of the federal government meant clear sailing for their legislation inimical to property. "Usurpation may rear its crest in each State, and trample upon the liberties of the people, while the national government could legally do nothing more than behold its encroachments with indignation and regret. A successful faction may erect a tyranny on the ruins of order and law, while no succor could constitutionally be afforded by the Union to the friends and supporters of the government,"[133] Hamilton complains. Reminding his countrymen of Shays's Rebellion, he emphasizes that the threat of democratic insurrections is not merely speculative and that the outcome of the convulsions in Massachusetts might have been different if the malcontents had been headed by a Caesar or a Cromwell.[134]

The damage done by democratic excesses within one state is not likely to be confined to that particular state. Domestic factions may not only endanger the peace and liberty of other states,[135] but may also lead to an overthrow of free government in other states by peaceful infiltration: "Who can predict what effect a despotism, established in Massachusetts, would have upon the liberties of New Hampshire or Rhode Island, of Connecticut or New York?" Hamilton asks apprehensively.[136]

4. Seeing, like Madison, the individual's rights threatened by democratic excesses in the states, Hamilton wants free government secured through a federal guarantee of the state constitutions.[137] Unlike Madison, Hamilton fears that factions in one state may cause trouble in other states rather than being absorbed and neutralized. Therefore, his remedy against factions is less that of a territorial power-balance and more that of a concentration of power in the national government.

Since to Hamilton the federal government under the Articles is so totally deficient in power that its quality as a government can be denied altogether, he feels that there exists an absolute necessity for an entire change of the system.[138] "Let us break the fatal charm which

---

[133] 21, 126.   [135] 9, 47.

[134] 21, 127.   [136] 21, 127.

[137] Hamilton's conception of the Union as a means to an end follows specifically from 1, 6, where he speaks of "the utility of the UNION to . . . prosperity," and from 20, 124, where he calls the Union "the parent of tranquility, freedom, happiness." Of course, the quality of the Union as a mere means follows also from Hamilton's conception of government as a means.

[138] 23, 143.

has too long seduced us from the paths of felicity and prosperity,"[139] Hamilton asks his compatriots, for "the evils we experience do not proceed from minute or partial imperfections, but from fundamental errors in the structure of the building, which cannot be amended otherwise than by an alteration in the first principles and the main pillars of the fabric."[140] How far there was effected in the Constitution "an entire change" of the "radically vicious and unsound" system of the Articles of Confederation[141] shall now be seen.

IV

1. Free government being an ideal, Hamilton concedes that the plan of the Convention is a compound as much of the errors and prejudices, as of the sense and wisdom, of the delegates, a compromise of many dissimilar interests and inclinations. It has no claim to absolute perfection.[142] Not expecting "to see a perfect work from imperfect man," Hamilton has praise for the Constitution. The system it establishes, "though it may not be perfect in every part, is, on the whole, a good one; it is the best that present views and circumstances of the country will permit."[143]

The "entire change"[144] that was effected by the Constitution consists in the creation of the Union. Not being ratified, as were the Articles, merely by the "several legislatures,"[145] but "by the PEOPLE" of America, irrespective of state boundaries,[146] the Constitution transforms a league under international law into a nation. More specifically, the radical alterations of the Articles of Confederation mean to Hamilton the grant of "new and extensive powers . . . to the national head, and . . . a different organization of the federal government—a single body being an unsafe depository of such ample authorities."[147] The Constitution, while concentrating power in the federal head as a remedy against democratic tyranny in the states,

---

[139] 15, 88-89.

[140] 15, 89.

[141] 22, 104.

[142] 85, 570-71.

[143] 85, 570. See also 68, 441. It is interesting to note Hamilton's opinion on the Constitution at a later date, when on Feb. 7, 1802, he wrote to Gouverneur Morris: "Mine is an odd destiny. Perhaps no man . . . has sacrificed or done more for the present Constitution than myself; and contrary to all anticipations of its fate, as you know from the very beginning, I am still laboring to prop the frail and worthless fabric." HAMILTON'S WORKS, x, 425.

[144] 22, 140; 23, 143.

[145] 21, 125; 22, 140-41.

[146] 22, 140.

[147] 84, 564.

diminishes the probability of too much democracy on the national level by taking power away from Congress. The achievement of free government in the Constitution thus boils down to a restriction of popular government in favor of the protection of the individual's rights. It is brought about mainly by two factors: the creation of a stronger national government and the dethronement of an all-powerful legislature.

Calling the principle of legislation for states, as recognized by the Articles, "the parent of anarchy,"[148] Hamilton considers a concentration of power in the national government as starting with the extension of the laws of the federal government to the individual citizens of America.[149] If the federal government can act directly upon individuals, the *status quo ante* of an *imperium in imperio* is abolished, since a state whose citizens are subject to another state's jurisdiction does not exercise *imperium*. The question as to the relation between the Union and the states is thus only one of the *degree* of consolidation, and its answer depends upon the extent of the powers that are granted to the federal government. Although Hamilton denies that under the Constitution there would be an entire consolidation of the states into one complete national sovereignty and gives the assurance that the plan of the Convention aims only at a partial consolidation,[150] the fact remains that, due to extensive grants of power to the national government, a consolidation exists to a high degree.

Hamilton's assurance that the state governments retain all the

---

[148] 16, 95. If in addition to this quotation one takes into account Hamilton's opinion that, in a strict sense, there existed no government of the Confederation, it admits of no doubt that Hamilton considered the states under the Articles as being in a state of nature, or anarchy. When on June 12, 1787, he said in the Federal Convention that he denied the doctrine that the states were thrown into a state of nature and admitted that the states met now on an equal footing, he can have meant only that *within each state* there did not exist a state of nature. This, however, does not preclude the existence of such a state *among* the different commonwealths, i.e., a living together under (anarchic) international law.

[149] 23, 143. More elaborately, Hamilton says in 15, 91: "If we still adhere to the design of a national government, or, what is the same thing, of a super-intending power, . . . we must resolve to incorporate into our plan those ingredients which may be considered as forming the characteristic difference between a league and a government; we must extend the authority of the Union to the persons of the citizens—the only proper objects of government." Whether he speaks of "the laws of the federal government" (23, 143) or of "the authority of the Union" (15, 91), it amounts to the same thing.

[150] 32, 194.

rights of sovereignty that they had before, and that were not exclusively delegated to the United States,[151] is a mere truism. If the
states retain the powers not delegated, then the Union has *all* the
powers that were given to it. In spite of his recognizing residuary
powers in the states,[152] Hamilton emphasizes the high degree of
power-concentration in the national government. He becomes the
advocate of national power. Asserting his power doctrine, Hamilton
stresses that if the national government possesses a certain power,
this power is absolute and may be exercised with utmost rigor: "It
is both unwise and dangerous to deny the federal government an
unconfined authority, as to all those objects which are intrusted to
its management."[153] We shall now consider the powers Hamilton
wants to be invested in the national government. In this consideration we shall always keep in mind that, since the Union is regarded
by Hamilton as a remedy against democratic excesses in the states,
any grant of power to the national government can be viewed as a
grant for the achievement of free government.

2. The principal purposes of the Union are such things as the
common defense, the preservation of public peace against internal
convulsions, and the regulation of commerce.[154] The powers necessary to meet other exigencies of the Union are thus closely connected
with those more immediately concerned with the control of too
much democracy. From among the latter, the power of taxation
appears to be especially relevant. Hamilton's comments on it reflect
the leitmotiv of power-concentration.[155] The lack of a national taxing power under the Articles is held responsible for the fact that the
government of the Union has gradually dwindled into a state of
decay, approaching nearly to annihilation, and a strong federal
taxing power is considered as being conducive to the happiness of
the people.[156] Seeing in money the "vital principle of the body
politic . . . which sustains its life and motion, and enables it to
perform its most essential functions," the author of the Report on

---

[151] 32, 194. "This exclusive delegation, or rather this alienation, of State sovereignty," he continues, "would only exist in three cases: where the Constitution
in express terms granted an exclusive authority to the Union; where it granted
in one instance an authority to the Union, and in another prohibited the States
from exercizing the like authority; and where it granted an authority to the
Union, to which a similar authority in the States would be absolutely and totally
contradictory and *repugnant*." For a similar point of view, see 82, 534-35.

[152] See essay 23; 17, 103. [154] 23, 142. [156] 30, 183.

[153] 23, 145. [155] Essays 30 to 36.

Manufactures and advocate of a National Bank holds that a complete power to procure an adequate supply of money may be regarded as an indispensable ingredient in every constitution.[157] The federal government must, with regard to taxation, have the power to achieve its object, namely, public justice and credit.[158] It must be able to exercise its taxing power free from any control by the state governments, and only give regard "to the public good and the sense of the people."[159] Independence from the states will give to the national government "energy and stability, dignity or credit, confidence at home and respectability abroad," and enable it to fulfill "the purposes of its institution . . . , the public happiness."[160]

Hamilton could have stated the purpose of power-delegation to the federal government in no clearer language. Power is concentrated in the Union in order that there may be an energetic and stable government that can provide for the individual's happiness by checking democratic excesses in the states. Hamilton pronounces this doctrine of *happiness through national power* in an even more direct language. Referring to the democratic convulsions in Pennsylvania and Massachusetts, he warns that a restriction of national power with respect to the establishment of an army in time of peace is not advisable, because an army is essential to the security of the society from internal convulsions.[161] Hamilton trusts that "the citizens of America have too much discernment to be argued into anarchy" and that experience has wrought a deep and solemn conviction in the public mind that greater energy in government is essential to the welfare and prosperity of the community."[162] He maintains that it is better to hazard the abuse of power by the government than to embarrass the government and endanger the public safety by impolitic restrictions on the legislative authority of the nation.[163]

In view of Hamilton's assertion of national power with respect to the enumerated subjects, it is not surprising that in contradistinction to Madison[164] he sees in the necessary and proper clause and in

[157] 30, 182.   [159] 31, 190.   [161] 25, 157-58.
[158] 30, 184-85.   [160] 30, 186.   [162] 26, 160.

[163] 26, 159. Hamilton expresses his doctrine of *happiness through national power* clearly in 26, 159, where he speaks of "the happy mean which marks the salutary boundary between POWER and PRIVILEGE, and combines the energy of government with the security of private rights."

[164] Speaking of the necessary and proper clause, Madison says that "without the *substance* of this power, the whole Constitution would be a dead letter"

the supremacy clause nothing but declaratory norms. "The constitutional operation of the intended government would be precisely the same, if these clauses were entirely obliterated, as if they were repeated in every article. They are only declaratory of a truth which would have resulted by necessary and unavoidable implication from the very act of constituting a federal government, and vesting it with certain specified powers."[165] The necessary and proper clause, "though it may be chargeable with tautology or redundancy, is at least perfectly harmless."[166] It was written into the Constitution only because the Convention foresaw the tendency of the state governments to sap the foundations of the Union and did not want, with respect to so cardinal a point as that of national power, to leave anything to construction.[167] The supremacy clause is "a truth which flows immediately and necessarily from the institution of federal government."[168] Since "a LAW, by the very meaning of the term, includes supremacy," the laws that the national government may enact "pursuant to the powers intrusted to it by its constitution must necessarily be supreme" over the states and individuals.[169]

In view of Hamilton's strong assertion of national power it would be wrong to suppose that he favors an absolute absorption of the

(44, 292); without the supremacy clause, the Constitution would "have been evidently and radically defective" (44, 295).

[165] 33, 199.   [166] 33, 200.

[167] 33, 200. Hamilton's conception of the clause can be seen in two interpretations, both of which contain strong assertions of national power. On the one hand, one may argue that if the power to pass all laws necessary and proper, etc., is included in each specific power of the federal government, even if there was no necessary and proper clause, this must be even more the case if there is such a clause. The clause would then become an ingredient part of each specific power-grant to the federal government. On the other hand, one may simply state that the clause contains a re-assertion of powers that have already been asserted in the enumerated *leges speciales*. It would then have the quality of a reminder of (existing) national power. In both cases the clause does not lose its merely declaratory character. It is interesting to note that another advocate of national power, Marshall, accepted in McCulloch v. Maryland, Madison's rather than Hamilton's conception of the clause by considering it as constitutive and not as declaratory. Had Marshall considered the clause as merely declaratory, he could have made an even stronger argument for national power.

[168] 33, 202.

[169] 33, 201. Connected with Hamilton's rather Austinian conception of law, this quotation boils down to the proposition "national law through national power," which means nothing else than "justice through national power" or "happiness through national power." For the connection for Hamilton between law, justice, and happiness, see *supra,* pp. 141 ff.

states by the Union. Emphasizing again and again the competences of the state governments,[170] he leaves no doubt that "if the federal government should overpass the just boundaries of its authority and make tyrannical use of its powers, the people, whose creature it is, must appeal to the standard they have formed [in the federal pact] and take such measures to redress the injury done to the Constitution."[171] In spite of all his recognition of state power, unavoidable for an advocate of a federal state, there can, however, be no doubt that Hamilton is above all an advocate of national power. The passage just quoted further precludes us from thinking that Hamilton's advocacy of federal power as a remedy against too much democracy makes him an opponent to popular government as such. A believer in free government, Hamilton is opposed to democracy only in so far as it impinges on the freedom of the individual. He is happy that the Constitution will rest "on the solid basis of the CONSENT OF THE PEOPLE," that "the streams of national power . . . flow immediately from that pure, original fountain of all legitimate authority."[172] He praises "the conformity of the proposed Constitution to the true principles of republican government"[173] because it provides for the exercise of the national legislative power by the representatives of the people and for an election of the executive and other officials by the people.[174] Furthermore, and this shows that Hamilton had no leanings toward monarchy or aristocracy, he praises the Constitution for containing that "cornerstone of republican government,"[175] namely, a prohibition of titles of nobility. When Hamilton further calls the people the natural guardians of the Constitution[176] and admits their right to amend or abolish that law by some solemn and authoritative act,[177] he clearly states his belief in popular government.

3. The control of democratic excesses in the states through the

---

[170] For instance, in 17, 103; 26, 163; 27, 169; 28, 174; 31, 191; 32, 193; 32, 194; 33, 202; 34, 208; 59, 386; 81, 530; 82, 535; 84, 562.

[171] 33, 200.   [172] 22, 141.   [173] 1, 6.

[174] Essays 68, 76, 77, 78. In his "Brief of Argument on the Constitution," written in 1788, Hamilton says that the United States under the Constitution is "*a representative democracy*. 1. House of representatives directly chosen by the people. . . . 2. Senate indirectly chosen by them. . . . 3. President indirectly chosen by them. . . . Thus legislative and executive representatives of the people. 4. Judicial power, representatives of the people indirectly chosen. . . . 5. All officers indirect choice of the people." HAMILTON'S WORKS, II, 92-93.

[175] 84, 557.   [176] 16, 100.   [177] 78, 509.

national government[178] does not necessarily preclude such excesses on the national level. Hamilton is careful to stress that the Federal Convention has taken precaution against danger from that end. The Constitution, while concentrating power in the nation, deconcentrates power from the national department most liable to democratic excesses, namely, Congress. Two other departments are made powerful instead, the Supreme Court and the president.

With a view toward creating a judiciary that would constitute a balance against Congress, the Convention provided for the independence of the courts from Congress. Hamilton opposes vesting supreme judicial power in a branch of the legislative body because this would verge upon a violation of that "excellent rule," the separation of powers.[179] Besides, due to the propensity of legislative bodies to party division, there is "reason to fear that the pestilent breath of faction may poison the fountains of justice."[180] Hamilton therefore praises the Constitution for establishing courts that are separated from Congress. He is pleased to note that to this organizational independence there is added a financial one.[181]

Another factor contributing to the independence of the judiciary is the judges' right to hold office during good behavior. It is in connection with his advocacy of that "excellent barrier to the encroachments and oppressions of the representative body,"[182] that "citadel of the public justice,"[183] that Hamilton pronounces judicial review as being part of the Constitution. Judicial review is another barrier against too much democracy. Exercised by state courts before the Federal Convention met,[184] and taken for granted by the majority of the members of the Convention,[185] as well as by the ratifying con-

[178] For Hamilton, "the control of democratic excesses" is nearly identical to "the control of faction," i.e., the control of an overbearing majority. He considers the Union as a remedy against "domestic faction and convulsions" (6, 27), a "barrier against domestic faction and insurrection" (9, 47). Also 85, 568.

[179] 81, 524.   [181] Essay 79.   [183] 78, 505.

[180] 81, 525.   [182] 78, 503.

[184] For precedents of judicial review, see Corwin, THE DOCTRINE OF JUDICIAL REVIEW (1914), 71-75.

[185] Definitely asserting a right of judicial review in the Federal Convention were: Gerry and King of Massachusetts; Wilson and Gouverneur Morris of Pennsylvania; Martin of Maryland; Madison and Mason of Virginia; Dickinson of Delaware; Rutledge and Charles Pinckney of South Carolina; Williamson of North Carolina; Sherman of Connecticut. See Farrand, RECORDS, I, 97 (Gerry), 100 (King); II, 73 (Wilson), 76 (Martin), 78 (Mason), 299 (Dickinson and Morris), 428 (Rutledge), 248 (Pinckney), 376 (Williamson), 28 (Sherman), 93 (Madison); III, 220 (Martin)

ventions in the states,[186] judicial review is expounded by Hamilton as a doctrine.[187] What Corwin calls the progress of constitutional theory between the Declaration of Independence and the meeting of the Philadelphia Convention[188] reaches climax and conclusion in essay seventy-eight of the *Federalist*.

Starting out from the premise that "a constitution is, in fact, and must be regarded by the judges, as a fundamental law"[189] (we may assume that he means a constitution providing for free government[190]), Hamilton considers judicial review as a means of preserving that constitution and, thereby, free government. To be more concrete, when Hamilton considers the judiciary both as a barrier to the encroachments and oppressions of the representative body and as the citadel of public justice, i.e., the citadel for the protection of the individual's life, liberty, and property, he states that judicial review means a curb on the legislature's encroachments upon individual rights. Parallel to every denial of legislative power in essay seventy-eight goes an assertion of vested rights.[191]

[186] Judicial review was dealt with in the Pennsylvania convention by Wilson, in Elliot, *op. cit.*, II, 417, 454; in the New York convention by Ellsworth, *ibid.*, II, 336-37; in the North Carolina convention that did not ratify, *ibid.*, IV, 87, 93, 94, 152, 165, 167, 192; in Massachusetts, Samuel Adams referred to judicial review, *ibid.*, II, 142, and so did other speakers, *ibid.*, II, 97-98, 100-106, 110-11, 113-18, 154, 167, 171-74. In the Virginia convention judicial review was alluded to by Henry, Randolph, Pendleton, Nicholas, Mason, Madison, Marshall, Granger. *Ibid.*, III, 182, 309; 197, 208, 431; 287, 498; 409; 441; 484-85; 503; 514. For the opinion that the courts under the Constitution could not declare an act of Congress void, see *ibid.*, I, 545; II, 314-15, 318, 321-22; IV, 175.

[187] 78, 505.

[188] AMERICAN HISTORICAL REVIEW (1924-25), XXX, 511 ff.

[189] 78, 506.

[190] This assumption is justified by Hamilton's theory according to which individuals, when leaving the state of nature, conclude the constitutional compact in order to be protected in their rights by a government in which they may participate, i.e., in order to live in a free government. On the other hand, it follows from essay 78.

[191] Essay 78. As if he wanted to leave no doubt about the fact that judicial review means to him mainly a means for the preservation of the primacy of the protection principle before the participation principle (free government), Hamilton, whenever he speaks of the necessity of independent courts and judicial review, is careful to mention both the restriction of the legislature and the ensuing protection of individual rights closely together, in order to keep the reader aware of the fact that he wants the legislature restricted by the judiciary for the protection of vested rights. In 78, 505, he says, for instance, in one paragraph: "Independence of the courts is . . . essential in a limited Constitution . . . which contains certain specified exceptions to the legislative authority; such . . .

Hamilton's statement that the power of the courts to prevent encroachments upon individual rights *de lege ferenda* and *de lege lata*[192] does not mean that the judiciary is superior to the legislature, because "the power of the people is superior to both,"[193] can only to a superficial reader appear as a denial of a superiority of the courts over Congress. Of course, it says that both judiciary and legislature are inferior to the people. This, however, by no means implies that the judiciary may not be superior to the legislature or vice versa. Hamilton leaves no doubt that the courts are superior to Congress when he confers upon them the status of an "intermediate body between the people and the legislature" with the function "to keep the latter within the limits assigned to their authority."[194] If the people are superior to the legislature, and the courts stand between the people and the legislature, the courts must be as superior to the legislature as they are inferior to the people. Without that superiority, they would be in no position to keep the legislative body within the limits of legislative jurisdiction. In essay seventy-eight, Hamilton enthrones the courts over Congress. His statement that the judiciary is, beyond comparison, the weakest of the three departments of power[195] has only the purpose of lulling the suspicions of the democratic element against the conservative judges. It does not

as that it shall pass no bills of attainder, no *ex-post-facto* laws and the like. Limitations of this kind can be preserved in practice only through the medium of the courts of justice, whose duty it must be to declare all acts contrary to the . . . Constitution void. Without this, all the reservations of particular rights or privileges would amount to nothing." Similarly, he says in another passage that the "independence of the judges is . . . requisite to guard the Constitution and the rights of individuals from the effects of those ill humors which . . . have a tendency . . . to occasion . . . serious oppressions of the minor party" (78, 508). In 78, 509 Hamilton calls the judges the "faithful guardians of the Constitution" against "legislative invasions of it, . . . instigated by the major voice of the community." Since he speaks of a constitution providing for the protection of the individual's rights, the concomitance of legislative restrictions and the protection of individual rights is evident. So it is a few lines below, when Hamilton calls "the independence of the judges . . . an essential safeguard against . . . the injury of the private rights of particular classes of citizens by unjust and partial laws" (78, 509). In a clear polemic against too much democracy in the state legislatures, Hamilton says that "the benefits of the integrity and moderation of the judiciary have already been felt in more States than one; and though they may have displeased those whose sinister expectations they may have disappointed, they must have commanded the esteem and applause of all the virtuous and disinterested."

[192] 78, 509.   [194] 78, 506.   [195] 78, 504.
[193] 78, 506.

detract from the powerful position the judiciary has under the Constitution.

Although he considers a power-concentration in the legislature as despotism, Hamilton does not perceive a strong judiciary as a threat to free government. He admits that individual oppression may now and then proceed from the courts, but he is emphatic in adding that the general liberty of the people can never be endangered from that quarter.[196] With the judges who unite integrity with knowledge,[197] power is in good hands. As the "bulwarks of a limited Constitution against legislative encroachments,"[198] they will use that power for the protection of the individual's rights rather than for infringements upon those rights.

Through judicial review vested rights are protected not only from the legislature. They are also protected from the executive. An executive act that is sanctioned by the courts and—since it is the duty of the judges to declare void legislative acts contrary to the Constitution[199]—that is thus in conformity with the will of the people as laid down in the Constitution, cannot be an act of oppression. Consequently, a power-concentration in the executive is not likely to do harm to the protection of individual rights. On the contrary, it is conducive to free government. Considering an energetic executive a prerequisite for good government, a steady administration of the laws, the protection of property, and the security of liberty,[200] Hamilton praises the Constitution for creating a powerful executive by providing for its unity,[201] duration,[202] and adequate support,[203] and by fitting it out with extensive powers.[204]

4.   In conclusion it may be said that the Constitution creates free government by providing, while fundamentally accepting popular government, for a remedy as well as for a preventive against democratic excesses. That remedy is supplied by a concentration of power in the national government. While accepting the federal character of the new system, the Constitution eliminates the *imperium in imperio.* The preventive against democratic excesses consists in a deconcentration of power from Congress, by giving the courts the power of judicial review and by making the executive strong. The concomitance of a territorial concentration of power in the national

[196] 78, 504.   [199] 78, 509.   [202] Essays 71 and 72.
[197] 78, 511.   [200] 70, 454.   [203] Essay 73.
[198] 78, 508.   [201] Essay 70.   [204] Essays 74 through 77.

government and, as it is, mainly in the legislature, and the institutional deconcentration of power from that department are by no means contradictory. Too much democracy, being abolished in the states through a concentration of power in the national legislature, is prevented from occurring on the national level by restraining Congress from becoming oppressive, through the institution of judicial review.[205]

[205] When Corwin, THE DOCTRINE OF JUDICIAL REVIEW, 66, says that those who denied the power of judicial review under the Constitution, on the grounds that the necessary and proper clause rendered the power of Congress practically unlimited, could base their claim especially on Hamilton's essay 33, he creates the impression that what Hamilton says in that essay is in contradiction to what he says in essay 78. This is far from being the case. Essay 33, containing a strong assertion of national legislative power (as a remedy against democratic excesses in the states), and essay 78, containing proof of the necessity of restricting Congress (in order to prevent democratic excesses on the national level), are, if viewed as advocating features of the new Constitution that are conducive to free government, absolutely in harmony with each other. Both being written from an identical motive, namely, distrust of absolute democracy, they are advocating what for Hamilton are the two main features of the Constitution securing free government, namely, national power and judicial review.

CHAPTER SEVEN

The Federalist on Peace

I

1. The *Federalist* denies, on the whole, the possibility of peace among nations.[1] Under neighborly conditions, the probability of tensions increases. Experience teaches that peace among independent neighboring states cannot be expected, since neighborhood makes nations natural enemies.[2] Men are ambitious and grasping[3] and so are nations.[4] The first thing to be considered shall be the opinion of the *Federalist* on the threats to peace from individual behavior.

Peace is endangered by monarchs. Jay regrets that such rulers "will often make war when their nations are to get nothing by it, but for purposes and objects merely personal, such as a thirst for military glory, revenge for personal affronts, ambition, or private compacts to aggrandize or support their particular families or partisans."[5] Hamilton complains that animosities can take their origin entirely in private passions, in the attachments, enmities, interests, hopes and fears of leading individuals. "Men of this class," he feels, "whether the favorites of a king or of a people, have in too many instances abused the confidence they possessed; and assuming the pretext of some public motive, have not scrupled to sacrifice the

---

[1] Compare 34, 206. [3] 6, 27. [5] 4, 18. Compare also 5, 26.
[2] 6, 27; 6, 33; 8, 41. [4] 6, 27 ff.

177

national tranquility to personal advantage or personal gratifica-
tion."[6] Thus Pericles, in compliance with the resentment of a prosti-
tute, at the expense of much of the blood and treasure of his countrymen, attacked, vanquished, and destroyed the city of the Samnians.
The same man, stimulated by private pique against the Megaren-
sians, or to avoid a prosecution with which he was threatened as an
accomplice in a supposed theft of the statue of Phidias, or to get
rid of the accusations prepared to be brought against him for dis-
sipating the funds of the state in the purchase of popularity, was
the primitive author of the Peloponnesian War.[7] Cardinal Wolsey,
permitted by his vanity to aspire to the papacy, in order to secure
the favor of Charles V, precipitated England into a war with France,
contrary to the plainest dictates of policy, and at the hazard of the
safety and independence of England and of Europe in general.[8] After
pointing out the disastrous role played by Madame Maintenon, the
Duchess of Marlborough, and Madame Pompadour in European
tensions, Hamilton remarks that "to multiply examples of the agency
of personal considerations in the production of great national events,
either foreign or domestic, . . . would be an unnecessary waste of time.
Those who have but a superficial acquaintance with the sources from
which they are to be drawn, will themselves recollect a variety of instances; and those who have a tolerable knowledge of human nature
will not stand in need of such lights, to form their opinion either of
the reality or extent of that agency."[9]

International tensions do not only derive from the behavior of
individuals. Just as the authors point out the dangers to individual
freedom from majority rule, they show the threat to peace from
popular actions. "It is too true," remarks Jay, "however disgraceful
it may be to human nature, that nations in general will make war
whenever they have a prospect of getting any thing by it."[10] Hamilton stresses causes of hostility that have a general and almost constant operation upon the collective bodies of society, such as love of
power, the desire of equality and safety,[11] and competition of commerce between commercial nations.[12]

This dangerous disposition of the people exists under a republican
form of government as much as under a monarchy. Hamilton takes
issue with those "visionary and designing men" who, against all

[6] 6, 28.   [9] 6, 29.   [11] 6, 27.
[7] 6, 28.   [10] 4, 18.   [12] 6, 30.
[8] 6, 28-29.

experience, claim that the genius of republican government is pacific, because the spirit of commerce has a tendency to soften the manners of men and to extinguish those inflammable humors that have so often kindled wars.[13] The argument that commercial republics will never be disposed to waste themselves in ruinous contentions with each other, since they will be governed by a spirit of mutual amity and concord, is encountered by Hamilton in an emphatic manner. "Is it not . . . the true interest of all nations to cultivate the same benevolent and philosophic spirit?" he asks, continuing,

> if this be their true interest, have they in fact pursued it? Has it not, on the contrary, invariably been found that momentary passions, and immediate interests, have a more active and imperious control over human conduct than general or remote considerations of policy, utility, or justice? Have republics in practice been less addicted to war than monarchies? Are not the former administered by *men* as well as the latter? Are there not aversions, predilections, rivalships, and desires of unjust acquisitions, that affect nations as well as kings? Are not popular assemblies frequently subject to the impulse of rage, resentment, jealousy, avarice, and of other irregular and violent propensities? Is it not well known that their determinations are often governed by a few individuals in whom they place confidence, and are, of course, liable to be tinctured by the passions and views of those individuals? Has commerce hitherto done any thing more than change the objects of war? Is not the love of wealth as domineering and enterprising a passion as that of power or glory? Have there not been as many wars founded upon commercial motives since that has become the prevailing system of nations, as were before occasioned by the cupidity of territory or dominion? Has not the spirit of commerce, in many instances, administered new incentives to the appetite, both for the one and for the other?[14]

In support of his argument Hamilton mentions the experience of Sparta, Athens, Rome, and Carthage, saying that these republics were as often involved in wars as their monarchical neighbors. Venice and the Dutch Provinces are given as further examples.[15] As to England, where "the representatives of the people compose one branch of the national legislature," where "commerce has been for ages the predominant pursuit," Hamilton states that "few nations, nevertheless, have been more frequently engaged in war; and the wars in which that kingdom has been engaged have, in numerous instances, proceeded from the people."[16] He arrives at the conclusion

[13] 6, 29-30. [15] 6, 30-31. [16] 6, 31.
[14] 6, 30.

that there have been almost as many popular as royal wars[17] and
states that "the cries of the nation and the importunities of their
representatives have, upon various occasions, dragged their monarchs
into war, or continued them in it, contrary to their inclinations, and
sometimes contrary to the real interests of the state."[18]

2. On the whole it can be said that the authors' skepticism concerning individual freedom under popular government is matched
by their apprehension of popular threats to international peace. The
republican form of government and commercial interests are by no
means a safeguard against international hostilities. War among
independent sovereign states is considered natural, especially in the
case of neighboring nations. This raises the question whether the
danger of war decreases among sovereign members of a confederation.

II

1. The authors admit that through confederation, the member
states decrease the probability of future tensions among themselves.[19]
Still, the existence of a genuine harmony is questioned. This is not
surprising in view of the fact that within a confederation, sovereign
states are neighbors. Thus the *Federalist* admits on the whole the
possibility of wars among confederated states. History is used to
support this thesis.[20] In the Amphictyonic league,[21] peace did hardly
exist because the more powerful members tyrannized successively
over all the rest.[22] In the end, the smaller states, although theoretically possessing equal rights, were reduced to mere satellites.[23] The
Achaean league[24] was destroyed not only by Macedon, but by the
usurpations of its different members. After its re-establishment, it
was again weakened through internal feuds.[25] The old feudal systems
were plagued by a similar disunity.[26] Between the eleventh and
fifteenth centuries, Germany had "many of the important features
of a confederacy,"[27] but was the scene of furious wars between the

[17] 6, 31.   [19] 6, 33.   [20] Essays 18, 19, 20.
[18] 6, 31.
[21] Compare Madison's essay "Of Ancient & Modern Confederacies," MADISON'S
WRITINGS, II, 371-73.
[22] 18, 108. Compare also 43, 383.   [23] 18, 108.
[24] Compare "Of Ancient & Modern Confederacies," MADISON'S WRITINGS, II, 373-74.
[25] 18, 111.   [26] 17, 104.   [27] 19, 114.

different princes and states.[28] Later, the German "confederacy" saw many wars among the princes and the states, and the German annals are crowded with the bloody pages that describe them.[29] The situation in the United Netherlands was characterized by disunity among the various provinces.[30]

This pessimistic picture raises the question as to the causes of the tensions among sovereign members of confederacies. It should first be stressed that the form of government is considered rather irrelevant. Tensions existed in the most different types of confederacies, be it the Greek leagues, which were composed of republics, the United Netherlands, a confederation of aristocratic republics, or the German empire, which included monarchies, bishoprics, and republics.[31] Their causes are identical to those applying to states that are absolutely independent, namely, greed, the quest for glory and conquest, etc. The *Federalist* brands the ambition and jealousy of the more powerful members of the Amphictyonic council,[32] the corruption of their statesmen,[33] their mutual jealousies, fears, hatreds, and injuries that resulted in the Peloponnesian War.[34] Likewise, complaint is made about the oppression of the weak states by the strong, the jealousies, pride, separate views, and clashing pretensions of sovereign bodies within the German empire.[35] In the union of Utrecht, the jealousy among the provinces is said to have prevented harmony among the confederated states.[36] This description of older confederacies and their problems again demonstrates that tensions among the members of the confederacies are a consequence of individual as well as popular behavior. Since this behavior derives from the weakness of man and since human nature cannot be changed,[37] it is suggested that matters could be improved by a better organization of the structure of federal government. A discussion of various federal systems and their problems is used to support that suggestion.

2.   The feudal order is considered a most primitive form of con-

---

[28] 19, 113. Compare also 80, 517.   [29] 19, 115-16.   [30] 20, 121; 20, 124.

[31] On the other hand, it is admitted that a similar form of government of the member states is likely to reduce the possibility of tensions (43, 282).

[32] 18, 108.   [34] 18, 108.   [36] 20, 121.

[33] 18, 107.   [35] 19, 115-16.

[37] While the *Federalist* is often stressing the shortcomings of human nature, the whole work does not contain a suggestion on how human nature itself can be improved, but restricts itself to a discussion of how the consequences of human shortcomings can be checked. Compare, in this connection, B. F. Wright, *op. cit.*, 3; Alpheus T. Mason, "The Federalist—A Split Personality," *loc. cit.*, 625.

federation. While Hamilton admits that "the ancient feudal systems were not, strictly speaking, confederacies," he maintains that "they partook of the nature of that species of association."[38] There was a common head, or sovereign, whose authority extended over the whole nation, and a number of subordinate vassals, or feudatories, who had large portions of land allotted to them, and numerous trains of inferior vassals, who cultivated land upon the tenure of fealty or obedience to the persons whose land they occupied. Each principal vassal was "a kind of sovereign" within his particular demesnes. The consequences of this situation were a continual opposition to the authority of the sovereign and frequent wars between the great feudatories themselves. The power of the head of the nation was commonly too weak, either to preserve the public peace or to protect the people against the oppressions of their immediate lords.[39] Only seldom was the sovereign a man of ability who could command the obedience of his vassals. On the whole, the power of the barons triumphed over that of the prince.[40] In many instances his dominion was entirely thrown off, and the great fiefs were erected into independent principalities or states.[41] Due to the great power and the sovereignty of the vassals, the feudal order was largely one of anarchy.[42]

The *Federalist* maintains that the various governments in a confederation could be compared to the feudal baronies.[43] The weaknesses of various confederations are pointed out and the reasons for disunity in them are given. As in the case of the feudal system, the independence of the member states is generally regarded as the cause of tensions, leading to the final destruction of the confederation.[44]

First, the *Federalist* deals with classic confederations like the Amphictyonic and Achaean leagues. The former was a confederacy of sovereign republics, each of which had an equal vote in the federal council[45] and equal rights, irrespective of power and extension.[46] The Amphictyonic council possessed general jurisdiction over all matters concerning the confederacy and could "propose and resolve whatever it judged necessary for the common welfare of

[38] 17, 104.

[39] Here again is pointed out the different function of federalism. Compare *supra*, pp. 35-36, 37-38.

[40] 17, 104; 45, 300.   [42] 17, 104-5.   [43] 17, 105.
[41] 17, 104.

Greece."[47] Aside from the right to make war and to admit new members, it had an important function for the preservation of peace among the states: It could decide controversies between the members, and had authority to fine the guilty state and to make use of the federal forces against rebellious member states. Also, the Amphictyons as the guardians of religion and the temple of Delphos had jurisdiction over controversies between the inhabitants and those who came to consult the oracle. As a further guarantee for peace, the Amphictyons took an oath mutually to defend and protect the united cities, to punish the violators of this oath, and to inflict vengeance on sacrilegious despoilers of the temple.[48] According to the *Federalist*, "this apparatus of powers seems amply sufficient for all general purposes" of the confederacy.[49]

However, the practice was different. It hardly reflected the theoretical power relation between the federation and its members. The functions of the council were not actually administered by an independent federal organ, since its members were not elected by the people of Greece, but appointd by the various states. This of necessity weakened the government of the confederacy. Furthermore, the laws of the council were not directly binding upon individuals, but only upon the various governments. The administration of federal policy was thus left to the member states. This meant a further strengthening of the members and a weakening of the confederate government. The right of the council to supervise state measures and to make the states adhere to federal law was, in view of the strong position of the states, of no great practical importance. Consequently, the confederacy was characterized by weakness and disorders, which finally brought about its fall. The more powerful members, instead of being kept in awe and subordination, tyrannized successively over all the rest, and it often happened that the deputies of the more powerful cities awed and corrupted their colleagues from the smaller cities and thus brought about decisions favoring their own interests.[50] Foreign powers promoted disunity among the member states. Times of peace were characterized by

[44] Hamilton had already in 1780 discussed the weaknesses of other federations, in his letter to James Duane of Sept. 3. HAMILTON'S WORKS, I, 213 ff. Later, this was done in greater detail by Madison. "Of Ancient & Modern Confederacies," MADISON'S WRITINGS, II, 369 ff.

[45] 18, 106.   [47] 18, 106.   [49] 18, 107.

[46] 18, 108.   [48] 18, 106-7.   [50] 18, 107.

"domestic vicissitudes, convulsions, and carnage."[51] Even in the midst of defensive and dangerous wars, the members never acted in concert and were eternally the dupes or hirelings of the common enemy.[52]

This continuous disunity resulted in the destruction of the league. Since the *Federalist* maintains that a confederacy with a weak central government would always be agitated by internal dissensions which could never fail to bring on fresh calamities from abroad,[53] the end of the Amphictyonic league appears to be quite natural. When the council imposed a fine upon the Phocians for having ploughed up some consecrated ground belonging to the temple of Apollo, the Phocians, being abetted by Athens and Sparta, refused to submit to the degree. Thereupon, Thebes and other cities undertook to maintain the authority of the Amphictyons. But, being the weaker party, they invited the assistance of Philip of Macedon. The latter, who had secretly fostered the contest, "gladly seized the opportunity of executing the designs he had long planned against the liberties of Greece. By his intrigues and bribes he won over to his interests the popular leaders of several cities; by their influence and votes, gained admission into the Amphictyonic council; and by his arts and arms, made himself master of the confederacy."[54]

The Achaean league met with a similar fate in spite of the fact that its organization was superior to that of its Amphictyonic counterpart because of the greater intimacy of the union. It also was composed of Greek republics.[55] The cities composing the league retained their municipal jurisdiction and appointed their own officers. All cities enjoyed perfect equality and were represented in a senate. Aside from having jurisdiction over foreign relations, the senate appointed the chief magistrate or praetor, who commanded the armies of the confederacy. With the advice and consent of ten of the senators, the praetor administered the government during the recess of the senate. Also, he had a share in the deliberations of the senate, when assembled.[56] We miss a remark on the power of the confederacy to secure peace among its members. This is probably due to the fact that only imperfect monuments remain of "this curious political fabric," especially of its "interior structure and regular operation." The authors maintain that the Achaean league could cast more light on the "science of federal government" than similar experiments.[57]

[51] 18, 107.   [54] 18, 108-9.   [56] 18, 109.
[52] 18, 107.   [55] 18, 109.   [57] 18, 110.
[53] 18, 108.

They assume that the league came very close to a genuine federal structure—which probably implies the existence of federal powers that could secure peace among the member states—and this assumption is buttressed by a description of the conditions within the league.

All cities had the same laws, customs, weights, measures, and money. They probably were compelled to receive the same laws and usages. For instance, when Lacedaemon was brought into the league, its admission was attended with an abolition of the institutions and laws of Lycurgus, and with the adoption of those of the Achaeans. The fact that the Amphictyonic confederacy, of which Lacedaemon had been a member, had left her in the full exercise of her government and legislation is considered as proof of "a very material difference in the genius" of the two confederacies, which is obviously due to the different degree of state sovereignty.[58]

The restriction of state sovereignty in the Achaean league meant that under that system, "there was infinitely more of moderation and justice in the administration of its government, and less of violence and sedition in the people, than were to be found in any of the cities exercising *singly* all the prerogatives of sovereignty."[59] In support of this thesis, one refers to the Abbé Mably, who said that "the popular government, which was so tempestuous elsewhere, caused no disorders in the members of the Achaean republic, *because it was there tempered by the general authority and laws of the confederacy.*"[60]

In spite of these advantages, the *Federalist* warns not to conclude too hastily that faction did not agitate the particular cities or that due subordination and harmony reigned in the Achaean league.[61] The contrary is displayed in the vicissitudes and fate of the republic. The authors conclude by describing the fall of the league, pointing out how foreign nations took advantage of the discord among the member states.[62]

In modern confederations, the want of a strong federal government is again held responsible for tensions among the members. As to the situation in Germany, it is emphasized that under the feudal order the vassals could become independent sovereigns because the force of imperial authority was insufficient to restrain them and to preserve unity and tranquility.[63] Anarchy was the result. Wars were carried on between the different princes. The imperial authority

[58] 18, 109-10.
[59] 18, 110.
[60] 18, 110.
[61] 18, 110.
[62] 18, 110-12. See also 45, 300.
[63] 19, 113.

declined until it was almost extinct and merely symbolic.[64] After a
description of the weak central government and the resultant war
among the member states, similar shortcomings in the existing
German confederacy, the successor of the feudal system, are pointed
out.[65] Again, tensions and a state of anarchy are predicted.

The German empire is described as a "federal system,"[66] a "community of sovereigns."[67] Governmental power is exercised by the
imperial diet as the representation of the member states, the
emperor, the imperial chamber, and the aulic council. The diet
possesses the general power of legislating for the empire. Aside from
other competences, it has that of securing peace among the member
states. It can subject disobedient states to the ban of the empire, by
which the party is degraded from its sovereign rights and loses its
possessions.[68] Federal competences are matched by prohibitions to
the states that are likely to be conducive to peace. "The members of
the confederacy are expressly restricted from entering into compacts
prejudicial to the empire; from imposing tolls and duties on their
mutual intercourse, without the consent of the emperor and diet;
from doing injustice to one another; or from affording assistance or
retreat to disturbers of the public peace. And the ban is denounced
against such as shall violate any of these restrictions. The members
of the diet, as such, are subject in all cases to be judged by the
emperor and diet."[69]

The emperor, who can veto resolutions of the diet, has the right
to grant privileges not injurious to the states and to watch over the
public safety.[70] Finally, the highest judicial bodies, the imperial
chamber and the aulic council, have jurisdiction over controversies
that concern the empire or that happen among its members.[71]

"From such a parade of constitutional powers, in the representatives and head of this confederacy," the *Federalist* concludes, "the
natural supposition would be, that it must form an exception to the
general character which belongs to its kindred systems," and that the
internal tensions that are evident in other systems do not exist here.
However, one hastens to add that nothing would be further from the
reality,[72] and one supports that statement by describing the conditions actually existing within the empire.

Again, the root of the evil is seen in "the fundamental principle"

[64] 19, 113-14.   [67] 19, 115.   [70] 19, 114-15.
[65] 19, 114.   [68] 19, 114.   [71] 19, 114; 80, 517-18.
[66] 19, 114.   [69] 19, 114.   [72] 19, 115.

on which the empire rests, "that the empire is a community of sovereigns, and that the laws are addressed to sovereigns."[73] There is no genuine federal government. The members of the diet are not elected by the people of the empire, but are appointed by the different governments, virtually for a role as ambassador. They represent the interests of their states rather than those of the empire. Furthermore, federal laws are not directly binding upon the inhabitants of the member states, their execution being left to the states.[74] Since the ban of the empire did, in practice, amount to no more than an empty threat,[75] the empire was a "nerveless body, incapable of regulating its own members, insecure against external dangers, and agitated with unceasing fermentations in its own bowels."[76] German history is described as "a history of wars between the emperor and the princes and states; of wars among the princes and states themselves; of the licentiousness of the strong, and the oppression of the weak; . . . of requisitions of men and money disregarded, or partially complied with; of attempts to enforce them, altogether abortive, or attended with slaughter and desolation, involving the innocent with the guilty; of general imbecility, confusion, and misery."[77] Examples of this disorder are supplied. In the sixteenth century the emperor, with one part of the empire on his side, was engaged against the other princes and states. The king of Prussia was more than once pitted against the imperial sovereign, and commonly proved an overmatch for him. Controversies and wars among the members of the German confederacy have been common,[78] and foreign intrigues contributed to them.[79] For instance, during the Thirty Years' War, the emperor, with one half of the empire, was fought by Sweden and the other half of the empire.[80]

The *Federalist* also mentions the possibility of securing peace by decreasing the power of the members through the formation of districts comprising several states. Since it was impossible to maintain order among the sovereigns, the empire was divided into a number of districts, each of which had its own interior organization and was supposed to enforce the execution of federal law against delinquent and contumacious members. However, in the opinion of the *Federalist*, this experiment only demonstrates more fully the radical vice of the German constitution, too great an independence of the

[73] 19, 115.
[74] 19, 115.
[75] 19, 115-18.
[76] 19, 115.
[77] 19, 115. Also 80, 517-18.
[78] 19, 115-16.
[79] 19, 115; 19, 118.
[80] 19, 115-16.

various states and too weak a federal power, each circle being a minia-
ture picture of the deformities of that "political monster," the empire. "They either fail to execute their commissions, or they do it
with all the devastation and carnage of civil war."[81] The German
empire furnishes further proof that a confederacy composed of
sovereign states is not likely to secure peace among its members.[82]

Poland, as "a government over local sovereigns" being "unfit for
self-government," is another example of the calamities flowing from
a confederate form of government.[83] Switzerland "scarcely amounts
to a confederacy" because the cantons have no common treasury,
no common troops, no common coin, no common judiciary, nor any
other common mark of sovereignty. Nevertheless, that country is
sometimes cited as an instance of the stability of federal institutions.[84] The cantons are said to be kept together by the few sources
of contention among a people of such simple and homogeneous
manners; by the mutual aid they stand in need of, for suppressing
insurrections and rebellions; and by the necessity of some regular
and permanent provision for accommodating disputes among the
cantons.[85] In the case of such disputes, the parties at variance shall
each choose four judges out of the neutral cantons, who, in case
of disagreement, choose an umpire. This tribunal, under an oath
of impartiality, pronounces definitive sentence, which all the cantons are bound to enforce.[86]

As far as the practice of Swiss government is concerned, the
Federalist complains that "whatever efficacy the union may have had
in ordinary cases, it appears that the moment a cause of difference
sprang up, capable of trying its strength, it failed. The controversies on the subject of religion, which in three instances have kindled
violent and bloody contests, may be said, in fact, to have severed the
league. The Prostestant and Catholic cantons have since had their
separate diets, where all the most important concerns are adjusted,
and which have left the general diet little other business than to
take care of the common bailages." The religious diversity produced opposite alliances with foreign powers, which were hardly
conducive to the peace in Switzerland. Berne, at the head of the
Prostestant association, was allied with the United Provinces, and
Lucerne, at the head of the Catholic association, with France.[87]

The United Netherlands, "a confederacy of republics, or rather of

[81] 19, 116. Also 19, 117.　　　[84] 19, 118.　　　[86] 19, 118-19.
[82] 19, 118.　　　　　　　　　　[85] 19, 118.　　　[87] 19, 119.
[83] 19, 118.

aristocracies,"[88] is composed of seven co-equal and sovereign states, and each state or province consists of equal and independent cities. In all important decisions, unanimity of both provinces and cities is required. The provinces are represented in the States-General by deputies appointed by them. In fact, they are also represented in the executive, the stadholder of the union being also stadholder of the several provinces. Other federal organs are a council of state, a chamber of accounts, and five colleges of admiralty.[89]

The competences of the States-General[90] do not appear to be relevant for the peace among the provinces. This is different in the case of prohibitions to the provinces, which are restrained, unless with the general consent, from entering into foreign treaties, from establishing imposts injurious to others, or charging their neighbors with higher duties than their own subjects.[91] However, the most important right for the promotion of peace is vested in the stadholder. Aside from other powers, he has authority to settle disputes between the provinces, when other methods fail.[92]

In spite of these far-reaching powers of the federal government, as "delineated on parchment,"[93] and in spite of the identity of federal and provincial executives,[94] in practice there exists "imbecility in the government; discord among the provinces; foreign influence and indignities; a precarious existence in peace, and peculiar calamities from war."[95] Again, the strong position of the provinces and the absence of a strong federal power are held responsible for this situation.[96] "The union of Utrecht reposes an authority in the States-General, seemingly sufficient to secure harmony, but the jealousy in each province renders the practice very different from the theory," an author is quoted.[97] Aside from jeal-

---

[88] 20, 119.   [89] 20, 119-20.

[90] For an enumeration of these competences, see 20, 120. Among the competences are the authority to enter into treaties and alliances; to make war and peace; to raise armies and equip fleets; to ascertain quotas and demand contributions; to appoint and receive ambassadors; to provide for the collection of duties on imports and exports; to regulate the mint; to govern as sovereigns the dependent territories.

[91] 20, 120.

[92] For the competences of the stadholder, see 20, 120-21.

[93] 20, 121.

[94] 20, 120.

[95] 20, 121.

[96] Thus the delegates to the States-General are appointed by the governments of the various provinces rather than being elected by the people of the United Netherlands. They are, therefore, mere ambassadors of their respective provinces.

[97] 20, 121.

ousy, the existing system of contributions causes tensions between the provinces. The constitution of the union "obliges each province to levy certain contributions; but this article never could, and probably never will, be executed; because the inland provinces, who have little commerce, cannot pay an equal quota. In matters of contribution, it is the practice to waive the articles of the constitution. The danger of delay obliges the consenting provinces to furnish their quotas, without waiting for the others; and then to obtain reimbursement from the others, by deputations, which are frequent, or otherwise, as they can."[98] "It has more than once happened," the *Federalist* continues, "that the deficiencies had to be ultimately collected at the point of the bayonet, a thing practicable, though dreadful, in a confederacy where one of the members exceeds in force all the rest, and where several of them are too small to mediate resistance; but utterly impracticable in one composed of members several of which are equal to each other in strength and resources, and equal singly to a vigorous and persevering defence."[99]

Tensions among the provinces are nourished by foreign powers.[100] Thus the United Netherlands confirm all the lessons derived from previously examined confederacies.[101] Consequently, it is not considered necessary, in the case of the United Netherlands, to draw attention to the evil mentioned in the case of all the other confederations, i.e., the independence of the member states. As in other confederations, the fall of the United Netherlands appears to be inevitable due to popular convulsions, dissensions among the states, and the actual invasion of foreign troops.[102]

3.   The discussion of various "federal precedents" in the *Federalist* is a rather elaborate one. It is justified on the grounds that "experience is the oracle of truth; and where its responses are unequivocal, they ought to be conclusive and sacred."[103] This leaves us to ask which, according to the *Federalist*, are the main problems of confederations outside America, and what lessons can be learned from them. To sum up: All confederacies were based upon international treaties, under which the federal organs, legislative, executive, and judicial, had more or less comprehensive powers that appeared to be sufficient for the preservation of peace among the member states. Nevertheless, political life within these federations was characterized

---

[98] 20, 121-22. [100] 20, 123. [102] 20, 124.
[99] 20, 122. [101] 20, 119. [103] 20, 124.

by strife and war among the members and between the states and the federal government. The cause for these conditions is seen in the fact that the federal compact was nothing but an international treaty under which the member states remained sovereign. This precluded a central power that could further the interests of the union, as well as the immediate validity of federal laws upon the individuals. The execution of federal laws was left to the member states, which, however, ignored those laws whenever their particular interests demanded it. Such behavior went unchallenged because the federal government did not have an effective way of enforcing its will upon the member states. The *Federalist* thus arrives at the conclusion that "the important truth" that can be learned from the experience of other federations, "is that a sovereignty over sovereigns, a government over governments, a legislation for communities, as contradistinguished from individuals, as it is a solecism in theory, so in practice it is subversive of the order and ends of civil polity, by substituting *violence* in place of *law,* or the destructive *coercion* of the *sword* in place of the mild and salutary *coercion* of the *magistracy.*"[104]

III

1. The remedy for the tensions within confederations is seen in the abolition of state sovereignty and an increase of federal power. On the whole, this amounts to a direct validity of federal laws for the individual and a federal power to enforce such laws, i.e., to the creation of a genuine federal government. The anarchic condition of might is replaced through a state of right and law, and peace is secured.

> Government implies the power of making laws. It is essential to the idea of a law, that it be attended with a sanction. . . . If there be no penalty annexed to disobedience, the resolutions or commands which pretend to be laws will, in fact, amount to nothing more than advice or recommendation. This penalty, whatever it may be, can only be inflicted in two ways: by the agency of the courts and ministers of justice, or by military force; by the COERCION of the magistracy, or by the COERCION of arms. The first kind can evidently apply only to men; the last kind must of necessity, be employed against bodies politic, or communities, or States.

[104] 21, 124. See also 15, 92; 16, 95; Madison's speech of June 7, 1788, before the convention of Virginia. MADISON'S WRITINGS, v, 137 ff.

It is evident that there is no process of a court by which the observance of the laws can, in the last resort, be enforced. Sentences
may be denounced against them for violations of their duty; but
these sentences can only be carried into execution by the sword.
In an association where the general authority is confined to the
collective bodies of the communities that compose it, every breach
of the laws must involve a state of war; and military execution must
become the only instrument of civil obedience. Such a state of
things can certainly not deserve the name of government, nor
would any prudent man choose to commit his happiness to it.[105]

Internal peace is thus, according to the *Federalist,* a prerequisite for
individual happiness.

2.   The establishment of a strong federal power poses the problem
of federal despotism. The *Federalist* denies that despotic government
is likely to exist under a federal constitution, since "federal bodies"
have a tendency "rather to anarchy among its members, than to
tyranny in the head."[106] This re-assures those who fear that an
abolition of tensions among the members of a confederation might
be bought at too high a price, namely, a dictatorship of the national
government. The federal state appears as being ideally suited for the
preservation of peace.

IV

In the preceding pages, an attempt has been made to show how
the general problem of peace is seen in the *Federalist.* Considering
past experience and the opinions of philosophers,[107] the authors

[105] 15, 91-92. See also 16, 98.

[106] 18, 112. "There is, in the nature of sovereign power," writes Hamilton in
15, 92-93, "an impatience of control, that disposes those who are invested with
the exercise of it, to look with an evil eye upon all external attempts to restrain
or direct its operations. From this spirit it happens, that in every political association which is formed upon the principle of uniting in a common interest a
number of lesser sovereignties, there will be found a kind of eccentric tendency
in the subordinate or inferior orbs, by the operation of which there will be a
perpetual effort in each to fly off from the common centre. This tendency is not
difficult to be accounted for. It has its origin in the love of power. Power controlled or abridged is almost always the rival and enemy of that power by
which it is controlled or abridged." See also 45, 299.

[107] The *Federalist* mentions Montesquieu and Abbé de Mably. However, these
two were not the only philosophers consulted by the authors. Comp. *infra.,*
chapter ten.

arrive at certain conclusions. Owing to the nature of man, which is no better in republics than in monarchies or other forms of government, the *Federalist* denies the possibliity of a peaceful co-existence of independent states, especially if these states are neighbors. A federal treaty under the norms of international law is admitted to bring about certain advantages for the peace among the confederating states. However, owing to the sovereignty of the members of such a confederacy, tensions continue to exist and in many cases will result in war. The solution of the problem is seen in the transfer of sovereignty from the states to the union, i.e., in the creation of a federal state that is not likely to develop into a centralized state.

The authors' opinion on the function of federalism to secure peace within a confederacy also applies to the situation in the United States. In the following, it shall be seen how, according to the *Federalist,* peace appears to be improbable among independent American states, under the Articles of Confederation, and how it can be secured under the Constitution.

V

1. We shall first consider the dangers arising from a dissolution of the Confederation under the Articles, i.e., from a possible creation of thirteen independent nations or several smaller confederacies. The first alternative, the creation of thirteen independent nations, is strongly condemned, because it would make wars among the new nations inevitable.[108] "A man must be far gone in Utopian speculations who can seriously doubt that, if these States should be wholly disunited, . . . the subdivisions into which they might be thrown would have frequent and violent contests with each other," writes Hamilton, and he adds, "to presume a want of motives for such contests as an argument against their existence, would be to forget that men are ambitious, vindictive, and rapacious."[109] The fact that these states were once united would by no means alter the situation: "To look for a continuation of harmony between a number of independent, unconnected sovereignties in the same neighborhood, would be to disregard the uniform course of human events and to set at defiance the accumulated experience of ages."[110] Exist-

---

[108] 41, 264.   [109] 6, 27. See also 45, 298.   [110] 6, 27.

ing feelings of friendship, due to former union, would be set off
through neighborhood, which would increase the possibilities of
tension. All the causes of international tensions would apply in
America.[111] Perpetual peace among the states, though dismem-
bered and alienated from each other, cannot be expected in spite of
the fact that they have a republican form of government. Likewise,
it would be wrong to suppose that commercial republics, like the
American states, "will never be disposed to waste themselves in
ruinous contentions with each other," that "they will be governed
by mutual interest, and will cultivate a spirit of mutual amity and
concord."[112] The experience of other nations, whose situation was,
with respect to the form of government and the occupation of
their citizens, similar to that of the American states, it mentioned as
a warning. Finally, the Americans are asked:

> What reason can we have to confide in those reveries which would
> seduce us into an expectation of peace and cordiality between the
> members of the present confederacy, in a state of separation? Have
> we not already seen enough of the fallacy and extravagance of
> those idle theories which have amused us with promises of an
> exemption from the imperfections, weaknesses, and evils incident
> to society in every shape? Is it not time to awake from the de-
> ceitful dream of a golden age, and to adopt as a practical maxim
> for the direction of our political conduct that we, as well as the
> other inhabitants of the globe, are yet remote from the happy
> empire of perfect wisdom and perfect virtue?[113]

Unfortunately, there would exist further causes of war deriving
from the American situation.[114] Hamilton first mentions the probability of territorial disputes.[115] Vast tracts of unsettled territory
would be claimed by the various states. Serious and animated discussion concerning the rights to the lands that were ungranted at
the time of the Revolution, the Crown lands, would continue. The
states within the limits of whose colonial governments these lands
were comprised have claimed them as their property, whereas others
have contended that the rights of the crown devolved upon the
Union. Disputes would exist especially with respect to that part of
the Western territory that was under the jurisdiction of the king
of Great Britain, till it was relinquished in the peace treaty, since
it could be maintained that the Confederacy acquired that land by
compact with a foreign power.[116] Hamilton praises the prudent

[111] 7, 34; 41, 263.   [113] 6, 32-33. See aso 41, 263; 45, 298.   [115] 7, 34.
[112] 6, 29-30.   [114] 41, 263.   [116] 7, 34-35.

policy of Congress to appease this controversy, by prevailing upon the states to make cessions to the United States for the benefit of the whole. He expresses hope that through a continuation of the Union an amicable termination of this dispute would come about. On the other hand, he fears that dismemberment of the Confederacy would revive the dispute and create others on the same subject.[117] On the whole, he perceives of "the wide field of Western territory" as "an ample theatre for hostile pretensions, without any umpire or common judge to interpose between the contending parties."[118]

Commercial competition would be another cause for tensions among the new states.[119]

> The States less favorably circumstanced would be desirous of escaping from the disadvantages of local situation, and of sharing in the advantages of their more fortunate neighbors. Each State . . . would pursue a system of commercial policy peculiar to itself. This would occasion distinctions, preferences, and exclusions, which would beget discontent. The habits of intercourse, on the basis of equal privileges, to which we have been accustomed since the earliest settlement of the country, would give a keener edge to those causes of discontent than they would naturally have independent of this circumstance. *We should be ready to denominate injuries those things which were in reality the justifiable acts of independent sovereignties consulting a distinct interest.* The spirit of enterprise, which characterizes the commercial part of America, has left no occasion of displaying itself unimproved. It is not at all probable that this unbridled spirit would pay much respect to those regulations of trade by which particular States might endeavor to secure exclusive benefits to their own citizens. The infractions of these regulations on one side, the efforts to prevent and repel them, on the other, would naturally lead to outrages, and these to reprisals and wars.[120]
>
> The opportunities which some States would have of rendering others tributary to them by commercial regulations would be impatiently submitted to by the tributary States. The relative situation of New York, Connecticut and New Jersey, would afford an example of this kind. New York, from the necessity of revenue, must lay duties on her importations. A great part of these duties must be paid by the inhabitants of the two other States in the capacity of consumers of what we import. New York would neither be willing nor able to forego this advantage. Her citizens would not consent that a duty paid by them should be remitted in favor of the citizens of her neighbors; nor would it be practicable . . . to distinguish the customers in our own markets. Would Connecti-

[117] 7, 35.   [119] 7, 37. See also 11, 68.   [120] 7, 37.
[118] 7, 35.

cut and New Jersey long submit to be taxed by New York for her exclusive benefit? Should we be long permitted to remain in the quiet and undisturbed enjoyment of a metropolis, from the possession of which we derived an advantage so odious to our neighbors, and, in their opinion, so oppressive? Should we be able to preserve it against the incumbent weight of Connecticut on the one side, and the co-operating pressure of New Jersey on the other? These are questions that temerity alone will answer in the affirmative.[121]

The public debt of the Union is considered a further cause of collision. The apportionment, in the first instance, and the progressive extinguishment afterwards would be alike productive of ill-humor and animosity. It would hardly be possible to agree upon a rule of apportionment satisfactory to all, because scarcely any can be proposed that is entirely free from real objections. These, as usual, would be exaggerated by the adverse interest of the parties. Some states, either because they are less impressed with the importance of national credit, or because their citizens have little, if any, immediate interest in the question, feel an indifference, if not repugnance, to the payment of the domestic debt at any rate. These states would be inclined to magnify the difficulties of a distribution. Other states, whose citizens are creditors to the public beyond the proportion of the state in the total amount of the national debt, would be anxious for some equitable and effective provision. The procrastinations of the former would excite the resentments of the latter. The settlement of a rule would, in the meantime, be postponed by real differences of opinion and affected delays. The citizens of the interested states would clamor, and the peace of the states would be hazarded to the contingency of internal contention.[122]

Even if the difficulties of agreeing upon a rule could be surmounted, and the apportionment made, there would still be room to suppose that the rule agreed upon would, upon experiment, be found to bear harder upon some states than upon others.

Those which were sufferers by it would naturally seek for a mitigation of the burden. The others would as naturally be disinclined to a revision, which was likely to end in an increase of their own incumbrances. Their refusal would be too plausible a pretext to the complaining States to withhold their contributions, not to be embraced with avidity; and the non-compliance of these States

[121] 7, 37-38.   [122] 7, 38-39.

with the engagements would be a ground of bitter discussion and altercation. If even the rule adopted should in practice justify the equality of its principle, still delinquencies in payments on the part of some of the States would result from a diversity of other causes—the real deficiency of resources; the mismanagement of their finances; accidental disorders in the management of the government; and, in addition to the rest, the reluctance with which men commonly part with money for purposes that have outlived the exigencies which produced them, and interfere with the supply of immediate wants. Delinquencies, from whatever causes, would be productive of complaints, recriminations, and quarrels. There is, perhaps, nothing more likely to disturb the tranquility of nations than their being bound by mutual contributions for any common object that does not yield an equal and coincident benefit. For it is an observation, as true as it is trite, that there is nothing men differ so readily about as the payment of money.[123]

State laws in violation of private contracts, "as they amount to aggressions on the rights of those States whose citizens are injured by them," are another source of hostility. These "atrocious breaches of moral obligation and social justice" are likely to result in a war "not of *parchment*, but of the sword."[124]

Not only can it be expected that in case of disunion there would exist special causes for war among the American states. Also, the consequences of such a war would be more serious in America than they commonly are, due to the absence of regular military establishments. It is admitted that the disciplined armies of European nations always bore a malignant aspect to liberty and economy. Nevertheless, these armies are credited with having rendered sudden conquests impracticable and of preventing that rapid desolation that used to mark the progress of war prior to their introduction. Fortifications served the same ends. The nations of Europe are encircled with chains of fortified places, which mutually obstruct invasion, or slow it down, since a comparatively small force of disciplined troops, acting on the defensive, is able to impede and finally to frustrate the enterprise of one much more considerable.[125] In America, "the scene would be altogether reversed. The jealousy of military establishments would postpone them as long as possible. The want of fortifications, leaving the frontiers of one State open to another, would facilitate inroads. The popular States would, with little difficulty, overrun their less populous neighbors. Conquests would

[123] 7, 39-40.   [124] 7, 40.   [125] 8, 41-42.

be desultory and predatory. PLUNDER and devastation ever march in the train of irregulars. The calamities of individuals would make the principal figure in the events which would characterize our military exploits."[126]

This precarious condition would only be a temporary one. However, the individual citizen would not be better off in the ensuing period. Since "safety from external danger is the most powerful director of national conduct,"[127] America would sooner or later establish standing armies. The weaker states would first have recourse to them, to put themselves in an equal position with their more potent neighbors. They would endeavor to supply the inferiority of population and resources by a more regular and effective system of defense, by disciplined troops, and by fortifications. And since small states, or states of less natural strength, with the assistance of disciplined armies, have often triumphed over large states, or states of greater natural strength, neither the pride nor the safety of the more important American states would permit them long to submit to this mortifying and adventitious superiority. As a consequence, thirteen American nations, equipped with standing armies and fortifications, would be facing each other, and peace would be perpetually endangered.[128]

Again the *Federalist* points to the dangers by which the internal peace is threatened from abroad, concluding that "America, if not connected at all, or only by the feeble tie of a simple league, offensive and defensive, would, by the operation of such jarring alliances, be gradually entangled in all the pernicious labyrinths of European politics and wars."[129]

2.   The creation of thirteen unconnected sovereignties is considered "a project too extravagant and too replete with danger to have many advocates."[130] However, prospects do not appear brighter if the Union is divided into several independent confederations,[131] an

---

[126] 8, 42.   [128] 8, 43-44; 8, 46; 41, 263-65.

[127] 8, 42.   [129] 7, 40; see also 11, 66.   [130] 13, 77.

[131] On the one hand, the *Federalist* speaks of an indefinite number of possible federations (2, 8; 4, 20; 4, 21-22; 13, 76; 13, 79); on the other hand, it mentions, more concretely, the possibility of "two, or three, or even four Confederacies" (28, 172), or of three confederacies (2, 12; 4, 21; 4, 22; 13, 78). The last alternative of three confederacies, being composed, respectively, of the four Northern states, the four Middle states, and the five Southern states, is considered to be the most probable possibility. (13, 77.) See, however, 13, 78.

"extraordinary" plan,[132] which has some advocates.[133] The motives for tension would be the same.[134] Like Great Britain before the unification of Scotland and England, America would be plagued by jealousy among the different confederacies. "Instead of their being 'joined in affection' and free from all apprehension of different 'interests,' envy and jealousy would soon extinguish confidence and affection, and the partial interests of each confederacy, instead of the general interests of all America, would be the only objects of their policy and pursuits. Hence, like most other *bordering* nations, they would always be either involved in disputes and war, or live in the constant apprehension of them."[135]

Even if the confederations were of about equal strength, which is improbable, a continuance of such equal strength appears to be doubtful. "Independent of those local circumstances which tend to beget and increase power in one part and to impede its progress in another, we must advert to the effects of that superior policy and good management which would probably distinguish the government of one above the rest, and by which their relative equality in strength and consideration would be destroyed. For it cannot be presumed that the same degree of sound policy, prudence, and foresight would uniformly be observed by each of these confederacies for a long succession of years," warns Jay.

> Whenever, and from whatever causes, it might happen, and happen it would, that any one of these nations or confederacies should rise on the scale of political importance much above the degree of her neighbors, that moment would those neighbors behold her with envy and fear. Both those passions would lead them to countenance, if not to promote, whatever might promise to diminish her importance; and would also restrain them from measures calculated to advance or even to secure her prosperity. Much time would not be necessary to enable her to discern these unfriendly dispositions. She would soon begin, not only to loose confidence in her neighbors, but also to feel a disposition equally unfavorable to them. Distrust naturally creates distrust, and by

[132] 2, 8.

[133] 2, 8. Strangely enough John Jay, who in the *Federalist* strongly opposes a dissolution of the Union into confederacies, was accused by James Monroe of promoting such a dissolution. Letter to Madison of August 14, 1786. Warren, THE MAKING OF THE CONSTITUTION, 25. This work gives a detailed description of the then existing danger of the formation of several confederacies. *Ibid.*, 23-30, 45.

[134] The *Federalist* often does not distinguish between a dissolution into thirteen independent states or one into several confederacies. 6, 27; 7, 37; 7, 38; 8, 43.

[135] 5, 23-24.

nothing is good-will and kind conduct more speedily changed than by invidious jealousies and uncandid imputations, whether expressed or implied.[136]

Envisaging coming events, the *Federalist* mentions which one of the different confederacies was likely to become more powerful.

The North is generally the region of strength, and many local circumstances render it probable that the most Northern of the proposed confederacies would, at a period not very distant, be unquestionably more formidable than any of the others. No sooner would this become evident than the *Northern Hive* would excite the same ideas and sensations in the more southern parts of America which it formerly did in the southern parts of Europe. Nor does it appear to be a rash conjecture that its young swarms might often be tempted to gather honey in the more blooming fields and milder air of their luxurious and more delicate neighbors.[137]

A division of the Union into several independent confederacies appears thus to be as dangerous to peace as a division into thirteen independent states.[138] The new confederacies would "neither love nor trust one another, but on the contrary would be a prey to discord, jealousy, and mutual injuries."[139] The strength of the various confederacies would be so much reduced as to make them *"formidable only to each other."*[140]

It is improbable that the confederacies would form alliances, offensive or defensive, and thereby secure peace.[141] Different commercial interests would result in treaties between the various confederations and foreign powers. It probably would happen that the foreign nation with which, for instance, the Southern confederacy is at war would be the one with which the Northern confederacy

[136] 5, 24-25.

[137] 5, 25. On the probable development toward two confederations, compare 13, 77-78.

[138] 41, 265; 59, 388.

[139] 5, 25. In the same essay, the following passage can be found: "Nay, it is far more probable that in America, as in Europe, neighboring nations, acting under the impulse of opposite interests and unfriendly passions, would frequently be found taking different sides. Considering our distance from Europe, it would be more natural for these confederacies to apprehend danger from one another than from distant nations, and therefore that each of them should be more desirous to guard against the others by the aid of foreign alliances, than to guard against foreign dangers by alliances between themselves." (5, 26.)

[140] 5, 25; 41, 263.

[141] Compare the passage quoted in note 139 on this page.

would be the most desirous of preserving peace and friendship. An alliance so contrary to the immediate interest of these confederations would not therefore be easy to form, nor, if formed, would it be observed and fulfilled with perfect good faith. Such an alliance would hardly be conducive to peace among the states.[142]

Foreign nations would contribute to tensions among the several confederacies in order to prevent America from becoming a great power. Due to their distance from Europe, it would be more natural for these confederacies to apprehend danger from one another than from distant nations. Therefore, each of them should be more desirous to guard against the other by the aid of foreign alliances, than to guard against foreign dangers by alliances between themselves.[143]

3. In summary it can be said that the *Federalist* admits that America is not free from tendencies that in other parts of the world have led to international conflicts. As a matter of fact, it is stressed that under American conditions, tensions are likely to increase rather than to diminish. The dangers arising from a dissolution of the Union into thirteen independent states or several confederacies are discussed at great length and described in the darkest colors. The authors are thus not at all content with merely pointing out the insufficiency of the existing system to preserve peace, a topic that will now be discussed.

VI

1. An American confederacy, in distinction to a mere alliance between American states or confederacies, secures certain advantages for the preservation of peace.[144] However, even such a confederacy is torn by tensions. The evils of the existing Confederation are, on the whole, similar to those described in other confederacies.[145] They hardly differ from those that are feared in case of a dissolution of the Union.[146] As a matter of fact, it appears open to doubt whether the system under the Articles of Confederation actually differs from a mere military alliance.[147]

Under the Articles, there exists such a high degree of state sovereignty as to warrant the assumption of a mere alliance. The United

[142] 5, 25-26; 7, 40; 15, 90-91.
[143] 5, 26.
[144] 8, 41; 8, 43; 8, 46; 14, 79; 15, 86; 15, 91; 45, 298.
[145] 37, 226.
[146] 15, 91.
[147] 15, 90-91.

States,[148] although her government theoretically possesses far-reaching powers,[149] has "reached almost the last stage of national humiliation," since, due to "material imperfections" of the national system, which make the existence of the Union a precarious one, conditions come close to a state of anarchy.[150] On the whole, "the great and radical vice in the construction of the existing Confederation is in the principle of LEGISLATION for STATES or GOVERNMENTS, in their CORPORATE or COLLECTIVE CAPACITIES, and as contradistinguished from the INDIVIDUALS of which they consist."[151] Although this form of legislation does not apply to all matters over which the federal government has jurisdiction, it applies to the important ones. Therefore, whereas in theory the laws of the federal government are binding upon the member states, in practice they do not amount to more than mere recommendations that can be ignored at will.[152] Under these conditions, peace among the states and between the states and the Union is not likely to exist.

Human shortcomings contribute their own part to tensions. The *Federalist* takes issue with those who believe that a sense of common interest would prevent breaches by the states of the regulations of the federal authority. Disproved by "the lessons from the best oracle of wisdom, experience,"[153] such optimism betrays an ignorance of the true springs by which human conduct is actuated and belies the original inducements to the establishment of civil power. Government was instituted because the passions of men will not conform to the dictates of reason and justice without constraint.[154] Under the Articles, the ambitions of individual politicians often endanger internal peace,[155] as do popular assemblies. "Has it been found that bodies of men act with more rectitude or greater disinterestedness than individuals?" asks Hamilton, commenting on the

[148] "The United States of America" was the official name of the nation as much under the Articles as it is under the Constitution.

[149] Theoretically, the federal government under the Articles possessed quite a few competences. In practice, however, these competences did hardly amount to anything, due to the fact that federal laws were not binding directly upon the citizens of the states, but only upon the governments of the states. Therefore, the *Federalist* often speaks of an invigoration of competences that were already vested in the national government under the Articles of Confederation. 40, 255; 45, 303; probably also 18, 106.

[150] 15, 86-87.

[151] 15, 89. See also 15, 93; 15, 94; 16, 95; 23, 143.

[152] 15, 89-90; 30, 183-84.

[153] 15, 92.

[154] 15, 92.

[155] 15, 93; 16, 96; 59, 388.

American situation. "The contrary of this has been inferred by all accurate observers of the conduct of mankind; and the inference is founded upon obvious reasons. Regard to reputation has a less active influence, when the infamy of a bad action is to be divided among a number, than when it is to fall singly upon one. A spirit of faction, which is apt to mingle its poison in the deliberations of all bodies of men, will often hurry the persons of whom they are composed into improprieties and excesses, for which they would blush in a private capacity."[156]

2.   As to the relation between the states and the Union, conditions under the Articles are not encouraging.

> If . . . the measures of the Confederacy cannot be executed without the intervention of the particular administrations, there will be little prospect of their being executed at all. The rulers of the respective members, whether they have a constitutional right to do it or not, will undertake to judge of the propriety of the measures themselves. They will consider the conformity of the thing proposed or required to their immediate interests or aims; the momentary conveniences or inconveniences that would attend its adoption. All this will be done; and in a spirit of interested and suspicious scrutiny, without that knowledge of national circumstances and reasons of state, which is essential to a right judgment, and with that strong predilection in favor of local objects, which can hardly fail to mislead the decision. The same process must be repeated in every member of which the body is constituted; and the execution of the plans, framed by the councils of the whole, will always fluctuate on the discretion of the ill-informed and prejudiced opinion of every part. Those who have been conversant in the proceedings of popular assemblies; who have seen how difficult it often is, where there is no exterior pressure of circumstances, to bring them to harmonious resolutions on important points, will readily conceive how impossible it must be to induce a number of such assemblies, deliberating at a distance from each other, at different times, and under different impressions, long to coöperate in the same views and pursuits.[157]

What could be expected from a system under which the compliance of thirteen states was a prerequisite for the execution of all important measures of the federal government actually happened. The measures of the Union were not executed; the delinquencies of the states matured into an extreme, which arrested all the wheels

[156] 15, 92; See also 15, 86; 15, 93; 16, 96; 45, 299.
[157] 15, 93-94.

of the national government. Congress scarcely possessed the means of keeping up the forms of administration.[158]

> Things did not come to this desperate extremity at once. The causes which have been specified produced at first only unequal and disproportionate degrees of compliance with the requisitions of the Union. The greater deficiencies of some States furnished the pretext of example and the temptation on interest to the complying, or to the least delinquent States. Why should we do more in proportion than those who are embarked with us in the same political voyage? Why should we consent to bear more than our proper share of the common burden? These were suggestions which human selfishness could not withstand, and which even speculative men, who looked forward to remote consequences, could not, without hesitation, combat. Each State, yielding to the persuasive voice of immediate interest or convenience, had successively withdrawn its support.[159]

The result was a state of anarchy,[160] characterized by tensions[161] between states and Union.

Also, the Articles of Confederation did not prevent tensions among the states themselves.[162] First of all, peace was endangered by territorial disputes. Vast tracts of unsettled territory within the boundaries of the United States were claimed by several of the states.[163] Particular controversies are referred to. The dispute between Connecticut and Pennsylvania, respecting the land at Wyoming, proved that an easy accommodation of such differences could not be expected. The Articles of Confederation obliged the parties to submit the matter to the decision of a federal court. The submission was made, and the court decided in favor of Pennsylvania. But Connecticut gave strong indications of dissatisfaction with that determination; nor did she appear to be entirely resigned to it, until, by negotiation and management, something like an equivalent was found for the loss she was supposed to have sustained.[164]

---

[158] 15, 94. See also 16, 97.   [160] 16, 95.

[159] 15, 94-95.   [161] 15, 94-95.

[162] 80, 518. Hamilton admits that the Articles of Confederation provide for a mode of settlement of disputes between the states. However, he claims that under the Articles the federal government is able to settle only boundary disputes (80, 518). Compare Robert Granville Caldwell, "The Settlement of Interstate Disputes," AMERICAN JOURNAL OF INTERNATIONAL LAW (1920), XIV, 38 ff., and A. H. Snow, "The Development of the American Doctrine of Jurisdiction of Courts over States," PUBLICATIONS OF THE AMERICAN SOCIETY FOR JUDICIAL SETTLEMENT OF INTERNATIONAL DISPUTES (1911), No. 4.

[163] 7, 34-37.   [164] 7, 36.

In a controversy between New York and the district of Vermont, the claim of New York was contested by the states not interested as well as by those that had a definite interest in the matter. Two motives preponderated in that opposition: one, a jealousy entertained of the future power of New York; and the other, the interest of certain individuals of influence in the neighboring states, who had obtained grants under the actual government of Vermont. States like New Hampshire, Massachusetts, and Connecticut, which brought forward claims in contradiction to those of New York, seemed more solicitous to dismember that state than to establish their own pretensions. New Jersey and Rhode Island discovered a warm zeal for the independence of Vermont, as did Maryland. Being small states, they saw with an unfriendly eye the perspective of the growing importance of New York. Fortunately, New York refrained from asserting its rights by force.[165]

Commercial competitions were another source of contention, owing to the fact that the regulation of interstate commerce was not vested in the federal government, but belonged to the jurisdiction of the states.[166] State sovereignty prevented the Union from being a reliable trading partner. This discouraged trade agreements between the Union and foreign nations. Since, on the other hand, the states were interested in foreign trade, they made their own arrangements. Such arrangements would often be incompatible with good relations among the states and "contrary to the true spirit of the Union." In many instances, interstate tensions were the result.[167] State regulations impeding interstate commerce, such as those providing for a tariff on transit goods, or the regulations of commercial states providing for a collection of an indirect revenue from their uncommercial neighbors,[168] proved to be further sources of animosity and discord.[169]

The public debt of the Union was another cause for friction owing to dissimilar views on the general principle of discharging the debt. The citizens of some states were less interested in the payment of the Union debt than those of others, which resulted in a difference in willingness to pay.[170]

Finally, state laws in favor of debtors, "fraudulent" laws, proved to be detrimental to the good relations between the states,[171] since they affected the citizens of other states. Thus "in consequence of

[165] 7, 36-37.
[166] 22, 131; 42, 274.
[167] 22, 132.
[168] 42, 274. See also 11, 65.
[169] 22, 132.
[170] 7, 38-39; 30, 185
[171] 80, 518.

the enormities perpetrated by the Legislature of Rhode Island,"
Connecticut showed a disposition to retaliation.[172]

Aside from the above-mentioned reasons for differences among
the states, other causes are pointed out.[173] On the whole, the *Federalist* describes tensions that exist, under the Articles, between the
states and the Union and among the states. However, the authors
are not content with a mere description of the experienced shortcomings of the existing system. Claiming that more satisfactory
conditions can hardly be expected, they envisage a future that is
even dimmer than the present situation.

3.   Although the existing chaos is so bad as to make the "natural
death" of the Confederacy inevitable, conditions may still get worse
and result in a civil war and the "violent death" of the Confederation. The principle of legislation for states in their political capacities, considered by Hamilton "the parent of anarchy,"[174] must have
for its consequence the failure of the states to obey federal law. A
use of force is then the only constitutional means by which the
federal government can execute its laws.[175] Nevertheless, it appears
doubtful whether "so odious an engine of government," in its application to America,

> would even be capable of answering its end. If there should not be
> a large army constantly at the disposal of the national government, it would either not be able to employ force at all, or, when
> this could be done, it would amount to a war between parts of the
> Confederacy concerning the infractions of a league, in which the
> strongest combination would be most likely to prevail, whether
> it consisted of those who supported or of those who resisted the
> general authority. It would rarely happen that the delinquency to
> be redressed would be confined to a single member, and if there
> were more than one who had neglected their duty, similarity of
> situation would induce them to unite for common defence. Independent of this motive of sympathy, if a large and influential State
> should happen to be the aggressive member, it would commonly
> have weight enough with its neighbors to win over some of them
> as associates to its cause. Specious arguments of danger to the
> common liberty could easily be contrived; plausible excuses for
> the deficiencies of the party could, without difficulty, be invented
> to alarm the apprehensions, inflame the passions, and conciliate
> the good-will even of those States which were not chargeable with

[172] 7, 40.

[173] 30, 185; 42, 276. The possibility of tensions among the states is stressed in
the case of naturalization. 42, 276.

[174] 16, 95.   [175] 16, 95.

any violation or omission of duty. This would be the more likely
to take place, as the delinquencies of the larger members might be
expected sometimes to proceed from an ambitious premeditation
in their rulers, with a view to getting rid of all external control
upon their designs of personal aggrandizement; the better to effect
which it is presumable they would hamper beforehand with the
leading individuals in the adjacent States. . . . When the sword is
once drawn, the passions of men observe no bounds of moderation.
The suggestions of wounded pride, the instigations of irritated
resentment, would be apt to carry the States against which the
arms of the Union were exerted, to any extremes necessary to
avenge the affront or to avoid the disgrace of submission. The first
war of this kind would probably terminate in the dissolution of
the Union.[176]

4. Again, the authors point to the role foreign nations play in
tensions among the American states. These nations are said to be
interested in preventing the establishment of a strong America by
attempting to promote interstate tensions. Not only would they foster the commercial antagonism between the states through their
intrigues,[177] they would even be willing to participate in a war
among the states, in order to bring about the end of the confederacy,
"from the firm union of which they had so much to fear."[178]

5. In summary, it can be said that the conditions under the Articles of Confederation are depicted as being about as bad as those
envisaged in the case of a dissolution of that union. Like its various
counterparts, the existing Confederation appears to be plagued by
tensions. Again, the high degree of state sovereignty is held responsible for the situation.[179] How peace will exist, according to the
Federalist, under the Constitution with its stronger federal government will now be considered.

VII

1. The *Federalist* denies that common culture and heritage, as well
as previous unification, would prevent tensions between the various

[176] 16, 96-97. See also 11, 65; 11, 68; 22, 132; 42, 274.
[177] 11, 62 ff.
[178] 16, 96-97.
[179] On the conditions under the Articles in general see Hamilton's letter to
James Duane of Sept. 3, 1780, HAMILTON'S WORKS, I, 213 ff.; Madison's "Vices of
the Political System of the United States," MADISON'S WRITINGS, II, 391 ff.

parts of America. On the other hand, it maintains that there are factors that are conducive to unity. Indeed, the existence of such factors appears to be of sufficient importance to be stressed right after the first essay, which describes the purpose of the whole undertaking. Consequently, the following essays must be under the impression of the idea of union, which is proclaimed as an American faith and appears throughout the work as being ideally suited to American exigencies. It is doubtful whether in American political literature there can be found a similarly strong confession of faith in the Union. Jay asks his countrymen to stay united and proclaims a concept of union that was used before him by Patrick Henry and later by Lincoln, namely, that the Union is older than the institutions formally establishing it.[180] He is happy to note that

> independent America was not composed of detached and distant territories, but that one connected, fertile, wide-spreading country was the portion of our western sons of liberty. Providence has in a particular manner blessed it with a variety of soils and productions, and watered it with innumerable streams, for the delight and accommodation of its inhabitants. A succession of navigable waters forms a kind of chain round its borders as if to bind it together; while the most noble rivers in the world, running at convenient distances, present them with highways for the easy communication of friendly aids, and the mutual transportation and exchanges of their various commodities.[181]

To the idea of the unity of the country, Jay adds that of the unity of the people: "With equal pleasure I have often taken notice, that Providence has been pleased to give this one connected country to one united people—a people descended from the same ancestors, speaking the same language, professing the same religion, attached

---

[180] Henry's words were: "The distinctions between Virginians, Pennsylvanians, New Yorkers and New Englanders are no more. I am not a Virginian, but an American. . . . All distinctions are thrown down. All America is thrown into one mass." Edmund Burnett, ed., LETTERS OF THE MEMBERS OF THE CONTINENTAL CONGRESS, I, 14. Later, Lincoln stated: "Union is perpetual . . . much older than the Constitution. It was formed in fact, by the Articles of Association in 1774, . . . matured and continued by the Declaration of Independence in 1776. It was further matured and continued by the Articles of Confederation in 1778. And finally, in 1787, one of the declared objectives for ordaining and establishing the Constitution was 'to form a more perfect Union,'" Richardson, ed., MESSAGES AND PAPERS OF THE PRESIDENTS (1896-99), VI, 7. Although Henry made his statement in order to get more votes for Virginia in Congress, it constitutes a strong assertion of the idea of the American nation.

[181] 2, 8-9.

to the same principles of government, very similar in their manners and customs, and who, by their joint counsels, arms, and efforts, fighting side by side throughout a long and bloody war, have nobly established general liberty and independence."[182] To complete this picture of American unity, Jay finally complements the concept of one country and one people through that of one nation:

> This country and this people seem to have been made for each other, and it appears as if it was the design of Providence, that an inheritance so proper and convenient for a band of brethren, united to each other by the strongest ties, should never be split into a number of unsocial, jealous, and alien sovereignties. . . . To all general purposes we have uniformly been one people; each citizen everywhere enjoying the same national rights, privileges, and protection. As a nation we have vanquished our common enemies; as a nation we have formed alliances, and made treaties, and entered into various compacts and conventions with foreign states.[183]

In view of the fact that the Union appears to be naturally suited to American conditions, any other form of government must be treason to the American cause, if not a denial of the will of God. Consequently, the opinion of those who favor state sovereignty can be considered as something unnatural and irresponsible. "Was, then, the American Revolution affected, was the American Confederation formed, was the precious blood of thousands split, and the hard-earned substance of millions lavished," Madison asks, "not that the people of America should enjoy peace, liberty and safety, but that the government of the individual States, that particular municipal establishments, might enjoy a certain extent of power and be arrayed with certain dignities and attributes of sovereignty?"[184] The Articles of Confederation realize the idea of union in an insufficient way, since, due to the fact that the Confederation was based upon a ratification of the governments of the states, the latter retained their sovereignty. By contrast, the Constitution corresponds to Jay's idea of union. Being adopted by the American people, it establishes a state in which sovereignty is transferred to the federal government. Thereby, one of the chief purposes of union, peace, is achieved.[185]

2. The *Federalist* points out that under the Articles, where the laws of the Union are binding upon the states only, obedience to

---

[182] 2, 9.   [183] 2, 9.   [184] 45, 298-99.

[185] For the fact that freedom and security were other purposes of union, see *supra*, pp. 35-36.

federal law can only be secured through the force of arms. The conclusion is reached that

> if it be possible at any rate to construct a federal government capable of regulating the common concerns and preserving the general tranquility, it must be founded, as to the objects committed to its care, upon the reverse of the principle contended for by the opponents of the proposed Constitution. It must carry its agency to the persons of the citizens. It must stand in need of no intermediate legislation; but must itself be empowered to employ the arm of the ordinary magistrate to execute its own resolutions. . . . The government of the Union, like that of each State, must be able to address itself immediately to the hopes and fears of individuals; and to attract to its support those passions which have the strongest influence upon the human heart. It must, in short, possess all the means, and have a right to resort to all the methods, of executing the powers with which it is intrusted, that are possessed and exercized by the governments of the particular States.[186]

The new Constitution corresponds to these requirements. It grants ample powers to the federal government and provides that federal laws are directly binding upon the inhabitants of the states. In the following, the legislative competences of the federal government will be dealt with first and then the means for the execution of those laws will be considered.

The *Federalist* discusses the powers of the federal government in a more or less detailed manner. Only those powers that, in the opinion of the authors, are especially conducive to the preservation of peace will be of concern here. However, it should be pointed out that actually all federal powers, since they strengthen the federal government and thereby diminish the *imperium in imperio,* are likely to decrease tensions between the federal government and the states as well as among the states themselves.[187] As to the competences that appear to be especially conducive to peace, it should be stressed that the *Federalist* often fails to emphasize their function to preserve peace. But such emphasis does not appear to be necessary, because it was indirectly given when, in their criticism of the Articles, the authors maintained that the want of certain federal powers was endangering peace. Therefore, it appears to be justified to consider as relevant for the preservation of peace all those federal powers

---

[186] 16, 98-99. See also 15, 91; 23, 141.
[187] 37, 227.

the absence of which, under the Articles, was regretted by the authors.[188]

3. As to the relation between the states and the Union, tensions were largely due to the failure of the former to fulfill their payment obligations. Therefore, the right of the federal government to tax the individual citizens directly appears as "the most important of the authorities proposed to be conferred upon the Union."[189] Since "money is, with propriety, considered as the vital principle of the body politic; as that which sustains its life and motion, and enables it to perform its most essential functions, a complete power . . . to procure a regular and adequate supply of it . . . may be regarded as an indispensable ingredient in every constitution," writes Hamilton, with the American situation in mind. He adds that the absence of such a power will make the government sink into a fatal atrophy, and, in a short course of time, let it perish, because a weak federal government would be unable to assert itself vis-à-vis the states.[190] Here is a distinct recognition of the peace principle, if we take into account the opinion that the main peril to peace derives from the failure of the states to pay their quotas.[191] This is confirmed by the remark that a system under which the national income depends upon requisitions, i.e., under which tax laws are not directly binding upon the citizens of the states, tends "to enfeeble the Union, and sow the seeds of discord and contention between the federal head and its members."[192] In another passage, a taxation of the citizens by the federal government is considered necessary for "securing the public peace against . . . domestic violence,"[193] as well as "against future invasions of the public peace by . . . domestic convulsions."[194]

An abuse of the federal taxing power, resulting in new tensions with the states, is not to be expected. The Constitution precludes discriminatory taxation by providing that direct taxes must be in proportion to the number of the inhabitants of the states. Indirect taxes, "all duties, imposts, and excises shall be UNIFORM through-

---

[188] As well as those powers, the absence of which the authors regretted in case of the existence of independent American states or confederacies. Compare *supra*, pp. 193 ff.

[189] 33, 199.

[190] 30, 182-83.

[191] Compare *supra*, p. 206 f.

[192] 30, 185. Compare also 33, 200; 36, 220.

[193] 31, 190.

[194] 34, 205.

out the United States."[195] The taxing powers of the Union and the
states are so clearly defined that, as to the interference of the
revenue laws of the Union and of its members, there can be no
clashing or repugnancy of authority. The laws cannot, therefore, in
a legal sense, interfere with each other.[196] According to Article 1,
Section 8, clause 1, Congress has the power to lay and collect taxes,
duties, imposts, and excises, just as, under the second clause of the
tenth section of the same article, it is prohibited to the states, without the consent of Congress, to lay any imposts or duties on imports and exports, except for the purpose of executing its inspection laws. Since under Section 9, clause 5, Congress shall lay no tax
or duty on articles exported from any state, the indirect taxing
power of Congress is restricted to the imposition of duties on imports. On the other hand, the states are permitted to impose taxes on
all other articles, with the exception of imports and exports.[197] As
to direct taxes, the power of the federal government is not exclusive.

It is not likely that tensions will result from the different competences of the Union and the states. The "necessary and proper
clause"[198] as well as the "supremacy clause"[199] of the Constitution
will prevent collisions, since these clauses leave no doubt about
the competences of the federal government.[200] "To argue upon
abstract principles," writes Hamilton, that a coördinate authority
cannot exist, "is to set up supposition and theory against fact and
reality."[201] In practice, there is little reason to apprehend any in-
convenience resulting from taxation by two authorities, because "in
a short course of time, the wants of the States will naturally reduce
themselves within *a very narrow compass;* and in the interim, the
United States will, in all probability, find it convenient to abstain
wholly from those objects to which the particular States would be
inclined to resort."[202] Besides, the federal competences are so comprehensive as to eliminate the possibility of a restriction of federal
power by the states and the tensions connected with it. This situation would not only exist in the present, but also in the future:

> We must bear in mind that we are not to confine our view to the
> present period, but to look forward to remote futurity. Constitu-
> tions of civil government are not to be framed upon a calcula-
> tion of existing exigencies, but upon a combination of these with

[195] 36, 220.   [196] 36, 220-21.   [197] 32, 195-96.
[198] Art. 1, Sec. 8, cl. 18, U.S. Constitution.
[199] Art. 6, cl. 2, U.S. Constitution.
[200] Essay 33.   [201] 34, 203.   [202] 34, 204.

the probable exigencies of ages, according to the natural and tried course of human affairs. Nothing, therefore, can be more fallacious than to infer the extent of any power, proper to be lodged in the national government, from an estimate of its immediate necessities. There ought to be a capacity to provide for future contingencies as they may happen; and as these are illimitable in their nature, it is impossible safely to limit that capacity. It is true, perhaps, that a computation might be made with sufficient accuracy to answer the purpose of the quantity of revenue requisite to discharge the subsisting engagements of the Union, and to maintain those establishments which, for some time to come, would suffice in time of peace. But would it be wise, or would it not rather be the extreme of folly to stop at this point, and to leave the government intrusted with the care of the national defence in a state of absolute incapacity to provide for the protection of the community against future invasions of the public peace, by foreign war or domestic convulsions?[203]

Doubts raised against the national taxing power and fears of such "specters" as a double set of revenue officials, a duplication of their burdens by double taxation, and the "frightful forms of odious and oppressive poll-taxes," are eliminated.[204] On the whole, the constitutional provisions concerning taxation appear to be conducive to the prevention of tensions between the federal government and the states. We may conclude our discussion about the function of federal power to secure peace between the Union and its component parts, since the *Federalist* hardly stresses that function in connection with federal powers, other than taxation.[205] An investigation will now be made into how, according to the *Federalist*, the powers of the federal government are likely to preserve peace among the states.

As to territorial disputes, the Constitution contains several provisions that are considered to be peace-preserving. "The general precaution, that no new States shall be formed, without the concurrence of the federal authority, and that of the States concerned, is consonant to the principles which ought to govern such transactions. The particular precaution against the erection of new States, by the partition of a State without its consent, quiets the jealousy of the larger States; as that of the smaller is quieted by a like precaution, against a junction of States without their consent."[206] The power of Congress to dispose of and make all needful rules and

[203] 34, 204--5.　　　[204] 36, 221-23.

[205] Compare *supra*, pp. 211-12. Also, Madison in the Virginia Convention on June 5, 7, 11, and 12, 1788. MADISON'S WRITINGS, v, 135 ff.

[206] 43, 281.

regulations respecting the territory or other property belonging to the United States, with a provision that nothing in the Constitution shall be so construed as to prejudice any claims of the United States, or of any particular state, is considered by Madison "a power of very great importance." The proviso annexed "is proper in itself, and was probably rendered absolutely necessary by jealousies and questions concerning the Western territory."[207] Finally, the *Federalist* interprets the provision that the federal government shall protect each state against invasion to mean that each state shall be protected "not only against foreign hostility, but against ambitious or vindictive enterprises of its more powerful neighbors."[208]

The power of the federal government to regulate interstate commerce is a further means to alleviate tensions among the states. It brings relief to the states that import and export through other states, from the "improper contributions levied on them by the latter," which "would nourish unceasing animosities, and not improperly terminate in serious interruptions of the public tranquility."[209] "An unrestricted intercourse between the States themselves will advance the trade of each by an interchange of their respective productions, not only for the supply of reciprocal wants at home, but for exportation to foreign markets. The veins of commerce in every part will be replenished, and will acquire additional motion and vigor from a free circulation of the commodities of every part. Commercial enterprise will have much greater scope, from the diversity in the productions of different states." In case of economic emergency, such as a bad harvest or unproductive crop, the state suffering can call to its aid the staple of another state.[210]

The problem of the payment of the public debt, which under the Articles marred relations among the states, will be solved because Congress will have the power to consider all debts contracted and engagements entered into, before the adoption of the Constitution.[211]

Similarly, state legislation favoring debtors will not be permitted. Since the Constitution provides that no state shall pass any law impairing the obligations of contract, tensions produced by such

[207] 43, 281-82.   [208] 43, 283.   [209] 42, 274.

[210] 11, 68. Compare also Madison's statements in the Virginia Convention of June 11, 1788 and June 24, 1788. MADISON'S WRITINGS, v, 163, 232.

[211] 43, 285-86. Compare in this connection Madison's speeches in the first Congress of Feb. 11 and 18, 1790. MADISON'S WRITINGS, v, 438 ff., as well as Hamilton's reports on the public credit of Jan. 14 and Dec. 13, 1790. HAMILTON'S WORKS, II, 227 ff., 337 ff.

legislation under the Articles will not continue to come into existence.[212]

Aside from the federal powers just mentioned, which are considered especially important for the preservation of peace, the *Federalist* mentions other powers as being relevant "for the harmony and proper intercourse among the States."[213] Among them are the power to coin money and to regulate its value, as well as that of foreign coin; to provide for the punishment of counterfeiting the current coin and securities of the United States; to fix the standard of weight and measures; to establish a uniform rule of naturalization and uniform laws of bankruptcy; to prescribe the manner in which the public acts, records, and judicial proceedings of each state shall be proved, and the effect they shall have in other states; and to establish post offices and post roads.[214]

On the whole, it can be said that the *Federalist* more explicitly mentions the function of federal power to preserve peace among the states, than its function to maintain good relations between the Union and the states. Often, no clear distinction is drawn between the two. Federal power is credited with being able to secure peace among the states as well as between the Union and its members. Its peace-preserving function is thus underlined.[215] This leads to the question of the execution of federal law. Again, such an execution is carried out in a manner that is conducive to peace.

4. Execution of federal law is preceded by court action, "the majesty of the national authority" being "manifested through the medium of the courts of justice."[216] The work of the courts contributes to good relations between the states and the Union.[217] The authors, feeling that disobedience to the law is not likely to happen under a government of laws, encounter the argument that any state could at any time obstruct the execution of federal law and bring the matter to the same issue of force as under the Articles, by pointing out "the essential difference between a mere NON-COMPLIANCE and a DIRECT and ACTIVE RESISTANCE":

If the interposition of the State legislatures be necessary to give

---

[212] 44, 289; 44, 291. [213] 42, 273. [214] 42, 273-78.

[215] This applies to the cases here discussed, where a stronger national government is conducive both to the peace among the states and to peace between the states and the federal government.

[216] 16, 98-99.

[217] Former plans of union did not provide for a federal judiciary, although the Albany Plan of Benjamin Franklin came possibly close to such an institution.

effect to a measure of the Union, they have only NOT TO ACT, or to ACT EVASIVELY, and the measure is defeated. This neglect of duty may be disguised under affected but unsubstantial provisions, so as not to appear, and of course not to excite any alarm in the people for the safety of the Constitution. The State leaders may even make a merit of their surreptitious invasions of it on the ground of some temporary convenience, exemption, or advantage. But if the execution of the laws of the national government should not require the intervention of the State legislatures, if they were to pass into immediate operation upon the citizens themselves, the particular governments could not interrupt their progress without an open and violent exertion of an unconstitutional power. No omissions or evasions would answer the end. They would be obliged to act, and in such manner as would leave no doubt that they had encroached on the national rights. An experiment of this nature would always be hazardous in the face of a constitution in any degree competent to its own defence, and of a people enlightened enough to distinguish between a legal exercise and an illegal usurpation of authority. The success of it would require not merely a factious majority in the legislature, but the concurrence of the courts of justice and of the body of the people. If the judges were not embarked in a conspiracy with the legislature, they would pronounce the resolutions of such a majority to be contrary to the supreme law of the land, unconstitutional, and void. If the people were not tainted with the spirit of their State representatives, they, as the natural guardians of the Constitution, would throw their weight into the national scale and give it a decided preponderancy in the contest. Attempts of this kind would not often be made with levity or rashness, because they could seldom be made without danger to the authors, unless in cases of a tyrannical exercise of the federal authority.[218]

Tensions between the Union and the states can also be brought about by state laws that are incompatible with national laws. Here again, the Constitution provides for a remedy. According to the *Federalist,* there are only two alternatives at the disposal of the national government for the prevention of collisions between the laws of the states and those of the Union, namely, either a "direct negative on the State laws, or an authority in the federal courts to overrule such as might be in manifest contravention of the articles of Union." The Constitution prefers the second alternative, which is likely to be "most agreeable to the States" and probably more conducive to peace,[219] by permitting judicial review of state laws.[220]

[218] 16, 99-100.   [219] 80, 516.

[220] Compare in this connection Oliver Wendell Holmes' statement of 1913, in which he stresses the necessity of a judicial review of state laws for the preservation of the Union. Oliver Wendell Holmes, COLLECTED LEGAL PAPERS (1920), 295-96.

Aside from judicial review, other federal functions appear to be furthering the cause of peace. There is, first, the competence of federal courts for all cases to which the Union is a party. "Controversies between the nation and its members or citizens, can only be properly referred to the national tribunals," writes Hamilton, continuing that "any other plan would be contrary to reason, to precedent, and to decorum."[221] Similarly, the power of the federal courts of determining cases between two states, between one state and the citizens of another, and between the citizens of different states, is considered "essential to the peace of the Union."[222]

5. In view of the far-reaching competences of the federal government that appear to be conducive to peace, the question arises whether the name "federal state" is not a misnomer and whether the term "unitary state" would be more appropriate. The *Federalist* leaves no doubt about the answer and stresses the federal character of the Constitution. The legislative competences of the Union are "few and defined," those remaining with the state governments, "numerous and indefinite."[223] The former, which will be exercised principally on such objects as war, peace, negotiation, foreign commerce, and taxation, will strengthen the government of the Union especially in times of war and emergency. The latter, being concerned with "all the objects which, in the ordinary course of affairs, concern the lives, liberties, and properties of the people, and the internal order, improvement, and prosperity of the State," will make the governments of the states more important in peace and normal times.[224] Furthermore, the danger of an absorption of the states by the Union is decreased through the fact that the state governments, being closer to the people, will have the unqualified support of the people in thwarting inroads by the national government upon states' rights.[225] Effective opposition to the national government will be facilitated by the large extension of the country.[226] An encroachment upon states' rights by federal courts does not appear to be possible because the judges exercise merely judicial, and no political, power.[227]

It has been asked whether the *Federalist*'s emphasis upon the federal character of the Constitution was not prompted by the idea to lull the suspicions of those who felt the Constitution estab-

---

[221] 80, 516.
[222] 80, 517.
[223] 45, 303.

[224] 45, 303.
[225] 17, 102; 28, 174; 46, 309; 46, 311.

[226] 28, 174.
[227] Essay 78.

lished a consolidated system. These doubts seem to be justified in view of far-reaching and elastic clauses through which the federal government can be further strengthened, such as the supremacy and the necessary and proper clauses. In later years, these doubts were vindicated by an increasingly nationalistic interpretation of the Constitution. Nevertheless, the *Federalist* basically preserves the federal character of the new state. Federalism appears to be ideally suited for the maintenance of peace in America.

VIII

In the second part of this chapter, an attempt was made to show how the authors of the *Federalist* see the problem of the preservation of peace in America. The experience of various confederations, including that of the United States under the Articles of Confederation, leads them to certain conclusions. Since man in America, as in other parts of the world, is not able to grow above the limits set to him by nature and cannot overcome his egoism, peace appears to be as improbable among thirteen independent American states as among several American confederacies. Although a confederation, like that under the Articles, offers certain advantages for the preservation of peace, it is probable that there will exist internal tensions owing to the high degree of sovereignty that remains with the states. In order to improve conditions, the authors advocate the ratification of the Constitution, which provides that federal laws are directly binding upon the inhabitants of the states, and which transfers sovereignty from the states to the Union, while also leaving with the states sufficient powers to prevent a development toward a unitary state.

CHAPTER EIGHT

The Federalist on Security

In the preceding chapter, it was shown how federalism is considered a means for the preservation of peace. While tensions within a confederation were considered likely to bring about its destruction, it was pointed out that foreign nations often fostered such tensions. Foreign powers appeared as intriguing against the federation, making use of the principle *divide et impera*.[1]

It is evident that such an indirect interference in the affairs of a confederation will often be hard to distinguish from more direct actions foreign powers may undertake in order to promote their own interests. This is recognized by the authors of the *Federalist* when they warn of "foreign intrusions and intrigues"[2] and speak of "the preservation of peace and tranquility . . . against dangers from *foreign arms and influence,*"[3] and thus mention more indirect and more direct hostile acts in one breath, indicating the close connection between the two. In the following, we shall be concerned only with open hostilities. An attempt will be made to show how in the *Federalist* federalism appears as a means for obtaining security from foreign nations. Again, we shall separate statements of a more theoretical and historical nature from those that are connected with the situation in America. A first part, dealing with the problem of se-

---

[1] The principle *divide et impera* is mentioned at 7, 40. Compare also 11, 63.
[2] 19, 115.   [3] 3, 13.

curity in general and suggesting the federal form of government as a solution for that problem, will be followed by a second part, which shows how the authors view with apprehension the possibility of foreign attacks against independent or loosely confederated American states and how in their opinion the more perfect Union under the Constitution will repel foreign aggression and be conducive to security from other nations.

I

1. As was shown above, the *Federalist* denies the probability of peace among independent nations. Human shortcomings, such as ambition, vindictiveness, and greed are held responsible for international tensions. The authors stress that these tensions are due not only to the attitude of monarchs, but also to that of the people themselves. War among republics is considered as natural a phenomenon as war among monarchies. The existence of international tensions is taken for granted.[4]

Under these conditions, the members of the international community are likely to form protective alliances. According to the *Federalist,* such alliances can be of a different type. They can be of a military or political nature. We are here concerned with the latter. Political alliances, in turn, fall into two categories. On the one hand, different states may form a union in order to prevent tensions among themselves. Thus the union between England and Scotland was formed to remove the animosities among the inhabitants of the two states, as well as the jealousies and differences between the two kingdoms.[5] Similarly, more than two states may enter a confederacy in order to prevent tensions among themselves, as has been done by the members of various confederacies throughout history. Federalism appears here as a means for the preservation of peace among the federating states, as was shown in the previous chapter. On the other hand, states may form an alliance in order to protect themselves from third powers which remain outside the alliance. Thus the union between England and Scotland was partly formed in order that "the whole island, being joined in affection and free from all apprehensions of different interest, will be *enabled to resist all its enemies.*"[6] In a similar manner, several states may enter a confed-

---

[4] Compare *supra,* pp. 177 ff.   [5] 5, 23.   [6] 5, 23.

cration in order to have security from the attacks of third powers. Federalism appears here as a means for the security of the federating states on the international scene.

The *Federalist* states the security function of federalism in quite a general way. "The utility of a Confederacy," writes Hamilton, "as well to suppress faction and to guard the internal tranquility of the States, as to increase their external force and security, is in reality not a new idea. It has been practised upon in different countries and ages, and has received the sanction of the most approved writers on the subjects of politics."[7] The *Federalist*, holding that safety from external danger is the most powerful director of national conduct[8] and that security against foreign danger is one of the primitive objects of civil society,[9] proceeds to point out the security motive in the formation of several confederacies. The Achaean league and the Lycian confederacy were the result of numerous and powerful external causes by which the component parts were pressed together.[10] After the end of the Achaean league through Macedonian conquest, the former members of the league re-united in order to shake off the foreign yoke and were joined by other Greek states in order to be secure from external enemies.[11] One of the reasons why the German confederacy, in spite of its inherent weakness and shortcomings, has not yet fallen apart, is "the weakness of most of its members, who are unwilling to expose themselves to the mercy of foreign powers; the weakness of most of the principal members, compared with the formidable powers all around them."[12] The Swiss cantons "are kept together by the peculiarity of their topographical position; by their individual weakness and insignificancy; by the fear of powerful neighbors, to one of which they were formerly subject."[13] In the United Netherlands, "the surrounding powers impose an absolute necessity of union to a certain degree, at the same time that they nourish by their intrigues the constitutional vices which keep the republic in some degree always at their mercy."[14]

While the *Federalist* does not deny the possibility of a federation

---

[7] 9, 49.   [8] 8, 42.   [9] 41, 261.
[10] 45, 300.   [11] 18, 111.
[12] 19, 117.   [13] 19, 118.
[14] 20, 123. Compare also 20, 121: "It was long ago remarked by Grotius, that nothing but the hatred of his countrymen to the house of Austria kept them from being ruined by the vices of their constitution."

of larger states, the examples supplied indicate that it is assumed that as a rule only smaller nations will enter a confederation for reasons of security. This assumption seems to be confirmed by a more direct statement of Hamilton. Quoting Montesquieu, he refers to a confederate republic as "a convention by which several smaller *states* agree to become members of a larger *one,* which they intend to form." This confederacy is "a kind of assemblage of societies that constitute a new one, capable of increasing, by means of associations, till they arrive to such a degree of power as to be able to provide for the security of the united body. A republic of this kind" is "able to withstand an external force."[15] It thus appears as if the purpose of federation is primarily one of defense, and not of aggression: Several smaller states combine in order that the new federation may be in a position to provide for the security of its members as well as for that of the federation as a whole, and not for purposes of aggrandizement. Also, it appears as if the federation would not be more powerful than other states. The smaller states seem to combine merely in order that their common strength might be on a par with that of other nations, not necessarily greater. The security motive thus prompts smaller states to unite in order to create a new member of the international community. World federalism, motivated by a quest for security, is not yet suggested in the *Federalist.*

2. Concluding our analysis of the *Federalist*'s opinion on the security motive for federation, it may be said that the people living in independent states, especially those living in small neighboring nations, realize their precarious situation and the dangers threatening from other powers. As a result, they enter a federal union in order to be able, through common strength, to defend themselves against foreign ambitions. This raises the question as to the type of confederation that can fulfill the purpose of federation, namely, security.

II

1. The Papers by no means maintain that any type of confederacy can guarantee security from foreign danger. On the contrary, it appears doubtful whether the end of the federal compact can be at-

[15] 9, 50-51.

tained in many cases. The experiences of various confederacies are used in support of this skepticism. Confederations, so goes the argument, did not only fail to prevent foreign intrigues among their members. They also failed to prevent a direct participation of foreign powers in conflicts among those members and were unable to thwart the conquest of the federation and its members by the enemy.[16]

Thus the Greek confederacy, associated under the Amphictyonic council, was by no means safe from foreign influence and attack. "Even in the midst of defensive and dangerous wars with Persia and Macedon, the members never acted in concert, and were, more or fewer of them, eternally the dupes and hirelings of the common enemy."[17] When the Phocians, being abetted by Athens and Sparta, refused to submit to a decree of the Amphictyonic council, the Thebans and other cities, in their attempts to enforce the decree, invited the assistance of Philip of Macedon, who had secretly fostered the contest among the members of the Amphictyonic league. He gladly seized the opportunity of executing the designs he had long planned against the liberties of Greece. By his intrigues and bribes he won over to his interests the popular leaders of several cities. By their influence and votes, he gained admission to the Amphictyonic council, and by his arts and arms he made himself master of the confederacy.[18]

The Achaean league was in a similar predicament. Dissensions among its members were fostered by the Romans.

Calicrates and other popular leaders became mercenary instruments for inveigling their countrymen. The more effectually to nourish discord and disorder the Romans had, to the astonishment of those who confided in their sincerity, already proclaimed universal liberty (this was but another name more specious for the independence of the members on the federal head) throughout Greece. With the same insidious views, they now seduced the members from the league, by representing to their pride the violation it committed on their sovereignty. By these arts this union, the last hope of Greece, the last hope of ancient liberty, was torn into pieces; and such imbecility and distraction introduced, that the arms of Rome found little difficulty in completing the ruin which their arts had commenced. The Achaeans were cut to pieces, and Achaia loaded with chains, under which it is groaning at this hour.[19]

---

[16] Compare *supra*, pp. 183f., 185, 187, 188, 190.
[17] 18, 107.   [18] 18, 107-8.   [19] 18, 112.

The history of Germany is seen as a history of foreign intrusions and intrigues.[20] "Previous to the peace of Westphalia, Germany was desolated by a war of thirty years, in which the emperor, with one half of the empire, was on one side, and Sweden, with the other half, on the opposite side. Peace was at length negotiated, and dictated by foreign powers; and the articles of it, to which foreign powers are parties, made a fundamental part of the German constitution."[21] Germany's neighbors are interested in a continuation of this state of affairs. They would not suffer a revolution that, by increasing national power, would give to the empire the force and pre-eminence to which it is entitled. Foreign nations have long considered themselves as interested in the changes made by the events in Germany. On various occasions, they betrayed their policy of perpetuating her anarchy and weakness.[22]

Poland is another confederation in which the various member states were not secure from outside powers. The authors regret to say that "it has long been at the mercy of its powerful neighbors; who have lately had the mercy to disburden it of one third of its people and territories."[23] Likewise Switzerland was plagued by the interference of foreign nations, when the United Provinces united with the Protestant cantons, and France, with the Catholic ones. Finally, it is stated that foreign powers nourish by their intrigues the constitutional vices that keep the republic of the United Netherlands in some degree always at their mercy.[24] On the whole, it may be said that under none of the older confederations examined in the *Federalist* was there achieved security from foreign powers. This leaves us to examine the "constitutional vices" that are held responsible for the possibility of foreign interference and the absence of security.

2.   The main cause of insecurity from foreign danger is a want of power in the government of the confederacy or, what amounts to the same thing, too much sovereignty in the member states. For instance, the government of the Amphictyonic league theoretically possessed the powers essential for the security of the league. The council had a general authority to propose and resolve whatever it judged necessary for the common welfare of Greece, as well as the power to declare and carry on war.[25] However, far reaching and sufficient as

[20] 19, 115.   [22] 19, 117-18.   [24] 20, 123.
[21] 19, 116.   [23] 19, 118.   [25] 18, 106.

these powers may appear, in practice they could hardly be exercised, due to the fact that the members of the federal government were appointed by the governments of the member states and that the laws and decrees of the confederate government were binding only upon the component political units, and not upon the individual citizens. This high degree of state sovereignty proved detrimental to security. Even in the midst of defensive and dangerous wars, the members never acted in concert.[26] The weakness of the confederate government and resultant internal dissensions are held responsible for bringing on calamities from abroad.[27] The conquest of the league by Philip of Macedon is attributed to the "fallacious principle" on which the league was founded, namely, the sovereignty of the member states. "Had Greece," it is stated, "been united by a stricter confederation, and persevered in her union, she would never have worn the chains of Macedon; and might have proved a barrier to the vast projects of Rome."[28]

The situation was similar in the case of the Achaean league. The powers of the confederate senate that are relevant for the security of the league are quite numerous. The senate had the sole and exclusive right of peace and war; of sending and receiving ambassadors; of entering into treaties and alliances; of appointing a chief magistrate or praetor, who commanded the armies of the confederacy.[29] Nevertheless internal dissensions facilitated the fall of the confederation, when foreign states attacked. Although the *Federalist* does not state in so many words that state sovereignty was responsible for the end of the Achaean league, we may assume that the authors believed this to have been the case, because they often hint at internal dissensions in that league that appear to be possible only under a weak federal government.

In the German confederation, the national diet possesses powers that are important for the security from foreign danger. It has the right of making war and peace, contracting alliances, assessing quotas of troops and money, and constructing fortresses.[30] Also, the members of the confederacy are expressly restricted from entering into compacts prejudicial to the empire.[31] However, the *Federalist* warns not to assume from this variety of national competencies that security from foreign nations is achieved. "The fundamental principle on which it rests, that the empire is a community of sovereigns,

[26] 18, 107.
[27] 18, 108.
[28] 18, 109.
[29] 18, 109.
[30] 19, 114.
[31] 19, 114.

and that laws are addressed to sovereigns, renders the empire a nerveless body, . . . insecure against external dangers."[32] Even "if the nation happens, on any emergency, to be more united by the necessity of self-defence, its situation is still deplorable. Military preparations must be preceded by so many tedious discussions, arising from the jealousies, pride, separate views and clashing pretensions of sovereign bodies, that before the diet can settle the arrangements, the enemy are in the field; and before the federal troops are ready to take it, are retiring into winter quarters."[33] Local sovereignty is held responsible for the fact that the small body of national troops, which has been judged necessary in time of peace, is defectively kept up, badly paid, infected with local prejudices, and supported only by irregular and disproportionate contributions to the treasury.[34]

In the case of Poland, the fact that the country has been at the mercy of its powerful neighbors is attributed to its being "a government over local sovereigns,"[35] i.e., to the want of power in the national government. The experience of that country is considered a striking proof of the calamities flowing from a government that is "equally unfit for self-government and self-defence."[36] Finally, the alliance of the Catholic Swiss cantons with France and of the Protestant cantons with the United Netherlands, which made foreign interference in Swiss affairs possible, is attributed to the fact that the Swiss confederacy is bare of any common mark of sovereignty, because sovereignty rests with the cantons.[37]

As to the United Netherlands, the situation is not much different. This "confederacy of republics"[38] has, "as delineated on parchment,"[39] a quite acceptable government. The sovereignty of the union is represented by the States-General, consisting of deputies appointed by the provinces.[40] The States-General have authority over all matters that appear relevant for the security of the confederation. They have the authority to enter into treaties and alliances; to make war and peace; to raise armies and equip fleets; to ascertain quotas and demand contributions; to appoint and receive ambassadors; to execute treaties and alliances already formed. In turn, the component provinces are restrained from entering into foreign treaties without the consent of the general government. To secure the safety of the confederacy further, the confederacy is

[32] 19, 115.   [35] 19, 118.   [38] 20, 119.
[33] 19, 116.   [36] 19, 118.   [39] 20, 121.
[34] 19, 116.   [37] 19, 118-19.   [40] 20, 120.

equipped with a strong executive, who is also heading the different provinces. He has the right to give audiences to foreign ambassadors and to keep agents for his particular affairs at foreign courts. In his military capacity, he commands the federal troops, provides for garrisons, and in general regulates military affairs. He disposes of all appointments, from colonels to ensigns, and of the governments and posts of fortified towns. In his marine capacity he is admiral-general, and he superintends and directs everything relative to naval forces and other naval affairs. He presides in the admiralties, appoints lieutenant-admirals and other officers, and establishes councils of war.[41] In spite of all these powers vested in the government of the confederacy for the sake of security, the federal government is branded with imbecility. Its weak position results in "foreign influence and indignities; a precarious existence in peace, and peculiar calamities from war."[42] Foreign nations take advantage of the situation due to the high degree of state sovereignty. Sir William Temple is quoted as saying that foreign ministers elude matters taken *ad referendum*, by tampering with the provinces and cities. In 1726, the treaty of Hanover was delayed by these means for a whole year. Instances of a like nature are numerous and notorious.[43] Naturally, the surrounding powers nourish by their intrigues the constitutional vices of the United Netherlands in order to be able to exercise a certain control over that federation.[44]

3. To summarize, it can be said that the experiences of various confederations, such as the Amphictyonic league, the Achaean league, the German empire, Poland, Switzerland, and the United Netherlands, demonstrate to the authors of the *Federalist* that a confederacy of sovereign states, no matter how large the powers delegated to the federal authority are, has a strong tendency toward anarchy[45] and is in no position to provide for security from foreign danger. The dependence of the federal authority on the governments of the member states is detrimental to the security of the whole and its parts. According to Hamilton, it is not possible that a government that, due to its dependence upon the states, is only half-supplied and always necessitous, can fulfill the purposes of its institution. It can neither provide for the security or support the reputation of the commonwealth, nor can it ever possess energy or stability, dignity or credit, confidence at home or respectability

41 20, 121.   43 20, 122.   45 18, 112; 19, 118.
42 20, 121.   44 20, 123.

abroad.[46] Jay complements these doubts by pointing out that "a confederacy of little consideration or power" will, if it should commit an international wrong, not even be able to have its acknowledgements, explanations, and compensations accepted by the insulted nation.[47] Its demonstration of good will will be of no avail for the security of its members. In general, the *Federalist* denies that half-hearted attempts at confederation—due to the desire of the confederating states to retain as much sovereignty as possible—are likely to achieve one of the proclaimed ends of the federal compact, namely, security.

III

1.   As a remedy against this state of insecurity, the *Federalist* suggests the creation of a strong federal government and the abolition of state sovereignty. "A government ought to contain in itself every power requisite to the full accomplishment of the objects committed to its care, and to the complete execution of the trusts for which it is responsible, free from every other control but a regard to the public good and to the sense of the people," writes Hamilton, and he continues saying that "the duties of superintending the national defence and of securing the public peace against foreign . . . violence involve a provision for casualties and dangers to which no possible limits can be assigned."[48] A dependence of the federal government upon the governments of the component states is considered inadmissible, as far as security from foreign nations is concerned. Madison complements his collaborator's unequivocal assertion of federal power for the sake of security in a similar language. "Energy in government," he writes, "is essential to that security against external . . . danger, and to that prompt and salutary execution of the laws which enter into the very definition of good government. Stability in government is essential to national character and to the advantages annexed to it."[49] Centrifugal tendencies that are supported by the sovereignty of the states and are likely to result in an unstable government are incompatible with the security of a confederation.

The same attitude can be concluded from statements made by Jay. The creation of a strong federal government is to be recommended

---

[46] 30, 186.   [47] 3, 17.   [48] 31, 190.   [49] 37, 227.

for two main reasons. First, Jay considers a decrease of state authority necessary to prevent provocations of foreign nations by the members of the confederacy, since such provocations are likely to result in retaliatory measures. Such *"just* causes of war," due to "designed or accidental violations of treaties and the law of nations," are "less to be apprehended under one general government than under several lesser ones, and in that respect the former most favors the *safety* of the people."[50] Furthermore, a strong federal government is considered to afford vastly more security against such just causes of war that proceed from direct and unlawful violence committed by the members of the confederacy, because such violent acts are caused more frequently by the passions and interests of a part than of the whole of the confederation.[51] Second, Jay feels that an increase of power in the federal government is necessary in order to repel hostility from abroad, i.e., in order to protect the confederacy from foreign action that is due to "pretended"[52] causes of war and the aggressive spirit of the enemy. He points out that Britain would be in bad shape "if the English militia obeyed the government of England, if the Scotch militia obeyed the government of Scotland, and if the Welsh militia obeyed the government of Wales." He doubts whether in an invasion these three governments would be able to operate against the enemy so effectually as a single government of Britain would. The same applies to the British navy. Again, Jay advances the proposition that unity creates strength. The prestige of that navy is attributed to the fact that one national government had called forth all the national means and materials for forming fleets. If, instead, England, Scotland, Wales, and Ireland would regulate their own fleets, these four parts of the British empire would soon dwindle into comparative insignificance, and the prowess of the British fleet would never have been celebrated.[53]

2. In summary, it may be said that in the *Federalist* a strong federal government is considered to be as necessary for security from foreign danger as for peace within the federation or for free government. Only a government that is not impeded by the sovereignty of its member states is in a position to guarantee security. A concentration of power in the federal government must raise the question whether that government might become so strong as to be oppressive to the member states and their people. This question can be an-

[50] 3, 16.   [51] 3, 16.   [52] 4, 18.   [53] 4, 20-21.

swered in the negative. Hamilton, the advocate of national power, admits that even in the case of superintending national defense and securing the public peace against foreign violence, the federal governernment, in spite of its far-reaching powers, would still be controlled by a due regard for the public good and the sense of the people.[54] Likewise, Jay emphasizes that since the safety of the whole is the interest of the whole, the federal government will take into consideration the interests of the parts as much as those of the whole and "extend the benefit of its foresight and precaution to each" of the members of the federation.[55] In a word, federalism appears to be ideally suited for the security of the federated states while, at the same time, guaranteeing a great degree of freedom to each of the individual states.

IV

In the preceding pages an attempt has been made to show how the *Federalist* sees the general problem of security. Taking into account the experience of international relations, including the relations of confederations with foreign states, the authors arrive at certain conclusions. War among nations—monarchies and republics alike—is, owing to the nature of man, considered inevitable. The desire for survival prompts independent nations, especially weaker nations, to form protective alliances through political federation, in order to be protected from foreign powers. While the authors admit that through confederation a greater degree of security can be achieved, they do by no means maintain that any form of federation will guarantee security. On the contrary, it is stressed that under most of the known confederations, security did not actually exist. This failure is attributed to the fact that in these confederations, sovereignty had largely remained with the component states. This made the federal government dependent upon the governments of the states and thus deprived the former of those powers that are indispensable for security purposes. As a remedy, the authors suggest a decrease of state power matched by an increase of national power. This amounts to a transfer of sovereignty from the states to the federation, without, however, jeopardizing the existence of the component parts. The conclusions reached with respect to the security function of federalism

[54] 31, 190.   [55] 4, 20.

are applied to American conditions, as will be shown in the following pages, which will examine how according to the *Federalist* the Confederation under the Articles was entered in order to be secure from foreign powers; how the system under the Articles of Confederation proved to be inadequate; and how the more perfect Union under the Constitution is believed to achieve security.

V

1.   Although the authors of the *Federalist* are largely concerned with proving that the government under the Articles of Confederation is inadequate for the achievement of security, they do not hesitate to answer those enemies of an American union that propose the formation of various confederacies or even of thirteen independent states.[56] Consequently, the problem of security in these hypothetical cases is amply dealt with. Its discussion serves as a means to demonstrate to the American people the alternatives of a more perfect Union and their disastrous consequences. Also, that discussion serves as a steppingstone to attacks on the existing federal system, which is considered not much better than a possible dissolution of the Union. As a matter of fact, the reader of the *Federalist* will often not know whether the work, when dealing with the problem of security in the case of thirteen independent states, does not actually speak of the members of the existing Confederation. It is conceivable that this ambiguous mode of expression was chosen on purpose. For, considering the fact that the majority of the American people were probably opposed to a dissolution of the existing Confederation, the authors, when describing the hazards of security in the case of thirteen independent states, actually point to the insecurity under the Articles of Confederation. Since these Articles had virtually left the independence of the states intact, a persuasion of the reader that thirteen independent American nations could not be secure was likely to amount to a persuasion that the thirteen states, as confederated under the Articles, could not be secure either.

The *Federalist* leaves no doubt that, in case of a dissolution of the existing Confederation into thirteen states or into three or four confederacies, there could be no security from foreign danger.[57] Jay's language is unequivocal on that point. "Leave America divided into

[56] 2, 9.   [57] 85, 568.

thirteen, or, if you please, into three or four independent governments—what armies could they raise and pay—what fleets could they
ever hope to have?" he asks, and continues in a skeptical vein: "If
one was attacked, would the others fly to its succor, and spend their
blood and money in its defence? Would there be no danger of their
being flattered into neutrality by its specious promises, or seduced by a
too great fondness for peace to decline hazarding their tranquility
and present safety for the sake of neighbors, of whom perhaps they
have been jealous, and whose importance they are content to see diminished." Such conduct, Jay adds, would not be wise, but it would,
nevertheless, be natural. To support his argument, he refers to the
history of the states of Greece and of other countries that abounds
with such instances, saying that it is not improbable that what has so
often happened would, under similar circumstances, happen again.[58]
Even if the other states or confederacies were willing to rally to the
help of the invaded state or confederacy, it would hardly be of much
help, because no one would know how, and when, and in what proportion aids of men and money could be afforded; who would command the allied armies, and from whom orders should be received;
who should settle the terms of peace, and in the case of disputes what
umpire should decide between them and compel acquiescence.[59]

Not only is it maintained that America divided into different nations would be in bad shape in case of a foreign attack. It is stated
also that weakness and divisions at home would invite dangers from
abroad, irrespective of provocations by American states or confederacies of foreign nations.[60] Foreign powers will view the American scene realistically and act accordingly, always trying to take
advantage of the existing situation. "If they find us either destitute
of an effectual government (each State doing right or wrong, as to its
rulers may seem convenient), or split into three or four independent
and probably discordant republics or confederacies, one inclining to
Britain, another to France, and a third to Spain, and perhaps played
off against each other by the three, what a poor, pitiful figure will
America make in their eyes! How liable would she become not only
to their contempts but to their outrage; and how soon would dear-
bought experience proclaim that when a people or family so divide,
it never fails to be against themselves."[61] Foreign nations would be
interested in keeping America divided. By their "arts and policy and

[58] 4, 21.   [59] 4, 21.   [60] 5, 23.   [61] 4, 22.

practices,"[62] they would keep the mutual jealousies of the different American nations perpetually inflamed in order that these confederacies might be "formidable only to each other,"[63] an easy prey for foreign powers. Disunion would add another victim to the triumphs of Europe, which had succeeded in extending her dominion over the earth.[64]

2. Aside from statements of a more general nature, the *Federalist* points out more specific disadvantages ensuing from disunion. American commerce is cited as a case in point. "In a state so insignificant our commerce would be a prey to the wanton intermeddlings of all nations at war with each other; who, having nothing to fear from us, would with little scruple or remorse supply their wants by depredations on our property as often as it fell in their way,"[65] writes Hamilton. He is afraid lest in a state of disunion there would exist combinations of European jealousy to restrain the growth of American commerce. Since it would be in the power of the maritime nations, availing themselves of the universal impotence of America, to prescribe the conditions of America's political existence, these foreign nations,

> as they have a common interest in being our carriers, and still more in preventing our becoming theirs, . . . would in all probability combine to embarrass our navigation in such a manner as would in effect destroy it, and confine us to a PASSIVE COMMERCE. We should then be compelled to content ourselves with the first price of our commodities, and to see the profits of our trade snatched from us to enrich our enemies and persecutors. That unequalled spirit of enterprise, which signalizes the genius of the American merchants and navigators, and which is in itself an inexhaustible mine of national wealth, would be stifled and lost, and poverty and disgrace would overspread a country which, with wisdom, might make herself the admiration and envy of the world.[66]

Hamilton then proceeds to point out the problems arising from a dissolution of the Confederacy with respect to the rights that for the time being belong to the Union, such as the rights concerning the fisheries and navigation on the Western lakes and on the Mississippi. In case of a dissolution, those rights would pose delicate questions, which foreign nations would not fail to solve in their own interest.

[62] 5, 23. [64] 11, 69; 41, 264. [66] 11, 66.
[63] 5, 25. [65] 11, 65.

Spain would be disposed to monopolize navigation on the Mississippi, just as France and Britain would cause trouble with respect to the fisheries and try to eliminate the American competition that has been able to undersell those nations in their own markets.[67]

3.   The insecurity of thirteen independent American nations or several confederacies, envisaged by the authors of the *Federalist,* must raise the question as to whether the situation could be improved through an alliance. The *Federalist* is skeptical on this possibility.[68] Since the proposed confederacies will be distinct nations, each of them would have its commerce with foreigners to regulate by distinct treaties, and as their productions and commodities are different and proper for different markets, so would those treaties be essentially different. Different commercial concerns must create different interests, and of course different degrees of political attachment to and connection with foreign nations. Consequently, it is very probable that one state, being at war with a foreign nation, will not be aided by the other confederacies, because the interests of these confederacies might be to preserve peace and friendship with the foreign nation at war. Since the different confederacies would have different interests, they would apprehend danger from one another rather than from foreign nations, and, therefore, be desirous to guard against the others by the aid of foreign alliances, rather than to guard against foreign dangers by alliances between themselves.[69] This might result in the invitation of foreign sea and land forces to America, and it might be hard to persuade these forces to depart.[70] Small as the probability of alliance between American nations is, the *Federalist* maintains that even if such an alliance came into existence, it would hardly be able to guarantee security.[71]

4.   The authors are not satisfied with merely pointing out the insecurity resulting from a dissolution of the existing Confederation. In order to boost their argument on the necessity of union, they do not just maintain that, for the sake of security, union is necessary now. They make reference to the past in an attempt to appeal to the American patriots' emotions. The *Federalist* states that the American Union has been consecrated by the "mingled blood" that American "citizens have shed in defence of their sacred rights" against the

---

[67] 11, 66-67.   [69] 5, 25-26. See also 7, 40; 15, 91.   [71] 15, 91.
[68] 5, 25; 15, 91.   [70] 5, 25-26.

English.[72] It is stressed that years back Americans united in order to gain security from foreign danger.[73] As early as 1774, "well-grounded apprehensions of imminent danger induced the people of America to form the memorable Congress of 1774."[74] That Congress, which was composed of wise and experienced men who were interested in public liberty and prosperity, recommended such measures as they thought prudent and advisable for the defense of the rights of the colonists against England, and experience proved their wisdom.[75]

Similarly, the Articles of Confederation were adopted in order to gain security from foreign danger. "A strong sense of the value and blessings of union induced the people, at a very early period, to institute a federal government to preserve and perpetuate it," says Jay, maintaining that the Americans formed the government under the Articles of Confederation "almost as soon as they had a political existence and at a time when their habitations were in flames and when many of their citizens were bleeding, in the middle of hostility and desolation."[76] According to the *Federalist,* the security motive is evident in certain provisions of the Articles. Under Article 3, the objects of the Union among the states are "their common defence, security of their liberties, and their mutual and general welfare."[77] Article 8 provides that all charges of war and all other expenses that shall be incurred for the common defense shall be defrayed out of the common treasury.[78] Madison praises the Articles for giving to the government of the Confederation the power over war and defense.[79] In view of these powers and the purpose of the Articles, the question arises whether the existing Confederation was in a position to provide for security from foreign nations.

VI

1. In the opinion of the *Federalist,* security was by no means guaranteed under the Articles, in spite of the fact that "the distance of the United States from the powerful nations of the world gives them the same happy security" as that enjoyed by England because of her insular position and maritime resources.[80] Rather, the United States offers the spectacle of a nation that, as Madison puts it, "finds

[72] 14, 84.
[73] 45, 300.
[74] 2, 11.
[75] 2, 11.
[76] 2, 9-10.
[77] 41, 269.
[78] 41, 269.
[79] 41, 261; 45, 303.
[80] 41, 263.

that she is held in no respect by her friends; that she is the derision
of her enemies; and that she is a prey to every nation."[81] Hamilton
complements the statement of his collaborator, saying that it seems
impossible that foreign nations can either respect or confide in the
present American government, a situation that jeopardizes American
security.[82] "We may indeed be said to have reached almost the last
stage of national humiliation," writes Hamilton, continuing, "there
is scarcely anything that can wound the pride or degrade the character of an independent nation which we do not experience."[83] He
then proceeds to enumerate conditions that demonstrate the weakness of the United States on the international scene. Valuable and
important territories and posts, which, by express stipulation, ought
to have been surrendered long since to the United States, are still in
the possession of a foreign power, retained to the prejudice of American interests no less than to that of American rights. Although the
United States is by nature and compact entitled to a free participation in the navigation on the Mississippi, Spain excludes her from it.
The United States is in no position to prevent aggression, since she
has "neither troops, nor treasury, nor government." America does
not enjoy that "safeguard against foreign encroachments," "respectability in the eyes of foreign powers." The imbecility of the government of the Union even forbids foreign nations to deal with the
United States. American ambassadors abroad are the mere pageants
of a mimic sovereignty.[84]

2.   This deplorable position of the United States vis-à-vis foreign
powers can be attributed to the same factors that were held responsible for the threat to peace and free government. The "mimic
sovereignty" of the government of the Union or, as Madison puts
it, "the want of a due sense of national character,"[85] prevents the
United States from playing a respected role in international affairs.
Owing to "material imperfections" of the system under the Articles,[86]
which left state sovereignty intact, the government of the Union has
been in no position to guarantee security from foreign powers.[87]
This is demonstrated by a variety of examples.

[81] 62, 405.   [83] 15, 87.   [85] 63, 407.
[82] 22, 139.   [84] 15, 87-88. See also 22, 136.   [86] 15, 87.
   [87] Compare 46, 305-6: "The federal administration, though hitherto very defective in comparison with what may be hoped under a better system, had, during
the war, and particularly whilst the independent fund of paper emissions was in
credit, an activity and importance as great as it can well have in any course of

For instance, the strong position of the states is believed to facilitate war with foreign nations. Jay stresses that "not a single Indian war has yet been occasioned by aggressions of the present federal government, feeble as it is; but there are several instances of Indian hostilities having been provoked by the improper conduct of individual States, who, either unable or unwilling to restrain or punish offences, have given occasion to the slaughter of many innocent inhabitants." He fears that since the neighborhood of Spanish and British territories, bordering on some states and not on others, naturally confines the causes of quarrel more immediately to the borderers, the bordering states will under the impulse of sudden irritation, and a quick sense of apparent interest or injury, be likely, by direct violence, to excite war with these nations, if these states are independent of the government of the Union.[88]

The independence of the states not only facilitates an outbreak of war but also impedes war efforts once the Union is engaged in hostilities. The War of Independence is cited as a case in point.[89]

> [Since] the power of raising armies, by the most obvious construction of the articles of Confederation, is merely a power of making requisitions upon the States for quotas of men [writes Hamilton], this practice, in the course of the late war, was found replete with obstruction to a vigorous and to an economical system of defence. It gave birth to a competition between the States which created a kind of auction for men. In order to furnish the quotas required of them, they outbid each other till bounties grew to an enormous and unsupportable size. The hope of a still further increase afforded an inducement to those who were disposed to serve to procrastinate their enlistment, and disinclined them from engaging for any considerable periods. Hence, slow and scanty levies of men, in the most critical emergencies of our affairs; short enlistments at an unparalleled expense; continual fluctuations in the troops, ruinous to their discipline and subjecting the public safety frequently to the perilous crisis of a disbanded army.[90]

measures which had for their object the protection of every thing that was dear, and the acquisition of every thing that could be desirable to the people at large. It was, nevertheless, invariably found, after the transient enthusiasm for the early Congresses was over, that the attention and attachment of the people were turned anew to their own particular governments; that the federal council was at no time the idol of popular favor; and that opposition to proposed enlargements of its powers and importance was the side usually taken by the men who wished to build their political consequence on the prepossessions of their fellow-citizens."

[88] 3, 16.   [89] 15, 89-90.   [90] 22, 133.

While Hamilton considers such a system of raising troops uneco-
nomical and unlikely to create that vigor of government that is
necessary for a successful conduct of war, he also complains about
disadvantages resulting from the unequal distribution of the burdens
of war, another consequence of state sovereignty. Owing to their
greater distance from the theater of war, certain states were reluctant
to supply their quotas.[91] The result was a weakening of the all-out
war effort. Hamilton is not satisfied with merely demonstrating the
shortcomings of the Articles in the conduct of war, as actually experienced in the War of Independence. He also emphasizes that a
similar situation would exist in a future war if the system of requisitions of men, as existing under the Articles of Confederation, is retained.[92] The absence of a national army is regretted in the *Federalist*
again and again and is considered as one of the great constitutional
defects that are likely to jeopardize American security.[93]

To the detriment of national security, the system of obtaining
troops through the requisition of quotas is matched by a similar procedure for raising funds for the national government. The Union suffers not only from a want of troops but also from the lack of a treasury.[94] The *Federalist* regrets that the government of the United States,
while possessing ample theoretical powers for raising money, is, in
practice, in no position to do so. Experience has shown that "the
principle of regulating the contributions of the States to the common
treasury by QUOTAS" is repugnant "to an adequate supply of the
national exigencies."[95] We may assume that defense from foreign
danger falls into the category of "national exigencies." At any rate,
the relevance of a national treasury for national security, or, what
amounts to the same thing, the incompatibility of the method of
requisition of monetary funds for such security, is stated by Hamilton in a more direct language. In essay thirty, he writes:

> The present Confederation, feeble as it is, intended to repose in
> the United States an unlimited power of providing for the
> pecuniary wants of the Union. But proceeding upon an erroneous
> principle, it has been done in such a manner as entirely to have
> frustrated the intention. Congress, by the articles which compose
> that compact . . . are authorized to ascertain and call for any sums
> of money necessary, in their judgment, to the service of the United
> States; and their requisitions, if conformable to the rule of ap-

[91] 22, 133.   [92] 30, 186.
[93] 41, 261; 45, 303-4. See also 16, 95-96; 25, 156-57.
[94] 15, 87; 15, 89-90; 45, 303-4.   [95] 21, 127; 45, 303.

portionment, are in every constitutional sense obligatory upon the States. These have no right to question the propriety of the demand; no discretion beyond that of devising the ways and means of furnishing the sums demanded. But though this be strictly and truly the case; though the assumption of such a right would be an infringement of the articles of Union; though it may seldom or never have been avowedly claimed, yet in practice it has been constantly exercized, and would continue to be so, as long as the revenue of the Confederacy should remain dependent on the intermediate agency of its members. What the consequences of this system have been, is within the knowledge of every man the least conversant in our public affairs, and has been amply unfolded in different parts of these inquiries. It is this which has chiefly contributed to reduce us to a situation, which affords ample cause both of mortification to ourselves, and of triumph to our enemies.[96]

Hamilton maintains that a government that, due to the sovereignty of its member states, is only half-supplied and always in need, cannot provide for security. In case of war, it would, since it could hardly depend on requisitions, be driven to the expedient of diverting the funds already appropriated from their proper objects to the defense of the states, as happened under the Articles. This would result in a loss of public credit at the very moment when credit is most necessary for national security.[97] The want of credit with foreign nations is not only detrimental in case of war. It can also induce other nations to attack the United States. Madison brands the state legislatures for passing laws providing for paper money, feeling not only that such legislation involves hardship and injustice for Americans, but also that "the subjects of foreign powers might suffer from the same cause, and hence the Union be discredited and embroiled by the indiscretion of a single member."[98]

The vulnerability of the Confederation follows also from the treaty power of the national government. Under the present system, Jay complains, it is possible for the states not to fulfill treaties of the United States. Thus many states actually infringed, through legislation, upon the provisions of the treaty of peace with Britain. This situation cannot be satisfactory to foreign nations, and, therefore, cannot be conducive to American security from such nations, since infringements of treaties constitute just causes of war.[99] "The treaties of the United States, under the present Constitution," Hamilton

[96] 30, 183-84.   [98] 44, 290-91.   [99] 3, 14-15.
[97] 30, 186-87; 15, 88.

complements Jay's misgivings, "are liable to the infractions of thirteen different legislatures, and as many different courts of final
jurisdiction, acting under the authority of those legislatures. The
faith, the reputation, the peace of the whole Union, are thus continually at the mercy of the prejudices, the passions, and the interests
of every member of which it is composed. Is it possible that foreign
nations can either respect or confide in such a government? Is it
possible that the people of America will longer consent to trust their
honor, their happiness, their safety, on so precarious a foundation?"[100] Madison also regrets that the Articles of Confederation
"contain no provision for the case of offences against the law of
nations; and consequently leave it in the power of any indiscreet
member to embroil the Confederary with foreign nations."[101]

Commerce is a case in point. Hamilton complains that the want of
power in the national government to regulate commerce has already
operated as a bar to the formation of beneficial treaties with foreign
powers. Foreign nations are reluctant to conclude commercial
treaties with the United States for fear that the engagements on the
part of the Union might at any moment be violated by it members.[102]

3. In summary, it may be said that the Articles of Confederation,
though adopted in order to make America safe from foreign danger,
did not actually achieve the desired end. Due to the sovereignty of
the states, the United States offered the spectacle of a nation without a government. This was not only of great disadvantage in case
of foreign aggression, but was also likely to incite foreign attacks.
Thus conditions under the Confederation were, as far as security is
concerned, not much better than those envisaged for the case of a
dissolution of the existing Union into independent states or confederacies. As a matter of fact, the discussions of the *Federalist* often
leave doubt as to whether they are dealing with the conditions under
the Articles or with those existing in case of a dissolution of the
Union. No more devastating verdict on the shortcomings of the
Articles and their ability to provide for security could have been
rendered. Union, in order to guarantee safety from foreign powers,
must, therefore, be more perfect than that existing under the present system. The national government must be sovereign. This was
accomplished in Philadelphia, where the Founding Fathers framed
a Constitution under which security could be achieved.

[100] 22, 139.   [101] 42, 272.   [102] 22, 131.

VII

1. According to the *Federalist,* a more perfect Union is a prerequisite for security from foreign danger. Swayed by enthusiasm for the Union, Madison at one point even goes so far as to claim that union itself, irrespective of its armed strength, would guarantee security. "America united," he writes, "with a handful of troops, or without a single soldier, exhibits a more forbidding posture to foreign ambition than America disunited, with a hundred thousand veterans ready for combat."[103] Union is for Madison a "bulwark against foreign danger,"[104] "essential to the security of the people of America against foreign danger."[105] Likewise, Hamilton sees in the Union "the guardian of the common safety."[106] For Jay, Union affords the Americans "the best security that can be devised against *hostilities* from abroad."[107]

The new Constitution, establishing a more perfect Union, is believed to guarantee American security. The authors' hopes soar high. Comments on the situation as it would exist under the new system stand in sharp contrast to those made on security under the Articles of Confederation. "By a steady adherence to the Union, we may hope, erelong, to become the arbiter of Europe in America, and to be able to incline the balance of European competitions in this part of the world as our interests may dictate," writes Hamilton.[108] Taking issue with the arrogance of Europe, he continues: "It belongs to us to vindicate the honor of the human race, and to teach that assuming brother, moderation. Union will enable us to do it. Disunion will add another victim to his triumphs. Let Americans disdain to be the instruments of European greatness! Let the thirteen States, bound together in a strict and indissoluble Union, concur in erecting one great American system, superior to the control of all transatlantic force and influence, and able to dictate the terms of the connection between the old and new world!"[109] Madison expresses a similar optimism.[110] Jay's essays, written at the very beginning of the *Federalist* enterprise, have the hope for security through Union as a keynote, and, with it, the belief in American greatness.[111]

According to Jay, a stronger national government will render foreign attacks more difficult and less probable. Just causes of war

[103] 41, 263.
[104] 14, 79.
[105] 45, 298.
[106] 23, 144.
[107] 3, 14.
[108] 11, 65.
[109] 11, 69.
[110] Compare 62, 405; 62, 407; 63, 407.
[111] Essays 2-5.

"are less to be apprehended under one general government than under several lesser ones." A national government will be more observant of the law of nations and international obligations, since the best men of the whole nation will serve in it. "The administration, the political counsels, and the judicial decisions of the national government will be more wise, systematical, and judicious than those of individual States, and consequently more satisfactory with respect to other nations, as well as more *safe* with respect to us."[112] Whereas the passions of the people in the states of a loose confederation can easily get out of hand and provoke war with foreign nations over slight incidents, through direct and unlawful violence of the states, this danger would be obviated by a "national government, whose wisdom and prudence will not be diminished by the passions which actuate the parties immediately interested."[113]

The national government will not only give fewer causes of war. It will also be in a better position to settle international disputes amicably. Its members "will be more temperate and cool, and . . . will be more in capacity to act advisedly than the offending State. The pride of states, as well as of men, naturally disposes them to justify all their actions, and opposes their acknowledging, correcting, or repairing their errors and offences. The national government, in such cases, will not be affected by this pride, but will proceed with moderation and candor to consider and decide on the means most proper to extricate them from difficulties which threaten them."[114]

Not only would a more perfect Union prevent or conclude wars deriving from just causes, i.e., from the behavior of a state that is wrong under international law, but also it would make war deriving from unjust and pretended causes less probable. Jay expresses hopes that the American people consider union and a strong national government necessary for the prevention of foreign attacks that are prompted by nothing but the desire for conquest and expansion. The more perfect Union, he feels, would discourage any foreign plans of aggression.[115]

[112] 3, 15.   [113] 3, 16.   [114] 3, 16-17.

[115] After having pointed out the rivalry of the United States with other nations, such as France and Britain, and Spain, Jay writes: ". . . it is easy to see that jealousies and uneasiness may gradually slide into the minds and cabinets of other nations, and that we are not to expect that they should regard our advance-ment in union, in power and consequence by land and by sea, with an eye of in-

2. The greater security the United States would enjoy under the Constitution is due to an increase of national power. "Security against foreign danger is one of the primitive objects of civil society. It is an avowed and essential object of the American Union," writes Madison, and he expresses satisfaction that the powers requisite for attaining national security are effectually confided to the federal councils.[116] "Under a vigorous national government, the natural strength and resources of the country, directed to a common interest, would baffle all the combinations of European jealousy to restrain our growth,"[117] adds Hamilton, noting gladly that the new Constitution vests powers in the national government that are conducive to security. Jay notes, reminding his countrymen of the past, that "as a nation we have made peace and war; as a nation we have vanquished our common enemies; as a nation we have formed alliances, and made treaties and entered into various compacts and conventions with foreign states,"[118] and he looks forward to a state of security under a strong national government.

The powers of the new government that are conducive to security are manifold. There is, first of all, the power over matters of defense. Hamilton takes issue with those opponents of the Constitution who suggest that defense ought to be provided for by the states under the direction of the Union. He feels that such an arrangement would amount to "an inversion of the primary principle of our political association, as it would in practice transfer the care of the common defence from the federal head to the individual members: a project oppressive to some States, dangerous to all and baneful to the Confederacy."[119] Since the territories of Britain, Spain, and the Indian nations do not border only on particular states, but encircle the whole Union from Maine to Georgia, the danger of foreign attack, though in different degrees, is common. Consequently, the means of guarding against it ought to be the object of

difference and composure. The people of America are aware that inducements to war may arise out of these circumstances, as well as from others not so obvious at present, and that whenever such inducements may find fit time and opportunity for operation, pretences to color and justify them will not be wanting. Wisely, therefore, do they consider union and a good national government as necessary to put and keep them in *such a situation* as, instead of *inviting* war, will tend to repress and discourage it. That situation consists in the best possible state of defence, and necessarily depends on the government, the arms, and the resources of the country" (4, 19).

[116] 41, 261.   [117] 11, 65.   [118] 2, 9.   [119] 25, 153.

common councils.[120] Hamilton is glad that the power of defense is vested in the national government, feeling that it would be improper to put restraints on the national legislature.[121] Fears about the Constitution's permitting military peace establishments are met by Hamilton's remark that a prohibition to raise troops in times of peace would make the United States the most extraordinary spectacle that the world has yet seen, that of a nation incapacitated by its Constitution to prepare for defense before it is actually invaded.[122] In his advocacy of a comprehensive defense power, Hamilton is seconded by Madison, who agrees that the framers of the Constitution acted wisely when they gave Congress "an INDEFINITE POWER of raising TROOPS, as well as providing fleets; and of maintaining both in PEACE, as well as in war."[123] The Virginian considers a national power of defense so obvious a necessity that he does not even feel like devoting space to its discussion.[124]

To the advantage of security, the direct method of providing for defense is matched by a direct procedure of raising revenue, the latter being largely complementary to the former. "Shall the Union be constituted the guardian of the common safety? Are fleets and armies and revenues necessary to this purpose?" Hamilton asks, asserting that "the government of the Union must be empowered to pass all laws, and to make all regulations which have relation to them."[125] He proposes that the "federal government ought to possess the power of providing for the support of the national forces, for the expense of raising troops, of building and equipping fleets, and for all other expenses in any wise connected with military arrange-

[120] 25, 153. Compare also 23, 144: "If the circumstances of our country are such as to demand a compound instead of a simple, a confederate instead of a sole, government, the essential point which will remain to be adjusted will be to discriminate the OBJECTS, as far as it can be done, which shall appertain to the different provinces or departments of power; allowing to each the most ample authority for fulfilling the objects committed to its charge. Shall the Union be constituted the guardian of the common safety? Are fleets and armies and revenues necessary to this purpose? The government of the Union must be empowered to pass all laws, and to make all regulations which have relation to them. . . . Not to confer in each case a degree of power commensurate to the end, would be to violate the most obvious rules of prudence and propriety, and improvidently to trust the great interests of the nation to hands which are disabled from managing them with vigor and success."

[121] 25, 155.   [124] See Madison's discussion at 41, 261-62.
[122] 25, 156.   [125] 23, 144; 25, 153; 41, 261.
[123] 41, 261.

ments and operations,"[126] and he is happy to note that under the new Constitution there will be, as far as revenue is concerned, "a change of the fallacious and delusive system of quotas and requisitions," as it exists under the Articles. For Hamilton, there can be no substitute for this *"ignis fatuus"* in finance, "but that of permitting the national government to raise its own revenues by the ordinary methods of taxation authorized in every well-ordered constitution of civil government."[127] Therefore, he lauds the Constitution because it provides for the taxation of individuals rather than for requisitions from the states.[128] In like manner, Madison praises the new system, because "the power of levying and borrowing money, being the sinew of that which is to be exerted in the national defence," is properly vested in the national government.[129] He is glad to note that just as the present Congress has the authority to require of the states indefinite supplies of money for the common defense, the future Congress will have the power to require, for the same purpose, indefinite supplies of money from individual citizens.[130] According to the *Federalist,* a national power of taxation would also restore national credit. If the national government has the right to create new funds upon new objects of taxation, it will be able to borrow as far as its necessities might require, including those of national security. Foreigners, as well as Americans, could then reasonably repose confidence in the engagements of the United States, and the country would have friends in cases of emergency, such as wars and disputes with foreign nations.[131]

The credit of the United States with foreign nations will be further enhanced by the provision that the treaties of the United States shall be the supreme law of the land. The supremacy clause will eliminate many possibilities of international tensions. Answering the opponents of that clause, Jay writes that "these gentlemen

[126] 30, 182.   [127] 30, 184.

[128] Essays 30 and 31. At 31, 190, Hamilton writes: "A government ought to contain in itself every power requisite to the full accomplishment of the objects committed to its care, and to the complete execution of the trusts for which it is responsible, free from every other control but a regard to the public good and to the sense of the people. As the duties of superintending the national defence and of securing the public peace against foreign and domestic violence involve a provision for casualties and dangers to which no possible limits can be assigned, the power of making that provision ought to know no other bounds than the exigencies of the nation and the resources of the community."

[129] 41, 267.   [130] 45, 304.

[131] 30, 187. See also, on credit, 43, 285-86; 44, 289-90.

would do well to reflect that a treaty is only another name for a bargain, and that it would be impossible to find a nation who would make any bargain with us, which should be binding on them *absolutely,* but on us only so long and so far as we may think proper to be bound by it." While he admits that ordinary laws may be altered or cancelled by the legislature, he emphasizes that treaties cannot be repealed by the legislature at pleasure. Since they are made not by only one of the contracting parties, but by both, it follows, "that as the consent of both was essential to their formation at first, so must it ever afterwards be to alter or cancel them."[132] If Jay thus puts treaties beyond the reach of the national legislature, Madison lauds the Constitution for guaranteeing the fulfillment of international treaties by the states. The supremacy clause is for Madison absolutely necessary to prevent a situation where treaties of the United States with foreign nations would be valid in some states and not in others, depending upon the character of the respective state constitutions.[133]

The treaty power of the federal government is not restricted to political issues. It extends over the whole area of international relations. It comprises, for instance, matters of commerce. The regulation of foreign commerce by the national government is hailed as a proper innovation[134] under the new Constitution.[135] The states will no longer be able to violate commercial treaties the United States has concluded with foreign nations, and an important source of international irritation will be eliminated.[136] The *Federalist* mentions quite a few other instances concerning intercourse with foreign nations, where the regulation by the national government—properly provided for by the Constitution—is considered to be conducive to the security of the United States, such as the right to send and receive ambassadors, other public ministers, and consuls, or the right to define and punish piracies and felonies committed on the high seas and offenses against the law of nations.[137]

3.   The Constitution not only vests comprehensive powers in the national government in order to promote security, but also provides for an effective administration of all matters that are relevant for the safety of the United States from foreign powers. There is, first, the institution of a federal judicial system. The judicial authority of

---

[132] 64, 421.   [134] 45, 303.   [136] 22, 131.
[133] 44, 296.   [135] 42, 272.   [137] 42, 270.

the Union extends to all cases "which involve the PEACE of the CONFEDERACY, [whenever] they relate to the intercourse between the United States and foreign nations."[138] National courts are considered to be better guardians of good relations with foreign nations than the courts of the states. Since "the peace of the WHOLE ought not to be left at the disposal of a PART," and since "the Union will undoubtedly be answerable to foreign powers for the conduct of its members," the responsibility for an injury of foreign interests should always be accompanied by the faculty for preventing it.[139] The Constitution takes this into full consideration. Hamilton defends its provisions in that respect:

> As the denial or perversion of justice by the sentences of courts, as well as in any other manner, is with reason classed among the just causes of war, it will follow that the federal judiciary ought to have cognizance of all causes in which the citizens of other countries are concerned. This is not less essential to the preservation of the public faith, than to the security of the public tranquility. A distinction may perhaps be imagined between cases arising upon treaties and the laws of nations and those which may stand merely on the footing of the municipal law. The former kind may be supposed proper for the federal jurisdiction, the latter for that of the States. But it is at least problematical, whether an unjust sentence against a foreigner, where the subject of controversy was wholly relative to the *lex loci*, would not, if unredressed, be an aggression upon his sovereign, as well as one which violated the stipulations of a treaty or the general law of nations. And a still greater objection would result from the immense difficulty, if not impossibility, of a practical discrimination between the cases of one complexion and those of the other. So great a proportion of the cases in which foreigners are parties, involve national questions, that it is by far most safe and most expedient to refer all those in which they are concerned to the national tribunals.[140]

Hamilton defends the Constitution for not providing for a trial by jury in civil cases, feeling that it would be ineligible particularly in cases that concern the public peace with foreign nations, i.e., in most cases where the question turns around the laws of nations. Since juries do not generally possess a thorough knowledge of the laws and usages of nations, there would always be a danger that the rights of other nations might be infringed by their decisions, so as to afford occasions of reprisal and war.[141]

Aside from promoting security through its provisions concerning

[138] 80, 515.   [139] 80, 517.   [140] 80, 517.   [141] 83, 548-49.

the federal judiciary, the Constitution further insures the safety of America from foreign powers by the creation of a strong executive. "Energy in the executive is . . . essential to the protection of the community against foreign attacks," writes Hamilton, adding that the Romans were often obliged to take refuge in the absolute power of a single man in order to be protected from the invasions of external enemies who menaced the conquest and destruction of Rome.[142] He praises the Constitution for providing for an energetic executive.[143] Advocating duration of office, Hamilton expresses concern lest "a change of the chief magistrate, at the breaking out of a war, or at any similar crisis, for another, even of equal merit, would at all times be detrimental to the community, inasmuch as it would substitute inexperience to experience, and would tend to unhinge and set afloat the already settled train of the administration."[144] Strengthened through unity, duration of office, and adequate financial support, the American president is in a good position to exercise with vigor many of the national powers that are, as was shown, necessary for national security. The president plays an important role in the national defense, being commander-in-chief of the army and navy of the United States and of the militia of the several states when they are called into the actual service of the United States. Even those of the opponents of the Constitution, Hamilton writes, who, "in other respects, coupled the chief magistrate with a council, have for the most part concentrated the military authority in him alone," because "of all the cares or concerns of government, the direction of war most peculiarly demands those qualities which distinguish the exercise of power by a single hand. The direction of war implies the direction of the common strength; and the power of directing and employing the common strength, forms a usual and essential part in the definition of the executive authority."[145] Aside from his power in matters of defense, the president also possesses the right to make treaties, with the advice and consent of the Senate.

The mode of concluding treaties is discussed by Jay and Hamilton at some length. Both are glad that the Constitution does not provide for a participation of the House of Representatives in the treaty-making process and thus again show their skepticism of democracy. "A popular assembly, composed of members constantly coming and going in quick succession," writes Jay, "must necessarily be inadequate to the attainment of those great objects, which require to be

[142] 70, 454.   [143] Essays 70-73.   [144] 72, 472.   [145] 74, 482.

steadily contemplated in all their relations and circumstances, and which can only be approached and achieved by measures which not only talents, but also exact information, and often much time, are necessary to concert and execute."[146] Likewise, Hamilton feels that the fluctuating and multitudinous composition of the House makes it unlikely that the lower branch of the national legislature will possess the qualities essential for the proper execution of the treaty-making power. For him, "accurate and comprehensive knowledge of foreign politics; a steady and systematic adherence to the same views; a nice and uniform sensibility to national character; decision, *secrecy*, and despatch, are incompatible with the genius of a body so variable and numerous."[147]

The power to make treaties should also not be vested in the Senate alone, since this would relinquish the benefits of the constitutional agency of the president in the conduct of foreign negotiations. The argument that the Senate could employ the president in this capacity is encountered by Hamilton, who maintains that the chief executive, as a ministerial agent of the Senate, could not be expected to enjoy the confidence and respect of foreign powers in the same degree as the constitutional representatives of the nation and would not be able to act with an equal degree of weight and efficacy. "While the Union would," he adds, "from this cause, lose a considerable advantage in the management of its external concerns, the people would lose the additional security which would result from the coöperation of the executive."[148]

The treaty power should be in the president and the Senate, as provided for by the Constitution. "The power of making treaties is an important one, especially as it relates to war, peace, and commerce," writes Jay, continuing that, therefore, "it should not be delegated but in such a mode, and with such precautions, as will afford the highest security that it will be exercised by men qualified for the purpose, and in the manner most conducive to the public good."[149] Both presidents and senators are, due to constitutional requirements of age and the mode of election, likely to be persons of high caliber.[150] They will "always be of the number of those who best understand our national interests, whether considered in relation to the several States or to foreign nations, who are best able to promote those interests, and whose reputation for integrity inspires and merits confidence."[151]

[146] 64, 418.   [148] 75, 487-88.   [150] 64, 417-18.
[147] 75, 488.   [149] 64, 417.   [151] 64, 418.

Quite properly, the power to negotiate treaties is vested in the president. Since, in the negotiations of treaties, secrecy and dispatch are requisite, the president should be able to act and negotiate "in such manner as prudence may suggest," i.e., following largely his own judgment and that of his close advisers.[152] Like a commander in the field, the president will often have to seize moments as they pass, and will have to act irrespective of public opinion. "Should any circumstance occur which requires the advice and consent of the Senate, he may at any time convene them."[153] Jay thus emphasizes that, in spite of the president's independence from the Senate when he is engaged in "preparatory and auxiliary measures which are not otherwise important in a national view, than as they tend to facilitate the attainment of the objects of the negotiation," the participation of the Senate in the treaty-making process is required and not to be ignored.[154] Hamilton, who, on the whole, appears in the *Federalist* as an advocate of executive power, agrees with Jay as to the restriction of the president's treaty power. Arguing that the power of making treaties could not very well be exclusively vested in the executive, since treaties are, after all, laws, he expresses himself in favor of a check on the president by the Senate. While he admits that "the qualities elsewhere detailed as indispensable in the management of foreign negotiations, point out the Executive as the most fit agent in those transactions," he hastens to add that, on the other hand, "the vast importance of the trust, and the operation of treaties as laws, plead strongly for the participation of the whole or a portion of the legislative body in the office of making them."[155] He then proceeds to point out that it would be "utterly unsafe and improper" to entrust the treaty power exclusively "to an elective magistrate of four years' duration," who might—not being a hereditary monarch—use his power for his own advantage and to the detriment of his country.[156]

Although the treaty power is vested in the national government, the *Federalist* stresses that even though the good of the whole will

---

[152] 64, 419.   [153] 64, 420.

[154] 64, 420. He writes that "the Constitution provides that our negotiations for treaties shall have every advantage which can be derived from talents, information, integrity, and deliberate investigations, on the one hand, and from secrecy and despatch on the other," indicating his satisfaction about the necessary collaboration between the executive and the Senate.

[155] 75, 486.   [156] 75, 486-87.

be more and more an object of attention, as the United States increasingly assumes a national form and a national character, the interests of the states ought not to be neglected. The government of the United States should never forget that "the good of the whole can only be promoted by advancing the good of each of the parts or members which compose the whole."[157] In accordance with the federal principle, the Senate plays largely the role of a protector of the rights and interests of the states. Thus the Founding Fathers, when vesting, for the sake of security, the power to make treaties in the national government, confirmed the survival of the federal idea under the Constitution: Just as the states originally enter the Union in order to have security from foreign nations, so it would be the task of the new national government to protect its members from foreign danger, and the states would have an important voice in the definition of that danger and of security.

4.   The federal idea is obvious not only in the treaty power of the United States. It can be found also in connection with most of the national powers and institutions that are relevant for security. Madison sums up the whole idea of the protection of the states through the Union rather well when, commenting on the provision that the federal government shall protect each state against invasion, he states that "a protection against invasion is due from every society to the parts composing it."[158] In the same paragraph, he connects security from foreign nations with peace among the federated states. "The latitude of the expression here used," he continues to comment on the provision concerning the invasion of the states, "seems to secure each State, not only against foreign hostility, but against ambitious or vindictive enterprises of its more powerful neighbors," adding that "the history, both of ancient and modern confederacies, proves that the weaker members of the union ought not to be insensible to the policy of this article."[159] National power is thus not only of advantage for the security of the states from foreign powers, but also, again for the sake of the states, important for the peace among the component parts of the Union. To make things complete, the *Federalist* also stresses that national establishments for the sake of security are by no means incompatible with the freedom of the individual. A national power of defense

[157] 64, 422.   [158] 43, 283.   [159] 43, 283.

and a national army are not considered detrimental to that freedom, even though they exist in times of peace. On the contrary, the *Federalist* believes that individual freedom would be jeopardized considerably more, were the power of defense vested in the individual states. Hamilton admits that "the violent destruction of life and property incident to war, the continual effort and alarm attendant on a state of continual danger, will compel nations the most attached to liberty to resort for repose and security to institutions which have a tendency to destroy their civil and political rights. To be more safe, they at length become willing to run the risk of being less free."[160] However, he adds that, while the existence of standing armies under the new Constitution is problematical and uncertain, "standing armies must inevitably result from a dissolution of the Confederacy. Frequent war and constant apprehension, which require a state of as constant preparation, will infallibly produce them."[161] A similar situation would exist if the states, united in a confederacy, would have the right to maintain armies. "As far as an army may be considered as a dangerous weapon of power," he warns, "it had better be in those hands of which the people are most likely to be jealous [the national government!] than in those of which they are least likely to be jealous [the State governments!]. For it is a truth, which the experience of ages has attested, that the people are always most in danger when the means of injuring their rights are in the possession of those of whom they entertain the least suspicion."[162] This passage shows more than merely the connection between security from foreign danger and the freedom of the individual from his government. It recognizes that a national army, although a definite necessity, is not supposed to be dangerous to the individual's rights. Also, it shows that the compatibility of a national army with the freedom of the individual is largely based upon the alertness of the people of the states not to let that army become destructive of their rights. This fundamentally amounts to a recognition of a right of the people—of the states as well as of the Union—to check upon the military establishments of the Union with a view to preventing possible infringements upon their rights. It is stressed in the *Federalist* that Congress "will be *obliged,* . . . once at least in every two years, to deliberate upon the

[160] 8, 42.
[161] 8, 42-43.
[162] 25, 154.

propriety of keeping a military force on foot; to come to a new resolution on the point; and to declare their sense of the matter, by a formal vote in the face of their constituents. They are not *at liberty* to vest in the executive department permanent funds for the support of an army, if they were even incautious enough to be willing to repose in it so improper a confidence."[163]

Thus we find also in the *Federalist*'s discussion of the more perfect Union as a means for security from foreign danger that, no matter how strong its advocacy of national power may be, the commentary on the Constitution always stresses that consolidation is neither planned nor necessary for purposes of security. Federalism is considered as ideally suited for the protection of America from foreign danger.

VIII

In the second part of this chapter, an attempt was made to show how the Papers see the problem of the security of the United States from foreign nations. Taking into account the experience of various confederacies, including the United States under the Articles of Confederation, the authors arrive at conclusions that are relevant for their evaluation of the situation in their country. The authors stress that the Union under the Articles of Confederation was largely adopted in order to bring the colonists' struggle with England to a successful conclusion, and remind their countrymen that a dissolution of the existing Union would be a step back into a condition that was previously discarded for not being compatible with American security. In the hypothetical case of a dissolution into thirteen independent states or several confederacies, American interests are seen at the mercy of foreign powers. The situation under the Articles of Confederation was also highly precarious, as far as security from other nations was concerned. Owing to the high degree of sovereignty the states retained when entering the federal compact, it appears doubtful whether the existing Union is conducive to safety from outside powers at all, in spite of the rather comprehensive powers that are vested in the federal government for purposes of defense. The situation will be different under the new Constitution. The work of the Convention of Philadelphia

[163] 26, 163. See also 41, 264-65, where Madison expresses quite similar thoughts.

creates a more perfect Union by making the acts of the national government directly binding upon the individuals in the states. Through an increase of the legislative competences of the national government and the establishment of a federal judicial system as well as of a strong executive, certain institutions are created that are likely to achieve security for the United States and her component parts.

CHAPTER NINE

Analysis of the Federalist—
Conclusions

In the preceding chapters, an attempt has been made to analyze the *Federalist* as a treatise on free government in peace and security. It has been shown how Jay, Madison, and Hamilton conceived of federalism and the more perfect Union as a means for the protection of the individual—be it from his government, from tensions among the federated states, or from foreign nations. Regardless of whether the authors were concerned with free government, or peace, or security, they were always primarily interested in the individual's freedom and welfare.[1] The whole work is thus a classic

---

[1] From what we have seen in our analysis of the *Federalist*, it seems hardly necessary to point out that the term "welfare" is by no means used in that work in the sense of "welfare state." On the contrary, the word is connected with individualism rather than collectivism, and has a strong liberal connotation. "Public welfare" means nothing else. It implies only the individuals' freedom from public restraint. It exists if the individual is free in the pursuit of his happiness, i.e., if he enjoys the protection of his life, liberty, and property. "Welfare" thus has a liberal (in the genuine sense of the word!), but not at all an equalitarian meaning. Compare *supra*, pp. 116-17, 146-48. "Welfare" is, in the *Federalist*, as much the end of government as the other values described on these pages.

of liberalism, an expression of America's English heritage and her western tradition.[2]

I

1.   This concern with man's well-being justifies a few remarks on the *Federalist*'s opinion of human nature. Clearly, the question must arise whether the authors' advocacy of federalism and the more perfect Union was for them a matter of convenience or, rather, of necessity. In other words: Did Hamilton, Madison, and Jay recommend the adoption of the Constitution because they felt that man was fundamentally good or because he was bad? The answer to that question has been supplied largely in the preceding chapters. Federalism and the more perfect Union, combined with an institutional separation of powers, have been shown to be *remedies against* foreign danger, tensions within the confederation, and governmental oppression. Since these various threats to the individual are due to human behavior, a strictly optimistic view of the nature of man must be out of the question. On the other hand, since the *Federalist* advocates some form of popular government, an absolutely pessimistic evaluation of man also does not appear to be possible. Therefore, we may say that Jay's opinion of human nature, mentioned above, is characteristic of the whole work, since that opinion is largely matched by Jay's junior collaborators.

2.   Like Jay, Madison refrains from committing himself absolutely on the nature of man. His statement, "what is government itself, but the greatest of all reflections on human nature? If men were angels, no government would be necessary,"[3] gives us an indication about the criteria by which the Virginian judges his fellow beings. They are those of rationality, government being the result of man's reflections, and ethics, men being no angels.

While complaining of human passions,[4] Madison does not deny that man is a reasonable being. Although he fears that the argu-

---

[2] See *infra,* chapter ten.   [3] 51, 337.

[4] Madison is against frequent appeals to the people by means of a referendum because "the passions, . . . not the reason of the public would sit in judgment" (49, 331). Complaining about the Council of Censors in Pennsylvania, he says that "passions, not reason must have presided over their decisions" (50, 334). He remarks that "in all very numerous assemblies, . . . passion never fails to wrest the sceptre from reason" (51, 361). See also 42, 274.

ments of the adversaries of the Constitution "may inflame the passions of the unthinking," he is, at the same time, confident that "cool and candid people will at once reflect" that the Constitution is a good one.[5] Trusting that "the cool and deliberative sense of the community ought, in all governments, and actually will, in all free governments, ultimately prevail," Madison is afraid lest "the people, stimulated by some irregular passion, . . . may call for measures which they themselves will afterwards be the most ready to lament and condemn."[6] If "the reason of man, like man himself, is timid and cautious when left alone," it is existent nevertheless.[7] Madison's judgment of man from an ethical point of view is also rather noncommittal. He refers to the "caprice and wickedness of man"[8] and the "infirmities and depravities of the human character"[9] and regrets that there is a certain "degree of depravity in mankind which requires a certain degree of circumspection and distrust."[10] On the other hand, he recognizes "other qualities in human nature which justify a certain portion of esteem and confidence,"[11] such as patriotism and the love of justice,[12] sensibility to marks of honor and esteem, confidence and gratitude.[13]

3.   Like his collaborators, Hamilton shows a certain reluctance to draw a one-sided picture of human characteristics. Complaining of the "folly and wickedness of mankind"[14] and of the fact that "momentary passions, and immediate interests have a more active and imperious control over human conduct than general or remote considerations of policy, utility, or justice,"[15] Hamilton also considers human nature under the criteria of rationality and ethics.[16]

Hamilton's statement that government has been instituted "because the passions of men will not conform to the dictates of reason . . . without restraint"[17] indicates a policy of noncommitment. While Hamilton, like Madison, deplores human passion, he admits that man has reason, a dualism one comes across again and again in his *Federalist*.[18] As to the New Yorker's evaluation of man

---

[5] 41, 260.   [9] 37, 232.   [13] 57, 372.
[6] 63, 409-10.   [10] 55, 365.   [14] 78, 510.
[7] 49, 329.   [11] 55, 365.   [15] 6, 30.
[8] 57, 373.   [12] 10, 59.

[16] He speaks, as was just shown, of man's folly, passion, and reasonable consideration, and, on the other hand, of man's wickedness.

[17] 15, 92.

[18] Hamilton speaks of "the passions . . . of the reasoner" (31, 189); of "men of upright . . . tempers" who have "opportunities of remarking how . . . the great

from an ethical point of view, he pessimistically states that "men are ambitious, vindictive, and rapacious,"[19] governed by "private inclinations and interests,"[20] and liable to "cabal, intrigue, and corruption."[21] Nevertheless, he counts upon their pride and virtue.[22] Writing that the "supposition of universal venality in human nature is little less an error . . . than the supposition of universal rectitude,"[23] Hamilton views "human nature as it is, without flattering its virtue or exaggerating its vices."[24]

4.   Through their use of rather neutral statements, Madison and Hamilton preclude themselves from asserting that man is, on the whole, unreasonable and bad or, for that matter, reasonable and good. Both authors admit that there are good people among the bad and reasonable people among those that are passionate, and vice versa. This noncommittal policy is both logical and politic. It places the authors in an advantageous strategic position, by permitting them either to condemn or to praise men, just as it might suit their purpose. As adherents of free government, the authors have to describe man in a way that justifies the individual's protection from popular government as well as his participation in government. If man is irrational and bad, popular government may be irrational and bad and should, for the sake of the individual, be restricted. On the other hand, popular government is justified if man is rational and good enough to be trusted with self-government. Similarly, the Articles of Confederation can be attacked for being a demonstration of the caprice and wickedness of man, as Madison puts it, and of democracy. "If Shays had not been a *desperate debtor*," who, motivated by an unethical egoism, did not want to fulfill his legal obligations, "it is much to be doubted whether Massachusetts would have been plunged into a civil war,"[25] says Hamilton, and he adds that popular assemblies like those in the states, with their legislation detrimental to private rights, are "frequently subject to the impulse of rage, resentment,

interests of society are sacrificed to the vanity . . . of individuals, who have credit enough to make their passions . . . interesting to mankind" (70, 458). People "sometimes err," but "the wonder is that they so seldom err as they do" (71, 465). While speaking of the "passions of mankind" (27, 168; 76, 493), "the passions of the community" (65, 424), and the "heats and ferments" of the people (68, 442), Hamilton admits that there are men "of calm and dispassionate feelings" (24, 100).

[19] 6, 27.   [22] 66, 435.   [24] 76, 496.
[20] 76, 495.   [23] 76, 495.   [25] 6, 29.
[21] 68, 442.

jealousy, avarice, and of other irregular and violent propensities."[26] On the other hand, when advocating the Constitution, the authors need not be reluctant to praise man. Madison can praise the framers for their work and credit them with qualities that justify esteem and confidence. Since the Constitution creates a representative form of government, Hamilton remarks that "the institution of delegated power implies, that there is a portion of virtue and honor among mankind, which may be a reasonable foundation of confidence; and experience justifies the theory."[27] He does not refrain from expressing his trust in the members of Congress,[28] the executive,[29] and the judiciary.[30]

5.   No matter how often the authors admit that there are people who are sufficiently reasonable and good to be trusted with self-government, the *Federalist* entertains, on the whole, a rather pessimistic view of human nature. This raises the question of whether the contributors to this American classic believe that man can be improved. The answer is in the negative. No millennium is foreseen in which human selfishness would disappear and in which it would be possible to live happily without the restraints of a government. All kinds of men, whether poor or rich, whether of common or aristocratic stock, are selfish and always will be. On the other hand, it follows from the present analysis of the Papers that the authors are confident that enlightened reason could check selfish passions. Hamilton is glad to note that "the science of politics, . . . like most other sciences, has received great improve-

[26] 6, 30.   [27] 76, 495.

[28] 26, 164; 67, 435. With respect to the treaty power of the president, Hamilton remarks, in order to justify the co-function of the Senate: "An avaricious man might be tempted to betray the interests of the state to the acquisition of wealth. An ambitious man might make his own aggrandizement, by the aid of a foreign power, the price of his treachery to his constituents. The history of human conduct does not warrant that exalted opinion of human virtue which would make it wise in a nation to commit interests of so delicate and momentous a kind, as those which concern its intercourse with the rest of the world, to the sole disposal of a magistrate created and circumstanced as would be a President of the United States" (75, 487). See also 72, 471.

[29] Essays 67-77. His expressions of trust in the executive stand in contrast to such pessimistic views as, for instance, the one mentioned in the preceding note. This is another indication of Hamilton's policy of noncommitment as to the nature of man.

[30] 79, 511, as well as in all the essays dealing with the judiciary. The judges rank first, as far as Hamilton's evaluation of man is concerned.

ment."[31] Discovered and expanded by enlightened reason, it has provided man with forms of government that, while unable to improve human nature, are likely to protect man from the disadvantages of his own selfish passions. Fortunately, people now understand "the efficacy of various principles . . . which were either not known at all, or imperfectly known to the ancients." From among those principles, Hamilton mentions "the regular distribution of power into distinct departments; the introduction of legislative balances and checks; the institution of courts composed of judges holding their offices during good behavior; the representation of the people in the legislature by deputies of their own election." While he stresses that "these are wholly new discoveries, or have made their principal progress toward perfection in modern times," he hastens to add that federalism is also one of the new "powerful means by which the excellence of republican government may be retained and its imperfections lessened or avoided"[32] and lauds the more perfect Union as it would exist under the Constitution.

The more perfect Union is thus considered a most important, if not the most important, means for checking the consequences of human egoism. It is established in order to preserve individual freedom, which largely amounts to the right to pursue one's own interests, be they of an ideal, or of a material nature. This central significance of the Union makes appropriate a few remarks on the *Federalist*'s view of the nature of that Union.

II

1.   Whereas Jay, who contributed a rather appealing and patriotic notion of the American Union, does not give us any hint as to its legal nature, his collaborators do provide such information. This by no means implies, however, that Hamilton and Madison agree on the nature of the Union. On the contrary, they advance quite conflicting opinions.

For Madison, the new Union comes into being through a federal compact. The relevant passage reads:

The Constitution is to be founded on the assent and ratification of the people of America, given by deputies elected for the spe-

[31] 9, 48. (Madison uses the term "political science" at 37, 229).
[32] 9, 48-49.

cial purpose. . . . This assent and ratification is to be given by the people, not as individuals composing one entire nation, but as composing the distinct and independent States to which they respectively belong. It is to be the assent and ratification of the several States, derived from the supreme authority in each State— the authority of the people themselves. The act, therefore, establishing the Constitution, will not be a *national,* but a *federal* act. . . . Each State, in ratifying the Constitution, is considered as a sovereign body, independent of all others, and only to be bound by its own voluntary act. In this relation, then, the new Constitution will, if established, be a *federal,* and not a *national* Constitution.[33]

This rather federal concept of the constituent act is matched by Madison's opinions on the main characteristics of the Constitution. First of all, the new Union in his judgment does not differ too much from its predecessor under the Articles of Confederation. He emphasizes again and again that the new law will merely "revise" and "reduce" the Articles by decreasing their federal or centrifugal features[34] or, what amounts to the same thing, that it will merely "invigorate" the Articles, as far as the national or centripetal tendencies are concerned.[35] "The truth is," the Virginian says in essay forty, "that the great principles of the Constitution proposed by the Convention may be considered less as absolutely new, than as the expansion of principles which are found in the articles of Confederation."[36] He stresses that the powers of the new national government are "few and defined,"[37] and throughout the pages of his essays there is evident a strong feeling for states' rights.[38]

Still, it is conceivable that nationalists could take issue with a federalistic interpretation of Madison's concept of the nature of the Union, as expressed in the *Federalist.* They might exploit Madison's speaking of "the people of America" and argue that when he later refers to "the people composing the . . . States," he has in mind merely the *form* in which the ratification of the Constitution was to take place, whereas in *essence* that ratification was performed by the people of America, irrespective of state boundaries.[39] They could

[33] 39, 246-47.
[34] 40, 251; 40, 253. See also his letter to Noah Webster of Oct. 12, 1804. MADISON'S WRITINGS, VIII, 163, 166.
[35] 40, 255; 45, 303.   [36] 40, 255.   [37] 45, 303.
[38] See *supra,* pp. 132 ff.
[39] Compare Marshall's language in McCulloch v. Maryland: "It is true, they assembled in their several states [for ratification]—and where else could they have assembled? No political dreamer was ever wild enough to think of breaking

marshal support for their thesis by referring to Madison's emphasis
on the necessity of a strong national government, to his qualifying
the territorial power-division so as to be compatible with the national government's quality as a power, to the fact that the Virginian considers the Union as one republic, and not as a mere
league under international law.[40] They can point to rather nationalistic statements that were made by the father of the Constitution
in the Philadelphia Convention and in the *Federalist* itself.[41]
Finally, it can be argued that from the character of the *Federalist*
as a piece of propaganda, it can be concluded that Madison expressed himself ambiguously in order to dissipate accusations that
the Constitution was creating a consolidation of the states.[42]

Those in favor of states' rights, on the other hand, can reject the
nationalists' distinction between formal and material ratification as
hair-splitting. They can add that when Madison stressed that ratification was to be made by the people of the states, he wanted to
specify and qualify his dictum that the Constitution would be ratified by the people of America and to emphasize that there did not
actually exist such a thing as an American people. They can support this view by showing that to Madison society is an intrastate
phenomenon;[43] that there will exist no consolidation under the
Constitution;[44] that the Virginian felt the Union would result from

down the lines which separate the states, and of compounding the American
people into one common mass. Of consequence, when they act, they act in their
States. But the measures they adopt do not, on that account cease to be the
measures of the people themselves, or become the measures of the State governments." 4 Wheaton 316, 402 (1819).

[40] See *supra,* esp. pp. 132 ff.

[41] In Philadelphia, Madison stated: "There is a gradation of power in all
societies, from lowest corporation to highest sovereign. The states never possessed
the essential rights of sovereignty. These were always vested in Congress [even
under the Articles of Confederation]." Farrand, ed., RECORDS, I, 471. In the
Federalist, Madison states: ". . . if . . . the Union be essential to the happiness
of the people of America, is it not preposterous, to urge as an objection to a
government, without which the objects of the Union cannot be attained, that
such a government may derogate from the importance of the governments of the
individual States? Was, then, the American Revolution effected, was the American
Confederacy formed, was the precious blood of thousands spilt, and the hard-
earned substance of millions lavished, not that the people of America should
enjoy peace, liberty and safety, but that the government of the individual States,
that particular municipal establishments, might enjoy a certain extent of power,
and be arrayed with certain dignities and attributes of sovereignty?" (45, 298-99.)

[42] 39, 245.   [43] See *supra* p. 114.

a compact between independent states;[45] that he refers to the sovereignty of the states.[46] Aside from being able to furnish ample proof for their arguments from the pages of the *Federalist*, the advocates of states' rights can also point to particularistic statements that were made by Madison in the Virginia ratifying convention and to the fact that the Virginia Resolutions, containing a strong assertion of states' rights and the compact theory of the nature of the Union, were, after all, the work of the father of the Constitution.[47] Finally, they could argue that the propagandistic character of the *Federalist* accounts for some statements by Madison in the nationalistic vein rather than his expressions in favor of states' rights and that these nationalistic statements were largely prompted by the desire to convince the friends of a strong national government that the Constitution did not intend to leave too much sovereignty and power with the states.

2. Hamilton's concept of the nature of the Union is quite different. To begin with, the new Union would come into being through a national rather than a federal act. Brushing aside Madison's distinction between a ratification given by the people in the states and one given by those in the nation as "a distinction, more subtle than accurate,"[48] Hamilton, while regretting that the Articles of Confederation were not ratified by the people,[49] emphasizes that the new Union would rest "on the solid basis of THE CONSENT OF THE PEOPLE" of America,[50] irrespective of state boundaries.[51]

This nationalistic interpretation of the constituent act is matched by the New Yorker's conception of the main features of the new system. To begin with, he stresses that the new Union is quite dif-

[44] See *supra*, pp. 137 ff.; also 39, 299-300; 62, 402.

[45] 39, 247.

[46] 45, 300; 45, 303, among other passages.

[47] In the Virginia ratifying convention, Madison stated as to the constituent act: "Who are the parties to it? The people—but not the people as composing one great body; but the people as composing thirteen sovereignties: were it, as the gentleman asserts, a consolidated government, the assent of a majority of the people would be sufficient for its establishment . . . but, Sir, no State is bound by it, as it is, without its own consent." Elliot, *op. cit.*, III, 114-15. In the Virginia Resolutions Madison also called the powers of the federal government powers which are derived from "the compact to which the States are parties." MADISON'S WRITINGS, VI, 326.

[48] 9, 51.   [49] 22, 140-41.   [50] 22, 141.

[51] This seems to follow from Hamilton's discussion at 22, 140-41.

ferent from the old one. "The evils we experience do not proceed," he writes, "from minute or partial imperfections, but from fundamental errors in the structure of the building, which cannot be amended otherwise than by an alteration in the first principles and main pillars of the fabric."[52] Therefore, he wants "an entire change" of the "radically vicious and unsound" Union under the Articles, which would eliminate the existing centrifugal forces.[53] Hamilton does not emphasize so much that the powers of the national government are few and defined, as Madison does. Rather, he stresses that the government should be "trusted with all the powers which a free people *ought to delegate to any government.*"[54] Throughout Hamilton's essays, one can easily recognize a strong assertion of national power, as it would exist under the new Constitution.[55]

In spite of his very nationalistic comments on the new Union, it is conceivable that the advocates of states' rights would be able to argue that Hamilton was not actually as nationalistic as the nationalists would have it. They might contend that Hamilton, when speaking of the ratification by the state legislatures and distinguishing that type of ratification from a ratification by the people, does not say in so many words that "the people" would be the people of America. Thus, it is possible that Hamilton actually objects only to a ratification by the state *legislatures,* due to his deep distrust of these institutions, and not necessarily to a ratification by the people of the states. The states' rights advocates could support their claim that Hamilton was not too nationalistic by pointing out the New Yorker's repeated concessions to the federal idea in the *Federalist* Papers, where he also states expressly that "the plan of the Convention aims only at a partial union or consolidation" and even admits that "the State governments would clearly retain all the rights of sovereignty which they before had, and which were not . . . *exclusively* delegated to the United States."[56]

On the other hand, the nationalists would not find it too difficult to meet the arguments of the advocates of states' rights. They can say that the context in which Hamilton uses the term "the people" in connection with the ratification of the Constitution makes it pretty evident that he can have in mind only the American people.[57] They could point out Hamilton's staunch promotion of national power throughout his essays and even argue that his occasional concessions to the rights of the states were largely prompted

[52] 15, 89.   [54] 23, 145.   [56] 32, 194.
[53] 22, 140.   [55] See *supra,* esp. pp. 165 ff.   [57] 22, 140-41.

by a desire to reassure those who were afraid the Constitution would establish a consolidated form of government. Hamilton actually wanted a Union that had a considerably stronger national government than the one described in the *Federalist,* it could be maintained, and his great speech before the Philadelphia Convention[58] and other statements,[59] made when it was not necessary to be considerate of the feelings of the public, would furnish ample proof of that contention.

3.   The *Federalist* thus does not give a precise answer as to the nature of the Union. With respect to the establishment of the new system, Madison states in so many words that the constituent act is a contract between the sovereign states.[60] Still, when he refers to those who ratify the Constitution as "the American people," he creates doubts as to whether in substance, ratification might not be an expression of the will of the nation, in spite of the fact that in form it would definitely be an act of the people of the various states.[61] Hamilton's statements seem to be even more ambiguous. Strangely enough, the prophet of the nationalists does not even use the term "the American people" in his comments on ratification. When he writes that the people will ratify the Constitution, he—unlike Madison—refrains from saying whether he means the people of the states or the nation, a peculiar omission indeed of an advocate of the nationalist doctrine![62] If the authors' comments on the substance of the Constitution are considered, a similar ambiguity as to the nature of the Union is apparent. This ambiguity makes the *Federalist* a genuine equivalent of the Constitution it interprets.

[58] Speech of June 18. Farrand, RECORDS, I, 282 ff.

[59] For instance, Hamilton's statement to Gouverneur Morris in a letter of Feb. 27, 1802, that the Constitution is a "frail and worthless fabric," is often referred to as proof of his disappointment about the weak Union that was established under the Constitution. On the other hand, this passage could also be interpreted as meaning that he felt that the national government, in 1802, was not actually as strong as it could be under the Constitution, since he is writing that he is "still laboring to prop the frail and worthless fabric." One might even doubt whether his reference to the Constitution is necessarily a reference to the Union and the national government, since he always just speaks of the Constitution, and never of the Union. HAMILTON'S WORKS, X, 425.

[60] 39, 247.

[61] It could be argued that Madison possibly considered the states, as did Dr. Johnson (Farrand, RECORDS, I, 461), as "districts of people composing one political society."

[62] 22, 141.

In Philadelphia, Madison stated that the Convention was not confronted with "two extremes," namely, "a perfect separation and a
perfect incorporation of the thirteen States."[63] The same can be said
of the authors of the *Federalist*. In that work Hamilton, who appears
definitely as the greater nationalist, declares himself to be as little
in favor of a perfect incorporation of the thirteen states as Madison,
the champion of states' rights, is of a perfect separation of the states.
The Constitution being a "bundle of compromises,"[64] it seems only
natural if its classic commentary, the *Federalist,* refrains from committing itself on the nature of that law's greatest compromise, the
Union. In the last number of the *Federalist,* there can be found a
re-affirmation of the idea that the Constitution is a compromise and
that there is no clear-cut answer to the nature of the Union it
establishes. As if he wanted to assure both the nationalists and
the advocates of states' rights alike that the Constitution and its
Union offered some common ground for them to meet, Hamilton
states that "the compacts which are to embrace thirteen distinct
States in a common bond of amity and union, must as necessarily
be a compromise of as many dissimilar interests and inclinations.
How can perfection spring from such materials?"[65] Thus the
man who, throughout his essays, had given a highly nationalistic
version of the Constitution, in the end not only admits that the
more perfect Union would come into existence through a compact,
but even goes so far as to say that it would be created through a
whole number of compacts—a clear concession to the states' rights
concept of a contract theory of the nature of the Union!

III

1. The first part of this chapter has dealt with the *Federalist's*
evaluation of man and the nature of the Union. At the risk of being
repetitious, a summary of the present analysis of the papers as a
treatise on free government in peace and security now seems neces-

[63] Madison in the Federal Convention on June 26. Farrand, RECORDS, I, 423.

[64] The term is used by Alpheus T. Mason in "The Nature of Our Federal
Union Reconsidered," POLITICAL SCIENCE QUARTERLY (1950), LXV, 503. In a letter of
Dec. 20, 1787, Jefferson wrote Madison, concerning the new Constitution: "I am
captivated by the compromise of the opposite claims of the great and little States,
of the last to equal, and the former to proportional influence." JEFFERSON'S WRIT-
INGS, VI, 387.

[65] 85, 571.

sary in order to show, in a more concise as well as precise manner, points of agreement and disagreement between the authors and in order to demonstrate the "split personality" of the *Federalist*.[66]

We have seen that Jay, Madison, and Hamilton fundamentally agree on federalism and the more perfect Union as a means for peace and security. This agreement justifies us to deal with the *Federalist* as a treatise for peace and security, without expressly distinguishing between the particular authors' opinions on those subjects.[67] On the other hand, a distinction between the authors' comments on federalism and the more perfect Union as a means for the achievement of free government appears, due to differences of opinion, to be necessary and, therefore, has been made. On that subject, Hamilton and Madison, the two authors mainly concerned with the freedom of the individual from governmental control, are, while agreeing on fundamental ideals, of different opinions as to the realization of these ideals. Their evaluations, being largely concerned with the government set up by the Constitution, must have important consequences for an appraisal of American constitutionalism and the position of the individual in the state. Therefore, it seems worth our while to draw a comparison between these evaluations.

2. The two main contributors to the *Federalist,* being in agreement on the nature of man, see eye to eye with respect to the nature of free government. They believe that the state of nature is left by the individuals in order to have the *bellum omnium contra omnes* ended and the rule of force replaced by a rule of law. Through a voluntary compact, government is instituted for the protection of the individual. The people have the right to participate in government. Holding identical opinions as to the relation between people and government from a teleological point of view, both authors agree as to the static-factual aspect of that relation and consider

[66] For the meaning of "split personality," compare *supra,* pp. 19 ff. It is, of course, possible to carry the whole concept of the "split personality" even further by distinguishing between theory and reality on the one hand, and propaganda in the *Federalist* on the other, or, by distinguishing statements in the *Federalist* from statements made by the authors somewhere else, although, of course, the latter distinction does not actually amount to a split personality of the *Federalist,* which concerns us here. To distinguish between propaganda and theory and reality does not seem to be a worthwhile undertaking, since it is hard to say what in the *Federalist* was merely propaganda and what not.

[67] *Supra,* chapters seven and eight.

society as an intrastate phenomenon. With respect to the dynamic-legal relation between society and government, Hamilton and Madison reject an absolute dependence of the government upon the people as inconsistent with the principle of the individual's protection, and an absolute independence of the government from society as incompatible with the principle of popular participation in government. They propose a government that is sufficiently independent to protect the rights of the individual, one in which popular participation is restricted by a constitution, i.e., a government in which the liberal protection principle has primacy before the democratic participation principle. Aware of the possibility that a government may abuse its powers, Madison and Hamilton admit the right of revolution. Both authors have a similar conception of law. Under the supreme natural law there are two sorts of positive law, namely, the superior and fundamental constitution, made by society, and the inferior and ordinary statute, made by the legislature. The Virginian and the New Yorker are in accord when they explain the protection principle to mean the protection of the individual's happiness and welfare, under which they understand his rights of life, liberty, and property, and the participation principle to mean popular government. The latter is a rule by the majority and may be the rule of an interested and overbearing majority, which suppresses the minority. Finally, the authors give the name "free government" to the form of government under which the discrepancy arising from the concomitance of the protection and participation principles is solved by giving the former the primacy over the latter. This is an ideal that may be realized under concrete governments. Parallel to this uniform belief in free government go identical opinions on the main threat to free government, factions. Free government exists to the degree that it controls factions.

This leads us to compare the theories concerning the realization of free government through concrete forms of government. Rejecting a direct democracy as existent in small states, Hamilton and Madison favor a representative popular government in a republic or, better, in a large republic. The state most conducive to free government is a federal republic with an institutional separation of powers. At this point, the opinions part. The authors conceive of federalism and the separation of powers in a different way.

Trusting that factions existing in one member state of the federation will be peacefully absorbed and neutralized by the other states, Madison sees in federalism a means for the creation of a system of federal power-balances. He admits that the internal power-division can be a qualified one only because the government must, after all, externally constitute a power. However, by pronouncing the doctrine of territorial power-balance, Madison emphasizes the value of the member states. In a word, federalism is to him an institution devised to protect the states within the federation. Although he recognizes that in a federal state sovereignty ultimately rests in the national government, federalism is not there for a power-concentration in the nation, but for a power-balance among the states. Hamilton's view is quite different. Having practically precluded himself from pronouncing a theory of power-balances by saying that factions within one member state may lead to war with other states, he puts the shock- or faction-absorbing function of the states in the background. Hamilton sees the remedy against factions in the states mainly in a strong national government. Federalism is a means for the creation of a system of power-concentration. Although he admits an internal power-division—something he has to do if he accepts federalism—Hamilton makes a strong assertion of national power. Federalism is to him a state-inimical rather than a state-friendly phenomenon, destined to slay that political monster, *imperium in imperio*. Federalism is there not so much for a power-balance among the states as for a concentration of power in the nation.

Similar differences exist with regard to the separation of powers. Madison sees in that institution a means for the creation of a system of balances in which the different departments counterpoise each other. And although his advocacy of such a system is, in view of the then existing all-powerful legislatures, mainly a polemic against these popular assemblies, it admits of no doubt that he is against a concentration of power in *any* department. His acceptance of judicial review thus does not result from a desire to strengthen the judiciary, but follows logically from the internal division and the external existence of governmental power. In a word, Madison wants the separation of powers for the sake of a genuine power-balance, and not so much for the deconcentration of power from the legislature in order that it may be concentrated in the judiciary or the executive. Hamilton, on the other hand, conceives of the purpose of the separation of powers quite differently. It does not lie in the creation of a power-balance, but in a deconcentration of power from the legislature, and he is not opposed to a powerful judiciary and executive. His acceptance of judicial review does not just follow from the concomitance of an internal division and an external existence of governmental power, but is the direct result of a desire to weaken the department in which democracy is most strongly reflected and to enthrone the judiciary over the legislative.

A comparative analysis of Madison's and Hamilton's conceptions of the purpose of federalism and the separation of powers tempts one to ask whether there is really a difference of opinion. Does it not amount to the same thing when Madison, while recognizing the supremacy of the national government, stresses the value of the states, and when Hamilton, while conceding the existence of the states, emphasizes the power of the national government? Does it make any difference whether Madison wants the separation of powers for the sake of a genuine power-balance or whether Hamilton wants it for a deconcentration of power from the legislature? Does a weakening of an omnipotent legislature through the strengthening of other departments *ipso facto* not constitute a genuine power-balance, just as such a balance must mean the weakening of an omnipotent legislature? To the former argument, concerning federalism, it may be answered that both authors can not be expected to express their differences of opinion more clearly and more absolutely than they do. Both accepting federalism, they are bound to make certain concessions from which a superficial observer may conclude agreement. Hamilton, stressing the importance of the national government, has to concede the existence of the states, just as Madison, emphasizing the importance of the states, has to concede that supreme power is lodged in the nation. Without these concessions, Madison could be branded as a believer in international rather than national federalism, whereas Hamilton could be blamed for believing in consolidation rather than federalism. To the argument concerning the separation of powers, one may reply that through a deconcentration of power from the legislature it only follows that there may, not that there must, be a genuine power-balance, one in which power is concentrated in *no* department. There may, however, also be a concentration of power in departments other than the legislative. This is desired by Hamilton, whereas it is only admitted by Madison, who is logically forced to do so. The differences between the opinions of Hamilton and Madison concerning federalism and the separation of powers may be subtle, but they are there. As a matter of fact, it seems open to doubt whether more than subtle dissimilarities can be expected of men who fundamentally agree on the ideal form of government and on the concrete government under which that ideal can best be realized. To expect of two believers in federalism and the separation of powers too divergent views as to the purpose of these institutions would come close to an outright denial that Hamilton and Madison are believing in these institutions. To conclude, it can be said that for Madison, free government can be achieved in a federal state with a separation of powers under the leitmotiv of power-balance, whereas for Hamilton this can be accomplished under the leitmotiv of power-concentration. Here is a split in the personality of the *Federalist* that casts its shadow over the authors' comments on the Articles of Confederation and the Constitution.

Hamilton and Madison agree that under the Articles there exists a crisis that is due mainly to too much democracy in the states. This crisis cannot be cured owing to fundamental errors of the existing system. Having come into being by a mere compact between the legislatures of the states, the United States under the Articles constitutes a mere league under international law. The national government, if such an expression is justified at all, is so bare of power that it is in no position to prevent democratic excesses in the states. Hamilton and Madison also agree on the remedy for the situation. Both want the national government strengthened so that it may be in a position to protect the individual's rights from democratic despotism. But their opinions on the nature of the necessary change again differ. Madison, who conceives of federalism as a means for a balance of powers among the states, is reluctant in his nationalism. Evaluating the system under the Articles, he arrives at the conclusion that nothing but a reduction of the centrifugal tendencies of the Articles is desirable. Hamilton, on the other hand, conceiving of federalism mainly as a means for power-concentration in the national government, and stressing the necessity of a strong nation, is an ardent nationalist who wants a complete change in the highly defective Articles, which permit the *imperium in imperio*.

The dualism between the more moderate Madison and the more radical Hamilton continues in their opinion on the nature of the new Union, with Hamilton appearing as the stronger nationalist. Since both authors disagree on the very nature of the Union, i.e., on the character of the constituent act, it is not surprising that on the whole the personality of the *Federalist* remains split when we consider Hamilton's and Madison's comments on how the new system is going to work. Although they both agree that the structure of the Union is corrected by the Constitution in so far as a loose league of states is transformed into a nation through grants of power to the national government, and although there is general agreement that the main purpose of these grants is to enable a stronger national government to check democratic excesses in the states, Hamilton pronounces the doctrine of happiness through national power more emphatically than does his collaborator. For proof of this, aside from comparing the general attitude of the authors as to the national government's power, we need consider only their different opinions on the necessary and proper and supremacy clauses. Hamilton, anxious to maintain the power of the national government whenever he can do so, considers both clauses as merely declaratory. On the other hand, Madison is not that unequivocal. Only hinting at the declaratory quality of the necessary and proper clause, he considers both clauses as constitutive rather than declaratory. This means that without these clauses the federal government would not possess as much power as it would under the Hamiltonian interpretation.

In view of the fact that Hamilton stresses more emphatically that it is national power above all through which the people's happiness can be achieved, it is not surprising that he conceives of federalism as existent under the Constitution primarily as a device to concentrate power in the national government, whereas Madison sees it primarily as a means for the creation of a system of power-balances. Both authors agree that the main threat to free government is factions and that a constitution providing for free government must furnish a remedy against factions. Madison sees factions in one state outbalanced by those in other states, and, to make the picture of his state protagonism and his system of power-balances complete, he sees the states as a counterpoise to the federal government. Hamilton, on the other hand, sees power concentrated in the Union and factions in or among the states prevented through a strong national government.

Parallel to this dualism on federalism under the Constitution is a different conception of the separation of powers under the new fundamental law. It corresponds to the authors' theoretical opinions on that institution. Hamilton, who wants power concentrated in Congress, creates the potentially greater danger of democratic excesses on the national level than does Madison, who is reluctant to announce the doctrine of national power. Consequently, Hamilton must be more anxious to restrict Congress. The power that is granted to that body through the constituent act by the people in the states must be kept within proper bounds on the national level. The anxiety to prevent Congress from democratic excesses is reflected in the New Yorker's emphasis on the concentration of power in the Supreme Court through the right to review legislative acts. By elevating the Court over Congress, Hamilton elevates the robe over the popular vogue and deprives the latter of its mobocratic sting. Madison need not be that emphatic about the necessity of restricting Congress and making the Court strong. Not having advocated a territorial concentration of power in the national legislature, he can, while accepting judicial review, be satisfied with the creation through the separation of powers of a system of genuine power-balances, under which power is concentrated in no department.

In spite of their disagreement on the nature of the main features of the Constitution, namely, the Union, federalism, and the separation of powers, Hamilton and Madison agree in their over-all evaluation of the new system. It is not perfect, but good.[68] Their different evaluations of various constitutional institutions does not cast any doubt on the authors' fundamental agreement that the Constitution realizes their ideal of free government to a high degree.

3. The split personality of the *Federalist* can be considered the root of the dualism that became so characteristic of American constitutional development. The disagreement over the nature of the Union may have contributed to nullification and secession or, for that matter, to the fight against these institutions. Likewise, Hamilton's and Madison's differing opinions on federalism were used when the Supreme Court interpreted the Constitution and largely account for that Court's oscillation between dual federalism and nationalism.[69] Also, the authors' different conceptions of the separation of powers seem to mark the beginning of a struggle between the legislative, executive, and judicial branches of government, evident throughout American history.

This leads us to ask whether the ambiguity with which the *Federalist* comments upon important features of the Constitution had a definite effect upon American constitutionalism. Was it an evil,

[68] See *supra*, pp. 132-33, 165.
[69] For the doctrine of dual federalism, compare Edward S. Corwin, THE TWILIGHT OF THE SUPREME COURT (1934).

or was it a blessing? It is probable that the Civil War could have been prevented, had the *Federalist* given a clear answer as to the nature of the more perfect Union and of federalism, as provided for by the Constitution.[70] That war is obviously the most outstanding example of the disadvantages resulting from the ambiguous language of the *Federalist*. Similarly, there were times when the relatively strong position of the judiciary, or executive, or the legislature was strongly attacked as being detrimental to various interests. It is possible that a great many controversies on the relative strength of the three departments could have been avoided, had the *Federalist* defined their respective powers more distinctly. On the other hand, it should not be overlooked that the ambiguity of the Papers could also be a blessing. The authors' varying opinions have made possible different interpretations of the Constitution by other people. One could now apply either Hamiltonian or Madisonian doctrines and still maintain that one followed the principles of the classical commentary. This broad scope of interpretation made the Constitution a rather flexible document that could easily be adapted to new conditions as they might exist in the future. Thus, the split personality has definite advantages. Its existence can be considered a happy accident and a gift of Providence, for there is no evidence that the authors introduced it intentionally or were aware of it when they produced the essays.[71] On the other hand, we know that they wanted the Constitution to last. Madison states in number forty-one that the Constitution creates "a system of government, meant for duration."[72] He is seconded by Hamilton. The latter, feeling that in Philadelphia there was framed "a government for posterity as well as ourselves,"[73] stresses that the work of the Federal Convention is not only "framed upon calculations of existing exigencies, but upon a combination of these with the probable exigencies of ages, according to the natural and tried course of human affairs."[74] This desire to have the Constitution last for ages appears quite natural in view of the fact that throughout their essays the authors attack the mutability of laws that are destructive of private rights and create a state of legal insecurity and that have been showered upon the people by legislators who, intoxicated by their own power, tried to please the whims of ever-changing majorities.

[70] See *infra*, pp. 283 ff.; Alpheus T. Mason, "The Nature of Our Federal Union Reconsidered," *loc. cit.*, 512 ff.

[71] See *supra*, pp. 19 ff.

[72] 41, 268.   [73] 34, 208.   [74] 34, 204.

Thus the Constitution automatically became, owing to its different interpretation by its chief commentators, a rather flexible law. On the other hand, the authors of its classical commentary emphasize that this law was to be immune from popular fluctuations. The rigidity and flexibility of the Constitution are not necessarily incompatible. As a matter of fact, the authors probably did not think that there was a conflict between the two and felt confident that there would be none in the future evolution of the United States.[75] On the other hand, their experience with the progressivism of absolute democracy, the majoritarian excesses in the states, and the violence of Shays's Rebellion, made them apprehensive of progressive ideas that had demonstrated a tendency to infringe upon the rights of the individual and could become destructive of the values of the Constitution. Consequently, an urgent need was felt for institutions that, while permitting gradual change and adaption to new conditions, could prevent a revolutionary, or even an evolutionary, replacement of these values and thus preserve the ideals of the Constitution. These means were mainly two, namely, a rather rigid process of constitutional amendment and the conservative—and conserving—institution of judicial review.

IV

1. The Constitution is, on the one hand, lauded by the authors for providing for amendments. On the other hand, it is praised for making the amending process a rather rigid one.

In the last number of the *Federalist,* Hamilton notes that the Constitution, once it is adopted, can be amended. He stresses that, whereas the ratification of the Constitution requires the assent of all the states, subsequent amendments would require only the consent of three-fourths of the members of the Union, happily concluding that there can be "no comparison between the facility of affecting an amendment, and that of establishing in the first instance a

---

[75] The many expressions of hope that the American people would, through their system of government under the Constitution, set an example for the success of popular and republican government for the world, are one indication of that confidence. Compare *supra,* p. 3, note 1. In spite of their rather pessimistic view on human nature, the authors do not seem to entertain much doubt that the system devised at Philadelphia would work and that a happy political evolution was ahead.

complete Constitution."[76] Answering the argument that the national government might prevent amendments, the New Yorker emphasizes that "the intrinsic difficulty of governing thirteen States . . . will . . . constantly impose on the national rulers the necessity of a spirit of accommodation to the reasonable expectations of their constituents."[77] Whenever two-thirds of the states concur, Congress will be obliged to call a convention for proposing amendments,[78] which shall be valid when ratified by the legislatures of three-fourths of the states or by conventions of three-fourths thereof.[79] Although it may be difficult to muster the required majority for amendments that merely affect local interests, there can be no doubt that the situation would be different in the case of amendments concerning "the general liberty and security of the people."[80] Hamilton concludes by saying that Americans may, as far as their rights are concerned, "safely rely on the disposition of the State legislatures to erect barriers against the encroachments of the national government."[81]

Madison, feeling that experience will suggest useful alterations of the Constitution, notes with satisfaction that the law makes provision for amendments. He is also pleased with the particulars of the constitutional arrangement: "The mode preferred by the convention seems to be stamped with every mark of propriety. It guards equally against that extreme facility, which would render the Constitution too mutable; and that extreme difficulty, which might perpetuate its discovered faults."[82] Thus, while satisfied that the Constitution can be amended, the Virginian is also happy about the rigidity of the amending process. Similarly, he likes the idea that the general and state governments are equally enabled "to originate the amendment of errors, as they may be pointed out by the experience on one side, or on the other,"[83] and that the Constitution, by prohibiting amendments depriving a state of its equal suffrage in the Senate, contains "a palladium to the residuary sovereignty of the States."[84]

Thus the authors, while expressing satisfaction about the possi-

---

[76] 85, 572.   [77] 85, 573.

[78] Hamilton stresses that the wording of the Constitution is, "shall call a convention," and that nothing in this particular is left to the discretion of Congress. 85, 573.

[79] 85, 573.   [81] 85, 573.   [83] 43, 286.

[80] 85, 573.   [82] 43, 286.

[84] 43, 286-87. Compare, as to his idea of "residuary sovereignty," also 62, 402.

bility of change, consider the provisions concerning amendment as a bulwark for the preservation of fundamental values that are deemed necessary for a free government, namely, the rights of the states and the freedom of the individual. It appears that in their discussions, states' rights stand in the foreground. Hamilton discusses them at great length, and Madison mentions nothing but states' rights. However, this should not blind us to the fact that to both authors the preservation of those rights also amounts to a preservation of individual freedom. We know that Madison, in his essays, conceives of the states as playing an important role in the protection of the individual. Therefore, when he praises the Constitution for perpetuating the "residuary sovereignty" of the states, he need not, in so many words, stress the relevance of that sovereignty for the protection of the freedom of the individual, because that relevance is implicit. On the other hand, Hamilton, who in the *Federalist* pronounces a doctrine of happiness through national power, has to put greater emphasis on the importance of the states for the protection of the individual's rights. Consequently, when remarking on the amending process, he expressly relates the states to "the general liberty and security of the people." We may thus say that the *Federalist*, in commenting on amendments, points to the usefulness of the amending process to the preservation of the freedom of the individual. It is, however, in the *Federalist*'s comments on judicial review that the function of preserving that freedom is more fully stated.

2. Like the amending process, judicial review can adjust the Constitution to new conditions. Although the *Federalist* does not make a direct statement on that function of the judges, such a function can be concluded from other remarks. The Constitution is, according to the authors, supposed to last for generations. Consequently the judges, being the "guardians of the Constitution,"[85] will have to interpret that law with a view to preserving it. This means that they will have to interpret it in a manner that takes into account changed conditions that might exist in new environments and times. Chief Justice Marshall's later dictum, "We must never forget, that it is a *constitution* we are expounding, . . . a constitution, intended to endure for ages to come, and, consequently, to be adopted to the various *crises* of human affairs,"[86] largely reflects

[85] 78, 509.
[86] McCulloch v. Maryland, 17 U.S. (4 Wheat.), 316, 407, 515 (1819).

judicial guardianship of the Constitution by means of adjustment, as suggested in the *Federalist*.

On the other hand, the Papers conceive of judicial review as an important means for the preservation of the values of the Constitution. Again, this function follows from the role of the judges as the guardians of the Constitution. It is the "duty"[87] of the judges *not* to adjust the fundamental law to current vogues of public opinion, if these sentiments, as expressed in statutes, should conflict with the Constitution and the values for which that law stands.

From among these values, the freedom of the individual is considered to be of paramount importance. As a matter of fact, Hamilton's exposition of the doctrine of judicial review in the seventy-eighth essay amounts largely to an advocacy of the preservation of individual freedom from the progressivism of popular majorities and their infringements upon life, liberty, and property.[88] The protection of these rights is in good hands because the judges, due to the nature of their profession, are likely to be conservatives.[89]

The emphasis, in the discussions on judicial review, upon the preservation of the freedom of the individual, hardly implies that Hamilton wants judicial review exclusively for the protection of that freedom. Although there is no remark on the protection of the rights of the states—something the New Yorker did not forget in his comments on the amendment process—this omission does not mean that these rights should not be preserved through judicial review. Probably, such a remark was not considered necessary because the preservation of states' rights is stressed in connection with constitutional amendments or was felt to be out of place in a discussion that is concerned with the relation between the institutional branches of government, the legislative, executive, and judiciary, and was directed against a democratic rather than against a national despotism. Actually, it does not seem to be necessary to mention specifically that the states will be protected through judicial review. If the judges are the guardians of the Constitution, they are bound to preserve *all* the values of that law, including, of course, those of federalism and states' rights. It would be strange indeed if the guardians of the Constitution failed to preserve a principle that, since it is made partly immune even from constitutional amendment, can be considered a superior principle of the Constitution.

[87] 78, 509.   [88] See *supra*, pp. 170 ff.

[89] Hamilton speaks of the "integrity and moderation" of the judiciary. 78, 509.

3. The Founders' permanent exemption of a federal principle from abolition and alteration by the amending power of the United States throws a significant light on the relation of states' rights to the sovereignty of the people. Clearly, if the people cannot deprive the states of their "residuary sovereignty,"[90] equal suffrage in the Senate, the federal principle must be above the will of the people, as reflected in their power of amending the Constitution. This may be carried even further. It is unlikely that the authors of the *Federalist* wanted to apply the rule *expressio unius est exclusio alterius* here. Since they conceived of federalism as a mere means for the protection of the freedom of the individual, they must, in view of the immunity of the federal principle from the people, have felt even more strongly that the end federalism was supposed to achieve, namely, the protection of the individual's life, liberty, and property, had to be above the popular will and thus to be immune from the amending power.[91] Here is as good a proof as any of the idea that is ever present in the pages of the *Federalist,* namely, that American government was conceived to be a government of laws and not of men—a government of the Constitution!

The supremacy of the Constitution over the people furnishes us with an indication of the importance of the judiciary. As the natural —and only—interpreters of that law,[92] the judges, while being bound by the Constitution, are not bound by the will of the people, unless that will has become part of the Constitution. They thereby occupy that peculiar position assigned to them in the *Federalist,* being, of all people, closest to the Constitution and its revelations of justice.[93] The judges, being bound by the Constitution, are, thereby, also bound by certain principles of higher law of which the Constitution is a reflection.[94] For the *Federalist* indicates that the Constitution is not only the source, but also the recipient of superior law: Although Hamilton says that "by a limited Constitution, I understand one which contains certain specified exceptions to the legislative authority,"[95] his use of the term "limited" instead of "limiting" suggests also that the Constitution itself is limited by certain principles

---

[90] 43, 286-87.   [91] See *supra,* chapters five and six.   [92] 78, 506.

[93] Hamilton writes that "the courts were designed to be an intermediate body between the people and the legislature" (78, 506), i.e., between those who make the constitution and those who make ordinary law. Consequently, the judges are closer to the constitution than the members of the legislature.

[94] Compare Edward S. Corwin, "The 'Higher Law' Background of American Constitutional Law," HARVARD LAW REVIEW (1928-29) XLII, 149, 365.

[95] 78, 505.

that secure the protection of the states and, *a fortiori,* the rights of the individual, and that constitutional restrictions upon the legislative and amending power are only expressions of those higher law principles that rule the Constitution.[96] The judges thus are the guardians not only of the letter but also of the spirit of the Constitution.[97] This makes them truly platonic guardians who, while not being unwilling to take into account new conditions that may arise in the course of time, guarantee the preservation of the values of the Constitution and thus secure justice, which is referred to in the *Federalist* as the end of government.[98] For the judges' right to adjust the Constitution to new conditions—important as it may be—is by no means unrestricted. If the people, who, after all, possess the general power of amendment, are restricted in the exercise of that power with respect to certain rights of the states and of individuals, the judges, not at all possessing the right of formal amendment, must be even more careful to respect those rights, because they are, after all, nothing but interpreters of the Constitution.[99] This raises the question as to what recourse there is if constitutional rights are infringed upon by the government. In spite of all precautions that were taken for the preservation of the Constitution, it is conceivable that the judges may neglect their duty of protecting the values of the Constitution, improbable as this may be in the opinion of the *Federalist.*[100] Likewise, it is very possible that the executive will not abide by a judicial decision and will enforce measures that are in-

[96] Compare Gottfried Dietze, "America and Europe—Decline and Emergence of Judicial Review," VIRGINIA LAW REVIEW (1958) XLIV, 1233. Reprinted in SOUTH AFRICAN LAW JOURNAL (1959), LXXVI, 398.

[97] Answering those who fear that the judges will have "the power of construing the laws according to the *spirit* of the Constitution," Hamilton remarks that "in the first place, there is not a syllable in the plan under consideration which *directly* empowers the national courts to construe the laws according to the spirit of the Constitution. . . . I admit, however, that the Constitution ought to be the standard of construction for the laws . . ." (81, 523-24). Since there is also no word in the Constitution that the courts can construe the laws according to the letter of the Constitution, it can be assumed that for Hamilton, there is no difference between the letter and the spirit of the Constitution. (Consider the use of the word "however"!)

[98] The most direct statement can be found at 51, 340: "Justice is the end of government. It is the end of civil society."

[99] 78, 506.

[100] The judges were conceived in the *Federalist* as those people to whom the authors' pessimism concerning the nature of man did apply least. Compare essays 78-83.

compatible with the judges' interpretation of the Constitution and detrimental to the values protected by the law.[101] In such cases the judiciary, possessing "no influence over either the sword or the purse,"[102] and, as far as actual power is concerned, by far the weakest of the departments of government,[103] would be in no position to assure the realization of its protective measures. Then the people may take recourse to extraconstitutional, or, better, extralegal, though legitimate, means to seek redress for their grievances.

V

1. The *Federalist* admits a right of revolution. In view of the fact that its authors lived through the revolution against the mother country and actively participated in that movement,[104] this can hardly come as a surprise. We have seen that in the Papers a distinction is made between superior natural law and inferior positive law.[105] A recognition of such a distinction makes an admission of the right of revolution highly probable. Thus we find in the *Federalist* direct statements that sanction the institution of revolution. In essay forty-three, Madison justifies the rather revolutionary action of the Federal Convention in discarding the Articles of Confederation by "the transcendent law of nature and of nature's God, which declares that the safety and happiness of society are the objects to which all political institutions aim, and to which all such institutions must be sacrificed."[106] In another passage in an earlier essay, the Virginian, quoting the Declaration of Independence, expresses himself in favor of "the transcendent and precious right of the people to 'abolish or alter their governments as to them shall seem most likely to effect their safety and happiness.' "[107] Similar statements are made by Hamilton, who admits the exercise of a right of revolution if, under

---

[101] President Jackson's veto of the National Bank and Lincoln's suspension of the writ of habeas corpus come to mind immediately. See James D. Richardson, ed., A COMPILATION OF THE MESSAGES AND PAPERS OF THE PRESIDENTS, II, 582; VII, 3226.

[102] 78, 504.   [104] See *supra*, chapter three.

[103] 78, 504.   [105] See *supra*, pp. 116, 145-46.   [106] 43, 287.

[107] 40, 257. In his answer to "Pacificus" of April 22, 1793, Madison writes: "If there be a principle that ought not to be questioned within the United States, it is that every nation has a right to abolish an old government and establish a new one. This principle is not only recorded in every public archive, written in every American heart, and sealed with the blood of a host of American martyrs,

the Constitution, the government abuses its power. "If the representatives of the people," he writes in connection with a possible abuse of military establishments by the new government, "betray their constituents, there is then no resource left but in the exertion of that original right of self-defence which is paramount to all positive forms of government, and which against the usurpations of the national rulers, may be exerted with infinitely better prospect of success than against those of the rulers of an individual state."[108]

The admission in the *Federalist* of a right of revolution does not imply that the people should make use of that right frequently or for light causes. The authors warn their readers that it was all "too ticklish a business" when the people felt called on to exercise their sovereign powers and prerogatives.[109] It is much safer, argue Hamilton and Madison, to have confidence in the good judgment of the rulers than in the passions of an excited and dissatisfied people. Resort to revolution is admitted only in exceptional cases. One is hopeful that it would not be necessary at all under the Constitution. If the right of revolution is exercised, the revolutionaries should act "as the exigency may suggest and prudence justify"[110] and not commit excessive and unreasonable acts of violence.

The statements concerning the right of revolution reveal that rebellions against the established order are justified by natural and higher law principles. However, these principles are by no means considered the only justification. The authors, recognizing that in many instances the rulers will be able to claim the sanction of higher law as much as the revolutionaries, feel the necessity of a further, more tangible, justification. This is found in the contract theory of the state, to which the authors subscribe.[111] Under that theory, sovereignty is not totally transferred from the people to the government. The individuals, when entering society, retain their unalienable rights, which the government is supposed to protect. If these rights are infringed upon, the people may, as a last resort, have recourse to revolution.

but is the only lawful tenure by which the United States hold their existence as a nation." MADISON'S WRITINGS, VI, 164. Compare also *ibid.*, IX, 398.

[108] 28, 173. In the case of unjust election laws, the "citizens, . . . conscious of their rights, would . . . overthrow their tyrants, and . . . substitute men who would be disposed to avenge the violated majesty of the people" (60, 395).

[109] Compare Edwin Mims, Jr., THE MAJORITY OF THE PEOPLE (1941), 35. That work attempts to give a pro-majoritarian interpretation of the *Federalist*.

[110] 33, 200.   [111] See *supra*, pp. 112-13, 142.

2.   The admission of a right of revolution if the government should fail to fulfill its contractual obligations raises the question whether, in a like manner, the members of a federal state should possess a right of nullification or secession if they feel their rights are disregarded by the national government. The *Federalist* is not as explicit in its answer as it is in the case of revolution. However, the work does not, in so many words, deny the right of nullification and secession. As a matter of fact, from a reading of the Papers the conclusion could be drawn that these means against national oppression are possible.

First of all, Madison and Hamilton recognize a parallel between the contract through which the individuals establish civil society and government and the federal compact, by which the states create a federation with a federal government.[112] There is no reason to believe that the authors would admit a right of revolution under the former and, at the same time, deny such a right under the latter. As a matter of logic, owing to their admission of a parallel between the two types of compacts, they are forced to admit revolutionary action by the states as much as such an action by the individual citizens. The *Federalist* furnishes further evidence that the right of a "federal" revolution is not denied.

Even supporters of the nationalistic interpretation of the nature of the Union admit that Madison contributed to the later doctrines of nullification and secession.[113] This is due largely to Madison's comments in the *Federalist*. One adherent of the nationalistic doctrine stated that the "equivocal views of the Father of the Constitution, expressed in a series of essays designed to win ratification, provided the leaders of nullification and secession with exactly the formula, the destructive ammunition, they used in their abortive attempt to blow up the Union."[114] The Virginian's language on the nature of the federal compact; his opinion that the new Constitution amounts to nothing but a mere reduction of the centrifugal tendencies of the Articles of Confederation, to a mere invigoration of their centripetal features; his constant emphasis on the rights of the

---

[112] See *supra,* pp. 113, 142.

[113] Compare Edward S. Corwin, "National Power and State Interposition, 1787-1861," MICHIGAN LAW REVIEW (1912) x, 535.

[114] Alpheus T. Mason, "The Nature of Our Federal Union Reconsidered," *loc. cit.,* 517. At 519, Mason states: ". . . one may venture the suggestion that his numbers of the *Federalist* papers planted the verbal bomb that, after 1861, flared tragically."

states: All this must be water on the mills of the advocates of states' rights, of nullification and secession, no matter how the adherents of the nationalistic doctrine may try to use Madison's essays in support of their own arguments.

As for Hamilton, there can be no doubt that his essays contain strong assertions of national power. However, such assertions do not necessarily exclude nullification and secession. We should not forget that he actually refrains from favoring an outright consolidation in so many words, but always is careful to mention the continuing existence of the states and their rights. His admission that the federal Union comes into being by a compact and his emphasis, in his comments on the amending process, upon the importance of the states are indications that, no matter how powerful the national government might be, the federal character of the Constitution sets definite limits to an arbitrary exercise of power. Back in 1780, Hamilton shied off from the suggestion that Congress under the Articles of Confederation, in order to cope with the existing crisis, should assert and exercise discretionary power, because such a course then seemed to him to be "too bold an expedient."[115] It can hardly be said that his attitude is a different one in the *Federalist*. In spite of all his protagonism of national power, Hamilton does not proceed to proclaim a discretionary power of the national government. A statement made in connection with the states' right to revoke the federal compact, that it was a gross heresy "to maintain that a *party* to a *compact* has a right to revoke that *compact*,"[116] ought not to be interpreted exclusively as barring nullification and secession. It shows, of course, that Hamilton on the whole disliked nullification and secession as much as he disliked revolution. On the other hand, that statement hardly prohibits these institutions absolutely. Throughout his *Federalist,* the New Yorker is a strong advocate of the principle *pacta sunt servanda*. But advocacy of that principle means only that *all* parties to a contract are bound by it. It does not mean that if one party does not fulfill its contractual obligations, the other parties would have to fulfill theirs. In a word, Hamilton does not actually say that the states could not revoke the federal compact by means of nullification and secession if that compact is broken by the national government.[117]

[115] Letter to James Duane of Sept. 3, 1780. HAMILTON'S WORKS, I, 213.
[116] 22, 141.
[117] Compare his statement at 33, 200: "If the federal government should overpass the just bounds of its authority and make a tyrannical use of its powers,

For the authors of the *Federalist,* the nationalist Hamilton as much as the state-friendly Madison, the more perfect Union is nothing but a means to an end. That end is, aside from security from foreign powers and peace within the federation, the preservation of free government in the states and the nation. Due to the existence of a democratic despotism in the states at the time the essays were written, the authors maintain that the Union could be of great value for the protection of the individual from the oppression of the state governments. They do not go so far as to claim that *only* the national government could protect the individual, and they thus refrain from giving that government discretionary power. Should it happen, against all expectation, that the freedom of the individual was suppressed by the national government, the states could, like the individuals themselves, exercise the right of revolution as a last resort.

VI

These remarks conclude this analysis of the *Federalist*. It is not claimed that it is a complete analysis, covering all the problems raised and discussed in the Papers. The aim has been a moderate one, namely, to analyze the essays as a treatise for free government in peace and security and to show that these essays are a classic on federalism and constitutional democracy. We even omitted to mention some of the more technical aspects and details of the administration of a federal and constitutional government that are discussed by Hamilton, Madison, and Jay. It was felt that this omission did not seem to have a bearing upon an over-all evaluation of the *Federalist*. On the other hand, it is realized that an evaluation of the Papers as a classic on federalism and constitutional democracy can hardly be based upon a systematic analysis only. Therefore, it shall now be shown what place the *Federalist* occupies in political theory and in the literature on federalism and constitutionalism.

the people, whose creature it is, must appeal to the standard they have formed, and take such measures to redress the injury done to the Constitution as the exigency may suggest and prudence justify."

BOOK THREE

Theoretical Setting

CHAPTER TEN

The Federalist—
Its Roots and Contributions

As a classic on federalism and constitutional democracy, the *Federalist* was influenced by the political thinking and experience of earlier periods. At the same time, the work makes definite contributions to both federal and constitutional thought.

The preceding chapters have demonstrated that the Papers deal with various aspects of federalism. Aside from technical problems of organization and administration, the essays discuss such topics as the nature of the Union and the rights of the states. Above all, they are concerned with the function of federalism to attain security from foreign powers, peace within the federation, and the freedom of the individual from governmental oppression. The *Federalist* thus appears as a classic on federalism. However, due to the last-mentioned function, the essays also emerge as a treatise on the merits of limited government and, owing to their fundamentl acceptance of popular rule, as a classic on constitutional democracy.

In the following pages, it will be seen to what degree the authors were influenced by their environment, by political practice and theory, and an examination will be made of the Papers' contribution to federal and constitutional thought.

I

1.   In their discussion of federal problems, Hamilton, Madison, and
Jay were, of course, under the impact of their environment. They
all experienced the shortcomings of the existing federal system. During and after the War of Independence, it had become evident to
them that a loose confederation was detrimental to security, peace,
and the freedom of the individual.[1] While all the authors were in
favor of a more perfect Union, they differed as to the degree of national power. Jay's nationalism[2] can be explained through his activities in international politics. From his diplomatic assignments, he
saw the United States as one subject in international relations and
was likely to wish it to be strong through an increase of national
power. Hamilton's nationalism derives from similar roots. Born on
the island of Nevis, one of the British West Indies, he grew up in an
atmosphere in which the American colonies appeared like something the American continent constitutes geographically—a unit.
Therefore in later years he saw the states as being nothing but parts
of one whole, and he was not too inhibited in proclaiming the doctrine of national power. Madison, on the other hand, was born into
an America that, from his home in Virginia, appeared not as a har-
monious whole, but as something composed of a great variety of
local entities among which the Old Dominion seemed to play the
most important role. Madison was thus aware of and friendly toward American particularism from the beginning. Since that particularism was not tempered by sojourns abroad, as it was in the
case of Jay, it was likely to play an important part throughout the
Virginian's later life.

2.   In its discussion of federalism, the *Federalist* is also influenced
by the history of ancient and modern federations. Again and again,
their experiences are given as examples for the blessings and disadvantages of federal government. The Papers mention quite a few
institutions of a more or less federal character. The Amphictyonic
council, the Achaean league, the Lycian confederacy, the feudal
system, the German empire, Switzerland, the United Netherlands,
all are considered to illustrate the shortcomings of the Articles of

[1] See *supra*, pp. 75 ff., 82 ff., 93 ff.
[2] In a letter to Washington of Jan. 7, 1787, Jay expressed himself in favor of
reducing the states to mere administrative districts. JAY'S CORRESPONDENCE, III,
227-28.

Confederation and the blessings of the Constitution. Clearly, the use of such a variety of systems as demonstrations of federalism must raise doubts as to the correctness of the authors' appreciation of these systems. For although Hamilton and Madison had occupied themselves with the study of ancient and modern confederacies prior to the *Federalist* enterprise[3] and probably did not arbitrarily offer their evaluations merely in order to support the argument in favor of ratification, their analysis leaves much to be desired.[4] Still, the authors' comments on these confederacies show a good insight into the motives for federation and the essentials of federal organization.

There can be no doubt that there existed certain federal institutions in ancient times. Freeman has supplied ample information on Greek confederations.[5] These confederations seem to have resulted from many considerations, which were not merely of a political nature. Thus the Amphictyonic council derived from a voluntary association of cities mainly for religious ends, and its aims were limited to the common welfare and the declaration and cessation of war.[6] The Achaean league was a political union that was established chiefly for the prevention of external invasion and diplomatic impropriety.[7] The members of the Lycian confederacy, according to the geographer and historian Strabo, "used to consult about war, and peace, and alliance,"[8] which indicates that this confederacy, like the others, was motivated mainly by considerations of internal peace and security from foreign powers. The security motive seems to have been most important for the creation of unions against Macedon and Rome. However, largely due to organizational shortcomings

[3] See *supra*, pp. 80 ff., 90 ff.

[4] Compare Edward A. Freeman, HISTORY OF FEDERAL GOVERNMENT (1863), I, 143, n. 1: "On this subject of the Amphiktyonic Council, the eighteenth number of the "Federalist" should by all means be read. It is clear that the authors, Madison and Hamilton, had not the least notion of the true nature of the institution, but it is most curious to see the strong political sagacity of the authors struggling with their utter ignorance of facts. They were politicians enough to see the utter political nullity of the Council in Grecian history; they were not scholars enough to see that it never really pretended to any character from which anything but political nullity could be expected. Some of the particular comments and illustrations are most ingenious."

[5] Freeman, *op. cit.* On p. 219, Freeman even refers to the last 150 years of Greek independence as the "Federal period of Grecian history."

[6] Sobei Mogi, THE PROBLEM OF FEDERALISM (1931), I, 21.

[7] *Ibid.*, 22.

[8] Freeman, *op. cit.*, 209. That work contains a translation of Strabo's account of the constitution of the Lycian league on pp. 208-9.

(too little power in the federal government), Greek confederations were not very successful and in no position to prevent the end of Greek independence.

In Rome, there were no federal institutions. The empire continually expanded through treaties of alliance,[9] but never united its dependencies under a federal system.[10] Although Roman territories would often possess far-reaching autonomy, no political entities or states were recognized within the limits of the empire. Later, the Holy Roman Empire, for the sake of Christianity, exercised sovereignty over the various Christian nations, *regna,* but these bodies politic were considered merely legal or administrative units, not states. In essence, the Holy Roman Empire remained what its predecessor, the *Imperium Romanum,* had been, namely, a unitary state.[11]

On the other hand, with the increasing influence of the vassals, the feudal order approached a federal system. However, since the feuds were not recognized as states, one can only speak of traces of federalism. Still, it must be admitted that the motives for and the end of the feudal order are rather similar to those of federalism, namely, peace within and security from without.

Voluntary alliances that, for the sake of peace and security, existed in Germany from the thirteenth century[12] had definite similarities to leagues of states, and in many instances the federal principle can be recognized.[13] The German empire itself possessed certain federal characteristics. Prior to the Thirty Years' War, steps were taken, in the course of Imperial reform, toward the improvement of peace within Germany and security from foreign nations. In 1495, the Diet of Worms decreed that, for the sake of *Landfriede,* the *Reichsstände* were prohibited from exercising the right of self-help. Disputes among the members of the empire were to be sub-

[9] On the Roman *foedera aequa* and *non aequa,* see Ferdinand Walter, GE-SCHICHTE DES RÖMISCHEN RECHTS BIS AUF JUSTINIAN (3rd ed., 1860-61), I, 131-32, 328 ff.

[10] The Romans only established an "association of the conquered." See François Laurent, HISTOIRE DU DROIT DES GENS ET DES RELATIONS INTERNATIONALES (1850-70), III, 62.

[11] Compare, for instance, Ubertus von Lampugano, "Utrum omnes Christiani subsunt Romano Imperio?", ZEITSCHRIFT FÜR GESCHICHTLICHE RECHTSWISSENSCHAFT (1816), II, 246 ff.

[12] Otto Gierke, DAS DEUTSCHE GENOSSENSCHAFTSRECHT (1868-1913), I, 296 ff.; II, 835 ff.

[13] For instance, the Rhenish City League and the Hanseatic League. Gierke, *op. cit.,* I, 476-81.

mitted to an Imperial court.[14] This measure, which was later complemented by acts providing for peace among the various religions,[15] was followed by laws that made it obligatory for the *Reichsstände* to protect members of the empire not only from other members, but also from the attacks of foreign powers.[16] The constitution of the empire survived the Thirty Years' War. However, in the course of time, Austria, Hanover, Saxony, and other members became, due to an increase of their power, virtually independent. Nevertheless, the empire continued to exist. The smaller states clung to it with increased intensity, recognizing that only through the empire could they enjoy protection from aggression. The idea of peace and security thus played an important part throughout the history of the German empire and its peculiar type of federal organization. Disintegration, which became characteristic of that empire and helped to bring about its decline, can be attributed, among other things, to the reasons that accounted for the fall of Greek confederations—a lack of power in the government of the Reich.[17]

The Swiss federation had its origin in the Eternal League that was formed in 1291 by the three original forest cantons, Schwyz, Uri, and Unterwalden, primarily with a view toward protection from Austria and the preservation of peace among the cantons.[18] Soon after the conclusion of the federal pact, the league was put to a test in the battle of Mogarten against the Austrians (1315). Thereafter, other cantons joined the confederation mainly for the purpose of peace and security.[19] Thus strengthened, the confederation succeeded in throwing off the Austrian yoke[20] and in securing formal recognition by that country.[21] Federation proved useful again in the fight against Charles the Bold, whose forces were decisively de-

[14] The *Reichskammergericht* was founded on that occasion.
[15] *Augsburger Reichsabschied* of 1555.
[16] *Exekutionsordnung* of 1555.
[17] For a good account of the German empire, see Fritz Hartung, DEUTSCHE VERFASSUNGSGESCHICHTE (5th ed., 1950).
[18] Erwin Ruck, SCHWEIZERISCHES STAATSRECHT (3rd ed., 1957), 2. On p. 1, this work supplies a valuable bibliography on the history of the Swiss confederation.
[19] Luzern joined in 1332, Zürich in 1351, Glarus in 1352, Zug in 1352, and Bern in 1353.
[20] Battles of Sempach (1386) and Näfels (1388).
[21] The Swiss confederation was recognized by Austria in the peace of 1412. In that peace, the Swiss still guaranteed the inviolability of Austrian territory in Switzerland. However, in the following years, more and more of that territory became Swiss (Aargau in 1415, Thurgau in 1460). Austria finally recognized the Swiss Confederation without qualification in the *Ewige Richtung* of 1474.

feated.[22] In the following years, the Swiss confederation became more and more independent of the German empire and, due to its strengthened position, could afford to disobey Imperial laws. This led to the Suebian War, in which the Swiss were again victorious. In the peace of Basel (1499), the confederation was recognized *de facto* to be "exempt" from the empire. In the Westphalian Peace Treaty, Swiss independence was acknowledged *de iure*. Switzerland thus furnishes an example of how federation can achieve and preserve independence.[23] However, the cantons, when participating in the federal enterprise, were also interested in the preservation of peace among themselves. The treaties of alliance, which, for want of a federal constitution, were binding the cantons together, and the decrees and orders that were adopted in their wake furnish proof of this.[24] The confederacy lasted until 1798, when it was conquered by Napoleon. This conquest brought to an end a confederation that ever since the seventeenth century, had been becoming increasingly characterized by an egoistic particularism of the cantons and thus did no longer possess the strength to resist foreign aggression.[25] Dis-

[22] Battles of Grandson (1476) and Nancy (1477). These Swiss victories resulted in the incorporation into the confederacy of the free cities of Freiburg and Solothurn in 1481.

[23] Compare W. E. Rappard, CINQ SIECLES DE SECURITE COLLECTIVE 1291-1798 (1945). The Swiss confederation was not based on a federal constitution, but on an alliance that was concluded through treaties. However, there was no treaty that would be binding upon all the cantons. Such a federal treaty was desired repeatedly in the 17th and 18th centuries, but, for political and religious reasons, was never realized. The core of the Confederacy was the original treaty between Schwyz, Uri, and Unterwalden. Besides, there existed leagues between the various cantons, though not between all of them. The leagues differed from one another in many respects. Nevertheless, all these leagues were no mere alliances, concluded for temporary emergencies, but were established on a permanent basis, in order to secure protection from foreign nations. Compare W. Liebeskind, "Altschweizerische Föderativsystems," ZEITSCHRIFT DES BERNISCHEN JURISTENVEREINS (1933), LXIX, 1 ff.; O. Hunziker, DER EIDGENÖSSISCHE BUNDESBRIEF VON 1291 UND SEINE VORGESCHICHTE NACH NEUEN FORSCHUNGSERGEBNISSEN (1934); B. Meyer, DIE ÄLTESTEN EIDGENÖSSISCHEN BÜNDE (1938); W. E. Rappard, DU RENOUVELLEMENT DES PACTES CONFEDERAUX 1351-1798 (1944).

[24] Best known among these are the *Pfaffenbrief* (1370), *Sempacherbrief* (1393), *Stanser Verkommnis* (1481), the four *Landfrieden* and the Treaty of Basel (1632), the *Defensionale* 1647-68. A collection of Swiss constitutional charters and documents provides P. Kläui, FREIHEITSBRIEFE, BUNDESBRIEFE, VERKOMMNISSE UND VERFASSUNGEN 1231-1815 (1952).

[25] See Ruck, *op. cit.*, 5.

integration was not surprising in view of the fact that under the Swiss confederation the cantons had retained their sovereignty, while there did not actually exist a federal government.[26]

As an example of a federation that "arose in the period of transition between medieval and modern history," Freeman mentions the United Provinces of the Netherlands,[27] which were formed during the struggle with Spain in 1579. If the defense against a foreign power was a strong motive for the creation of that union, the quest for security remained important throughout the following years, during the war of independence and, later, in the relations with the powers of Europe. It is probably no exaggeration to say that the union was mainly held together by the hatred for the house of Austria.[28] The constitution of the United Netherlands furnishes ample proof that considerations of security played an important part in the establishment of federal government.[29] At the same time, the act of union also resulted from the desire to have peace among the seven provinces.[30] However, it soon became evident that harmony could hardly exist in a federation that was based upon the principle of the sovereignty of its constituent parts and did not possess a strong federal government.[31] This want of harmony was detrimental to the international position of the United Netherlands. Whereas in the first half of the seventeenth century that federation was the leading Protestant power and a center of European politics, its prestige declined thereafter, until the federation came to an end in the Napoleonic era.

To conclude the survey of foreign federal systems prior to the formation of the American Union, we may say that these federations were formed mainly for the sake of peace and security. There

---

[26] The two institutions of federal government, the *Tagsatzung* and the *Vorort*, were not independent governmental organs, but merely common organs of the members of the confederation. Compare R. Joos, DIE ENTSTEHUNG UND RECHTLICHE AUSGESTALTUNG DER EIDGENÖSSISCHEN TAGSATZUNG BIS ZUR REFORMATION (1925).

[27] Freeman, *op. cit.*, 5.

[28] See John Lothrop Motley, THE RISE OF THE DUTCH REPUBLIC (Altemus ed., 1898), II, Part IV.

[29] *Ibid.*, II, 160-62.

[30] *Ibid.*, II, 160-62.

[31] The federal authority was mainly vested in the Estates General, which, however, were not superior to the Estates of the Provinces, but functioned merely as the representative and executive organ of the union. The members of the Estates General were bound by the instructions of the Estates of the Provinces.

are no indications that federalism was resorted to for the protection of the individual from the oppressions of the government.[32] Although freedom is often mentioned as an aim of federation, it is conceived not so much as freedom of the individual from the government, but, rather, as safety of the state from the aggressions of foreign powers. In a word, it suggests the security of the federated bodies politic or of the whole federation rather than the freedom of the individual citizen. The individual is free as long as his respective society is free. A function of federalism to make the individual safe from the infringements of his own government is not recognized. Another important feature of the federations under consideration is the principle employed in the organization of federal government. In all cases, the federal government was not strong enough to be really superior to the governments of the component parts, although a formal sovereignty was recognized in various instances. Due to the power and even the sovereignty of the members, the federal experiment proved to be not very successful. The ends of federalism, peace and security, were not achieved.

Federalism not only appeared in the practice of government prior to the writing of the *Federalist*. It had also been discussed by political theorists. However, no new concept of federalism was developed by them. As will be shown in the following pages, the theory of federalism remained within the scope of actual institutions. Aside from a recognition of the peace and security motives, there are found simply descriptions of rather loose types of federation, in which the component parts retained a high degree of sovereignty.

3.   Although confederations existed in Greece, no theory of federalism was developed. During the blossoming of Greek political life, each city and its surrounding territory formed a state by itself. The more powerful states ruled the scene, and their unions were usually prompted by the desire to expand their own sphere of influence.[33] It was from these city-states rather than from their confederations that political thinkers derived their ideas. Thus neither Plato nor Aristotle developed a concept of federalism. The latter, in his *Poli-*

---

[32] German Reich law, which prohibited individuals from exercising the right of self-defense, provided for the protection of the individual from other individuals rather than from the government. The same applies to the provisions of certain Swiss intercantonal treaties.

[33] The nature of these "leagues" is described by Polybius, HISTORIOE (Bekker ed., 1844), II, 37.

tics, discusses political life in the various cities, which, being self-sufficient, would enter treaties for the attainment of certain ends, but would never subordinate themselves to a common political organization.[34] Aristotle's concept of the state was incompatible with the federal idea, because for him the state existed for the realization of the good life and not "for the sake of alliance."[35] When, during the preponderance of Macedon and Rome, Greek policy was determined by organized federations, Greek political theory had passed its climax. Philosophers took a more negative attitude toward political life and do not seem to have been concerned with the new institutions. Even Polybius, who is full of praise for the Achaean league, did not recognize federalism, since he clung to the orthodox concept of the state. Although he recognized that the Achaean league formed a political entity that went beyond a mere league of friendship or alliance, and thus recognized its similarity to a state,[36] the fact that the people of the league did not live within the same walls precluded him from using the term "polis." The relation of the member states to the confederacy was not defined at all.[37]

In view of the fact that Greek philosophy, in spite of existing federations, did not develop a concept of federalism, it cannot be surprising that, in the absence of federal institutions, such a concept was not developed in Rome. Possibly, Roman political theory was not independent enough to bring forth concepts that had been of no concern to the Greeks, the Romans' teachers and masters.[38]

Thus the two authorities that mainly influenced medieval secular thinking, Aristotle and the *Corpus Iuris Civilis,* did not furnish theories that would have encouraged discussions of federalism in the Middle Ages. Existing institutions were not of the kind to bring about a consciousness of federal government and to stimulate a scholarly elaboration of that subject. Although the re-established Roman empire exercised control over various peoples and had a certain similarity to the central government of an organization of states, the theory of the legists considered that empire as a unitary state. Only a few thinkers, such as Engelbert von Volkersdorf[39] and

[34] Compare Aristotle's comments on the distinction between πόλις and συμμαχία. POLITICS, III, 9.

[35] Aristotle, POLITICS (Benjamin Jowett transl., 1923), III, 118-19.

[36] See Siegfried Brie, DER BUNDESSTAAT (1874), 10.

[37] *Ibid.,* 10.

[38] *Ibid.,* 11.

[39] "Engelberti abbatis Admontensis Liber de Ortu, Progressu et Fine imperii Romani," in BIBLIOTHECA VETERUM PATRUM (1577), XXV, chapters 15 and 17.

Dante,[40] had a notion of federalism. They ascribed to the emperor the realization of general prosperity and the fostering of the higher interests of the state and to the individual states the realization of the prosperity of the individual nations and care for the particular interests, and thus they approximated the idea of the federal state in an important respect.[41]

While the feudal order had certain similarities with federal systems, federalism was hardly discussed by thinkers of that period. Federal associations, which from the thirteenth century existed in Germany and neighboring countries, did not serve as a starting point for a federal theory either. Existing on too small a scale or for too short a time, they were unable to attract the attention of the Roman publicists.[42] Still, plans for the realization of the federal idea can be found. In 1300, Pierre Dubois proposed a world state under the leadership of France in order to break the power of the Pope.[43] Probably six years later, he asked for the creation of a federation or a league of states, headed by a council of prelates and sovereign princes. That council was to elect judges for the settlement of controversies between the members of the league. Peace among the states was desired for the conquest of the Holy Land and for security from the Turks.[44]

About a century later, George of Podiebrad, King of Bohemia, advanced a similar plan of union.[45] He wanted peace among the federated states and the elimination of war within the Christian community.[46] The princes were to promise mutual friendship and understanding and had to abstain from the exercise of self-help. A federal court was to settle controversies between the states.[47] Again, as in the case of Dubois' plan, the sovereignty of the members of the union was left intact.[48] Thus the effectiveness of the confedera-

---

[40] Dante, DE MONARCHIA, book 1, chapter 16.

[41] Brie, op. cit., 13. Mogi, op. cit., I, 24.

[42] Brie, op. cit., 14.

[43] Pierre Dubois, SUMMARIA BREVIS ET COMPENDIOSA DOCTRINA FELICIS EXPEDITIONIS GUERRARUM AT LITIUM REGNI FRANCORUM (1300).

[44] Pierre Dubois, DE RECUPERATIONE TERRE SANCTE (1306). For a description of Dubois' plan and references to the literature on that plan, see Wilhelm Samuel, DIE IDEE DES FÖDERALISMUS (Dissertation, Halle, 1928), 12-14.

[45] Compare E. Schwitzky, DER FÜRSTENBUND GEORG VON PODIEBRADS (1907), and M. Jordan, DAS KÖNIGTUM GEORGS VON PODIEBRAD (1861).

[46] Jordan, op. cit., 16, 99. Samuel, op. cit., 14. Schwitzky, op. cit., 13.

[47] Samuel, op. cit., 15.

[48] Ibid., 15.

tion under both plans depended upon the degree of community feeling, which, due to the sovereignty of the states, was subject to great fluctuations.

It may be said that since the thirteenth century the idea of federalism had been in the air. And while it was not elaborated by the majority of thinkers in the beginning, it was likely to be taken up by someone sooner or later and to become a subject of discussion for future generations. Bartolus, a Roman jurist, took a first step. He distinguished between *universitates* that were subject to no superior and *universitates* that recognized a superior, but made no distinction between *civitas, regnum,* and *imperium,* the differences between which were, from the point of view of human organization, merely quantitative.[49]

Bodin, though not favoring it, could no longer ignore federalism. In his major work, he emphasized the co-operative character of confederations and divided them into *foedera aequa* and *foedera iniqua.* Both types of union, being composed of sovereign states, were based on mere treaties of alliance. An unequal federation existed when one state "acknowledgeth the other to be superior in the treaty of alliance; which is of two sorts, that is to wit, when the one acknowledgeth the other to be superior for honour, and yet is not in his protection: or else the one receiuth the other into protection, and both the one and the other is bound to pay a certaine pention or to give certaine succours, or owe neither pention nor succours."[50] The members of the federation were absorbed into one common sovereignty, and thus Bodin's *foedera iniqua* are actually unitary states. Under an *aequum foedus,* on the other hand, one state "is in nothing superiour unto the other in the treatie; and that the one hath nothing above the other for their prerogative of honour, albeit that the one must do or give more or lesse than the other for aid that the one oweth unto the other."[51] Bodin criticized under this heading the position of the cantons of Switzerland, of the members of ancient leagues, and of the German states. All these confederacies could, in his opinion, not be called states, but only confederacies, which were formed mainly for purposes of defense. The "equal federation" is thus as much the result of Bodin's concept of sovereignty as is his "unequal federation." Obviously, the defender of undivided sover-

---

[49] Otto Gierke, JOHANNES ALTHUSIUS (1880), 14-15.

[50] Jean Bodin, THE SIX BOOKS OF COMMONWEALE (Richard Knolles transl., 1606), 73.

[51] *Ibid.,* 75.

eignty was unable to make concessions to a principle of quasi sovereignty.

The federal principle was considerably elaborated by Althusius. Whereas federalism was something Bodin could no longer afford to ignore, in view of the existence of various confederacies at his time, Althusius was enthusiastic about that institution and made the bond of union, *consociatio,* one of the cornerstones of his political thought. In distinction to Bodin, who was under the spell of a monarchical conception of sovereignty, Althusius explained the federal principle on the basis of popular sovereignty.[52] Like the Frenchman, he distinguished between a *confederatio plena,* under which the federated units were dissolved into a single state that alone exercised sovereign authority,[53] and the *confederatio non plena,* under which the component parts maintained their full sovereignty.[54] In the latter type, Althusius clearly recognized the peace and security motives.[55] The obligations of the confederates were laid down in definite laws that were accepted by the oath of the participating parties. These laws provided, first, for the mutual defense of the members against external and internal attacks and for the obligation to render assistance quickly and to be loyal allies in times of war and peace; second, for the friendly settlement of disputes between the members of the confederation through conciliation or arbitration, obliging them not to make war against each other and not to assist any one of the confederated states in attacking another; third, for contributions to common expenditure in war and for the equitable distribution of territorial gains or monetary indemnities, etc.[56]

A few decades after Althusius' publications, federal theory was again complemented by a concrete proposal for union. The chancellor of Henry IV, Sully, drafted a plan for a confederation of Christian states.[57] Its main purposes were the preservation of peace among the states and security from the Turks. The former was to be secured through the provision that the federation would punish all

[52] Johannes Althusius, POLITICA, METHODICE DIGESTA ATQUE EXEMPLIS SACRIS ET PROFANIS ILLUSTRATA (1603).

[53] *Ibid.,* chapter VII.   [54] *Ibid.,* chapter VII.

[55] The purpose of confederation concerned mainly three matters: "1. de defensione mutua contra vim et injuriam; 2. de concordia inter confederatos fovenda et conservanda; 3. de administratione communium jurium sociorum confederatorum." Johannes Althusius, POLITICA ETC. (5th ed., 1654), Chapter XVII. Sec. 33.

[56] *Ibid.,* Secs. 34-40. Compare Mogi, *op. cit.,* I, 28.

[57] For a discussion of that plan, see Samuel, *op. cit.,* 16 ff.

those members that were delinquent in obeying the verdicts of courts of arbitration, which were to settle disputes among the states. Also, peace was to be achieved through a conquest of the House of Austria, since Austrian policy was said to be opposed to any policy that aimed at a peaceful unification of Christian powers. Once peace in Europe was established, the confederation would be able to wage a successful war against the Turks. Under Sully's proposal, the members of the union remained sovereign states. However, their sovereignty was no longer as absolute as it had been under the plans of Dubois and Podiebrad. The states could not secede from the union and the confederation exercised a certain influence upon its members with respect to their conduct of foreign policy. Sully's plan seems to have been influenced by Althusius, who had felt that union should be perpetual. Also, Bodin's impact can be noticed, especially with respect to the advocacy of tolerance for the sake of peace among the states.[58] However, Sully's plan does not advance too far beyond Dubois' and Podiebrad's concepts of federation, since he advocates a confederacy of sovereign states, designed primarily for purposes of peace and defense.[59]

Whereas Althusius' idea of federalism was based upon corporations of lesser units, as were the concepts of his followers Hoenonius and Otto Casmannus,[60] Christoph Besold limited the idea of the *civitas composita* to cases in which a number of different *gentes* possessing different laws, were bound together in a single *corpus politicum* with a single *imperium*. The main example of this type of state was the German empire, a "state made up of states," in which the *majestas* belonged to the whole, but the members had the nature of subordinate and relative states.[61] Besold's theory found elaboration in Ludolph Hugo's work, *De statu regionum Germaniae,* published in 1661. At the beginnning of that work, Hugo stated that it was obvious that the German empire was governed by a twofold government, since the Reich as a whole forms one common state and the various territories of which it is composed possess special princes or magistrates, courts and assemblies, and, on the whole, a definite and special status, which is subordinate to that of the superior state.[62] He stressed that the German states were

[58] *Ibid.,* 18.   [59] *Ibid.,* 20-24.   [60] Mogi, *op. cit.,* 29-30.

[61] Christoph Besold, DISS. DE JURE TERRITORIUM (1624), Chapter IV, Secs. 2-3; DISS. PRAECOGN. PHILOS. COMPL., Chapter VIII, Secs. 1, 3-4. (cited by Gierke, *op. cit.,* 245).

[62] For a discussion of Hugo's thesis, see Brie, *op. cit.,* 16-20.

under a *subiectio civilis* and had thus to obey the measures of the general government. However, even under his system, the members of the confederation remained sovereign. They are considered as analogies of states, and no central power is directly binding upon their individual citizens. As to the motives for federation, those of peace and security again stand in the foreground.[63]

Hugo's theory was accepted rather enthusiastically, but it did not remain dominant for a long time. Due to its idea of compromise, it was liked neither by those who were in favor of imperial power, nor by those who favored the princes.[64] Hugo's main critic, Samuel Pufendorf, advanced quite a different concept of federal union. Following Grotius, who had stressed that in a confederation no general authority was nominally and legally transferred from the member states to the federal council,[65] Pufendorf showed, by clinging to the concept of indivisible sovereignty, the untenability of Ludolph Hugo's doctrine of a "state" composed of states. Pufendorf's "system of states," as he called a confederacy, was only an "irregular state," and not a state, as Ludolph Hugo would have it. It came into being when sovereign states united permanently for specific purposes, such as foreign intercourse and alliance, war and peace, with a full guarantee that their sovereignty would remain intact.[66]

The beginning of the eighteenth century saw another utopian plan of federal union. Discouraged by the wars in Europe, Saint-Pierre came forth in 1713 with his project for perpetual peace.[67] He suggested the formation of a federation of twenty-four states. The members were to send delegates to a "peace-senate," which would meet in a "peace-city." Even the more powerful members would be content with just one delegate, Saint-Pierre felt, since they would be interested only in the promotion of the welfare of the league and in its security. Thus peace did not have the destruction

---

[63] *Ibid.*, 16-20.

[64] The two leading schools of thought at that time were called "Cäsarianer" and "Fürstenianer."

[65] Hugo Grotius, DE JURE BELLI ET PACIS (1702), II, Chapter xv, Secs. 5-6; I, Sec. 7. See Mogi, *op. cit.*, I, 31.

[66] Samuel von Pufendorf (Severinus de Monzambano), DE STATU IMPERII GERMANICI (1667). In that work, Pufendorf criticized the nature of the German empire, which appeared to him as "irregulare aliquod corpus et monstro simile." In his later works, DE REPUBLICA IRREGULARI (1671), and DE SYSTEMATIBUS CIVITUM (1677), Pufendorf developed his theory of federalism. Of a "system of states" he speaks in DE JURE NATURAE ET GENTIUM (1672), Book VII, Chapter v, Sec. 16.

[67] Charles Castel de Saint-Pierre, PROJET POUR RENDRE LA PAIX PERPETUELLE EN EUROPE (1713). For a discussion of that plan, see Samuel, *op. cit.*, 28 ff.

of Austria as a prerequisite, as it did with Sully. A federal court had to settle disputes between the members of the confederation, and its verdicts were to be enforced by federal troops composed of contingents from the various member states. However, under Saint-Pierre's plan the states also retained their sovereignty.[68]

Later in the eighteenth century, federalism was discussed by Montesquieu in his brilliant, if at times obscure, comments on federal constitutions.[69] Criticizing federal unions for not having made progress since the days of Grotius, the Frenchmen argues that the federal form of government is important for the sake of security and mutual defense, especially in small republics.[70] A "confederate republic,"[71] he writes, "has all the internal advantages of a republican, together with the external force of monarchical government."[72] It is "a convention by which several petty states agree to become members of a larger one, which they intend to establish. It is a kind of assemblage of societies, that constitutes a new one, capable of increasing by means of further association, till they arrive at such a degree of power as to be able to provide for the security of the whole body."[73] While each of the confederates preserves its sovereignty, parts of its functions are transferred to the federal government for the sake of security. Thus a confederation, "able to withstand an external force, may support itself without any internal corruption."[74] Also, the federal form of government was likely to prevent internal threats that might endanger its existence, or the safety and peace of the component parts, being so constituted that "should a popular insurrection happen in one of the confederated states, the others are able to quell it," and "should abuses creep into one part, they are reformed by those that remain sound."[75] Montesquieu felt that petty republics could remain both internally happy and externally strong only by entering a federal union. He also suggested that it would be advisable for all the members of the con-

---

[68] Samuel, *op. cit.,* 30 ff.

[69] Montesquieu, ESPRIT DES LOIS (1748), Book IX, Chapters 1-3. Montesquieu sometimes uses the term "Etat" for the whole confederation ("Cette forme de gouvernement est une convention par laquelle plusieurs corps politiques consentent à devenir citoyens d'un Etat plus grand qu'ils veulent former"; "Cet Etat peut périr d'un côté sans périr de l'autre"). On the other hand, Montesquieu uses such terms as "société," "association," "confédération" without implying any difference in meaning.

[70] Thomas Nugent, transl., THE SPIRIT OF THE LAWS (Franz Neumann ed., 1949), 126 ff.

[71] *Ibid.,* 126. [73] *Ibid.,* 126. [75] *Ibid.,* 127.
[72] *Ibid.,* 126. [74] *Ibid.,* 127.

federacy to have the same form of government, preferably the republican one.

Rousseau also wrote on federalism, but the document was lost in
the early months of the French Revolution.[76] Still, we find some
comments in other writings. In the *Social Contract,* he points to the
security motive for federation.[77] In *Emile,* he speaks of leagues and
federations as a remedy against the insecurity of small states, feeling
that these forms of government, while "leaving each state master in
his own home, arm it against all unjust aggression from without."[78]
The advocate of the small state did not, however, envisage a sur-
rendering of sovereignty by the members of the federation. The only
federal system that was desirable for him was "one of federated self-
governing communes, small enough to allow each member an active
share in the legislation of the communes."[79]

Rousseau also advanced a plan for the establishment of peace in
Europe, characteristically written on the manuscript of the Abbé
de Saint-Pierre.[80] Rousseau felt that peace could be secured by
eliminating the rivalries among the European nations and urged
that this could be done "only by a confederative form of government
which, uniting nations by bonds similar to those which unite individuals, submits them all equally to the authority of the laws."[81]
For the sake of peace, Rousseau went rather far in his plan to restrict the members of the confederacy. "To form a solid and durable
confederation," he wrote, "all its members must be placed in such
a mutual state of dependence that not one of them alone may be in
a position to resist all of the others and that minor associations
which would have the power to injure the general body may meet
with sufficient hindrances to prevent their formation, without which
the confederation would be vain, and each would be really independent under an apparent subjection."[82] He wanted the contracting sovereigns to establish an irrevocable and perpetual alliance.
Their representatives in a permanent congress had to regulate differences between the contracting parties and to settle them by way

[76] Mogi, *op. cit.,* I, 37.

[77] Jean Jacques Rousseau, DU CONTRAT SOCIAL (Ed. 1762), 281-305.

[78] Rousseau, EMILE, in Vaughan, ed., THE POLITICAL WRITINGS OF ROUSSEAU (1915),
II, 158.

[79] T. H. Green, WORKS, PHILOSOPHICAL (1906), II, 398.

[80] Rousseau, EXTRAIT DU PROJET DE PAIX PERPETUELLE DE M. L'ABBE DE SAINT-
PIERRE (1760).

[81] *Ibid.,* in Vaughan, ed., THE POLITICAL WRITINGS OF ROUSSEAU (1915), I, 365.

[82] *Ibid.,* I, 373.

of arbitration or adjudication. In order to put an end to disputes that were constantly occurring in Europe, the act of federation was to guarantee the present possessions and rights of the contracting powers. No member was to be permitted under any pretext to take the law into his own hands, or to take up arms against his fellow members. Any ally refusing to carry out the decisions of the great alliance, or making preparations for war, or negotiating treaties contrary to the federal compact, or taking up arms to resist the federation or to attack any of her allies, was to be declared a common enemy and put under the ban of Europe.[83] In spite of all these provisions, however, Rousseau did not advance beyond the orthodox concept of federalism. Under his plan, also, the members of the confederacy remained sovereign states.

It was only close to the time when federalism became an issue in America that the idea of dual sovereignty, which Ludolph Hugo had touched upon, was taken up again. Johann Stephan Pütter, after having maintained in his earlier publications that the territories and cities of Germany were states, and that the empire also was a state, proceeded in 1777 to elaborate his ideas.[84] Pütter felt that just as several independent states could be merged into one large state, or, irrespective of their equality and independence, form leagues for their protection from foreign powers, it could happen that several states would "federate in a way that, on the one hand, each of them would retain, as far as its internal constitution is concerned, its own government with all its sovereign rights, whereas, on the other hand, all these states would have a common superior."[85] The fact that such a federal state could be formed from independent states, together with the example of Germany, where a unitary state had developed into a federation of sovereign states, led Pütter to the conclusion that the German states possessed, "as a rule, and on the whole, all the rights of sovereign governments,"[86] whereas, at the same time, they were subject to restrictions by the

[83] *Ibid.*, I, 374-76.

[84] Johann Stephan Pütter, BEYTRÄGE ZUM TEUTSCHEN STAATS—UND FÜRSTENRECHTE (1777), esp. *Beitrag* (contribution) II, "Von der Regierungsform des Teutschen Reichs und einigen davon abhängenden Grundsätzen des Teutschen Staatsrechts." His earlier publications dealing especially with the problem of federalism were ELEMENTA IURIS PUBLICI GERMANICI (1754), Secs. 121-122, and the preface to his INSTITUTIONES IURIS PUBLICI GERMANICI (1770).

[85] Pütter, BEYTRÄGE ETC., Contribution II, Secs. 9-14, 18.

[86] *Ibid.*, Contribution II, Secs. 14 and 25. Compare also contribution XI, esp. Secs. 10-12.

Reich.[87] This subordination of the sovereign states under a superior government appeared to him absolutely compatible with their quality as states.[88] The German constitution, so he felt, was very similar to the *systemate foederatarum civitatum*.[89] Pütter thus recognized the similarity between a state composed of states and a system of allied states, with respect to both their origin and their organization. There can be no doubt that he came very close to our modern concept of the federal state. Still, he did not yet see the type of federation that was created by the United States Constitution, with its divided sovereignty, the quasi sovereignty of the states, and the direct validity of federal laws upon the individual citizens in the states. All he did—and this was important enough in view of the preponderance over the centuries of the concept of indivisible sovereignty—was to state that the subordination of states under a federal government did not deprive them of their quality as states, that federalism was compatible with the existence of different types of states.

In our conclusion, we may say that prior to the American Constitution, federal theories and plans had the same major features as actually existing confederations. Authors would usually stress the security motive for federation, or the desire for peace, or both. An awareness of the function of federalism to protect the individual from his government can hardly be noticed. Montesquieu appears to be the only author who touched that problem. However, his statement about the states balancing popular faction in other states seems to be concerned with the maintenance of peace among the states rather than the protection of the individual from the oppressions of his government. Also, authors did not yet conceive of a federalism that would recognize the possibility of one state composed of other states whose sovereignty would, for the sake of common interests, be restricted and reduced to a quasi sovereignty by means of a supremacy clause. They did not yet envisage a federation in which the will of the federal government would be binding directly upon the individuals in the states with respect to certain matters. In a word, the closely knit federal state as we have known it since the adoption of the American Constitution was unknown to them.

Theories and plans for federation in colonial America can hardly be said to have deviated from federal theory and practice in other

[87] *Ibid.*, Contributions XVII and XVIII.
[88] *Ibid.*, Contribution II, Secs. 15-17.
[89] *Ibid.*, Contribution III, Sec. 27.

parts of the world.[90] The Articles of Confederation, as the first federal experiment comprising all America, are an example of the generally accepted concept of federalism, under which the members remained sovereign and the main function of federation was seen in the achievement of security from foreign nations and in the preservation of peace among the federated states. It remained for the Founding Fathers to broaden this orthodox conception of federalism, with respect to both the purpose and the nature of the federal state. They created, for the sake of free government as well as for the sake of peace and security, that more perfect Union under which national power was combined with a great deal of autonomy of the component parts. And the authors of the *Federalist* became the classic commentators on this new concept of federalism.

4. It cannot be denied that the exposition of federalism in the Papers was influenced by federal theory and practice that existed before the essays were written. Such authors as Grotius,[91] the Abbé de Mably,[92] and Montesquieu[93] are mentioned in connection with their remarks on federal government. The *Federalist* refers to several ancient and more modern federations and devotes whole numbers to their discussion. Of course, not all the sources upon which Jay, Hamilton, and Madison drew were likely to be mentioned in their essays.

Although it is open to doubt to what degree the authors' analyses of previous federal thought and practice are correct,[94] we may say that they had good insight into the major problems of federal government as it existed up to the American Revolution. They recognized, first of all, what had been the main purposes of federation so far, security and peace. They also clearly recognized the chief problem in the organization of federal government—insufficient power in the nation due to the sovereignty of the states. No matter how much the various federal systems might differ from each other, these main purposes and problems were always emphasized. They were also stressed in the discussion of the most recent attempt at federalism under the Articles of Confederation.

Small wonder, then, that Hamilton, Madison, and Jay were happy to note that under the new Constitution the major shortcomings of previous federal systems would be abolished. There would be no

[90] See *supra*, chapter two.
[91] 20, 121.
[92] 6, 33; 18, 110; 20, 123.
[93] 9, 49; 9, 50; 9, 53; 43, 282; 43, 285.
[94] See *supra*, p. 291.

imperium in imperio that could frustrate national efforts. For the sake of security from foreign powers and peace among the states, the national government would be strengthened. An old concept of federalism would thus be replaced by a new one. But the new type of federal government could do more than guarantee security and peace. Established in order to quell democratic despotism, which existed in some of the states, it could protect the individual citizens from governmental encroachments. Federalism was given a new meaning in America. The improvement of federal organization was matched by a broadening of the scope of federalism. In a word, federalism was elevated by the Americans to some form of constitutionalism. The *Federalist,* by expounding and stressing that aspect of federalism, thus becomes more than a classic on federal government. It becomes a classic on constitutional democracy.

II

1.   The Papers' quality as a treatise on free government can be explained partly by the authors' background. In each case there exist factors that, on the one hand, were likely to make Hamilton, Madison, and Jay cautious of democratic excesses while, on the other hand, they promoted an inclination toward popular government. Jay came from an old New York family. With the best education available, he grew up in a cultured atmosphere and became a member of the legal profession. These aristocratic features of his background were tempered by the fact that his family had been engaged in trade and commerce and thus was close to the political philosophy of the Whigs. Hamilton came of humble origin, being the illegitimate child of a West Indies merchant. This was likely to make him understand the desires of the common people for a share in the affairs of government. On the other hand, he became a member of the New York aristocracy through marriage. As an *arriviste* with an education from King's College that was supplemented by first-rate legal training, he would be skeptical about the advantages of democracy. Madison came from an old Virginian family, relatively prosperous and conservative. His father owned slaves in considerable number and was a leading Episcopalian. Another relative was president of the College of William and Mary and the first Episcopal bishop in Virginia. He received a good private education and attended Princeton. As a first-born, Madison was

entitled to share with his father the consideration as the head of an aristocratic family. However, these features were mitigated by others that were likely to make the Virginian susceptible to democratic ideas. The counties of the Piedmont region, including Orange, his home, were strongholds of democracy and centers of revolt against entails and primogeniture, slavery and the established church.

Though Jay and Hamilton were members of the bar, and Madison, a landed squire, their interests were less divergent than might be expected. In their formative years, the world of knowledge was still a unity, and the three received a well-rounded education quite naturally. Even during his military service as an artillery captain, Hamilton took time out to read the ancients, including Demosthenes, Plutarch, and Cicero. From among modern authors, he had read, at that time, Bacon's *Essays,* Hobbes's *Dialogues,* Millot's *History of France,* Ralt's *Dictionary of Trade and Commerce,* Robertson's *Charles V,* Rousseau's *Emile,* and Smith's *History of New York.* Before going into the practice of law, Hamilton had read Blackstone, Grotius, and Pufendorf.[95] Jay's breadth of knowledge was on a par with that of Hamilton.[96] Madison, who in his youth had instruction in Greek, Latin, arithmetic, geography, and miscellaneous literature, had the opportunity to avail himself of his father's voluminous library. There is evidence that he was familiar with the works of Plutarch, Demosthenes, Grotius, Coke, Diderot, the Abbé de Mably, Vattel, Pufendorf, and Bynkershoek.[97] The broad scope of the authors' reading—and they read, of course, more than we can actually prove—shows that they were genuine denizens of the age they lived in and that they were able to profit from the high-level intellectual atmosphere of their time, to which they, in turn, were destined to make valuable contributions.

Through their studies, Hamilton, Madison, and Jay were well equipped to evaluate governmental systems and their problems. Since the conditions in their own environment made them aware of democratic trends, they were likely to judge things from the point of view of conservatives who, while not opposed to the principle of popular government, had strong fears lest democratic rule might get out of hand and result in a majoritarianism that would be op-

[95] Hamilton's pay-book of the State Company of Artillery of Aug. 31, 1776, furnishes proof for the breadth of his intellectual interest. J. C. Hamilton, ed. WORKS (1851), I, 4 ff.

[96] See Beloff, *op. cit.,* xxvii-xxviii; Monaghan, *op. cit.,* 23 ff.

[97] See Burns, *op. cit.,* 3, 186-89.

pressive of the rights of the minority and be incompatible with free government.

2.   The history of Greece and Italy is a case in point. Again and again, the dangers of democracy, as it had existed in those parts of the world, are pointed out in the *Federalist*. "It is impossible," writes Hamilton, "to read the history of Greece and Italy without feeling sensations of horror and disgust at the distractions with which they were continually agitated, and at the rapid succession of revolutions by which they were kept in a state of perpetual vibration between the extremes of tyranny and anarchy."[98] His sentiments are complemented by Madison who, thinking of the republics of Greece, writes that pure democracies "have ever been spectacles of turbulence and contention; have ever been found incompatible with personal security or the rights of property; and have in general been as short in their lives as they have been violent in their deaths."[99] However, in the opinion of the *Federalist* it is not only a direct democracy that can be detrimental to the freedom of the individual. Representative democracy can also be dangerous to minority rights. Madison warns those who oppose a long term for senators that in Sparta and Rome the representatives of the people would have concentrated all power in their hands, had they not been checked by a more conservative upper chamber.[100] The situation in England is given as another example. The House of Lords, Madison argues, being a "hereditary assembly of opulent nobles," could have been expected to furnish proof of "aristocratic usurpations and tyranny." However, "the British history informs us that this hereditary assembly has not been able to defend itself against the continual encroachments of the House of Representatives; and that it no sooner lost the support of the monarch, than it was actually crushed by the weight of the popular branch."[101] We could provide many more examples to show how the *Federalist* uses historical data to demonstrate the dangers resulting from absolute majority rule. The distrust of a democratic despotism appears again and again in the discussions of the various types of government, irrespective of the specific topic with which the authors might be concerned.

Hamilton, Madison, and Jay were, of course, also influenced by the events in their own country. The struggle with the British had only recently been concluded. In that struggle, the colonists had

[98] 9, 47.   [100] 63, 415.
[99] 10, 58.   [101] 63, 415.

become more and more aware of the fact that an oppression by the representatives of the people was as possible as that by a monarch. While absolute monarchy was replaced by a limited monarchy in 1688, the English interpretation of Locke's philosophy tended increasingly to stress the doctrine of parliamentary supremacy. In the years prior to Independence, the acts of the English government that were considered oppressive by the Americans were acts of Parliament, not acts of the King. Thus, in spite of the general tendency during the colonial period to increase the power of the colonial legislature, the colonists were well aware of the dangers to the rights of the individual ensuing from a democratic institution. The slogan, "no taxation without representation" does not alter that fact.

The authors' concern over majority rule is, however, most evident in their comments on the conditions under the Articles of Confederation. The shortcomings of the democratic state constitutions with their concentration of power in the legislature are frequently pointed out. For instance, Madison criticizes the constitution of his home state along the lines of Jefferson's *Notes on Virginia*. Quoting from that work, he stresses that an elective despotism was not the government the colonists fought for in the War of Independence and that one hundred and seventy-three despots, the members of the Virginia legislature, would surely be as oppressive as one.[102] In a similar manner, Madison criticizes the conditions in Pennsylvania, where "the constitution had been flagrantly violated by the legislature in a variety of important instances."[103] For example, the principle of trial by jury had been violated. Executive power had been usurped. Cases belonging to the competence of the judiciary had been frequently drawn within legislative cognizance and determination.[104] The Virginian stresses that the conditions in Virginia and Pennsylvania are only examples of the shortcomings of democratic rule in the states generally, and his criticism of a majoritarian despotism can be noticed throughout his comments upon the conditions under the Articles of Confederation.[105] Hamilton's evaluation of these conditions is very similar. He also examines the democratic tendencies in the states and is disgusted with the increasing infringements upon the rights of the individual.[106]

On the whole, it may be said that the authors of the *Federalist* drew largely upon the experience of other governments in their attempts to demonstrate the dangers of absolute democracy and the

[102] 48, 324. [104] 48, 325-26. [106] *Supra*, pp. 162-63.
[103] 48, 325. [105] *Supra*, pp. 130 ff.

advantages of checks upon the ruling majority. This does not mean, however, that other governments were criticized only for their failure to check democracy. Monarchical and aristocratic tendencies were also denounced by men who, after all, believed in the principles of popular government. Likewise, it would be wrong to suppose that the authors merely criticized other institutions. On the contrary, these institutions would often be praised. It would even happen that one type of government would be criticized in one respect and lauded in another. English government, for instance, is denounced for its concentration of power in the House of Commons. On the other hand, it is largely depicted as a system under which free government is realized to a high degree. The concept of limited monarchy is heralded as a guarantor of the rights of Englishmen, rights of which Hamilton, Madison, and Jay were probably as proud as the inhabitants of the British Isles themselves. As a matter of fact, it would appear as if the English constitution was considered by the authors a great monument of freedom, if one rejected the idea that this constitution implied the supremacy of Parliament and accepted an interpretation of the English constitution as meaning the superiority of the English heritage and the common law. In a like manner, other institutions would be praised for their democratic features as well as for the safeguards they provided against a democratic despotism. In view of the authors' emphasis upon the problems of free government, it would be wrong to believe that they drew upon other governmental systems merely in order to bolster their argument in favor of that ideal. Often, matters of a rather technical and administrative nature are discussed at some length, and historical examples are used as illustrations. History obviously was a great teacher of the authors of the *Federalist*. This accounts for their rather practical approach to political issues. It should not lead us to believe, however, that Hamilton, Madison, and Jay were not also influenced by philosophers.

3.   Being a treatise on the theory as well as on the practice of free government, the *Federalist* draws heavily upon the writings of political theorists. Raynal, Delolme, Montesquieu, and Hume are, among others, expressly mentioned and quoted. But these writers do not exhaust the list of those whose impact on the Papers is obvious. Machiavelli and Hume; Hobbes and Rousseau; Harrington, Locke, and Montesquieu; Coke and Blackstone: They are probably the intellectual forebears of the *Federalist's* discussion of constitu-

tional democracy. What was said in connection with the historical roots of the *Federalist*'s concept of free government also holds true with respect to the philosophical origin of that concept: some of these authors were fundamentally accepted by Hamilton, Madison, and Jay, whereas others were fundamentally rejected. No one's philosophy was taken over completely or, for that matter, completely rejected.

There is, first, Machiavelli. His name is mentioned nowhere in the essays. However, there can be no doubt that the Papers, especially those written by Hamilton, show the influence of the Florentine. This is obvious, for instance, with respect to methodology. Machiavelli applied science to politics. He believed in an accurate and systematic description of public facts, in correlating these facts into laws. Through this correlation, he predicted the probability of future facts. This is what is done in the *Federalist*. Like the Florentine, the authors of the *Federalist* use language in a cognitive, scientific manner. It is always clear what they are talking about. Like Machiavelli, they assemble a large number of facts, based upon their knowledge of history and the political life of their own day. The authors—statesmen rather than philosophers, by Spinoza's definition[107]—have a certain contempt for people who devise forms of government in their closets.[108] Whenever a certain fact does not coincide with a rule they derived from sets of facts, they consider it an exception to that rule and not as something impossible, which it would have been under a deductive mode of thinking. Like Machiavelli, the authors of the *Federalist* are not interested mainly in isolated events, but in the laws they can conclude from them. Just as the Florentine was wondering whether something related by Livy or Thucydides, or something he observed in his own environment, was a unique action or rather an instance of a general pattern, in a like manner Hamilton, Madison, and Jay evaluated events within the framework of certain rules. For them, absolute democracy under the Articles of Confederation was bad, and majoritarianism would be bad in the future, because history had proved the rule that unrestricted popular government was detrimental to the freedom of the individual.

Aside from methodology, there exists a definite similarity between Machiavelli and the *Federalist* with respect to value judgments.

---

[107] Spinoza in the opening chapter of TRACTATUS POLITICUS (1677). Quoted by Benjamin F. Wright, *op. cit.*, 2.

[108] Compare Wright, *ibid.*, 2-3.

This can be seen in the evaluation of man. Machiavelli is trying to analyze not simply man, but political man, as do the authors of the *Federalist*. They are primarily interested in the relation of man to political phenomena, and not so much in his relations to his family and friends. Machiavelli's opinion of man is characterized by as much pessimism as that of the Papers.[109] Still, like Hamilton, Madison, and Jay, he does not maintain that man is absolutely bad.[110] Machiavelli's, as well as the *Federalist*'s judgment of man is not primarily a moral one. It is simply stated that, on the whole, all men are likely to make mistakes, that no man is always judicious and tempered and intelligent, and that, on the other hand, even the stupid have moments of insight. As it does to the authors of the *Federalist*, Machiavelli's evaluation of man applies to rulers and ruled alike.[111]

In view of this opinion of political man, it is not surprising that politics appears fundamentally as a struggle for power. Ethical behavior, though conceived to be possible, is not expected from men in politics. Man takes into consideration human nature and acts accordingly in his attempts to achieve political preponderancy. This thirst for power is one of the main reasons for political instability.[112] Political life is never static, but is in a process of continual change. It is an illusion to believe that a state could be perfect and last indefinitely. People can only strive to approach a certain ideal form of government, which, however, is not likely to last forever, because man's lust for power and the dynamic forces in society will bring about changes.[113]

Machiavelli, Hamilton, Madison, and Jay wrote for a definite

---

[109] In Chapter 17 of THE PRINCE, Machiavelli states: "In the general, men are ungrateful, inconstant, hypocritical, fearful of danger, and covetous of gain; whilst they receive any benefit by you, and the danger is at distance, they are absolutely yours, their blood, their estates, their lives, and their children (as I said before) are all at your service, but when mischief is at hand, and you have present need of their help, they make no scruple to revolt." Compare also Book I, Chapter 54 of the DISCOURSES: "The people, being deceived with a false imagination of good, do many times solicit their own ruin, and run the commonwealth upon infinite dangers and difficulties."

[110] In Book I, Chapter 27 of the DISCOURSES, Machiavelli writes that "it is so provided by Providence, that no man can be exquisitely wicked, no more than good in perfection."

[111] James Burnham, THE MACHIAVELLIANS—DEFENDERS OF FREEDOM (1943), 54. B. F. Wright, *op. cit.*

[112] Compare Burnham, *op. cit.*, 63.

[113] *Ibid.*, 62-63.

purpose. The Florentine's chief practical goal was the unification of Italy, and he made no bones about that goal, which he felt could be realized. The *Federalist* shows, in its attempt to bring about the more perfect Union in America, a similar realistic appreciation of existing conditions.

It need hardly be mentioned that Machiavelli did not influence each of the authors of the *Federalist* to an equal degree. As was said in the beginning, Madison was less under the spell of the Florentine than Hamilton. As an advocate of a genuine division of governmental power, the Virginian could hardly have agreed to Machiavelli's advocacy of a strong executive,[114] which was favored by the New Yorker. On the other hand, Machiavelli's proposal to balance opposed interests for the sake of liberty comes rather close to the Madisonian concept of a guarantee for freedom.[115] All in all, it can be said that Machiavelli's influence upon the *Federalist* can clearly be recognized. If the authors did not know the Italian, which seems highly improbable,[116] they were certainly Machiavellians in more than one respect.

[114] Machiavelli felt strongly that Italy could only be united by a prince. He was here obviously influenced by the example of other European countries, where unification had come about under the monarchical form of government. Compare Burnham, *op. cit.*, 36-37.

[115] Compare Burnham, *op. cit.*, 69 ff.

[116] On the question whether Hamilton knew Machiavelli, compare Alex Bein, DIE STAATSIDEE ALEXANDER HAMILTONS IN IHRER ENTSTEHUNG UND ENTWICKLUNG (1927), 173 ff. Bein proves that Hamilton knew Machiavelli, by comparing the writings of both. In the *Federalist*, some passages written by the New Yorker are very similar to passages written by Machiavelli. At 25, 158, Hamilton writes: "Wise politicians will be cautious about fettering the government with restrictions that cannot be observed, because they know that every breach of the fundamental laws, though dictated by necessity, impairs that sacred reverence which ought to be maintained in the breast of rulers towards the constitution of a country, and forms a precedent for other breaches where the same plea of necessity does not exist at all, or is less urgent and palpable." This statement is matched by one in Book I, Chapter 34 of the DISCOURSES: "E in una repubblica non vorrebbe mai accader cosa che con i modi straordinari s'avesse a governare. Perché, anchora che il modo straordinario per allora facesse bene, nondimeno lo esempio fa male, perché si mette una usanza di rompere gli ordini per bene, che poi sotto quel colore si rompono per male." The heading of Book I, Chapter 45 of the DISCOURSES says: "E cosa di malo esempio il non osservare una legge fatta e massime dallo autore di essa" etc. At 70, 454, Hamilton writes: "There is an idea which is not without its advocates, that a vigorous Executive is inconsistent with the genius of republican government." After saying that this opinion is wrong, he continues: "Every man the least conversant in Roman history, knows how often that republic was obliged to take refuge in the absolute power of a single

It has been suggested that the authors of the *Federalist* were made acquainted with Machiavelli by Hume,[117] and there is no doubt about the latter's direct influence upon the *Federalist*. Hume is quoted in the last essay, written by Hamilton, and his influence can be noted in many other places. This admission of Hume's impact is not surprising. While it was always a risky thing to admit one's sympathy for Machiavelli, the Scotsman was definitely *persona grata* in America. Even before Independence, there had existed complete accord between Hume and the colonists on the subject of liberty. Hume's *History of England* was like a mirror in which the Americans could see their own situation. The denunciation of King James, for depriving the colonies of their privileges and for introducing an arbitrary rule, was now applied to the rule of George III and his Parliament, who had associated in iniquity and provided an example, as Hume had warned in his early essay on the science of politics, that even free governments can become "the most ruinous and oppressive to their provinces."[118] Not only did Hume supply the colonists with ammunition for their fight for independence. He also showed a great deal of sympathy for the American cause.[119]

After Independence Hume, who had envisaged the difficulties of building a republic,[120] remained important for the people of the United States. His *History of England* and its story of authority and liberty provided the Founding Fathers with many examples of how governments, be they of the monarchical, the aristocratic, or the popular type, have a tendency toward despotism. It convinced them of the necessity of a well-founded constitution, which provided for a certain balance between authority and liberty. Thus partly due to Hume's writings, the men at Philadelphia, while rejecting absolute monarchy, were very much aware of the dangers arising from absolute democracy. Like Hume, they felt, for the sake of the freedom of the individual, a need for restricting majority rule.

man under the formidable title of Dictator," etc. Machiavelli, in Book I, Chapter 34 of the DISCOURSES, writes: "L'autorità dittatoria fece bene a non danno alla repubblica romana; e come le autorità che i cittadini si tolgono non quelle che sono loro dai suffragi liberi date, sono alla vita civile perniciose." "E però le repubbliche debbone fra i loro ordini avere un simile modo."

[117] Bein, *op. cit.*, 174.

[118] David Hume, "That Politics May Be Reduced to a Science," in Charles W. Hendel, ed., DAVID HUME'S POLITICAL ESSAYS (1953), 15.

[119] See Hendel, *op. cit.*, 1 ff.: "The Relevance of Hume's Political Writings to American Thought."

[120] *Ibid.*, lvii-lx.

This feeling became, of course, the keynote of the *Federalist*'s concept of free government. But this classic saw eye to eye with Hume in other respects also. It accepts some of his suggestions for the achievement of free government. Throughout Hume's *Essays* as well as in his *History of England,* the idea of a balance of powers is evident. That institution is considered by Hume not only to be a blessing for international relations,[121] but to have definite advantages for internal affairs. There is, for instance, Hume's rejection of democracy and his advocacy of a representative republic. "Democracies are turbulent, for however the people may be separated or divided, . . . their near habitation in a city will always make the force of popular tides and currents very sensible," he wrote, and continued that "in a large government which is modeled with masterly skill, there is compass and room enough to refine the democracy, from the lower people . . . to the higher magistrates. . . . At the same time, the parts are so distant and remote that it is very difficult, either by intrigue, prejudice or passion, to hurry them into any measure against the public interest."[122] In another passage, Hume wrote that "though it is more difficult to form a republican government in an extensive country than in a city, there is more facility once it is formed, of preserving it steady and uniform, without tumult and faction."[123] These passages appear to have been taken over into essay ten of the *Federalist* Papers, in which Madison points out the advantages of a large republic over a small democracy, as far as the freedom of the individual is concerned, and comes forth with his doctrine of the advantages of a balance of power.[124] Like

---

[121] Hume's essays "Of the Balance of Power" and "Of Public Credit." Compare Hendel, *op. cit.*, xxii.

[122] "The Perfect Commonwealth" in T. H. Green and T. H. Grose, HUME'S ESSAYS, MORAL, POLITICAL, AND LITERARY (1898), 492.

[123] *Ibid.*, 492.

[124] "Democracies have ever been spectacles of turbulence and contention. . . . A common passion or interest will, in almost every case, be felt by a majority of the whole; . . . and there is nothing to check the inducements to sacrifice the weaker party or an obnoxious individual" (10, 58). "The effect . . . is . . . to refine and enlarge the public views by passing them through the medium of a chosen body of citizens, whose wisdom may best discern the true interest of their country, and whose patriotism and love of justice will be least likely to sacrifice it to temporary or partial considerations." (10, 59.) "The greater number of citizens and extent of territory which may be brought within the compass of republican than of democratic government . . . renders factious combinations less to be dreaded in the former than in the latter." (10, 60.) It is interesting to note that the quotations from Hume, given *supra,* notes 122 and 123, also occur within one

Madison, Hume wanted a two-chamber system, which he felt was a prerequisite to free government.[125] "Divide the people into many separate bodies, and then they may debate with safety,"[126] he wrote. The higher offices of the republic, Hume felt, must be distributed so as not to be in the same hands. Not only was one legislative chamber to be checked by the others; the whole legislature was to be checked by the executive.[127] For Hume, any power in the state must be limited for the sake of the freedom of the individual as well as for the safety and well-being of the nation.[128]

Such a limitation can be achieved through the granting of governmental power by a constitution, since the very grant of power must then appear as a concession.[129] A government of law and not of men would be established. In his concept of the value of a constitution, Hume thus is in agreement with the authors of the *Federalist*. The constitution is a supreme law and as such restricts governmental power, be it of the monarchical or the democratic brand. The constitution guarantees the preservation of old values.[130]

The authors of the *Federalist* were influenced not only by Hume's political thought, but also by his methodology. Like Machiavelli, the Scotsman did not proceed from calculations, but from facts. He regarded speculative tenets and all vast pretensions of the human mind with skepticism and brought forth his convictions in politics not as dogmatic assertions, but as inferences and conclusions from experience and history. As has been seen, this was the procedure employed by Hamilton, Madison, and Jay. Like these authors, Hume examined the history of the ancients and that of England, feeling that this was a good means of exhibiting certain truths about

page. See in this connection Douglass Adair, " 'That Politics May Be Reduced to a Science': David Hume, James Madison, and the Tenth Federalist," HUNTINGTON LIBRARY QUARTERLY (1956-57), xx, 343-60.

[125] In "Idea of a Perfect Commonwealth," Hume stated that "all free governments must consist of two councils, a lesser and a greater or, in other words, of a senate and a people." Hendel, *op. cit.*, 152.

[126] *Ibid.*, 153.

[127] Compare Hendel, *op. cit.*, xxiv-xxv.

[128] *Ibid.*, xxii.

[129] ". . . a power, however great, when granted by law to an eminent magistrate is not so dangerous to liberty as an authority, however inconsiderable, which he acquires from violence and usurpation. For besides that the law always limits every power which it bestows, the very receiving it as a concession establishes the authority whence it is derived and preserves the harmony of the constitution. . . ." T. H. Green and T. H. Grose, ed., *op. cit.*, 379-80.

[130] Hendel, *op. cit.*, xxiv.

man in politics. By searching out facts and connections of fact, he reached his conclusions for the present. In short, Hume's approach is very similar to that of Machiavelli.

The obvious influence of these two thinkers upon the authors of the *Federalist* raises the question as to the relative degree of their influence. It is, of course, hard to say whether Machiavelli or Hume exercised a greater influence upon the Papers as a whole. However, it is probably correct to maintain that the Florentine's impact is greater in the essays written by Hamilton, whereas that of Hume can be noticed more in the Virginian's papers. On the other hand, it should not be overlooked that Machiavelli is evident in the writings of Madison, just as Hume is in those of Hamilton. It appears quite natural' that the different authors of the *Federalist* would, while recognizing the merits of political philosophers, draw from them in different ways.

Through their study of Machiavelli and Hume, the authors of the *Federalist* had been led to adopt a scientific method for the study of politics.[131] That method, applied to their evaluation of political institutions and experiments, led them to approve or disapprove the ideas of political philosophers. Such rejection or acceptance took place in varying degrees, depending largely upon the degree of extremeness of the respective philosophies. Thus men like Hobbes and Rousseau were rejected, while Harrington, Locke, and Montesquieu, as well as Coke and Blackstone, were largely accepted.

Hobbes's political philosophy is based fundamentally upon the idea of the individual's good. He believed that individuals leave the state of nature in order to have the *bellum omnium contra omnes* ended and the individual protected by the great *Leviathan,* the state.[132] As one author put it, Hobbes was a great individualist as well as a great utilitarian.[133] As such, he found acceptance by the authors of the *Federalist.* On the other hand, while there was agreement with the Englishman on the purpose of the social contract and the state, these authors found themselves unable to accept what is probably best known of Hobbes's philosophy, namely, his conception of the character and scope of political power. They definitely rejected the Hobbesian idea of absolute monarchy, being opposed

---

[131] At 21, 130, Hamilton speaks of "political arithmetic." The *Federalist* also refers to the "science of politics" (9, 48), and "political science" (37, 229).

[132] Compare George H. Sabine, A HISTORY OF POLITICAL THOUGHT (rev. ed., 1950), 464-67.

[133] *Ibid.,* 474-75.

not only to a monarchical form of government, but to any kind of absolutism. There can be no doubt that there are traces of Hobbesian monism, as one author called it,[134] in the *Federalist*. These traces can be found especially in Hamilton's essays, with their emphasis upon the advantages of a vigorous executive and a strong national government. However, even the New Yorker would not go so far as to agree with Hobbes upon such an important thing as the nature of the social contract. While Hobbes excluded the implication of a contract binding upon the ruler, Hamilton, believing in a more genuine interpretation of the principle *pacta sunt servanda* than Hobbes, felt that the social compact established a relationship under which both parties had definite rights and duties. He admitted what Hobbes denied, a right of revolution in the case of an abuse of governmental power. Despite his nationalism, Hamilton maintained that a federal pact created the same rights and duties for the contracting parties as a simple contract establishing a government. Consequently, he admitted a right of secession and nullification as much as a right of revolution, considering the former as nothing but federal variations of the latter. In the case of Madison, the statement about the influence of Hobbesian monism does, of course, not apply. The Virginian's essays express themselves too clearly in favor of a genuine balance of powers—be it with respect to a separation of executive, legislature, and judiciary or that of the national and state governments—to justify the argument that Hobbes exercised a great influence upon him. On the whole, it may be said that the English philosopher was accepted by the authors of the *Federalist* only in so far as his advocacy of the freedom and well-being of the individual is concerned. As soon as he created a potential threat to the rights of the individual, through his conception of the nature of the social compact and government, he was rejected.

In view of the fact that Hobbes was rejected for his advocacy of absolute government, it is not surprising that the proponent of absolute democracy, Rousseau, would meet the same fate. As a matter of fact, we may venture to say that Rousseau's ideas were even more rejected than those of Hobbes. The reason for this is obvious. By 1787, absolute monarchy was a thing of the past for most Americans. The War of Independence had severed the ties with a monarchy that, for all practical purposes, had ceased to be of the absolutist type decades ago. On the other hand, just as the danger of a

---

[134] Alpheus T. Mason, FREE GOVERNMENT IN THE MAKING (1949), 269.

monarchical absolutism had faded away, that of a democratic despotism had been continually in the ascendancy. It increased by leaps and bounds under the Articles of Confederation. Therefore, the Founding Fathers deemed it imperative to guard against it more than against anything else, while, at the same time, preserving the principles of popular government. The *Federalist* thus became primarily a treatise against the extremes of democracy and the resulting injustice to the rights of the individual. It is, therefore, not at all surprising that a philosopher like Rousseau should be more strongly rejected by the authors than Hobbes. The latter may have been objectionable for potentially endangering individual freedom through his theory of absolutism. Still, being an individualist himself, he was likely to find a certain degree of sympathy with individualists like Hamilton, Madison, and Jay, and could hope to enjoy their readiness to forgive him for mistakes that, after all, resulted from intentions to make the individual free. Rousseau, on the other hand, could hardly expect such a sympathetic understanding. It was inconceivable for our authors how an individual could be forced to be free, as Rousseau would have it. The very idea of a rule by the *volonté générale* for the well-being of the community rather than for that of the individual made them shudder with fright, since it destroyed the very foundations of their political ideals, which were based on the freedom of the individual's life, liberty, and property.

The rejection of the main exponents of monarchical and democratic absolutism for the sake of the individual quite naturally led the authors of the *Federalist* to follow philosophers that steered more of a middle course. As adherents of popular government, they were likely to agree with those who, while accepting democratic rule, would see to it that such a rule was, for the protection of the individual's rights, sufficiently checked.

Among these philosophers, James Harrington occupies an important place. Harrington, who at the same time was a close friend of Charles I and an advocate of republicanism, had experienced the despotism of republican as well as of monarchical government. In spite of his belief in republicanism, he was imprisoned by the republicans and rejected by Cromwell, who had been suspicious of him and tried to prevent the publication of *Oceana*. After the restoration of the Stuarts, Charles II sent Harrington to jail, accusing him of plotting to overthrow the monarchy, and Harrington spent years in the Tower of London. Misunderstood in his own age, he had in 1659 suggested the epitaph, "If this age fails me, the next will do me justice."[135] This prophecy was to come true, especially in the new world.

As early as the seventeenth century, Harrington's theories exercised a profound influence upon the governments of the proprietary colonies of Carolina, New Jersey, and Pennsylvania.[136] His popularity reached a peak in the struggle of the American colonies with the mother country.[137] Like Hume, he provided the colonists with ammunition for their arguments against the oppressions of Parliament, having brought forth the constitutional ideal of "a government of laws and not of men."[138] Harrington had arrived at this ideal through his study of history and the conditions in England during the seventeenth century. He felt that absolute monarchy was essentially a government of men. This situation would not necessarily change or improve once monarchy was replaced by a republic, an event that, due to the progressing distribution of property, was most likely to happen. For, as much as Harrington disagreed with Bodin and Hobbes, he saw eye to eye with them as far as the necessity of a strong state for the prevention of internal strife was concerned. Consequently, he felt that even under republican forms the government had to remain strong and, therefore, constituted a potential threat to the rights of the individual. Harrington was not at all satisfied with the democratic dogma that good men would automatically make good laws, believing that this principle was "the Maxim of a demagogue" and "exceedingly fallible."[139] Rather, he thought that "good orders . . . will make us good men."[140] Therefore, laws or a constitution had to be devised to decrease the possibility of an arbitrary and selfish exercise of governmental power. That constitution would skillfully and delicately balance and check

[135] James Harrington, THE ART OF LAWGIVING (1659). Quoted in Charles Blitzer, ed., THE POLITICAL WRITINGS OF JAMES HARRINGTON (1955), xxv.

[136] Blitzer, *op. cit.*, xi.

[137] James Otis acknowledged his debt to the "divine writings" of "the incomparable Harrington." John Adams is said to have been at once the most ardent and the most distinguished American disciple of the English theorist. During the Massachusetts constitutional convention of 1779 a motion was made and seconded to the effect "that the word 'Massachusetts' be expunged and that the word 'Oceana' be substituted." For further proof of the popularity of Harrington during this period, see Blitzer, *op. cit.*, xi-xiii.

[138] Harrington also uses the phrase, "an Empire of laws and not of men."

[139] Quoted by Blitzer, *op. cit.*, xxxviii.

[140] *Ibid.*, xxxviii.

power through the introduction of such devices as indirect elections, bicameralism, rotation in office, and the secret ballot, and thereby prevent a republican type of despotism.[141]

The idea of a government of laws and not of men, implying a subordination of the branches of government under a supreme law that eliminated the oppression of the individual, had many adherents among the Americans not only during their struggle with the mother country, but also in the following years. The distinction, recognized in some of the states after 1776, between a constitutional convention as the constitution-maker and the legislature as the ordinary lawmaker that was instituted by and thus subordinate to the constitution, is proof of that fact. By 1787, that distinction had become more and more accepted by leading Americans who had become increasingly aware of the incompatibility of the actually existing legislative supremacy with the Harringtonian principle, which, after all, was meant to guarantee the protection of the individual's freedom. In view of this, it seems only natural that the Philadelphia Convention was called for the sole purpose of correcting constitutional defects. In that Convention, the idea that, for the sake of liberty and justice, there should be established a government of laws and not of men was evident.

The authors of the *Federalist,* to whom Harrington's inductive method must have appealed as much as the methods used by Machiavelli and Hume,[142] show a definite belief in the principle of a government of laws and not of men. As a matter of fact, we may venture to say that this principle is paramount with them, since it is considered the very prerequisite of a free government. However, while the idea of a government of laws and not of men appears to be Harrington's most obvious influence upon the Papers, the Englishman's impact can be noted in other respects. His idea of checks and balances reappears in essay ten and other parts of the Papers, when the value of an equilibrium of political, religious, and economic forces is stressed, or the advantages of representative government are pointed out, or the merits of a rotation in office or of bicameralism are shown.

However, Harrington's philosophy, useful as it was for the authors of the *Federalist,* did not quite satisfy them. This was due to

---

[141] Among other things, he also proposed guarantees of religious liberty and liberty of conscience, the "agrarian law," universal military training, free public education.

[142] For a description of Harrington's method, see Blitzer, *op. cit.,* xxv ff.

the Englishman's failure to emphasize the necessity for a protection of private property. In his desire to seek a cure for the political disruption in his home country, Harrington had explored economic interests and their relationship to political developments. He had come to the conclusion that the disequilibrium between economic and political power is the basic cause for political disorder and instability. Therefore, he suggested a wide distribution of property and such things as a curtailment of primogeniture and agrarian laws that would prevent the passing of large estates to the eldest son alone if there were other heirs. This distribution of property was the very basis for his republican commonwealth. It is obvious that property does not appear to be too safe under such a plan. Our authors realized, of course, the Harringtonian truth about the close relation between the ownership of property and political power, as is evident in the pages of their essays.[143] However, they had experiences Harrington could not count among his own. They had seen, at close range, what could happen once people desirous of a more equal distribution of property succeeded in getting the upper hand in the government. They had known what to them appeared as outrageous infringements upon private property. Therefore, they were likely to look for a philosopher who would put greater emphasis upon the sacrosanctity of property and thus fill the gap that was left open by the great exponent of republican constitutionalism. That man was Locke.

It is probably no exaggeration to say that Locke exercised a greater influence upon American political thought during the revolutionary era than any other philosopher. His writings were the colonists' major work of reference in their struggle with the mother country. The Declaration of Independence was so close to the *Second Treatise of Government* in form, phraseology, and content that Jefferson was accused of copying from it.[144] Locke's influence can

---

[143] Needless to say that the authors of the *Federalist* do, by that recognition, not become economic materialists, just as Harrington cannot be classified as an economic materialist. (Sabine, *op. cit.*, 501.) For Hamilton, Madison, and Jay, the acquisition of property was motivated by ethical rather than materialistic considerations. They were, in that sense, Calvinists.

[144] These accusations seem to be unjustified. Jefferson simply stated the ideas of English constitutionalism to which Locke had given expression, ideas that were current at his time. Compare Carl Becker, THE DECLARATION OF INDEPENDENCE (1922), 79: "The lineage is direct: Jefferson copied Locke and Locke quoted Hooker. In political theory and in political practice the American Revolution drew its inspiration from the parliamentary struggle of the seventeenth century.

be seen in state declarations and constitutions.[145] His ideas were present in the Philadelphia Convention. They played an important role thereafter. Locke is the philosopher to whom the authors of the *Federalist* are most indebted for an exposition of constitutionalism and free government.

Locke's impact upon the Papers, or, for that matter, upon American thinking during this formative period, is too obvious to need detailed comment. Like most of the writers of his time, he proceeded from the assumption of a state of nature. However, he modified the then dominant trend strikingly by advancing the idea that property, which came into existence when man applied his labors to the gifts of nature, was a natural right that preceded civil society and was not created by it. The idea of the sacrosanctity of property thus stands at the very beginning of Locke's political thought. It remained prevalent throughout the further development of his system of government. According to the Englishmen, the individuals leave the state of nature by unanimously concluding a social contract. The government merely receives fiduciary power, or a "trust," which is to be exercised for the good of the community. The protection of property is represented as being the primary function of government, which was based upon the principles of majority rule and legislative supremacy. However, the legislature could not rule in an arbitrary manner. It had to exercise its function through laws that were properly promulgated and that applied equally to all groups. The powers of the other branches of government[146] were even more restricted. Although government was thus, for the sake of the freedom of the individual, definitely restricted, Locke realized that a government, in order to be able to fulfill its purpose, must be effective and have sufficient power and adequate discretion to exercise that power. However, it was not permitted to abuse that discretion and to betray the trust of the people. In such a case, the people possessed the right of revolution.

The philosophy of the Declaration was not taken from the French. It was not even new; but good old English doctrine newly formulated to meet a present emergency. In 1776 it was commonplace doctrine, everywhere to be met with, as Jefferson said, "whether expressed in conversation, in letters, printed essays, or the elementary books of public right." And in sermons also, he might have added."

[145] Thomas P. Peardon, ed., JOHN LOCKE, THE SECOND TREATISE OF GOVERNMENT (1952), xx.

[146] Locke distinguished legislative from executive and federative functions, the latter being concerned with foreign relations.

Except for the idea of legislative supremacy, all these Lockeian principles found expression in the *Federalist*. The authors' rejection of legislative supremacy was as natural as the Englishman's adoption of that institution. Power being concentrated in the executive under the Stuarts, the legislature would appear as the great liberator from absolutism, just as it did, a hundred years after the Glorious Revolution, in France.[147] Having experienced the oppressions of a monarchical absolutism under which power was concentrated in the executive, Locke, like the men of the French Revolution, was not suspicious of legislative power, since that power was, after all, exercised by the representatives of the people. In America, the situation was quite different. For reasons already mentioned,[148] the authors of the *Federalist* took a rather cautious attitude toward legislative supremacy. In their desire to secure free government, they were in favor of a system of government under which the legislature would not be more important than the other branches of government. This led them to follow the classic exponent of the separation of powers, Montesquieu. The Frenchman provided the additional machinery that was necessary to make a reality of the Harringtonian ideal of a government of laws and not of men, combined with the Lockeian concept of free government and the sacrosanctity of property.[149]

The idea of the separation of powers was, of course, not new. Plato and Polybius were concerned with it in their discussion of a mixed state, and the concept of a tempered or mixed monarchy was a familiar one during the Middle Ages. In England, the struggle between the crown and the courts of common law, and between the crown and Parliament, had given concrete importance to the separation of powers. Harrington had considered it a prerequisite for free government, and Locke had given it a subsidiary role in his theory of parliamentary supremacy. However, the idea of mixed government had never had a definite meaning. It had connoted a balancing of social and economic interests, or a sharing of power by such corporations as communes or municipalities. Often, the concept was proposed as a remedy against extreme centralization and as a reminder that a political organization would only work if there ex-

---

[147] See Gottfried Dietze, "Judicial Review in Europe," MICHIGAN LAW REVIEW (1957), LV, 548 ff.

[148] *Supra*, pp. 309 ff.

[149] Montesquieu's doctrine of the separation of powers is brought forth in Book XI of his *Spirit of the Laws* (1748), Books XI and XII containing the celebrated discussion of political and civil liberty.

isted some degree of comity and fair dealing between its various parts. It was Montesquieu who modified the ancient doctrines by making the separation of powers into a system of legal checks and balances between the parts of a constitution.[150]

Montesquieu's idea, which was derived inductively from a study of the English constitution, gained a great deal of popularity in America. After having been hailed by the colonists in their attempts to curb the powers and prerogatives of the royal governor, the principle of the separation of powers was a guiding light for the constitution-making that took place after independence had been declared. It was mentioned in the Virginia Declaration of Rights of 1776[151] and in the preamble of the constitution of Massachusetts of 1780,[152] and it thus found official recognition in America years before it was put down in the famous article 16 of the French Declaration of the Rights of Man and Citizen. The members of the Philadelphia Convention reaffirmed the validity of the Montesquieuian concept, the more so since the preceding years had shown a lapse in its strict observance, which was due largely to the belief that a strong legislature, considered by many as the great liberator from monarchical despotism, could not very well be destructive of the Frenchman's ideal, liberty.[153]

The *Federalist* accepts the framers' version of the separation of powers. Aware of the probability of legislative usurpations, the authors of that work desire a separation that would be likely to eliminate legislative supremacy. No matter how much Hamilton and Madison might disagree on certain aspects of the separation of powers,[154] they see eye to eye with respect to that major point. Montesquieu's influence on the Papers goes still further. Not only is his idea of a separation of the executive, legislative, and judicial branches accepted, but also, his concept of checks and balances.

[150] See Sabine, *op. cit.*, 558-59.

[151] Sect. 5.

[152] Sect. 30.

[153] Montesquieu maintained that a nation, in which the separation of powers is not carried out, has no constitution at all. He thus connected the separation of powers with the idea of constitutionalism. Compare in that connection the words of Art. 16 of the French Declaration of the Rights of Man and Citizen of Aug. 26, 1789: "Any society, in which the enforcement of rights is not guaranteed and the separation of powers not definitely stated, does not possess a constitution."

[154] As was shown above, Madison favored a more genuine separation of powers, being against concentration of governmental power in any department. Hamilton, on the other hand, in his desire to prevent a legislative despotism, did not mind a concentration of power in the executive and, especially, in the judiciary.

Whole essays are devoted to the discussion of the Frenchman's great innovation in the science of politics, and he is frequently quoted.[155] He seems indeed to have had a special fascination for the authors, especially for Madison, from whose pen came most of the discussions of the separation of powers. This popularity may have been due partly to Montesquieu's inductive method, which was likely to have a certain appeal to statesmen who were, in a way, suspicious of mere philosophical speculations. However, what probably accounts most for Hamilton's, Madison's, and Jay's sympathy for the Frenchman was the fact that he chose the English constitution as an example of the merits of a separation of powers. Montesquieu thus became the great foreign herald of the rights of Englishmen. These were the rights that our authors believed in, that they hoped would exist in the free government under the Constitution.

The rights of Englishmen were, on the whole, based upon the common law, as expounded by Coke and Blackstone. Since the *Federalist* is fundamentally a treatise on the rights of the individual, we arrive, finally, at the question whether that work was also influenced by these great legal philosophers. This question can be answered in the affirmative. Coke and Blackstone were known to the authors. The ideas of the former had played an important role in the colonists' struggle with England and had provided good arguments against the validity of acts of Parliament that were considered oppressive.[156] Blackstone, on the other hand, was the undisputed authority on the common law at the time the *Federalist* was written and during the preceding decades. There can be no doubt that the Englishmen's proclamation of the immemorial rights of Englishmen impressed the authors of the *Federalist*.

With respect to the important question about the most appropriate means to secure these rights, however, Coke was more likely to be acceptable than Blackstone. Coke's famous decision in Dr. Bonham's Case, in which he stated that "the common law will control Acts of Parliament, and sometimes adjudge them to be utterly void" as "against Common Right and Reason,"[157] is usually considered the *fons et origo* of judicial review. But, while his idea achieved a certain amount of political currency during the seven-

[155] Especially essays 47-51.

[156] For instance, James Otis invoked Coke's dictum in Dr. Bonham's Case in the *Writs of Assistance Case*. Quincy's Mass. Rep. 4 (1761), 469-85.

[157] Coke's Reports (1610), VIII, 118.

teenth century, in later years English judges were reluctant to venture to declare an act of Parliament void and proceeded according to the principle laid down by Blackstone, that "the power of parliament is absolute and without control."[158] While Blackstone's statement, probably made with the conviction that the representatives of the people would not harm the rights of the individual, was not disputed in England, it came under attack in America, after the acts of Parliament had become oppressive. It was acceptable in a limited monarchy where the representatives of the people, recognizing higher norms of natural and common law, would not become oppressive. However, the situation was different under a popular government where the majority was not restricted and, convinced of its infallibility, rejected the idea of being under a superior law. The authors of the *Federalist* were, as far as legislative supremacy was concerned, not likely to follow Blackstone. Rather, they would follow Coke, who had recognized the value of judicial review for individual freedom and was thus the forefather of a doctrine that found its classic exposition in the *Federalist*.

4.   This leads to a consideration of the Papers' contribution to the idea of government. It has been noted in the preceding pages that there were many factors bearing upon the authors' discussion of constitutionalism, environmental and historical as well as philosophical. In what, then, consists the originality of the essays?

Like the Founding Fathers, the authors of the *Federalist* were confronted with a genuinely democratic problem and succeeded in solving that problem. This alone constitutes enormous progress in the theory and practice of government as it existed up to their time. Former generations had been concerned largely with the question of how to restrict monarchical absolutism and had been confronted with the choice of monarchy or popular government. Hamilton, Madison, and Jay, on the other hand, conceived of popular government as the very premise for their arguments. They did not ask whether popular government should take the place of monarchy, as their predecessors had done. That question had been answered for them in 1776. Rather, they asked about the degree of democracy and majority rule. Their answer was that of men who believed in the individualism of the English heritage and their intellectual environment. They brought forth their own concept of free government,

[158] Cooley's Blackstone (2nd ed., 1872), 159.

under which the popular majority, while governing, was restricted by a constitution for the sake of the freedom of the individual and under which the democratic principle of popular participation in government, as a mere means, was subordinate to the liberal principle of the protection of the individual, as the end of government. Here was solved in a truly ingenious manner, prior to the French Revolution, the problem of democracy that was to plague continental nations throughout the nineteenth and twentieth centuries.

As a great new guarantee for the preservation of free government, the *Federalist* introduced the doctrine of judicial review. It is true that Coke already had suggested the control of legislative acts. However, his action was directed against a monarchical absolutism.[159] We cannot be sure whether his attitude would have been the same in case of a democratic lawgiver. In spite of his advocacy of a government of laws and not of men, Harrington had not thought of judicial review as a means to guarantee the supremacy of the constitution over a republican legislator. Locke, though believing that the legislature had to rule for the sake of the individual, also had failed to provide for judicial review as a safeguard for constitutionalism and free government. Montesquieu felt that a distribution of governmental power would be sufficient for the protection of the individual's liberty. All these philosophers obviously believed that government by the representatives of the people constituted no danger to the rights of the individual.

In America, James Otis had invoked Coke's dictum on judicial review in the *Writs of Assistance* case.[160] But, again, the question arises whether he would have done so if the colonists had been represented in Parliament. Even after legislative oppressions had become evident in some of the newly established American states, political thinkers did not suggest the introduction of judicial review. Turgot, in his criticism of American state constitutions,[161] did not mention judicial review as a possible remedy. Even John Adams, whose influence upon American conservatism is beyond any doubt,[162] restricted himself, in his answer to Turgot,[163] to a defense

[159] See Carl J. Friedrich, CONSTITUTIONAL GOVERNMENT AND DEMOCRACY (rev. ed., 1951), 105, 223.

[160] *Loc. cit.*

[161] Letter to Richard Price of March 22, 1778. Published in Richard Price, OBSERVATIONS ON THE IMPORTANCE OF THE AMERICAN REVOLUTION (1784), 90.

[162] For Adams' influence upon the *Federalist*, see Beloff, *op. cit.*, lxii.

[163] John Adams, DEFENCE OF THE CONSTITUTIONS OF GOVERNMENT OF THE UNITED STATES OF AMERICA (1787-88).

of the doctrine of the separation of powers and failed to introduce judicial review as its corollary.[164]

Although state courts had exercised judicial review after independence, and although that institution was accepted by many of the delegates to the Philadelphia Convention, it was not elaborated by them as a doctrine. This remained to be done in the *Federalist*. Conceiving of judicial review as a corollary to the separation of powers, as a means to secure the rights of the individual from legislative oppression, and as an institution to secure the supremacy of the constitution, the *Federalist* came to fill the gap that existed in the philosophies of Montesquieu, Locke, and Harrington, gaps that were due in all probability to those authors' naive belief that a representative democracy was not likely to infringe upon the freedom of the individual. The *Federalist*'s creation of the doctrine of judicial review for a democratic society cannot be evaluated too highly. A means for the protection of liberty, judicial review was destined to become one of the cornerstones of American constitutionalism, the blessings of which could be felt in many parts of the world.[165]

[164] This was pointed out by John Stevens (writing as 'A Farmer of New Jersey'), in OBSERVATIONS OF GOVERNMENT; INCLUDING SOME ANIMADVERSIONS ON MR. ADAMS'S DEFENCE OF THE CONSTITUTIONS OF GOVERNMENT OF THE UNITED STATES OF AMERICA AND ON MR. DE LOLME'S CONSTITUTION OF ENGLAND (1787).

[165] For the emergence of judicial review in Europe, see Gottfried Dietze, "America and Europe—Decline and Emergence of Judicial Review," *loc. cit.* Compare in this connection F. A. Hayek, THE CONSTITUTION OF LIBERTY (1960), 176 ff.

Conclusion

CHAPTER ELEVEN

The Federalist—
Values and Prospects

In the preceding pages, the main purpose has been not to interpret, but to analyze, the *Federalist*. Too much interpreting is being done these days, with a view to adjusting classic thought to modern use. Stimulating and interesting as interpretations may be, they are also fraught with danger. Often they are unobjective enough to justify questions about scholarship. In this time of rapid change, we should keep in mind that not everything new is necessarily also true. Attempts have been made in recent decades to reinterpret the formative period of American history. Charles A. Beard's economic interpretation of the Constitution, adjusting a great era to the designs and desires of his progressive contemporaries,[1] was by no means the respectable scholarship with which it has been credited by those who liked the Beardian doctrine and used it for their own purposes.[2] The so-called liberal school continued the process of adjusting interpretation, but their very use of the word "liberalism" was sympto-

[1] See Adair, "The Tenth Federalist Revisited," *loc. cit.*

[2] See *ibid.*; Brown, *op. cit.*; Forrest McDonald, WE THE PEOPLE (1958); B. F. Wright, *op. cit.*, 17 ff.

335

matic of the hypocrisy of their method, for during the formative
period liberalism meant anything but a protagonism of the welfare
state. Later, when the new type of liberalism became more and more
suspect, a need was felt for a new, more palatable name. The "New
Conservatism" was created. Needless to say, that conservatism is as
much new as it is not true, a defense of the New Freedom and the
New Deal, but by no means of conservatism! The two-hundredth
anniversary of Hamilton's birth appeared like a culmination of the
trend toward adjusting interpretation. Whereas in previous decades
liberal authors had been content with denying that Alexander Hamilton was a great American because he did not share their liberal
views,[3] they now attempted to show Hamilton as a new conservative,
who put the interests of the nation above those of the individual and
who, after all, was not opposed to the government's interference
with the freedom of the individual.[4]

In the present study of the *Federalist,* the interpretative method
has been rejected in favor of the analytical one, on the assumption
that the authors' own interpretation of the Constitution should not
be altered.[5] It has not been intended to provide startling news that
would please most readers but simply to show what stands written in
the *Federalist* in black and white. Although this approach might
not be as challenging and interesting as a more subjective one, the
method seems justified not only because the values of the *Federalist*
are timeless and important for this generation, but also because
these values seem in danger of being forgotten.

I

1.   What are these values? It has been shown in the preceding chapter that the *Federalist* broadened the orthodox concept of federalism
by maintaining that federalism was a means not only to achieve
peace and security, but also to guarantee the protection of the in-

---

[3] Woodrow Wilson, while admitting that Hamilton was a great man, denied
him the privilege of being considered a great American, because presumably "he
did not think in terms of American life." THE NEW FREEDOM (1913), 47.

[4] See, for instance, Broadus Mitchell, ALEXANDER HAMILTON (1957); Richard B.
Morris, ed., ALEXANDER HAMILTON AND THE FOUNDING OF THE NATION (1957). For an
argument against this view of Hamilton, see Gottfried Dietze, "Hamilton's Concept of Free Government," NEW YORK HISTORY (1957), XXXVIII, 351.

[5] See *supra,* pp. 31 ff.

dividual from the government. To insure that protection in a democratic society even further, the *Federalist* introduced the doctrine
of judicial review. These two contributions to the science of federalism and popular government point to the values of the work.

To begin, it may be said that justice, meaning the protection of
the rights of the individual, occupies a superior place. The authors
conceived of these rights as being part of human freedom as one
entity. This is not surprising. In the Declaration of Independence
as well as in the various state constitutions, the protection of property and the free use thereof was mentioned in one breath with such
rights as freedom of worship, freedom of the press, and other civil
rights. Quite naturally, the authors of the *Federalist* did not discriminate between economic and noneconomic rights. They by no means
suggested that the latter were superior to the former, feeling that all
of them were ingredient parts of the freedom of the individual. As
a matter of fact, it appears as if the Papers are actually more concerned with the protection of property than any other right. This
may be due to the fact that at that time property was more under
attack and that, consequently, a greater need was felt to stress its
sacrosanctity.[6] Perhaps also the authors, who shared the political
ideals of John Adams,[7] recognized a more fundamental value of
property.[8] At any rate, the rights of property rated for them at least
as high as the other rights of the individual.

2. For the sake of freedom, the authors advocated a popular government that promised to guarantee a high degree of the protection
of the individual, a government that was characterized by both
spatial and institutional divisions of power. Unlike thinkers of previous generations, they felt that federalism had more to offer than
merely security from foreign powers and peace among the federating
states, being also a means for the protection of the freedom of the

[6] For the thesis that the guarantee of human rights is a consequence of previous oppression and the ensuing fight against such oppression, see Georg Jellinek,
DIE ERKLÄRUNG DER MENSCHEN- UND BÜRGERRECHTE (1895).

[7] Beloff, *op. cit.*, lxii.

[8] In DEFENCE OF THE CONSTITUTIONS OF GOVERNMENT OF THE UNITED STATES OF
AMERICA, John Adams wrote: "Property is surely a right of mankind as really
as liberty. . . . The moment the idea is admitted into society, that property is
not as sacred as the laws of God, and that there is not a force of law and public
justice to protect it, anarchy and tyranny commence." Charles Francis Adams,
ed., THE WORKS OF JOHN ADAMS (1850-56), VI, 8-9.

individual from governmental interference. The separation of powers was conceived to serve similar aims. Again for the protection of the individual, an important American contribution to constitutional democracy was elaborated in the *Federalist* as the doctrine of judicial review.

3.   The function of federalism to secure the freedom of the individual was acknowledged to exist on a broad scale. In the *Federalist,* the more perfect Union is, of course, advocated primarily as a means for the prevention of oppressions by the state governments. But this emphasis is probably a mere accident, due to the fact that at the time the Papers were written, the citizens were oppressed by the legislatures of the states and not by Congress, because the latter was in no position to do so. Nowhere in the *Federalist* do we find a remark to the effect that the national government exercises an exclusive and absolute role in protecting the individual's rights. On the contrary, nothing appears as absolute as freedom itself. Therefore, federalism is conceived to serve as a means for the protection of the individual as much from the national government as from the state governments. In a word, the states are as much of a potential protector of the individual from the national government, as the national government is a protector of the individual from the states. This means that, should the national government become oppressive, the Constitution could be as much invoked against the actions of that government as it can be used against similar behavior by the states. The *Federalist* is a polemic against oppressive government in general and is directed as much against a majoritarianism on the national, as on the state, level. As a matter of fact, we may ask whether, *a fortiori,* Hamilton, Madison, and Jay, individualists as they were, might not have been much more afraid of the former than of the latter.

Federalism, conceived to be a prerequisite for the protection of the individual in a democratic society, is created by the Constitution and preserved by the interpreters of that law, the judges. The authors, aware of the contractual nature of the federal union and the probability of federal problems, advocate that the function of umpiring controversies arising from the complex of federalism should be vested in the body most likely to be impartial, the judiciary. Both state and national governments being of the popular type, the function of the judiciary to iron out federal issues amounts largely to the function of checking democracy, or the will of the majority, as reflected in the political branches of government. Again, the power of judicial review is a rather broad one, being restricted only by the letter and spirit of the Constitution.[9]

II

1. The discovery of the New World has been the outstanding event of modern history. When we ask what the major contribution of the New World to our civilization has been, we may answer that it lies in the field of government, or political science. The Americans were not only the first to emancipate themselves from the Old World. They were also the first to establish a popular republican government that worked. In doing so, they made an important contribution to modern constitutionalism. Not only did they lead the way in guaranteeing the individual's freedom by bills of rights,[10] but they also recognized the dangers of centralization and majoritarianism. At an early stage in their democratic experiment, the Americans succeeded in solving the major problem of democracy and decided to what degree the majority, while ruling, should be checked for the sake of minority rights. The *Federalist* gives the classic exposition of the importance of individual freedom and the important devices for protecting it, such as federalism and judicial review. This raises the question whether the ideals of Hamilton, Jay, and Madison were realized and to what degree they are still part of today's form of government. While we can reply to the former question in the affirmative, the latter question cannot be answered so easily. It should not be overlooked that the beliefs of the *Federalist* are about to become simply ideals, which correspond less and less to an actually existing situation.

The first consideration should be what happened to the authors' concept of free government. As was mentioned before, they conceived of free government as that form of popular government under which the democratic principle of popular participation in government, while accepted, was a mere means, inferior to the liberal principle of the protection of the individual, as the end. It appears doubtful whether this concept is still accepted today. American government is still called a "free government," but many people feel that too serious a shift has taken place in the relative importance of the participation and protection principles to justify speaking of an

[9] See *supra,* pp. 279 ff.
[10] See Jellinek, *op. cit.*

actual existence of the ideas of the *Federalist*. In an effort to secure the protection of the individual from the ruling majority, Chancellor Kent, fearful lest the people, [conscious of their power to govern, might get intoxicated with that power, and, making laws for their own sovereign pleasure only, might interfere with the rights of the minority, warned of an extension of suffrage to those who had no property. His statement, "there is no retrograde step in the rear of democracy,"[11] admitted the inevitable end of free government, as understood by the authors of the *Federalist*. If there is no retrograde step in the rear of democracy, the participation principle, i.e., democratic rule, must grow until it has relegated the idea of the protection of the individual from a primary to a secondary position, until the conditions the Constitution was designed to prevent are reinstituted, until there exists a democratic despotism under which the majority may trample upon the rights of the minority at discretion.[12] While the very fact of the adoption of the Constitution proves the untenability of Chancellor Kent's statement, his warning was justified. Ever since the Constitution was ratified, there has taken place, through the extension of suffrage, an increasing acceptance of mere majority rule and Rousseauistic philosophy. Freedom has become more and more considered to be the right to participate in government, rather than the right to be protected from the government, i.e., an individualistic concept of liberty has been largely replaced by a commune one.[13]

One of the consequences of this shift was a different evaluation of the individual's freedom from the government itself. That freedom, which for the authors of the *Federalist* had constituted a unity, became the victim of an increased atomization, which the nominalism inherent in popular government created in quite a few other fields. Discrimination was now made against the rights of property. The influx of poor European immigrants, who came to this country mainly for material gain, increased those Americans who considered an equal distribution of property more important than the sacrosantity of property. Property, which in the *Federalist* had been on a

---

[11] REPORTS OF THE PROCEEDINGS AND DEBATES OF THE CONVENTION OF 1821, AS-SEMBLED FOR THE PURPOSE OF AMENDING THE CONSTITUTION OF THE STATE OF NEW YORK (1821), 222.

[12] Compare Jacob Burckhardt, WELTGESCHICHTLICHE BETRACHTUNGEN (Kaegi, ed., 1941), 279. Sharing Ranke's doubts as to the value of the sovereignty of the people, Burckhardt felt that the French Revolution, which "considered itself the symbol of freedom," was actually "as fundamentally unfree as a forest fire."

[13] Compare Raoul E. Desvernine, DEMOCRATIC DESPOTISM (1936).

par with, if not superior to, the noneconomic rights of the individual, now became considered a right of second order.

Thus changes have occurred during the past decades that have challenged the very substance of the *Federalist*'s concept of free government. It may be added that what appeared to the authors as major means for the existence of freedom, federalism and judicial review, experienced a similar decline, which is not surprising in view of the fundamental shift from a primacy of individual protection to one of majority rule.

2. As to federalism, there has been a trend toward nationalism ever since the adoption of the Constitution. The power of the federal government has been continually increased at the cost of that of the states. This development was given a good start by one of America's great chief justices, John Marshall. Nationalists have exploited this fact, as well as Hamilton's nationalistic interpretation of the Constitution in the *Federalist,* to further their own designs. However, their version is actually a contortion of both Hamilton's and Marshall's concepts of nationalism. National power was for Hamilton by no means an end in itself, but was a mere means for securing the happiness of the individual, of which the protection of property constituted a prominent part. This is no different in the case of Marshall. It should not be overlooked that the man who brought forth the doctrine of implied powers[14] and started the nationalistic interpretation of the commerce clause[15] did so only after having established in judicial review an effective means for securing individual rights[16] and after having stressed the sacrosanctity of property.[17] For Marshall also the more perfect Union was nothing but a means for the protection of the freedom of the individual. He strictly followed Hamilton's doctrine of "happiness through national power," brought forth in the *Federalist,* and did not transcend that doctrine by favoring national power at the cost of individual rights.

We have doubts whether this can be said of more recent exponents of the nationalist doctrine. Ever since the problem of the nature of the Union was solved on the battlefield, nationalism has come to be considered an end in itself. Hamilton's doctrine in the

[14] McCulloch v. Maryland, 4 Wheaton 316 (1819).
[15] Gibbons v. Ogden, 9 Wheaton 1 (1824).
[16] Marbury v. Madison, 1 Cranch 137 (1803).
[17] Fletcher v. Peck, 6 Cranch 87 (1810).

Federalist was misunderstood as often as it was invoked. The advocate of free government appeared more and more as an advocate of nationalism.[18] The dangers of this development were hardly recognized.[19] The nationalists' cause was enhanced when, after the beginning of the twentieth century, the United States emerged as a world power. The emergencies of World War I, the Great Depression, World War II, and the Cold War also contributed to a promotion of their designs. The trend away from federalism, however, was not due only to the factors just mentioned. Another cause that should not be overlooked was the broadening of democracy. When democracy became increasingly Rousseauistic in character, the general will of the nation gained in importance, to the detriment of the rights of the states. American federalism became replaced more and more by a federal melting pot, which absorbed and majorized the states.

The Supreme Court, umpire over the constitutional balance between national power and states' rights, did not halt this development. It was silent on the protection of states' rights in the period immediately following the Civil War.[20] Though later invoking the doctrine of dual federalism,[21] and showing some awareness of the necessity of checking infringements upon the states' rights, it did not harness the general trend toward nationalism. This brings us to the other institution contributed by the Americans to modern constitutionalism, judicial review.

[18] See Adair, "The Authorship of the Disputed Federalist Papers," *loc. cit.,* 111 ff. It is admitted that Hamilton was much more of a nationalist, when writing the *Federalist,* as was Madison, and that he became even more of a nationalist in his later years. Still, nationalism remained for him always a means for the advantage of the individual. It was never an end in itself. See Dietze, "Hamilton's Concept of Free Government," *loc. cit.*

[19] Before the Civil War, outstanding treatises warned of the dangers of centralization. See John Taylor's last books, CONSTRUCTION CONSTRUED, AND CONSTITUTIONS VINDICATED (1820), TYRANNY UNMASKED (1822), NEW VIEWS OF THE CONSTITUTION (1823). The classic work is John C. Calhoun, A DISQUISITION ON GOVERNMENT (1853). Another one of Calhoun's important contributions in this respect is A DISCOURSE ON THE CONSTITUTION AND GOVERNMENT OF THE UNITED STATES (1853). It is surprising that after the Civil War, no comparable works came forth. See, however, the recent study by Felix Morley, FREEDOM AND FEDERALISM (1959).

[20] First steps toward a recognition of states' rights were taken in the Slaughterhouse Cases, 16 Wallace 36 (1873), United States v. Cruikshank, 92 U.S. 542 (1876), and the Civil Rights Cases, 109 U.S. 3 (1883).

[21] For this doctrine, see Alfred H. Kelly and Winfred A. Harbison, THE AMERICAN CONSTITUTION—ITS ORIGINS AND DEVELOPMENT (1948), 683 ff., 738 ff, 786 ff. On p. 787, it is stated that " 'dual federalism' is apparently dead and beyond revival."

3.   With federalism as a means for the protection of the individual, the increasing elimination of the rights of the states was fraught with danger. Still it is conceivable, though unlikely, that the judges, while neglecting their duty to preserve the rights of the states, would have balanced that neglect by a very conscious exercise of judicial review over acts of the national government. But the judges failed to do so. Whereas the Supreme Court, throughout the nine-teenth and the early decades of the twentieth centuries, was indeed that "citadel of public justice," functioning as the "excellent barrier to the encroachment and oppressions of the representative body" that Hamilton wished it to be,[22] and that "stronghold and . . . bat-tery" from which Jefferson thought "all the works" of egalitarian democracy would be "beaten down and erased,"[23] it seems no longer to deserve these attributes. During the last decades the Supreme Court showed great reluctance to declare Acts of Congress unconsti-tutional.[24] Of course, this reluctance does not in itself imply the dis-appearance of judicial review as a governmental practice. American constitutional history has known a period longer than a mere quarter of a century in which the constitutionality of national laws was not contested by the Supreme Court.[25] Nevertheless, recent develop-ments indicate changes that warrant apprehensions concerning the very survival of judicial review as an institution. Throughout the years from Marbury v. Madison to Dred Scott, the acquiescence of the judiciary in acts of Congress implied a recognition of neither legislative supremacy nor majoritarianism, in spite of the fact that this was the epoch of the great debates that saw Congress at the apex of its prestige, and witnessed a substantial progress of democ-racy through the broadening of suffrage.[26] The rigorous exercise of judicial review in the years after the Civil War did not come as a surprise. Rather, it seems to have been a corollary to the further in-crease of egalitarian democracy.[27] Today, judicial acquiescence in

[22] 78,503; 78,505.

[23] Letter to John Dickinson of December 19, 1801. JEFFERSON'S WORKS, x, 302.

[24] The only cases being United States v. Lovett, 328 U.S. 303 (1946), U.S. ex rel. Toth v. Quarles, 350 U.S. 11 (1955), and Trop v. Dulles, 356 U.S. 86 (1958).

[25] There was a considerably longer lapse of time between Marbury v. Madison (1803) and the Dred Scott decision (1857).

[26] It was during this very period that the great jurists Joseph Story, James Kent, and Thomas M. Cooley advocated judicial review along the same lines as Chief Justice Marshall. Compare Story, *op. cit.*, i, 344 ff., 382 ff.; iii, 425 ff. (It is significant that Story dedicated his work to Marshall.) Kent, *op. cit.*, i, 295; Cooley, CONSTITUTIONAL LIMITATIONS (1868).

[27] From 1789 to 1864, the Supreme Court declared an act of Congress void in

congressional fiat must, by contrast, appear as the arrival of legislative supremacy. The Supreme Court seems to have abdicated its former position as the guardian of the individual's freedom with its capitulation before the American *volonté générale* in 1937.

This abdication can be attributed, in the main, to factors that are the result of the march of egalitarian democracy and the adjustment of juridical thinking to this march. Ever since the last decades of the past century, the ranks of those Americans who considered themselves underprivileged and believed in unrestricted majority rule have been swelled, as Justice Lurton complained, by the "great influx of an enormous mass of immigrants . . . wholly unfamiliar with the American constitutional idea . . . ," people who increased "the number of those voters who object to any restraint upon the will of the majority . . . ," people who, arriving from nations which rejected judicial review, considered the "power to annul a law as the usurpation of legislative authority."[28] There came to the fore political currents that attacked the very institution of judicial review, culminating in the New Deal.[29]

An opposition to judicial review by the majority of the people or by the political departments of government, no matter how vehement, does not necessarily amount to a disappearance of that institution. American history furnishes ample proof of this.[30] As long as

only two cases. From 1864 to 1885 in sixteen, from 1886 to 1906 in twelve, from 1906 to 1924 in twenty-three, and from 1924 to 1935 in seventeen cases. During the first seventy-five years of the Court's existence national judicial review was exercised only twice, whereas in the following seventy-one years this was done as often as sixty-eight times.

[28] Horace H. Lurton, "A Government of Laws or of Men?" NORTH AMERICAN REVIEW (1911), XCIII, 17.

[29] These currents were expressed, for instance, in Theodore Roosevelt's Square Deal. It is interesting to note that Roosevelt led the Bull Moose Party in a campaign that included a demand for the recall of judicial decisions. In 1912, he stated: "I contend that the people, in the nature of things must be better judges of what is the preponderant opinion than the Court, and that the Courts should not be allowed to reverse the political philosophy of the people." Roosevelt, "The Right of the People to Rule," OUTLOOK (March 23, 1912), 620. Compare in this connection the answers by Elihu Root, "The Importance of an Independent Judiciary," THE INDEPENDENT (1912), LXXII, 704, and William Howard Taft, POPULAR GOVERNMENT (1913), 163.

[30] For a few examples of animosity toward judicial action, compare the comments of various American presidents: Jefferson's letter to W. H. Torrance of June 11, 1815, JEFFERSON'S WRITINGS, XIV, 302-6; Jackson's veto of the Bank of the United States, in J. D. Richardson, comp., COMPILATION OF THE MESSAGES AND PAPERS OF THE PRESIDENTS (1869-99), II, 582; Lincoln's attitude toward the Dred

no constitutional amendments prohibited its exercise, there could be no doubt that judicial review did exist, provided it was not renounced by the judges themselves. As a matter of fact, the Supreme Court seemed for quite some time little impressed by the growing tendency toward majoritarianism and legislative supremacy. A considerably greater number of congressional statutes or parts thereof were found to be unconstitutional during the first thirty-five years of the present century, than in the same period preceding it.[31] The very threat of a potential growth of legislative majoritarianism seemed to stimulate the judiciary to stop legislative ambitions.[32] Stability was secured by testing what were conceivably acts of a majoritarian passion for their compatibility with the Constitution and those principles of the older law that were considered part of the American constitutional order.[33] But this general attitude of the Court was, in the end, challenged by the legal profession itself. There came about a new form of juridical thinking that was ideally suited to the march of egalitarian democracy. Stimulated by contemporary developmentalist and pragmatist philosophy that considered stability an impossible—even an undesirable—condition and elevated the concept of change into a principle of social theory,[34] sociological jurisprudence questioned the Court's skeptical attitude toward legislative fiat and, thereby, the institution of judicial review itself.

Oliver Wendell Holmes stated as early as 1881 that the law "should correspond with the actual feelings and demands of the community, whether right or wrong."[35] Three years later, he said: "Everyone instinctively recognizes that in these days the justification of a law for us cannot be found in the fact that our fathers always have followed it. It must be found in some help which the law

Scott decision, in Arthur B. Lapsley, THE WRITINGS OF ABRAHAM LINCOLN (Federal ed., 1905-06), II, 291 ff.

[31] See *supra*, page 343, note 27.

[32] Indeed, it seems justified to speak here of reaction and counter-reaction and the rule that dangers of legislative majoritarianism are being matched by tendencies toward a more rigorous exercise of judicial review. Such a rule would, of course, correspond to what was originally conceived to be the function of judicial review, namely, the restriction of the legislature representing the popular majority to within the limits set by superior constitutional and extraconstitutional law.

[33] For the fact that too much and too fast a lawmaking may lead to legal insecurity, compare Madison's statement at 62, 406. Hamilton made similar comments in the *Federalist*. 27, 167 and 85, 568.

[34] Fred V. Cahill, JUDICIAL LEGISLATION (1952), 21-31.

[35] Oliver Wendell Holmes, THE COMMON LAW (1881), 41-42.

brings toward reaching a social end which the governing power of the community has made up its mind it wants."[36] The necessity of a law which reflected the mutability of social conditions was thus linked up with a rejection of older law. Law was to be purged of "every word of moral significance,"[37] i.e., of *a priori* higher law standards. To make things complete, Holmes argued against judicial review. In his famous dissent in Lochner v. New York, he maintained "the right of the majority to embody their opinions in law," and cautioned the Court about its exercise of judicial review.[38] In 1913, the Boston Brahmin used a more direct language. "I do not think," he remarked, "that the United States would come to an end if we lost our power to declare an Act of Congress void."[39] This meant that the Constitution and the older and higher law were irrelevant if they conflicted with the wishes of the majority as reflected in the acts of Congress.[40] Here was a revolutionary concept of American government indeed. The supremacy of the American *volonté générale* was now recognized.

Sociological jurisprudence has had a great impact upon constitutional development in the United States. In a way, Holmes came to occupy in great measure the position of official judicial philosopher

[36] Oliver Wendell Holmes, "The Law in Science and Science in Law," COLLECTED LEGAL PAPERS (1920), 225. Compare also his statement, made in 1897: "It is revolting to have no better reason for a rule of law than that so it was laid down in the time of Henry IV. It is still more revolting if the grounds upon which it was laid down have vanished long since, and the rule simply persists from blind imitation of the past." "The Path of the Law," *ibid.*, 187.

[37] "I often doubt whether it would not be a gain if every word of moral significance could be banished from the law altogether, and other words adopted which should convey legal ideas uncolored by anything outside the law. We should lose the fossil records of a good deal of history and the majesty got from ethical associations, but by ridding ourselves of an unnecessary confusion we should gain very much in the clearness of our thought." Quoted in Harold R. McKinnon, "The Secret of Mr. Justice Holmes: An Analysis," AMERICAN BAR ASSOCIATION JOURNAL (1950), XXXVI, 264.

[38] Lochner v. New York, 198 U.S. 45, 75 (1905).

[39] "Law and the Court," COLLECTED LEGAL PAPERS (1920), 295-96.

[40] For Holmes' derisive attitude toward the Court's testing of legislative acts for their compatibility with older and higher law, see his dissent in Baldwin v. Missouri, 281 U.S. 586, 595 (1930), where he complains that one can see "hardly any limit but the sky" to the invalidation of legislative acts "if they happen to strike a majority of the Court as for any reason undesirable." The common law was for Holmes "not a brooding omnipresence in the sky but the articulate voice of some sovereign or quasi-sovereign that can be identified." Southern Pacific Co. v. Jensen, 244 U.S. 205, 222 (1917).

for the modern age. He can be considered not only "the starting point for almost all recent American legal writers,"[41] but also the judge who brought about the fundamental shift in the attitude of the Supreme Court toward judicial review. His philosophy, originally confined to a small minority of the Court, advanced as consistently within that body as did the idea of absolute democracy with the American people. In the middle 1920's, the famous minority of Holmes and Brandeis was strengthened by Stone. By the middle of the 1930's the minority favoring the Court's acceptance of New Deal legislation had increased to four judges. Finally, in 1937 the Court, faced with the threat of Roosevelt's court-packing plan, submitted to the demands of the popular majority. The "Cult of the Robe"[42] was replaced by a cult of the popular vogue. A landmark of American constitutionalism, the Court's traditional policy of protecting "the rights of the minor party" from "the superior force of an interested and overbearing majority"[43] through the invalidation of legislative fiat irrespective of the reaction of the other branches of government and the general public, had come to an end. It is one of the principles of limited democracy that majoritarian tendencies should be matched by an increased exercise of judicial review. Consequently, one would have expected that throughout the New Deal the judiciary would continue to meet an increased majoritarian challenge with an increased activity in the exercise of judicial review. Instead, weakened by a judicial philosophy that bore the mark of majoritarian democracy and was complementary to rather than preventive of a democratic despotism,[44] the Supreme Court capitulated.

Nothing the Court did in the ensuing years could minimize the importance of that capitulation, the decisive feature of which was the abandonment by the Court of the individual to the dangers of majoritarian oppression. The Court, it is true, set out on an ambitious program to protect noneconomic civil rights. In approaching these cases, the judges, often invoking older and natural law, have tended to assume that statutes regulating such rights are unconstitutional. While in almost all instances the regulatory measures were the product of local and state legislation, the Court did not refrain

[41] Cahill, *op. cit.*, 32.

[42] This term was first used by Jerome Frank as the title of an article which appeared in the SATURDAY REVIEW OF LITERATURE on Oct. 13, 1945, 12.

[43] 10, 54.

[44] Compare Desvernine, *op. cit.*

from exercising judicial review over national legislation. The recent
decision in the citizenship case is indeed a refreshing reminder of
the Court's tradition.[45] Still, for the time being, it is hardly more.
It does not conceal the decline of judicial review in the United
States. Aside from the reluctance of the Court to face a nationwide
unpopularity by challenging acts of Congress as distinguished from
state and local legislation, it is open to doubt whether the Court's
attitude actually amounts to a challenge of majoritarianism. Occasional invalidations of statutes that merely regulate noneconomic
rights are not likely to make the Court too unpopular, as long as the
judges refrain from invalidating laws that restrict the activities of
economic minorities. But throughout American history, it has appeared to be the very essence of judicial review that it has been
exercised *in spite of* popular disapproval and irrespective of whether
it was criticized by economic or noneconomic groups. Therefore, it
is hard to believe that judicial review is emerging from its period of
decline as long as the Court has not demonstrated its willingness to
face unpopularity by challenging legislative action also for the sake
of economic rights. The different evaluation of noneconomic and
economic rights appears to be arbitrary.[46] It is absurd to maintain
that the right to picket is more important than the right to work.
There is, aside from the Four Freedoms, a Fifth Freedom.[47] Of
course the latter occupies the position of a numerical minority vis-
à-vis its four brethren. But this is a symbol of importance rather
than irrelevance. It should not be overlooked that the juxtaposition
to the Four Freedoms may be interpreted to mean that from a qual-
itative point of view the Fifth Freedom is as important as the Four
Freedoms taken together and thus more important than any one of
the four. The only explanation for the judges' acquiescence in legislation harmful to the rights of economic minorities can be the fact
that they believe in legislative supremacy and majoritarianism.

III

1.   The arrival in the United States of majoritarianism and the ensuing decline of the institutions America contributed to modern

[45] Trop v. Dulles, 356 U.S. 86 (1958).

[46] See Earl Latham, "The Majoritarian Dilemma in the United States Supreme
Court," CONFLUENCE (No. 4, 1953), 22.

[47] Herbert Hoover, "The Fifth Freedom," an address of 1941, in ADDRESSES UPON
THE AMERICAN ROAD: WORLD WAR II, 1941-1945 (1946), 222.

constitutionalism does not detract from the importance of the *Federalist* for our own day. The values of the work still stand, a constant reminder of a great past. Sooner or later they might again be appreciated. This might help to spare the United States the fate of the European nations that learned their lessons about absolute democracy the hard way.

The plight of continental democracies and their final collapse can be attributed largely to the acceptance of the ideas of the French Revolution.[48] Although the dangers of these ideas were realized at a rather early stage by a few sages,[49] the great mass believed in the righteousness of French thought. That thought was different from that of the American Revolution and its concluding document, the Constitution. It advocated the very concepts the authors of the *Federalist* sought to fight, absolute democracy combined with legislative supremacy and centralization.

In America, the idea of limited democracy, which was started in 1776, after some absolutist aberrations under the Articles of Confederation became consolidated with the ratification of the Constitution. Higher, natural, and common law principles with their inherent protection of the rights of the individual strongly influenced the Founders. The Constitution was largely a transmutation of these principles into written norms and by no means, as Gladstone would have it, "struck off at a given moment."[50] The Founding Fathers were aware of the fallibility of human reason. They considered the Constitution good, but not perfect. The situation was quite different in France. Whereas the Americans had refused to reject the old order completely, the French revolutionaries favored a total break. The absolutism of the *ancien régime* was replaced by a new absolutism, that of the people, the nation. Having discovered their own divinity, the people felt that their will, as embodied in constitutions written by themselves, was the very embodiment of reason. The belief in the infallibility of the national *volonté générale* had inescapable conse-

---

[48] In spite of all attempts to restore the *ancien régime*, the vision of Kant came true: The French Revolution, having "discovered in human nature . . . an ability to improvement," was "a phenomenon in human history" which was "never forgotten." Immanuel Kant, DER STREIT DER FAKULTÄTEN IN DREI ABSCHNITTEN (1798), VII, 400. As to the hypnosis deriving from French codifications under Napoleon I, see Dietze, "America and Europe—Decline and Emergence of Judicial Review," *loc. cit.,* 1249 ff.

[49] For instance, Jacob Burckhardt, Friedrich Nietzsche, and José Ortega y Gasset.

[50] See *supra.,* p. 3, note 1.

quences. There was room neither for a check upon the nation, in the form of federalism, nor for a check upon the representatives of the nation, the legislature, in the form of judicial review, the national legislature having become the constituent power itself.

The existence of absolute democracy, combined with centralization and legislative supremacy, became characteristic not only of the constitutional development in France, but also of that of other countries, such as Italy and Germany.[51] It had ill effects in all these nations. The concept of legality more and more superseded that of legitimacy.[52] Everything the legislature did was accepted at face value. The question of legitimacy was no longer raised. A government of laws was replaced by a mere government of statutes.[53] A wrong of the state, of the legislative majority, came to be considered a contradiction in terms.[54] Few thinkers warned of this trend. They were not able to stem the tide and halt disaster. Mussolini, Hitler, and Pétain came to power under the legality of existing democratic

[51] The German *Rechtsstaat* (classic definition in Friedrich Julius Stahl, DIE STAATSLEHRE UND DIE PRINZIPIEN DES STAATSRECHTS [3rd ed., 1856], 137), implying the rule of legislative acts, was taken over by the Italians. See Carmelo Caristia, "Ventura e avventure di una formola: Rechtsstaat," RIVISTA DI DIRITTO PUBBLICO (1934), XXVI, 388. The unification of Italy resulted in the creation of a unitary state that became highly centralized under Mussolini. Imperial Germany was succeeded by the unitary state of the Weimar Republic, and the latter, by the centralized Third Reich.

[52] The distinction between legality and legitimacy was recognized by Lamennais as early as 1829. It is interesting to note that already at that time the connection between legislative majoritarianism and centralization was seen by a few Frenchmen, de Tocqueville being one of them. It was felt that the development of the law in France, characterized by a transformation of right into statutory legality, amounted to nothing but a means for a progressive centralization. See Carl Schmitt, DIE LAGE DER EUROPÄISCHEN RECHTSWISSENSCHAFT (1950), 31.

[53] The words of the French jurist Bugnet, "Je ne connais pas de droit civil; je n'enseigne que le Code Napoléon" (quoted in Julien Bonnecase, ECOLE DE L'EXEGESE EN DROIT CIVIL [2nd ed., 1924], 128), are characteristic of this development. The term *Rechtsstaat* (state of right) proved more and more to be a misnomer, since it degenerated more and more into a mere *Gesetzesstaat*.

[54] Hans Kelsen, HAUPTPROBLEME DER STAATSRECHTSLEHRE (1923), 249. It is realized, of course, that Kelsen's dictum could, from the point of view of his theory of law, not be different and did not necessarily amount to a denial of ethical values. Nevertheless, it afforded despotic rulers a means for demanding obedience from their subjects, including the jurists, and was, therefore, not unlikely to have dangerous consequences. It appears indeed ironical that Kelsen should have been one of the first to feel the injustice (the "wrong of the state" that could not exist according to his theory) of the Hitler regime.

constitutions.[55] Backed by a positivism that had developed as the inevitable result of the blind acceptance of the principle *vox populi vox dei*, the new Caesars were able to eliminate the freedom of the individual. Absolute democracy convicted itself.

This brought forth a definite reaction. Having become aware of the danger inherent in majoritarianism, the Europeans came to realize that there were values higher than those of the general will and acknowledged the necessity of limitations upon democracy.[56] The *Federalist*'s ideal of free government was now appreciated, as were the institutions proposed by Hamilton, Madison, and Jay for the realization of that ideal, federalism and judicial review.

2. The constitutional development in postwar Europe was characterized by federal trends. Even France, with its tradition of centralized government, was not free from them. As a reaction against centralization, which, especially under the Vichy regime, had proved to be detrimental to freedom, the Fourth Republic changed the prefectural system. Although the prefect remained the representative of the national government, he was to yield his place as the chief executive of the department to that local district's own elected officials. The process of decentralization was further advanced under the Fifth Republic, when the communes were strengthened and the probability of an oppressive national government decreased.[57] In Italy, the trend toward decentralization was even stronger than in France, taking the form of regionalism. Not content with just re-

[55] Mussolini was appointed Prime Minister by the King on Oct. 30, 1922, and obtained a 306 to 116 vote of confidence in the Chamber on Nov. 18. A week later, the Chamber granted him plenary powers by a vote of 275 to 90. Hitler was appointed Chancellor by President Hindenburg on Jan. 30, 1933, and got plenary powers through the Enabling Act of March 24 by the comfortable majority of 441 to 94. (No votes were cast by 81 communists and 26 socialists, who were imprisoned or in hiding.) Pétain received plenary powers from the regularly constituted assembly on July 10, 1940, by a vote of 569 to 80. Even if the communists, who were not present at the vote, had voted against this act, it would have passed with a comfortable majority.

[56] See Gottfried Dietze, "Natural Law in the Modern European Constitutions," NATURAL LAW FORUM (1956), I, 73. Italian translation in JUS, RIVISTA DI SCIENZE GIURIDICHE (1957), VIII (N.S.), 529.

[57] Compare Michel Debré, LA MORT DE L'ETAT REPUBLICAIN (1947), and LA REPUBLIQUE ET SES PROBLEMES (1952), 46-47; Stanley H. Hoffmann, "The Areal Division of Powers in the Writings of French Political Thinkers," in Arthur Maas, ed., AREA AND POWER (1959) 113.

creating the rights of communes and provinces as they existed prior to the fascist regime, the Italians set up new territorial subdivisions that roughly correspond to the old historic states of the Apennine peninsula, the regions. The latter were given a substantial degree of independence and autonomy.[58] The Germans went still further. Having learned under the third Reich the disadvantages of centralization to the rights of the individual, they not only re-instituted a unitary state with strong federal features after the pattern of the Weimar Republic, but they established a genuine federal state. Federalism was considered so important that it was put beyond the reach of the amending power and elevated to a superior principle of the Basic Law.[59]

3.   The general trend toward federalism was matched by one favoring judicial review.[60] Even France, with its strong tradition of legislative supremcy, took steps in that direction. Judicial review, which had been advocated by a small minority of jurists ever since World War I, was officially instituted a generation later. Although the Fourth Republic still showed a certain reluctance in establishing that institution in a strong fashion, the Fifth Republic corrected that shortcoming.[61] In the Italian Republic, a Constitutional Court possesses far-reaching powers of judicial review. That court, originally believed to be not too effective as a means for checking the political branches of government, soon proved to be a bulwark of individual freedom from governmental encroachment.[62] In Germany, judicial review had already been exercised during the Weimar period, though it was not officially established at that time. Of course, its existence was out of the question under the Hitler regime. However, once this regime had been defeated, judicial review was enthusiastically instituted on both the state and national levels.

[58] This applies especially to the so-called "autonomous" regions (Sicily, Sardinia, Valle d'Aosta, Trento-Alto Adige and Friuli Venezia), which, due to their geographic position and minority problems, were permitted an especially high degree of self-government. Compare Roberto Lucifredi, LA NUOVA COSTITUZIONE ITALIANA (1952), 240 ff.; Ferruccio Pergolesi, DIRITTO COSTITUZIONALE (1955), 400 ff.

[59] Art. 79 of the Basic Law.

[60] See Gottfried Dietze, "Judicial Review in Europe," MICHIGAN LAW REVIEW (1957), LV, 539.

[61] Under Articles 56-63 of the present constitution, an effective form of judicial review is established.

[62] See David Farrelly, "The Italian Constitutional Court," ITALIAN QUARTERLY (1957), I, 50; Carlo Esposito, LA COSTITUZIONE ITALIANA (1954), 263 ff.

During the past fifteen years it has proved an effective means for the protection of freedom.[63] German courts even broadened the orthodox concept of judicial review, maintaining that not only statutes and decrees, but also constitutional provisions themselves, may be incompatible with the principles of higher and natural law as embodied in the constitution. Aside from the acts of government, those of the constituent power, the people themselves, were subjected to review.[64] A far step from the dogma that the voice of the people is the voice of God!

4. The recognition by the Europeans of not merely one, but of both the outstanding American contributions to modern constitutionalism is hardly surprising. Having experienced the most dangerous combination of centralized power and majoritarianism, they saw in decentralization and control of the political branches of government complementary means for the protection of freedom. In the middle of the twentieth century, the old continent at last became convinced of the important truths proclaimed by the new world's great classic and recognized the value of American political institutions for individual liberty. The idea of an American mission for the world had gained substantial confirmation. But strangely enough, this new development in Europe took place at a time when both federalism and judicial review were undergoing a decline in the very country where they. were first adopted, the United States. This trend is as paradoxical as it is dangerous, and ought to be halted before it is too late. It is true, as the authors of the *Federalist* claimed, that an absence of federalism and judicial review is likely to spell despotism, be it that of the national government, or that of an oppressive majority, or, worst but most probable of all, that of a combination of both. There exists in this country a present danger of centralization and majoritarianism that, since it does not seem to be clear to many, ought to be pointed out. Such a warning will be unpopular in twentieth-century America. Still, I feel I can advance it, having experienced the disastrous consequences of centralized nationalism and the idea that right is what is useful for the people. That idea is as democratic as it was destructive of freedom under

[63] The Federal Constitutional Court is discussed by Taylor Cole, "The West German Federal Constitutional Court: An Appraisal After Six Years," JOURNAL OF POLITICS (1958), xx, 278.

[64] See Gottfried Dietze, "Unconstitutional Constitutional Norms?—Constitutional Development in Postwar Germany," VIRGINIA LAW REVIEW (1956), XLII, 1.

the new Caesars that came to power with popular sanction. I am unable to share the prevalent blind belief in the infallibility of popular government. There is no reason to trust human nature more today than did Hamilton, Madison, and Jay when they advocated the Constitution. And there is as little ground for abandoning the safeguards against human frailty that the Founding Fathers established for the sake of freedom.

With this note of warning I conclude. There has been too much talk these past years about what should be done in order to make the world safe for democracy, without serious thought about the meaning of that term. Also of concern should be the question of where popular government in America has gone and what type of democracy is being advocated. The foregoing may sound rather pessimistic. One could, of course, share the optimism fashionable today and enjoy the security that goes with being part of the crowd. This appears, at least on the surface, to be the way of the easy life. But this public philosophy is fraught with danger. Once we become members of the mass, we lose our identity and with it our quality as human beings. For a very dubious security we would have to give up our liberty, and this is too high a price to pay for something that results from human shortcomings rather than from humane thinking. Our pessimism is thus anything else but defeatism. At a time when justifications are found for everything people are doing, when the pursuit of happiness is said to mean the meager and shallow welfare of the masses rather than the freedom of the individual, we feel the need for expressing our belief in Hamilton's, Madison's, and Jay's concept of liberty, by emphasizing the values of the *Federalist,* American classic on federalism and free government.

SELECTED BIBLIOGRAPHY

SOURCES

Charles Francis Adams, ed., THE WORKS OF JOHN ADAMS (Boston, 1850-56).

Edmund C. Burnett, ed., LETTERS OF THE MEMBERS OF THE CONTINENTAL CONGRESS (Washington, 1921-36).

Jonathan Elliot, ed., THE DEBATES, RESOLUTIONS AND OTHER PROCEEDINGS IN CONVENTION ON THE ADOPTION OF THE FEDERAL CONSTITUTION (Washington, 1827-30).

Max Farrand, ed., THE RECORDS OF THE FEDERAL CONVENTION (New Haven, 1911).

John C. Fitzpatrick, ed., THE WRITINGS OF GEORGE WASHINGTON (Washington, 1931-44).

Paul Leicester Ford, ed., PAMPHLETS ON THE CONSTITUTION OF THE UNITED STATES (Brooklyn, 1888).

Worthington Chauncey Ford, ed., JOURNALS OF THE CONTINENTAL CONGRESS 1774-1789 (Washington, 1904-37).

Gaillard Hunt, ed., THE WRITINGS OF JAMES MADISON (New York, 1900-10).

Henry P. Johnston, ed., THE CORRESPONDENCE AND PUPLIC PAPERS OF JOHN JAY (New York, 1890-93).

Henry Cabot Lodge, ed., THE WORKS OF ALEXANDER HAMILTON (New York, 1904).

Memorial ed., THE WRITINGS OF THOMAS JEFFERSON (Washington, 1903-04).

Hezekiah Niles, ed., PRINCIPLES AND ACTS OF THE REVOLUTION (Baltimore, 1822).

Francis N. Thorpe, ed., THE FEDERAL AND STATE CONSTITUTIONS, COLONIAL CHARTERS AND OTHER ORGANIC LAWS OF THE STATE, TERRITORIES, AND COLONIES NOW AND HERETOFORE FORMING THE UNITED STATES OF AMERICA (Washington, 1909).

SECONDARY REFERENCES

George Bancroft, HISTORY OF THE FORMATION OF THE CONSTITUTION OF THE UNITED STATES OF AMERICA (New York, 1882).

Charles A. Beard, AN ECONOMIC INTERPRETATION OF THE CONSTITUTION (New York, 1913).

Carl L. Becker, THE DECLARATION OF INDEPENDENCE (New York, 1922).

Alex Bein, DIE STAATSIDEE ALEXANDER HAMILTONS IN IHRER ENTSTEHUNG UND ENTWICKLUNG (Munich and Berlin, 1927).

George C. S. Benson, THE NEW CENTRALIZATION (New York, 1941).

Albert J. Beveridge, THE LIFE OF JOHN MARSHALL (Boston and New York, 1916-19).

Irving Brant, JAMES MADISON (Indianapolis and New York, 1941-).

Robert E. Brown, CHARLES BEARD AND THE CONSTITUTION (Princeton, 1956).

James B. Bryce, THE AMERICAN COMMONWEALTH (London and New York, 1888).

Edward M. Burns, JAMES MADISON, PHILOSOPHER OF THE CONSTITUTION (New Brunswick, 1938).

William S. Carpenter, THE DEVELOPMENT OF AMERICAN POLITICAL THOUGHT (Princeton, 1930).

355

Thomas M. Cooley, A TREATISE ON THE CONSTITUTIONAL LIMITATIONS WHICH REST UPON THE LEGISLATIVE POWER OF THE STATES OF THE AMERICAN UNION (Boston, 1868).

Edward S. Corwin, THE DOCTRINE OF JUDICIAL REVIEW (Princeton, 1914).

Richard K. Cralle, ed., THE WORKS OF JOHN C. CALHOUN (New York, 1853-59).

William W. Crosskey, POLITICS AND THE CONSTITUTION IN THE HISTORY OF THE UNITED STATES (Chicago, 1953).

Max Farrand, THE FRAMING OF THE CONSTITUTION (New Haven, 1913).

Herman Finer, THEORY AND PRACTICE OF MODERN GOVERNMENT (Rev. ed., New York, 1950).

John Fiske, THE CRITICAL PERIOD OF AMERICAN HISTORY (Boston and New York, 1888).

Edward A. Freeman, HISTORY OF FEDERAL GOVERNMENT (London and Cambridge, 1863).

Carl J. Friedrich, CONSTITUTIONAL GOVERNMENT AND DEMOCRACY (Rev. ed., Boston, 1950).

Friedrich A. Hayek, THE CONSTITUTION OF LIBERTY (Chicago, 1960).

Richard Hofstadter, THE AMERICAN POLITICAL TRADITION AND THE MEN WHO MADE IT (New York, 1948).

Arthur N. Holcombe, OUR MORE PERFECT UNION (Cambridge, Mass., 1950).

Oliver W. Holmes, COLLECTED LEGAL PAPERS (New York, 1920).

Georg Jellinek, DIE LEHRE VON DEN STAATENVERBINDUNGEN (Berlin, 1882).

Merrill Jensen, THE ARTICLES OF CONFEDERATION (Madison, 1940).

James Kent, COMMENTARIES ON AMERICAN LAW (12th ed., Boston, 1873).

Alpheus T. Mason, FREE GOVERNMENT IN THE MAKING (New York, 1949),

——, SECURITY THROUGH FREEDOM (Ithaca, 1955).

Forrest McDonald, WE THE PEOPLE (Chicago, 1958).

Charles H. McIlwain, THE AMERICAN REVOLUTION (New York, 1923).

Broadus Mitchell ALEXANDER HAMILTON (New York, 1957).

Sobei Mogi, THE PROBLEM OF FEDERALISM (London, 1931).

Frank Monaghan, JOHN JAY (New York and Indianapolis, 1935).

Felix Morley, FREEDOM AND FEDERALISM (Chicago, 1959).

Allan Nevins, THE AMERICAN STATES DURING AND AFTER THE REVOLUTION (New York, 1924).

Vernon L. Parrington, MAIN CURRENTS IN AMERICAN THOUGHT (New York, 1927-30).

F. D. G. Ribble, STATE AND NATIONAL POWER OVER COMMERCE (New York, 1937).

Clinton L. Rossiter, SEEDTIME OF THE REPUBLIC (New York, 1953).

Joseph Story, COMMENTARIES ON THE CONSTITUTION OF THE UNITED STATES (Cambridge, Mass., 1833).

Carl B. Swisher, AMERICAN CONSTITUTIONAL DEVELOPMENT (2nd ed., Boston, 1954).

John Taylor, CONSTRUCTION CONSTRUED AND CONSTITUTIONS VINDICATED (Richmond, 1820).

Alexis de Tocqueville, DEMOCRACY IN AMERICA (4th ed., New York, 1845).

Charles Warren, THE MAKING OF THE CONSTITUTION (Boston, 1937).

Justus B. Westerkamp, STAATENBUND UND BUNDESSTAAT (Leipzig, 1892).

Woodrow Wilson, CONSTITUTIONAL GOVERNMENT IN THE UNITED STATES (New York, 1908).

WORKS CONCERNED EXCLUSIVELY WITH THE FEDERALIST

Various editions of the *Federalist* are listed in Paul L. Ford, A LIST OF EDITIONS OF THE FEDERALIST (Brooklyn, 1886), and in Henry Cabot Lodge, ed., THE WORKS OF ALEXANDER HAMILTON (New York, 1904), XI, xxxi-xl. These lists, however, are not complete. Professor Roy P. Fairfield of Ohio University informed me that he is preparing a new edition of the *Federalist* with a comprehensive bibliography. In the following list the reader will find a selection of studies that appear to be relevant for an understanding of the *Federalist*. Compare in this connection the references to the literature on the *Federalist* in Chapter One.

Douglass Adair, "The Authorship of the Disputed Federalist Papers," WILLIAM AND MARY QUARTERLY (1944), Third Series, I, 97-122; 235-64.

————, "The Tenth Federalist Revisited," WILLIAM AND MARY QUARTERLY (1951), Third Series, VIII, 48-67.

————, " 'That Politics May Be Reduced to a Science': David Hume, James Madison, and the Tenth Federalist," THE HUNTINGTON LIBRARY QUARTERLY (1957), XX, 343-60.

Mario d'Addio, "Il Federalista e il superamento del giusnaturalismo politici," in Gaspare Ambrosini, ed., IL FEDERALISTA (Pisa, 1955), 625-47.

Gaspare Ambrosini, introduction to his edition of IL FEDERALISTA (Pisa, 1955), ix-cxix.

Charles A. Beard, THE ENDURING FEDERALIST (Garden City, New York, 1948).

Max Beloff, introduction to his edition of THE FEDERALIST (Oxford, 1948), vii-lxvi.

Mabel G. Benson, SOME RHETORICAL CHARACTERISTICS OF THE FEDERALIST (Dissertation, Chicago, 1948).

Edward G. Bourne, "The Authorship of the Federalist," in his ESSAYS IN HISTORICAL CRITICISM (New York, 1901), 113-56.

————, "The Federalist Abroad," in his ESSAYS IN HISTORICAL CRITICISM (New York, 1901), 159-62.

Henry B. Dawson, introduction to his edition of THE FEDERALIST (New York, 1863), ix-lxxxix.

Martin Diamond, "Democracy and the Federalist: A Reconsideration of the Framers' Intent," AMERICAN POLITICAL SCIENCE REVIEW (1959), LIII, 52-68.

Gottfried Dietze, THE POLITICAL THEORY OF THE FEDERALIST (Dissertation, Princeton, 1952).

————, "Der Federalist und die Friedensfunktion des Föderalismus," JAHRBUCH DES ÖFFENTLICHEN RECHTS (1958), VII (N.F.), 1-47.

————, "Hamilton's Federalist—Treatise for Free Government," CORNELL LAW QUARTERLY (1957), XLII, 307-28, 501-18.

————, "Jay's Federalist—Treatise for Free Government," MARYLAND LAW REVIEW (1957), XVII, 217-30.

————, "Madison's Federalist—A Treatise for Free Government," GEORGETOWN LAW JOURNAL (1957), XLVI, 21-51.

Edward M. Earle, introduction to his edition of THE FEDERALIST (New York, 1937), v-xxv.

Albert Esmein, preface in Gaston Jèze, ed., LE FEDERALISTE (Paris, 1902), v-xxxviii.

Paul L. Ford, introduction to his edition of THE FEDERALIST (New York, 1898), vii-xli.

Aldo Garosci, IL PENSIERO POLITICO DEGLI AUTORI DEL "FEDERALIST," (Milan, 1954).

John C. Hamilton, introduction to his edition of THE FEDERALIST (Philadelphia, 1864), ix-cxxxviii.

Gaston Jèze, introduction to his edition of LE FEDERALISTE (Paris, 1902), xxxix-lv.

Wilhelm von Kiesselbach, DER AMERIKANISCHE FEDERALIST—POLITISCHE STUDIEN FÜR DIE DEUTSCHE GEGENWART (Bremen, 1864).

Henry Cabot Lodge, introduction to his edition of THE FEDERALIST (New York, 1888), xxiii-xlv.

Alpheus T. Mason, "The Federalist—A Split Personality," AMERICAN HISTORICAL REVIEW (1952), LVII, 625-43.

Kurt H. Nadelmann, "Apropos of Translations (Federalist, Kent, Story)," AMERICAN JOURNAL OF COMPARATIVE LAW (1959), VIII, 204-14.

Guglielmo Negri, "Il Federalista nella letteratura politico-giuridica," in Gaspare Ambrosini, ed., IL FEDERALISTA (Pisa, 1955), 611-24.

James B. Scanlan, THE CONCEPT OF INTEREST IN THE FEDERALIST (Dissertation, Chicago, 1956).

———, "The Federalist and Human Nature," REVIEW OF POLITICS (1959), XXI, 657-77.

Goldwin Smith, introduction to his edition of THE FEDERALIST (London, 1901), iii-ix.

Maynard Smith, THE PRINCIPLES OF REPUBLICAN GOVERNMENT IN THE FEDERALIST (Dissertation, The New School, 1951).

Gustavo R. Velasco, introduction to his second edition of EL FEDERALISTA (Mexico City, 1957), vii-xxiv.

Irvin Weaver, THE SOCIAL PHILOSOPHY OF THE FEDERALIST (Dissertation, Boston University, 1953).

Benjamin F. Wright, "The Federalist on the Nature of Political Man," ETHICS (1949), LIX (No. 2, Part II), 1-31.

OUTLINE OF CONTENTS

BOOK TWO: ANALYSIS

CONCLUSION

INDEX